UNITED STATES BANKRUPTCY CODE

Title 11 - United States Code

2026 Edition

Updated Through August 1, 2026

Michigan Legal Publishing Ltd.®

QUICK DESK REFERENCE SERIES™

Academic and bulk discounts available at
www.michlp.com

WE WELCOME YOUR FEEDBACK: info@michlp.com

ISBN-13: 978-1-64002-171-6

Table of contents

CHAPTER 1: GENERAL PROVISIONS

§101. Definitions

In this title the following definitions shall apply:

(1) The term "accountant" means accountant authorized under applicable law to practice public accounting, and includes professional accounting association, corporation, or partnership, if so authorized.

(2) The term "affiliate" means—

(A) entity that directly or indirectly owns, controls, or holds with power to vote, 20 percent or more of the outstanding voting securities of the debtor, other than an entity that holds such securities—

(i) in a fiduciary or agency capacity without sole discretionary power to vote such securities; or

(ii) solely to secure a debt, if such entity has not in fact exercised such power to vote;

(B) corporation 20 percent or more of whose outstanding voting securities are directly or indirectly owned, controlled, or held with power to vote, by the debtor, or by an entity that directly or indirectly owns, controls, or holds with power to vote, 20 percent or more of the outstanding voting securities of the debtor, other than an entity that holds such securities—

(i) in a fiduciary or agency capacity without sole discretionary power to vote such securities; or

(ii) solely to secure a debt, if such entity has not in fact exercised such power to vote;

(C) person whose business is operated under a lease or operating agreement by a debtor, or person substantially all of whose property is operated under an operating agreement with the debtor; or

(D) entity that operates the business or substantially all of the property of the debtor under a lease or operating agreement.

(3) The term "assisted person" means any person whose debts consist primarily of consumer debts and the value of whose nonexempt property is less than $256,800.

(4) The term "attorney" means attorney, professional law association, corporation, or partnership, authorized under applicable law to practice law.

(4A) The term "bankruptcy assistance" means any goods or services sold or otherwise provided to an assisted person with the express or implied purpose of providing information, advice, counsel, document preparation, or filing, or attendance at a creditors' meeting or appearing in a case or proceeding on behalf of another or providing legal representation with respect to a case or proceeding under this title.

(5) The term "claim" means—

(A) right to payment, whether or not such right is reduced to judgment, liquidated, unliquidated, fixed, contingent, matured, unmatured, disputed, undisputed, legal, equitable, secured, or unsecured; or

(B) right to an equitable remedy for breach of performance if such breach gives rise to a right to payment, whether or not such right to an equitable remedy is reduced to judgment, fixed, contingent, matured, unmatured, disputed, undisputed, secured, or unsecured.

(6) The term "commodity broker" means futures commission merchant, foreign futures commission merchant, clearing organization, leverage transaction merchant, or commodity options dealer, as defined in *section 761* of this title, with respect to which there is a customer, as defined in *section 761* of this title.

(7) The term "community claim" means claim that arose before the commencement of the case concerning the debtor for which property of the kind specified in *section 541(a)(2)* of this title is liable, whether or not there is any such property at the time of the commencement of the case.

(7A) The term "commercial fishing operation" means—

(A) the catching or harvesting of fish, shrimp, lobsters, urchins, seaweed, shellfish, or other aquatic species or products of such species; or

(B) for purposes of *section 109* and chapter 12, aquaculture activities consisting of raising for market any species or product described in subparagraph (A).

(7B) The term "commercial fishing vessel" means a vessel used by a family fisherman to carry out a commercial fishing operation.

(8) The term "consumer debt" means debt incurred by an individual primarily for a personal, family, or household purpose.

(9) The term "corporation"—

(A) includes—

(i) association having a power or privilege that a private corporation, but not an individual or a partnership, possesses;

(ii) partnership association organized under a law that makes only the capital subscribed responsible for the debts of such association;

(iii) joint-stock company;

(iv) unincorporated company or association; or

(v) business trust; but

(B) does not include limited partnership.

(10) The term "creditor" means—

(A) entity that has a claim against the debtor that arose at the time of or before the order for relief concerning the debtor;

(B) entity that has a claim against the estate of a kind specified in *section 348(d), 502*(f), 502(g), 502(h) or 502(i) of this title; or

(C) entity that has a community claim.

(10A) The term "current monthly income"—

(A) means the average monthly income from all sources that the debtor receives (or in a joint case the debtor and the debtor's spouse receive) without regard to whether such income is taxable income, derived during the 6-month period ending on—

(i) the last day of the calendar month immediately preceding the date of the commencement of the case if the debtor files the schedule of current income required by *section 521(a)(1)(B)(ii)*; or

(ii) the date on which current income is determined by the court for purposes of this title if the debtor does not file the schedule of current income required by *section 521(a)(1)(B)(ii)*; and

(B)

(i) includes any amount paid by any entity other than the debtor (or in a joint case the debtor and the debtor's spouse), on a regular basis for the household expenses of the debtor or the debtor's dependents (and in a joint case the debtor's spouse if not otherwise a dependent); and

(ii) excludes—

(I) benefits received under the Social Security Act (42 U.S.C. 301 et seq.);

(II) payments to victims of war crimes or crimes against humanity on account of their status as victims of such crimes;

(III) payments to victims of international terrorism or domestic terrorism, as those terms are defined in section 2331 of title 18, on account of their status as victims of such terrorism; and

(IV) any monthly compensation, pension, pay, annuity, or allowance paid under title 10, 37, or 38 in connection with a disability, combat-related injury or disability, or death of a member of the uniformed services, except that any retired pay excluded under this subclause shall include retired pay paid under chapter 61 of title 10 only to the extent that such retired pay exceeds the amount of retired pay to which the debtor would otherwise be entitled if retired under any provision of title 10 other than chapter 61 of that title.

(11) The term "custodian" means—

(A) receiver or trustee of any of the property of the debtor, appointed in a case or proceeding not under this title;

(B) assignee under a general assignment for the benefit of the debtor's creditors; or

(C) trustee, receiver, or agent under applicable law, or under a contract, that is appointed or authorized to take charge of property of the debtor for the purpose of enforcing a lien against such property, or for the purpose of general administration of such property for the benefit of the debtor's creditors.

(12) The term "debt" means liability on a claim.

(12A) The term "debt relief agency" means any person who provides any bankruptcy assistance to an assisted person in return for the payment of money or other valuable consideration, or who is a bankruptcy petition preparer under *section 110*, but does not include—

(A) any person who is an officer, director, employee, or agent of a person who provides such assistance or of the bankruptcy petition preparer;

(B) a nonprofit organization that is exempt from taxation under *section 501(c)(3)* of the Internal Revenue Code of 1986;

(C) a creditor of such assisted person, to the extent that the creditor is assisting such assisted person to restructure any debt owed by such assisted person to the creditor;

(D) a depository institution (as defined in section 3 of the Federal Deposit Insurance Act) or any Federal credit union or State credit union (as those terms are defined in section 101 of the Federal Credit Union Act), or any affiliate or subsidiary of such depository institution or credit union; or

(E) an author, publisher, distributor, or seller of works subject to copyright protection under title 17, when acting in such capacity.

(13) The term "debtor" means person or municipality concerning which a case under this title has been commenced.

(13A) The term "debtor's principal residence"—

(A) means a residential structure if used as the principal residence by the debtor, including incidental property, without regard to whether that structure is attached to real property; and

(B) includes an individual condominium or cooperative unit, a mobile or manufactured home, or trailer if used as the principal residence by the debtor.

(14) The term "disinterested person" means a person that—

(A) is not a creditor, an equity security holder, or an insider;

(B) is not and was not, within 2 years before the date of the filing of the petition, a director, officer, or employee of the debtor; and

(C) does not have an interest materially adverse to the interest of the estate or of any class of creditors or equity security holders, by reason of any direct or indirect relationship to, connection with, or interest in, the debtor, or for any other reason.

(14A) The term "domestic support obligation" means a debt that accrues before, on, or after the date of the order for relief in a case under this title, including interest that accrues on that debt as provided under applicable nonbankruptcy law notwithstanding any other provision of this title, that is—

(A) owed to or recoverable by—

(i) a spouse, former spouse, or child of the debtor or such child's parent, legal guardian, or responsible relative; or

(ii) a governmental unit;

(B) in the nature of alimony, maintenance, or support (including assistance provided by a governmental unit) of such spouse, former spouse, or child of the debtor or such child's parent, without regard to whether such debt is expressly so designated;

(C) established or subject to establishment before, on, or after the date of the order for relief in a case under this title, by reason of applicable provisions of—

(i) a separation agreement, divorce decree, or property settlement agreement;

(ii) an order of a court of record; or

(iii) a determination made in accordance with applicable nonbankruptcy law by a governmental unit; and

(D) not assigned to a nongovernmental entity, unless that obligation is assigned voluntarily by the spouse, former spouse, child of the debtor, or such child's parent, legal guardian, or responsible relative for the purpose of collecting the debt.

(15) The term "entity" includes person, estate, trust, governmental unit, and United States trustee.

(16) The term "equity security" means—

(A) share in a corporation, whether or not transferable or denominated "stock", or similar security;

(B) interest of a limited partner in a limited partnership; or

(C) warrant or right, other than a right to convert, to purchase, sell, or subscribe to a share, security, or interest of a kind specified in subparagraph (A) or (B) of this paragraph.

(17) The term "equity security holder" means holder of an equity security of the debtor.

(18) The term "family farmer" means—

(A) individual or individual and spouse engaged in a farming operation whose aggregate debts do not exceed $12,562,250 and not less than 50 percent of whose aggregate noncontingent, liquidated debts (excluding a debt for the principal residence of such individual or such individual and spouse unless such debt arises out of a farming operation), on the date the case is filed, arise out of a farming operation owned or operated by such individual or such individual and spouse, and such individual or such individual and spouse receive from such farming operation more than 50 percent of such individual's or such individual and spouse's gross income for—

(i) the taxable year preceding; or

(ii) each of the 2d and 3d taxable years preceding;

the taxable year in which the case concerning such individual or such individual and spouse was filed; or

(B) corporation or partnership in which more than 50 percent of the outstanding stock or equity is held by one family, or by one family and the relatives of the members of such family, and such family or such relatives conduct the farming operation, and

(i) more than 80 percent of the value of its assets consists of assets related to the farming operation;

(ii) its aggregate debts do not exceed $12,562,250 and not less than 50 percent of its aggregate noncontingent, liquidated debts (excluding a debt for one dwelling which is owned by such corporation or partnership and which a shareholder or partner maintains as a principal residence, unless such debt arises out of a farming operation), on the date the case is filed, arise out of the farming operation owned or operated by such corporation or such partnership; and

(iii) if such corporation issues stock, such stock is not publicly traded.

(19) The term "family farmer with regular annual income" means family farmer whose annual income is sufficiently stable and regular to enable such family farmer to make payments under a plan under chapter 12 of this title.

(19A) The term "family fisherman" means—

(A) an individual or individual and spouse engaged in a commercial fishing operation—

(i) whose aggregate debts do not exceed $2,568,000 and not less than 80 percent of whose aggregate noncontingent, liquidated debts (excluding a debt for the principal residence of such individual or such individual and spouse, unless such debt arises out of a commercial fishing operation), on the date the case is filed, arise out of a commercial fishing operation owned or operated by such individual or such individual and spouse; and

(ii) who receive from such commercial fishing operation more than 50 percent of such individual's or such individual's and spouse's gross income for the taxable year preceding the taxable year in which the case concerning such individual or such individual and spouse was filed; or

(B) a corporation or partnership—

(i) in which more than 50 percent of the outstanding stock or equity is held by—

(I) 1 family that conducts the commercial fishing operation; or

(II) 1 family and the relatives of the members of such family, and such family or such relatives conduct the commercial fishing operation; and

(ii)

(I) more than 80 percent of the value of its assets consists of assets related to the commercial fishing operation;

(II) its aggregate debts do not exceed $2,568,000 and not less than 80 percent of its aggregate noncontingent, liquidated debts (excluding a debt for 1 dwelling which is owned by such corporation or partnership and which a shareholder or partner maintains as a principal residence, unless such debt arises out of a commercial fishing operation), on the date the case is filed, arise out of a commercial fishing operation owned or operated by such corporation or such partnership; and

(III) if such corporation issues stock, such stock is not publicly traded.

(19B) The term "family fisherman with regular annual income" means a family fisherman whose annual income is sufficiently stable and regular to enable such family fisherman to make payments under a plan under chapter 12 of this title.

(20) The term "farmer" means (except when such term appears in the term "family farmer") person that received more than 80 percent of such person's gross income during the taxable year of such person immediately preceding the taxable year of such person during which the case under this title concerning such person was commenced from a farming operation owned or operated by such person.

(21) The term "farming operation" includes farming, tillage of the soil, dairy farming, ranching, production or raising of crops, poultry, or livestock, and production of poultry or livestock products in an unmanufactured state.

(21A) The term "farmout agreement" means a written agreement in which—

(A) the owner of a right to drill, produce, or operate liquid or gaseous hydrocarbons on property agrees or has agreed to transfer or assign all or a part of such right to another entity; and

(B) such other entity (either directly or through its agents or its assigns), as consideration, agrees to perform drilling, reworking, recompleting, testing, or similar or related operations, to develop or produce liquid or gaseous hydrocarbons on the property.

(21B) The term "Federal depository institutions regulatory agency" means—

(A) with respect to an insured depository institution (as defined in section 3(c)(2) of the Federal Deposit Insurance Act) for which no conservator or receiver has been appointed, the appropriate Federal banking agency (as defined in section 3(q) of such Act);

(B) with respect to an insured credit union (including an insured credit union for which the National Credit Union Administration has been appointed conservator or liquidating agent), the National Credit Union Administration;

(C) with respect to any insured depository institution for which the Resolution Trust Corporation has been appointed conservator or receiver, the Resolution Trust Corporation; and

(D) with respect to any insured depository institution for which the Federal Deposit Insurance Corporation has been appointed conservator or receiver, the Federal Deposit Insurance Corporation.

(22) The term "financial institution" means—

(A) a Federal reserve bank, or an entity that is a commercial or savings bank, industrial savings bank, savings and loan association, trust company, federally-insured credit union, or receiver, liquidating agent, or conservator for such entity and, when any such Federal reserve bank, receiver, liquidating agent, conservator or entity is acting as agent or custodian for a customer (whether or not a "customer", as defined in *section 741*) in connection with a securities contract (as defined in *section 741*) such customer; or

(B) in connection with a securities contract (as defined in *section 741*) an investment company registered under the Investment Company Act of 1940.

(22A) The term "financial participant" means—

(A) an entity that, at the time it enters into a securities contract, commodity contract, swap agreement, repurchase agreement, or forward contract, or at the time of the date of the filing of the petition, has one or more agreements or transactions described in paragraph (1), (2), (3), (4), (5), or (6) of *section 561(a)* with the debtor or any other entity (other than an affiliate) of a total gross dollar value of not less than $1,000,000,000 in notional or actual principal amount outstanding (aggregated across counterparties) at such time or on any day during the 15-month period preceding the date of the filing of the petition, or has gross mark-to-market positions of not less than $100,000,000 (aggregated across counterparties) in one or more such agreements or transactions with the debtor or any other entity (other than an affiliate) at such time or on any day during the 15-month period preceding the date of the filing of the petition; or

(B) a clearing organization (as defined in section 402 of the Federal Deposit Insurance Corporation Improvement Act of 1991).

(23) The term "foreign proceeding" means a collective judicial or administrative proceeding in a foreign country, including an interim proceeding, under a law relating to insolvency or adjustment of debt in which proceeding the assets and affairs of the debtor are subject to control or supervision by a foreign court, for the purpose of reorganization or liquidation.

(24) The term "foreign representative" means a person or body, including a person or body appointed on an interim basis, authorized in a foreign proceeding to administer the reorganization or the liquidation of the debtor's assets or affairs or to act as a representative of such foreign proceeding.

(25) The term "forward contract" means—

(A) a contract (other than a commodity contract, as defined in *section 761*) for the purchase, sale, or transfer of a commodity, as defined in *section 761(8)* of this title, or any similar good, article, service, right, or interest which is presently or in the future becomes the subject of dealing in the forward contract trade, or product or byproduct thereof, with a maturity date more than two days after the date the contract is entered into, including, but not limited to, a repurchase or reverse repurchase transaction (whether or not such repurchase or reverse repurchase transaction is a "repurchase agreement", as defined in this section) consignment, lease, swap, hedge transaction, deposit, loan, option, allocated transaction, unallocated transaction, or any other similar agreement;

(B) any combination of agreements or transactions referred to in subparagraphs (A) and (C);

(C) any option to enter into an agreement or transaction referred to in subparagraph (A) or (B);

(D) a master agreement that provides for an agreement or transaction referred to in subparagraph (A), (B), or (C), together with all supplements to any such master agreement, without regard to whether such master agreement provides for an agreement or transaction that is not a forward contract under this paragraph, except that such master agreement shall be considered to be a forward contract under this paragraph only with respect to each agreement or transaction under such master agreement that is referred to in subparagraph (A), (B), or (C); or

(E) any security agreement or arrangement, or other credit enhancement related to any agreement or transaction referred to in subparagraph (A), (B), (C), or (D), including any guarantee or reimbursement obligation by or to a forward contract merchant or financial participant in connection with any agreement or transaction referred to in any such subparagraph, but not to exceed the damages in connection with any such agreement or transaction, measured in accordance with *section 562*.

(26) The term "forward contract merchant" means a Federal reserve bank, or an entity the business of which consists in whole or in part of entering into forward contracts as or with merchants in a commodity (as defined in *section 761*) or any similar good, article, service, right, or interest which is presently or in the future becomes the subject of dealing in the forward contract trade.

(27) The term "governmental unit" means United States; State; Commonwealth; District; Territory; municipality; foreign state; department, agency, or instrumentality of the United States (but not a United States trustee while serving as a trustee in a case under this title), a State, a Commonwealth, a District, a Territory, a municipality, or a foreign state; or other foreign or domestic government.

(27A) The term "health care business"—

(A) means any public or private entity (without regard to whether that entity is organized for profit or not for profit) that is primarily engaged in offering to the general public facilities and services for —

(i) the diagnosis or treatment of injury, deformity, or disease; and

(ii) surgical, drug treatment, psychiatric, or obstetric care; and

(B) includes—

(i) any—

(I) general or specialized hospital;

(II) ancillary ambulatory, emergency, or surgical treatment facility;

(III) hospice;

(IV) home health agency; and

(V) other health care institution that is similar to an entity referred to in subclause (I), (II), (III), or (IV); and

(ii) any long-term care facility, including any—

(I) skilled nursing facility;

(II) intermediate care facility;

(III) assisted living facility;

(IV) home for the aged;

(V) domiciliary care facility; and

(VI) health care institution that is related to a facility referred to in subclause (I), (II), (III), (IV), or (V), if that institution is primarily engaged in offering room, board, laundry, or personal assistance with activities of daily living and incidentals to activities of daily living.

(27B) The term "incidental property" means, with respect to a debtor's principal residence—

(A) property commonly conveyed with a principal residence in the area where the real property is located;

(B) all easements, rights, appurtenances, fixtures, rents, royalties, mineral rights, oil or gas rights or profits, water rights, escrow funds, or insurance proceeds; and

(C) all replacements or additions.

(28) The term "indenture" means mortgage, deed of trust, or indenture, under which there is outstanding a security, other than a voting-trust certificate, constituting a claim against the debtor, a claim secured by a lien on any of the debtor's property, or an equity security of the debtor.

(29) The term "indenture trustee" means trustee under an indenture.

(30) The term "individual with regular income" means individual whose income is sufficiently stable and regular to enable such individual to make payments under a plan under chapter 13 of this title, other than a stockbroker or a commodity broker.

(31) The term "insider" includes—

(A) if the debtor is an individual—

(i) relative of the debtor or of a general partner of the debtor;

(ii) partnership in which the debtor is a general partner;

(iii) general partner of the debtor; or

(iv) corporation of which the debtor is a director, officer, or person in control;

(B) if the debtor is a corporation—

(i) director of the debtor;

(ii) officer of the debtor;

(iii) person in control of the debtor;

(iv) partnership in which the debtor is a general partner;

(v) general partner of the debtor; or

(vi) relative of a general partner, director, officer, or person in control of the debtor;

(C) if the debtor is a partnership—

(i) general partner in the debtor;

(ii) relative of a general partner in, general partner of, or person in control of the debtor;

(iii) partnership in which the debtor is a general partner;

(iv) general partner of the debtor; or

(v) person in control of the debtor;

(D) if the debtor is a municipality, elected official of the debtor or relative of an elected official of the debtor;

(E) affiliate, or insider of an affiliate as if such affiliate were the debtor; and

(F) managing agent of the debtor.

(32) The term "insolvent" means—

(A) with reference to an entity other than a partnership and a municipality, financial condition such that the sum of such entity's debts is greater than all of such entity's property, at a fair valuation, exclusive of—

(i) property transferred, concealed, or removed with intent to hinder, delay, or defraud such entity's creditors; and

(ii) property that may be exempted from property of the estate under *section 522* of this title;

(B) with reference to a partnership, financial condition such that the sum of such partnership's debts is greater than the aggregate of, at a fair valuation—

(i) all of such partnership's property, exclusive of property of the kind specified in subparagraph (A)(i) of this paragraph; and

(ii) the sum of the excess of the value of each general partner's nonpartnership property, exclusive of property of the kind specified in subparagraph (A) of this paragraph, over such partner's nonpartnership debts; and

(C) with reference to a municipality, financial condition such that the municipality is—

(i) generally not paying its debts as they become due unless such debts are the subject of a bona fide dispute; or

(ii) unable to pay its debts as they become due.

(33) The term "institution-affiliated party"—

(A) with respect to an insured depository institution (as defined in section 3(c)(2) of the Federal Deposit Insurance Act), has the meaning given it in section 3(u) of the Federal Deposit Insurance Act; and

(B) with respect to an insured credit union, has the meaning given it in section 206(r) of the Federal Credit Union Act.

(34) The term "insured credit union" has the meaning given it in section 101(7) of the Federal Credit Union Act.

(35) The term "insured depository institution"—

(A) has the meaning given it in section 3(c)(2) of the Federal Deposit Insurance Act; and

(B) includes an insured credit union (except in the case of paragraphs (21B) and (33)(A) of this subsection).

(35A) The term "intellectual property" means—

(A) trade secret;

(B) invention, process, design, or plant protected under title 35;

(C) patent application;

(D) plant variety;

(E) work of authorship protected under title 17; or

(F) mask work protected under chapter 9 of title 17;

to the extent protected by applicable nonbankruptcy law.

(36) The term "judicial lien" means lien obtained by judgment, levy, sequestration, or other legal or equitable process or proceeding.

(37) The term "lien" means charge against or interest in property to secure payment of a debt or performance of an obligation.

(38) The term "margin payment" means, for purposes of the forward contract provisions of this title, payment or deposit of cash, a security or other property, that is commonly known in the forward contract trade as original margin, initial margin, maintenance margin, or variation margin, including mark-to-market payments, or variation payments.

(38A) The term "master netting agreement"—

(A) means an agreement providing for the exercise of rights, including rights of netting, setoff, liquidation, termination, acceleration, or close out, under or in connection with one or more contracts that are described in any one or more of paragraphs (1) through (5) of *section 561(a)*, or any security agreement or arrangement or other credit enhancement related to one or more of the foregoing, including any guarantee or reimbursement obligation related to 1 or more of the foregoing; and

(B) if the agreement contains provisions relating to agreements or transactions that are not contracts described in paragraphs (1) through (5) of *section 561(a)*, shall be deemed to be a master netting agreement only with respect to those agreements or transactions that are described in any one or more of paragraphs (1) through (5) of *section 561(a)*.

(38B) The term "master netting agreement participant" means an entity that, at any time before the date of the filing of the petition, is a party to an outstanding master netting agreement with the debtor.

(39) The term "mask work" has the meaning given it in *section 901(a)(2)* of title 17.

(39A) The term "median family income" means for any year—

(A) the median family income both calculated and reported by the Bureau of the Census in the then most recent year; and

(B) if not so calculated and reported in the then current year, adjusted annually after such most recent year until the next year in which median family income is both calculated and reported by the Bureau of the Census, to reflect the percentage change in the Consumer Price Index for All Urban Consumers during the period of years occurring after such most recent year and before such current year.

(40) The term "municipality" means political subdivision or public agency or instrumentality of a State.

(40A) The term "patient" means any individual who obtains or receives services from a health care business.

(40B) The term "patient records" means any record relating to a patient, including a written document or a record recorded in a magnetic, optical, or other form of electronic medium.

(41) The term "person" includes individual, partnership, and corporation, but does not include governmental unit, except that a governmental unit that—

(A) acquires an asset from a person—

(i) as a result of the operation of a loan guarantee agreement; or

(ii) as receiver or liquidating agent of a person;

(B) is a guarantor of a pension benefit payable by or on behalf of the debtor or an affiliate of the debtor; or

(C) is the legal or beneficial owner of an asset of—

(i) an employee pension benefit plan that is a governmental plan, as defined in section 414(d) of the Internal Revenue Code of 1986; or

(ii) an eligible deferred compensation plan, as defined in section 457(b) of the Internal Revenue Code of 1986;

shall be considered, for purposes of *section 1102* of this title, to be a person with respect to such asset or such benefit.

(41A) The term "personally identifiable information" means—

(A) if provided by an individual to the debtor in connection with obtaining a product or a service from the debtor primarily for personal, family, or household purposes —

(i) the first name (or initial) and last name of such individual, whether given at birth or time of adoption, or resulting from a lawful change of name;

(ii) the geographical address of a physical place of residence of such individual;

(iii) an electronic address (including an e-mail address) of such individual;

(iv) a telephone number dedicated to contacting such individual at such physical place of residence;

(v) a social security account number issued to such individual; or

(vi) the account number of a credit card issued to such individual; or

(B) if identified in connection with 1 or more of the items of information specified in subparagraph (A)—

(i) a birth date, the number of a certificate of birth or adoption, or a place of birth; or

(ii) any other information concerning an identified individual that, if disclosed, will result in contacting or identifying such individual physically or electronically.

(42) The term "petition" means petition filed under *section 301, 302, 303* and 1504 of this title, as the case may be, commencing a case under this title.

(42A) The term "production payment" means a term overriding royalty satisfiable in cash or in kind—

(A) contingent on the production of a liquid or gaseous hydrocarbon from particular real property; and

(B) from a specified volume, or a specified value, from the liquid or gaseous hydrocarbon produced from such property, and determined without regard to production costs.

(43) The term "purchaser" means transferee of a voluntary transfer, and includes immediate or mediate transferee of such a transferee.

(44) The term "railroad" means common carrier by railroad engaged in the transportation of individuals or property or owner of trackage facilities leased by such a common carrier.

(45) The term "relative" means individual related by affinity or consanguinity within the third degree as determined by the common law, or individual in a step or adoptive relationship within such third degree.

(46) The term "repo participant" means an entity that, at any time before the filing of the petition, has an outstanding repurchase agreement with the debtor.

(47) The term "repurchase agreement" (which definition also applies to a reverse repurchase agreement)—

(A) means—

(i) an agreement, including related terms, which provides for the transfer of one or more certificates of deposit, mortgage related securities (as defined in section 3 of the Securities Exchange Act of 1934), mortgage loans, interests in mortgage related securities or mortgage loans, eligible bankers' acceptances, qualified foreign government securities (defined as a security that is a direct obligation of, or that is fully guaranteed by, the central government of a member of the Organization for Economic Cooperation and Development), or securities that are direct obligations of, or that are fully guaranteed by, the United States or any agency of the United States against the transfer of funds by the transferee of such certificates of deposit, eligible bankers' acceptances, securities, mortgage loans, or interests, with a simultaneous agreement by such transferee to transfer to the transferor thereof certificates of deposit, eligible bankers' acceptance, securities, mortgage loans, or interests of the kind described in this clause, at a date certain not later than 1 year after such transfer or on demand, against the transfer of funds;

(ii) any combination of agreements or transactions referred to in clauses (i) and (iii);

(iii) an option to enter into an agreement or transaction referred to in clause (i) or (ii);

(iv) a master agreement that provides for an agreement or transaction referred to in clause (i), (ii), or (iii), together with all supplements to any such master agreement, without regard to whether such master agreement provides for an agreement or transaction that is not a repurchase agreement under this paragraph, except that such master agreement shall be considered to be a repurchase agreement under this paragraph only with respect to each agreement or transaction under the master agreement that is referred to in clause (i), (ii), or (iii); or

(v) any security agreement or arrangement or other credit enhancement related to any agreement or transaction referred to in clause (i), (ii), (iii), or (iv), including any guarantee or reimbursement obligation by or to a repo participant or financial participant in connection with any agreement or transaction referred to in any such clause, but not to exceed the damages in connection with any such agreement or transaction, measured in accordance with *section 562* of this title; and

(B) does not include a repurchase obligation under a participation in a commercial mortgage loan.

(48) The term "securities clearing agency" means person that is registered as a clearing agency under section 17A of the Securities Exchange Act of 1934, or exempt from such registration under such section pursuant to an order of the Securities and Exchange Commission, or whose business is confined to the performance of functions of a clearing agency with respect to exempted securities, as defined in section 3(a)(12) of such Act for the purposes of such section 17A.

(48A) The term "securities self regulatory organization" means either a securities association registered with the Securities and Exchange Commission under section 15A of the Securities Exchange Act of 1934 or a national securities exchange registered with the Securities and Exchange Commission under section 6 of the Securities Exchange Act of 1934.

(49) The term "security"—

(A) includes—

(i) note;

(ii) stock;

(iii) treasury stock;

(iv) bond;

(v) debenture;

(vi) collateral trust certificate;

(vii) pre-organization certificate or subscription;

(viii) transferable share;

(ix) voting-trust certificate;

(x) certificate of deposit;

(xi) certificate of deposit for security;

(xii) investment contract or certificate of interest or participation in a profit-sharing agreement or in an oil, gas, or mineral royalty or lease, if such contract or interest is required to be the subject of a registration statement filed with the Securities and Exchange Commission under the provisions of the Securities Act of 1933, or is exempt under section 3(b) of such Act from the requirement to file such a statement;

(xiii) interest of a limited partner in a limited partnership;

(xiv) other claim or interest commonly known as "security"; and

(xv) certificate of interest or participation in, temporary or interim certificate for, receipt for, or warrant or right to subscribe to or purchase or sell, a security; but

(B) does not include—

(i) currency, check, draft, bill of exchange, or bank letter of credit;

(ii) leverage transaction, as defined in *section 761* of this title;

(iii) commodity futures contract or forward contract;

(iv) option, warrant, or right to subscribe to or purchase or sell a commodity futures contract;

(v) option to purchase or sell a commodity;

(vi) contract or certificate of a kind specified in subparagraph (A)(xii) of this paragraph that is not required to be the subject of a registration statement filed with the Securities and Exchange Commission and is not exempt under section 3(b) of the Securities Act of 1933 from the requirement to file such a statement; or

(vii) debt or evidence of indebtedness for goods sold and delivered or services rendered.

(50) The term "security agreement" means agreement that creates or provides for a security interest.

(51) The term "security interest" means lien created by an agreement.

(51A) The term "settlement payment" means, for purposes of the forward contract provisions of this title, a preliminary settlement payment, a partial settlement payment, an interim settlement payment, a settlement payment on account, a final settlement payment, a net settlement payment, or any other similar payment commonly used in the forward contract trade.

(51B) The term "single asset real estate" means real property constituting a single property or project, other than residential real property with fewer than 4 residential units, which generates substantially all of the gross income of a debtor who is not a family farmer and on which no substantial business is being conducted by a debtor other than the business of operating the real property and activities incidental thereto.

(51C) The term "small business case" means a case filed under chapter 11 of this title in which the debtor is a small business debtor and has not elected that subchapter V of chapter 11 of this title shall apply.

(51D) The term "small business debtor"—

(A) subject to subparagraph (B), means a person engaged in commercial or business activities (including any affiliate of such person that is also a debtor under this title and excluding a person whose primary activity is the business of owning single asset real estate) that has aggregate noncontingent liquidated secured and unsecured debts as of the date of the filing of the petition or the date of the order for relief in an amount not more than $3,424,000 (excluding debts owed to 1 or more affiliates or insiders) not less than 50 percent of which arose from the commercial or business activities of the debtor; and

(B) does not include—

(i) any member of a group of affiliated debtors under this title that has aggregate noncontingent liquidated secured and unsecured debts in an amount greater than $3,424,000 (excluding debt owed to 1 or more affiliates or insiders);

(ii) any debtor that is a corporation subject to the reporting requirements under section 13 or 15(d) of the Securities Exchange Act of 1934 (15 U.S.C. 78m, 78 *o*(d)); or

(iii) any debtor that is an affiliate of a corporation described in clause (ii).

(52) The term "State" includes the District of Columbia and Puerto Rico, except for the purpose of defining who may be a debtor under chapter 9 of this title.

(53) The term "statutory lien" means lien arising solely by force of a statute on specified circumstances or conditions, or lien of distress for rent, whether or not statutory, but does not include security interest or judicial lien, whether or not such interest or lien is provided by or is dependent on a statute and whether or not such interest or lien is made fully effective by statute.

(53A) The term "stockbroker" means person—

(A) with respect to which there is a customer, as defined in *section 741* of this title; and

(B) that is engaged in the business of effecting transactions in securities—

(i) for the account of others; or

(ii) with members of the general public, from or for such person's own account.

(53B) The term "swap agreement"—

(A) means—

(i) any agreement, including the terms and conditions incorporated by reference in such agreement, which is—

(I) an interest rate swap, option, future, or forward agreement, including a rate floor, rate cap, rate collar, cross-currency rate swap, and basis swap;

(II) a spot, same day-tomorrow, tomorrow-next, forward, or other foreign exchange, precious metals, or other commodity agreement;

(III) a currency swap, option, future, or forward agreement;

(IV) an equity index or equity swap, option, future, or forward agreement;

(V) a debt index or debt swap, option, future, or forward agreement;

(VI) a total return, credit spread or credit swap, option, future, or forward agreement;

(VII) a commodity index or a commodity swap, option, future, or forward agreement;

(VIII) a weather swap, option, future, or forward agreement;

(IX) an emissions swap, option, future, or forward agreement; or

(X) an inflation swap, option, future, or forward agreement;

(ii) any agreement or transaction that is similar to any other agreement or transaction referred to in this paragraph and that—

(I) is of a type that has been, is presently, or in the future becomes, the subject of recurrent dealings in the swap or other derivatives markets (including terms and conditions incorporated by reference therein); and

(II) is a forward, swap, future, option, or spot transaction on one or more rates, currencies, commodities, equity securities, or other equity instruments, debt securities or other debt instruments, quantitative measures associated with an occurrence, extent of an occurrence, or contingency associated with a financial, commercial, or economic consequence, or economic or financial indices or measures of economic or financial risk or value;

(iii) any combination of agreements or transactions referred to in this subparagraph;

(iv) any option to enter into an agreement or transaction referred to in this subparagraph;

(v) a master agreement that provides for an agreement or transaction referred to in clause (i), (ii), (iii), or (iv), together with all supplements to any such master agreement, and without regard to whether the master agreement contains an agreement or transaction that is not a swap agreement under this paragraph, except that the master agreement shall be considered to be a swap agreement under this paragraph only with respect to each agreement or transaction under the master agreement that is referred to in clause (i), (ii), (iii), or (iv); or

(vi) any security agreement or arrangement or other credit enhancement related to any agreements or transactions referred to in clause (i) through (v), including any guarantee or reimbursement obligation by or to a swap participant or financial participant in connection with any agreement or transaction referred to in any such clause, but not to exceed the damages in connection with any such agreement or transaction, measured in accordance with *section 562*; and

(B) is applicable for purposes of this title only, and shall not be construed or applied so as to challenge or affect the characterization, definition, or treatment of any swap agreement under any other statute, regulation, or rule, including the Gramm-Leach-Bliley Act, the Legal Certainty for Bank Products Act of 2000, the securities laws (as such term is defined in section 3(a)(47) of the Securities Exchange Act of 1934) and the Commodity Exchange Act.

(53C) The term “swap participant” means an entity that, at any time before the filing of the petition, has an outstanding swap agreement with the debtor.

(56A) The term “term overriding royalty” means an interest in liquid or gaseous hydrocarbons in place or to be produced from particular real property that entitles the owner thereof to a share of production, or the value thereof, for a term limited by time, quantity, or value realized.

(53D) The term “timeshare plan” means and shall include that interest purchased in any arrangement, plan, scheme, or similar device, but not including exchange programs, whether by membership, agreement, tenancy in common, sale, lease, deed, rental agreement, license, right to use agreement, or by any other means, whereby a purchaser, in exchange for consideration, receives a right to use accommodations, facilities, or recreational sites, whether improved or unimproved, for a specific period of time less than a full year during any given year, but not necessarily for consecutive years, and which extends for a period of more than three years. A "timeshare interest" is that interest purchased in a timeshare plan which grants the purchaser the right to use and occupy accommodations, facilities, or recreational sites, whether improved or unimproved, pursuant to a timeshare plan.

(54) The term "transfer" means—

(A) the creation of a lien;

(B) the retention of title as a security interest;

(C) the foreclosure of a debtor's equity of redemption; or

(D) each mode, direct or indirect, absolute or conditional, voluntary or involuntary, of disposing of or parting with—

(i) property; or

(ii) an interest in property.

(54A) The term "uninsured State member bank" means a State member bank (as defined in section 3 of the Federal Deposit Insurance Act) the deposits of which are not insured by the Federal Deposit Insurance Corporation.

(55) The term "United States", when used in a geographical sense, includes all locations where the judicial jurisdiction of the United States extends, including territories and possessions of the United States.

(Pub. L. 95–598, Nov. 6, 1978, 92 Stat. 2549; Pub. L. 97–222, § 1, July 27, 1982, 96 Stat. 235; Pub. L. 98–353, title III, §§ 391, 401, 421, July 10, 1984, 98 Stat. 364, 366, 367; Pub. L. 99–554, title II, §§ 201, 251, 283(a), Oct. 27, 1986, 100 Stat. 3097, 3104, 3116; Pub. L. 100–506, § 1(a), Oct. 18, 1988, 102 Stat. 2538; Pub. L. 100–597, § 1, Nov. 3, 1988, 102 Stat. 3028; Pub. L. 101–311, title I, § 101, title II, § 201, June 25, 1990, 104 Stat. 267, 268; Pub. L. 101–647, title XXV, § 2522(e), Nov. 29, 1990, 104 Stat. 4867; Pub. L. 102–486, title XXX, § 3017(a), Oct. 24, 1992, 106 Stat. 3130; Pub. L. 103–394, title I, § 106, title II, §§ 208(a), 215, 217(a), 218(a), title III, § 304(a), title V, § 501(a), (b)(1), (d)(1), Oct. 22, 1994, 108 Stat. 4111, 4124, 4126–4128, 4132, 4141–4143; Pub. L. 106–554, § 1(a)(5) [title I, § 112(c)(3), (4)], Dec. 21, 2000, 114 Stat. 2763, 2763A–393, 2763A–394; Pub. L. 109–8, title I, § 102(b), (k), title II, §§ 211, 226(a), 231(b), title III, § 306(c), title IV, §§ 401(a), 414, 432(a), title VIII, § 802(b), title IX, § 907(a)(1), (b), (c), title X, §§ 1004, 1005, 1007(a), title XI, § 1101(a), (b), title XII, § 1201, Apr. 20, 2005, 119 Stat. 32, 35, 50, 66, 73, 80, 104, 107, 110, 145, 170, 175, 186, 187, 189, 192; Pub. L. 109–390, § 5(a)(1), Dec. 12, 2006, 120 Stat. 2695; Pub. L. 111–327, § 2(a)(1), Dec. 22, 2010, 124 Stat. 3557; Pub. L. 116–51, § 2, Aug. 23, 2019, 133 Stat. 1075; Pub. L. 116–52, § 2, Aug. 23, 2019, 133 Stat. 1076; Pub. L. 116–54, § 4(a)(1), Aug. 23, 2019, 133 Stat. 1085; Pub. L. 116–92, div. A, title XVII, § 1736, Dec. 20, 2019, 133 Stat. 1819; Pub. L. 116–136, div. A, title I, § 1113(a)(4)(A), (b)(1)(A), (2)(A)(i), Mar. 27, 2020, 134 Stat. 311, 312; Pub. L. 117–151, § 2(a), June 21, 2022, 136 Stat. 1298; Pub. L. 119–27, § 11(b), July 18, 2025, 139 Stat. 457.)

Sections that reference this section: 104, 522, 546, 548, 707, 741

§102. Rules of construction

In this title—

(1) "after notice and a hearing", or a similar phrase —

(A) means after such notice as is appropriate in the particular circumstances, and such opportunity for a hearing as is appropriate in the particular circumstances; but

(B) authorizes an act without an actual hearing if such notice is given properly and if—

(i) such a hearing is not requested timely by a party in interest; or

(ii) there is insufficient time for a hearing to be commenced before such act must be done, and the court authorizes such act;

(2) "claim against the debtor" includes claim against property of the debtor;

(3) "includes" and "including" are not limiting;

(4) "may not" is prohibitive, and not permissive;

(5) "or" is not exclusive;

(6) "order for relief" means entry of an order for relief;

(7) the singular includes the plural;

(8) a definition, contained in a section of this title that refers to another section of this title, does not, for the purpose of such reference, affect the meaning of a term used in such other section; and

(9) "United States trustee" includes a designee of the United States trustee.

(Pub. L. 95–598, Nov. 6, 1978, 92 Stat. 2554; Pub. L. 98–353, title III, § 422, July 10, 1984, 98 Stat. 369; Pub. L. 99–554, title II, § 202, Oct. 27, 1986, 100 Stat. 3097.)

Sections that reference this section: None

§103. Applicability of chapters

(a) Except as provided in *section 1161* of this title, chapters 1, 3, and 5 of this title apply in a case under chapter 7, 11, 12, or 13 of this title, and this chapter, *sections 307, 362(o)*, 555 through 557, and 559 through 562 apply in a case under chapter 15.

(b) Subchapters I and II of chapter 7 of this title apply only in a case under such chapter.

(c) Subchapter III of chapter 7 of this title applies only in a case under such chapter concerning a stockbroker.

(d) Subchapter IV of chapter 7 of this title applies only in a case under such chapter concerning a commodity broker.

(e) Scope of Application.—

Subchapter V of chapter 7 of this title shall apply only in a case under such chapter concerning the liquidation of an uninsured State member bank, or a corporation organized under section 25A of the Federal Reserve Act, which operates, or operates as, a multilateral clearing organization pursuant to section 409 of the Federal Deposit Insurance Corporation Improvement Act of 1991.

(f) Except as provided in *section 901* of this title, only chapters 1 and 9 of this title apply in a case under such chapter 9.

(g) Except as provided in *section 901* of this title, subchapters I, II, and III of chapter 11 of this title apply only in a case under such chapter.

(h) Subchapter IV of chapter 11 of this title applies only in a case under such chapter concerning a railroad.

(i) Subchapter V of chapter 11 of this title applies only in a case under chapter 11 in which a debtor (as defined in *section 1182*) elects that subchapter V of chapter 11 shall apply.

(j) Chapter 13 of this title applies only in a case under such chapter.

(k) Chapter 12 of this title applies only in a case under such chapter.

(l) Chapter 15 applies only in a case under such chapter, except that—

(1) *sections 1505, 1513,* and *1514* apply in all cases under this title; and

(2) *section 1509* applies whether or not a case under this title is pending.

(Pub. L. 95–598, Nov. 6, 1978, 92 Stat. 2555; Pub. L. 97–222, § 2, July 27, 1982, 96 Stat. 235; Pub. L. 98–353, title III, § 423, July 10, 1984, 98 Stat. 369; Pub. L. 99–554, title II, § 252, Oct. 27, 1986, 100 Stat. 3104; Pub. L. 106–554, § 1(a)(5) [title I, § 112(c)(5)(A)], Dec. 21, 2000, 114 Stat. 2763, 2763A–394; Pub. L. 109–8, title VIII, § 802(a), Apr. 20, 2005, 119 Stat. 145; Pub. L. 111–327, § 2(a)(2), Dec. 22, 2010, 124 Stat. 3557; Pub. L. 116–54, § 4(a)(2), Aug. 23, 2019, 133 Stat. 1085; Pub. L. 116–136, div. A, title I, § 1113(a)(2), Mar. 27, 2020, 134 Stat. 311.)

Sections that reference this section: 523, 524, 901, 902, 943

§104. Adjustment of dollar amounts

(a) On April 1, 1998, and at each 3-year interval ending on April 1 thereafter, each dollar amount in effect under *sections 101(3), 101*(18), 101(19A), 101(51D), 109(e), 303(b), 507(a), 522(d), 522(f)(3) and 522(f)(4), 522(n), 522(p), 522(q), 523(a)(2)(C), 541(b), 547(c)(9), 707(b), 1182(1), 1322(d), 1325(b), and 1326(b)(3) of this title and section 1409(b) of title 28 immediately before such April 1 shall be adjusted—

(1) to reflect the change in the Consumer Price Index for All Urban Consumers, published by the Department of Labor, for the most recent 3-year period ending immediately before January 1 preceding such April 1, and

(2) to round to the nearest $25 the dollar amount that represents such change.

(b) Not later than March 1, 1998, and at each 3-year interval ending on March 1 thereafter, the Judicial Conference of the United States shall publish in the Federal Register the dollar amounts that will become effective on such April 1 under *sections 101(3), 101*(18), 101(19A), 101(51D), 109(e), 303(b), 507(a), 522(d), 522(f)(3) and 522(f)(4), 522(n), 522(p), 522(q), 523(a)(2)(C), 541(b), 547(c)(9), 707(b), 1182(1), 1322(d), 1325(b), and 1326(b)(3) of this title and section 1409(b) of title 28.

(c) Adjustments made in accordance with subsection (a) shall not apply with respect to cases commenced before the date of such adjustments.

(Pub. L. 95–598, Nov. 6, 1978, 92 Stat. 2555; Pub. L. 103–394, title I, § 108(e), Oct. 22, 1994, 108 Stat. 4112; Pub. L. 109–8, title I, § 102(j), title II, §§ 224(e)(2), 226(b), title III, § 322(b), title IV, § 432(c), title X, § 1002, title XII, § 1202, Apr. 20, 2005, 119 Stat. 35, 65, 67, 97, 110, 186, 193; Pub. L. 110–406, § 7, Oct. 13, 2008, 122 Stat. 4293; Pub. L. 117–151, § 2(b), June 21, 2022, 136 Stat. 1298.)

Sections that reference this section: None

§105. Power of court

(a) The court may issue any order, process, or judgment that is necessary or appropriate to carry out the provisions of this title. No provision of this title providing for the raising of an issue by a party in interest shall be construed to preclude the court from, sua sponte, taking any action or making any determination necessary or appropriate to enforce or implement court orders or rules, or to prevent an abuse of process.

(b) Notwithstanding subsection (a) of this section, a court may not appoint a receiver in a case under this title.

(c) The ability of any district judge or other officer or employee of a district court to exercise any of the authority or responsibilities conferred upon the court under this title shall be determined by reference to the provisions relating to such judge, officer, or employee set forth in title 28. This subsection shall not be interpreted to exclude bankruptcy judges and other officers or employees appointed pursuant to chapter 6 of title 28 from its operation.

(d) The court, on its own motion or on the request of a party in interest—

(1) shall hold such status conferences as are necessary to further the expeditious and economical resolution of the case; and

(2) unless inconsistent with another provision of this title or with applicable Federal Rules of Bankruptcy Procedure, may issue an order at any such conference prescribing such limitations and conditions as the court deems appropriate to ensure that the case is handled expeditiously and economically, including an order that—

(A) sets the date by which the trustee must assume or reject an executory contract or unexpired lease; or

(B) in a case under chapter 11 of this title —

(i) sets a date by which the debtor, or trustee if one has been appointed, shall file a disclosure statement and plan;

(ii) sets a date by which the debtor, or trustee if one has been appointed, shall solicit acceptances of a plan;

(iii) sets the date by which a party in interest other than a debtor may file a plan;

(iv) sets a date by which a proponent of a plan, other than the debtor, shall solicit acceptances of such plan;

(v) fixes the scope and format of the notice to be provided regarding the hearing on approval of the disclosure statement; or

(vi) provides that the hearing on approval of the disclosure statement may be combined with the hearing on confirmation of the plan.

(Pub. L. 95–598, Nov. 6, 1978, 92 Stat. 2555; Pub. L. 98–353, title I, § 118, July 10, 1984, 98 Stat. 344; Pub. L. 99–554, title II, § 203, Oct. 27, 1986, 100 Stat. 3097; Pub. L. 103–394, title I, § 104(a), Oct. 22, 1994, 108 Stat. 4108; Pub. L. 109–8, title IV, § 440, Apr. 20, 2005, 119 Stat. 114; Pub. L. 111–327, § 2(a)(3), Dec. 22, 2010, 124 Stat. 3557.)

Sections that reference this section: 106, 1181

§106. Waiver of sovereign immunity

(a) Notwithstanding an assertion of sovereign immunity, sovereign immunity is abrogated as to a governmental unit to the extent set forth in this section with respect to the following:

(1) *Sections 105*, 106, 107, 108, 303, 346, 362, 363, 364, 365, 366, 502, 503, 505, 506, 510, 522, 523, 524, 525, 542, 543, 544, 545, 546, 547, 548, 549, 550, 551, 552, 553, 722, 724, 726, 744, 749, 764, 901, 922, 926, 928, 929, 944, 1107, 1141, 1142, 1143, 1146, 1201, 1203, 1205, 1206, 1227, 1231, 1301, 1303, 1305, and 1327 of this title.

(2) The court may hear and determine any issue arising with respect to the application of such sections to governmental units.

(3) The court may issue against a governmental unit an order, process, or judgment under such sections or the Federal Rules of Bankruptcy Procedure, including an order or judgment awarding a money recovery, but not including an award of punitive damages. Such order or judgment for costs or fees under this title or the Federal Rules of Bankruptcy Procedure against any governmental unit shall be consistent with the provisions and limitations of section 2412(d)(2)(A) of title 28.

(4) The enforcement of any such order, process, or judgment against any governmental unit shall be consistent with appropriate nonbankruptcy law applicable to such governmental unit and, in the case of a money judgment against the United States, shall be paid as if it is a judgment rendered by a district court of the United States.

(5) Nothing in this section shall create any substantive claim for relief or cause of action not otherwise existing under this title, the Federal Rules of Bankruptcy Procedure, or nonbankruptcy law.

(b) A governmental unit that has filed a proof of claim in the case is deemed to have waived sovereign immunity with respect to a claim against such governmental unit that is property of the estate and that arose out of the same transaction or occurrence out of which the claim of such governmental unit arose.

(c) Notwithstanding any assertion of sovereign immunity by a governmental unit, there shall be offset against a claim or interest of a governmental unit any claim against such governmental unit that is property of the estate.

(Pub. L. 95–598, Nov. 6, 1978, 92 Stat. 2555; Pub. L. 103–394, title I, § 113, Oct. 22, 1994, 108 Stat. 4117; Pub. L. 111–327, § 2(a)(4), Dec. 22, 2010, 124 Stat. 3557.)

Sections that reference this section: None

§107. Public access to papers

(a) Except as provided in subsections (b) and (c) and subject to *section 112*, a paper filed in a case under this title and the dockets of a bankruptcy court are public records and open to examination by an entity at reasonable times without charge.

(b) On request of a party in interest, the bankruptcy court shall, and on the bankruptcy court's own motion, the bankruptcy court may—

(1) protect an entity with respect to a trade secret or confidential research, development, or commercial information; or

(2) protect a person with respect to scandalous or defamatory matter contained in a paper filed in a case under this title.

(c)

(1) The bankruptcy court, for cause, may protect an individual, with respect to the following types of information to the extent the court finds that disclosure of such information would create undue risk of identity theft or other unlawful injury to the individual or the individual's property:

(A) Any means of identification (as defined in section 1028(d) of title 18) contained in a paper filed, or to be filed, in a case under this title.

(B) Other information contained in a paper described in subparagraph (A).

(2) Upon ex parte application demonstrating cause, the court shall provide access to information protected pursuant to paragraph (1) to an entity acting pursuant to the police or regulatory power of a domestic governmental unit.

(3) The United States trustee, bankruptcy administrator, trustee, and any auditor serving under section 586(f) of title 28—

(A) shall have full access to all information contained in any paper filed or submitted in a case under this title; and

(B) shall not disclose information specifically protected by the court under this title.

(Pub. L. 95–598, Nov. 6, 1978, 92 Stat. 2556; Pub. L. 109–8, title II, §§ 233(c), 234(a), (c), Apr. 20, 2005, 119 Stat. 74, 75; Pub. L. 111–327, § 2(a)(5), Dec. 22, 2010, 124 Stat. 3557.)

Sections that reference this section: None

§108. Extension of time

(a) If applicable nonbankruptcy law, an order entered in a nonbankruptcy proceeding, or an agreement fixes a period within which the debtor may commence an action, and such period has not expired before the date of the filing of the petition, the trustee may commence such action only before the later of—

(1) the end of such period, including any suspension of such period occurring on or after the commencement of the case; or

(2) two years after the order for relief.

(b) Except as provided in subsection (a) of this section, if applicable nonbankruptcy law, an order entered in a nonbankruptcy proceeding, or an agreement fixes a period within which the debtor or an individual protected under *section 1201* or *1301* of this title may file any pleading, demand, notice, or proof of claim or loss, cure a default, or perform any other similar act, and such period has not expired before the date of the filing of the petition, the trustee may only file, cure, or perform, as the case may be, before the later of—

(1) the end of such period, including any suspension of such period occurring on or after the commencement of the case; or

(2) 60 days after the order for relief.

(c) Except as provided in *section 524* of this title, if applicable nonbankruptcy law, an order entered in a nonbankruptcy proceeding, or an agreement fixes a period for commencing or continuing a civil action in a court other than a bankruptcy court on a claim against the debtor, or against an individual with respect to which such individual is protected under *section 1201* or *1301* of this title, and such period has not expired before the date of the filing of the petition, then such period does not expire until the later of—

(1) the end of such period, including any suspension of such period occurring on or after the commencement of the case; or

(2) 30 days after notice of the termination or expiration of the stay under *section 362, 922, 1201*, or *1301* of this title, as the case may be, with respect to such claim.

(Pub. L. 95–598, Nov. 6, 1978, 92 Stat. 2556; Pub. L. 98–353, title III, § 424, July 10, 1984, 98 Stat. 369; Pub. L. 99–554, title II, § 257(b), Oct. 27, 1986, 100 Stat. 3114; Pub. L. 109–8, title XII, § 1203, Apr. 20, 2005, 119 Stat. 193.)

Sections that reference this section: 541

§109. Who may be a debtor

(a) Notwithstanding any other provision of this section, only a person that resides or has a domicile, a place of business, or property in the United States, or a municipality, may be a debtor under this title.

(b) A person may be a debtor under chapter 7 of this title only if such person is not—

(1) a railroad;

(2) a domestic insurance company, bank, savings bank, cooperative bank, savings and loan association, building and loan association, homestead association, a New Markets Venture Capital company as defined in *section 351* of the Small Business Investment Act of 1958, a small business investment company licensed by the Small Business Administration under *section 301* of the Small Business Investment Act of 1958, credit union, or industrial bank or similar institution which is an insured bank as defined in section 3(h) of the Federal Deposit Insurance Act, except that an uninsured State member bank, or a corporation organized under section 25A of the Federal Reserve Act, which operates, or operates as, a multilateral clearing organization pursuant to section 409 of the Federal Deposit Insurance Corporation Improvement Act of 1991 may be a debtor if a petition is filed at the direction of the Board of Governors of the Federal Reserve System; or

(3)

(A) a foreign insurance company, engaged in such business in the United States; or

(B) a foreign bank, savings bank, cooperative bank, savings and loan association, building and loan association, or credit union, that has a branch or agency (as defined in section 1(b) of the International Banking Act of 1978) in the United States.

(c) An entity may be a debtor under chapter 9 of this title if and only if such entity—

(1) is a municipality;

(2) is specifically authorized, in its capacity as a municipality or by name, to be a debtor under such chapter by State law, or by a governmental officer or organization empowered by State law to authorize such entity to be a debtor under such chapter;

(3) is insolvent;

(4) desires to effect a plan to adjust such debts; and

(5)

(A) has obtained the agreement of creditors holding at least a majority in amount of the claims of each class that such entity intends to impair under a plan in a case under such chapter;

(B) has negotiated in good faith with creditors and has failed to obtain the agreement of creditors holding at least a majority in amount of the claims of each class that such entity intends to impair under a plan in a case under such chapter;

(C) is unable to negotiate with creditors because such negotiation is impracticable; or

(D) reasonably believes that a creditor may attempt to obtain a transfer that is avoidable under *section 547* of this title.

(d) Only a railroad, a person that may be a debtor under chapter 7 of this title (except a stockbroker or a commodity broker), and an uninsured State member bank, or a corporation organized under section 25A of the Federal Reserve Act, which operates, or operates as, a multilateral clearing organization pursuant to section 409 1 of the Federal Deposit Insurance Corporation

Improvement Act of 1991 may be a debtor under chapter 11 of this title.

(e) Only an individual with regular income that owes, on the date of the filing of the petition, noncontingent, liquidated, unsecured debts of less than $526,700 and noncontingent, liquidated, secured debts of less than $1,580,125, or an individual with regular income and such individual's spouse, except a stockbroker or a commodity broker, that owe, on the date of the filing of the petition, noncontingent, liquidated, unsecured debts that aggregate less than $526,700 and noncontingent, liquidated, secured debts of less than $1,580,125 may be a debtor under chapter 13 of this title.

(f) Only a family farmer or family fisherman with regular annual income may be a debtor under chapter 12 of this title.

(g) Notwithstanding any other provision of this section, no individual or family farmer may be a debtor under this title who has been a debtor in a case pending under this title at any time in the preceding 180 days if—

(1) the case was dismissed by the court for willful failure of the debtor to abide by orders of the court, or to appear before the court in proper prosecution of the case; or

(2) the debtor requested and obtained the voluntary dismissal of the case following the filing of a request for relief from the automatic stay provided by *section 362* of this title.

(h)

(1) Subject to paragraphs (2) and (3), and notwithstanding any other provision of this section other than paragraph (4) of this subsection, an individual may not be a debtor under this title unless such individual has, during the 180-day period ending on the date of filing of the petition by such individual, received from an approved nonprofit budget and credit counseling agency described in *section 111(a)* an individual or group briefing (including a briefing conducted by telephone or on the Internet) that outlined the opportunities for available credit counseling and assisted such individual in performing a related budget analysis.

(2)

(A) Paragraph (1) shall not apply with respect to a debtor who resides in a district for which the United States trustee (or the bankruptcy administrator, if any) determines that the approved nonprofit budget and credit counseling agencies for such district are not reasonably able to provide adequate services to the additional individuals who would otherwise seek credit counseling from such agencies by reason of the requirements of paragraph (1).

(B) The United States trustee (or the bankruptcy administrator, if any) who makes a determination described in subparagraph (A) shall review such determination not later than 1 year after the date of such determination, and not less frequently than annually thereafter. Notwithstanding the preceding sentence, a nonprofit budget and credit counseling agency may be disapproved by the United States trustee (or the bankruptcy administrator, if any) at any time.

(3)

(A) Subject to subparagraph (B), the requirements of paragraph (1) shall not apply with respect to a debtor who submits to the court a certification that —

(i) describes exigent circumstances that merit a waiver of the requirements of paragraph (1);

(ii) states that the debtor requested credit counseling services from an approved nonprofit budget and credit counseling agency, but was unable to obtain the services referred to in paragraph (1) during the 7-day period beginning on the date on which the debtor made that request; and

(iii) is satisfactory to the court.

(B) With respect to a debtor, an exemption under subparagraph (A) shall cease to apply to that debtor on the date on which the debtor meets the requirements of paragraph (1), but in no case may the exemption apply to that debtor after the date that is 30 days after the debtor files a petition, except that the court, for cause, may order an additional 15 days.

(4) The requirements of paragraph (1) shall not apply with respect to a debtor whom the court determines, after notice and hearing, is unable to complete those requirements because of incapacity, disability, or active military duty in a military combat zone. For the purposes of this paragraph, incapacity means that the debtor is impaired by reason of mental illness or mental deficiency so that he is incapable of realizing and making rational decisions with respect to his financial responsibilities; and "disability" means that the debtor is so physically impaired as to be unable, after reasonable effort, to participate in an in person, telephone, or Internet briefing required under paragraph (1).

(Pub. L. 95–598, Nov. 6, 1978, 92 Stat. 2557; Pub. L. 97–320, title VII, § 703(d), Oct. 15, 1982, 96 Stat. 1539; Pub. L. 98–353, title III, §§ 301, 425, July 10, 1984, 98 Stat. 352, 369; Pub. L. 99–554, title II, § 253, Oct. 27, 1986, 100 Stat. 3105; Pub. L. 100–597, § 2, Nov. 3, 1988, 102 Stat. 3028; Pub. L. 103–394, title I, § 108(a), title II, § 220, title IV, § 402, title V, § 501(d)(2), Oct. 22, 1994, 108 Stat. 4111, 4129, 4141, 4143; Pub. L. 106–554, § 1(a)(5) [title I, § 112(c)(1), (2)], § 1(a)(8) [§ 1(e)], Dec. 21, 2000, 114 Stat. 2763, 2763A–393, 2763A–665; Pub. L. 109–8, title I, § 106(a), title VIII, § 802(d)(1), title X, § 1007(b), title XII, § 1204(1), Apr. 20, 2005, 119 Stat. 37, 146, 188, 193; Pub. L. 111–16, § 2(1), May 7, 2009, 123 Stat. 1607; Pub. L. 111–327, § 2(a)(6), Dec. 22, 2010, 124 Stat. 3557; Pub. L. 117–151, § 2(c), (i)(1)(A), June 21, 2022, 136 Stat. 1298, 1300.)

Sections that reference this section: 101, 111, 1328, 1501, 349, 362, 521, 727, 921

§110. Penalty for persons who negligently or fraudulently prepare bankruptcy petitions

(a) In this section—

(1) "bankruptcy petition preparer" means a person, other than an attorney for the debtor or an employee of such attorney under the direct supervision of such attorney, who prepares for compensation a document for filing; and

(2) "document for filing" means a petition or any other document prepared for filing by a debtor in a United States bankruptcy court or a United States district court in connection with a case under this title.

(b)

(1) A bankruptcy petition preparer who prepares a document for filing shall sign the document and print on the document the preparer's name and address. If a bankruptcy petition preparer is not an individual, then an officer, principal, responsible person, or partner of the bankruptcy petition preparer shall be required to—

(A) sign the document for filing; and

(B) print on the document the name and address of that officer, principal, responsible person, or partner.

(2)

(A) Before preparing any document for filing or accepting any fees from or on behalf of a debtor, the bankruptcy petition preparer shall provide to the debtor a written notice which shall be on an official form prescribed by the Judicial Conference of the United States in accordance with rule 9009 of the Federal Rules of Bankruptcy Procedure.

(B) The notice under subparagraph (A)—

(i) shall inform the debtor in simple language that a bankruptcy petition preparer is not an attorney and may not practice law or give legal advice;

(ii) may contain a description of examples of legal advice that a bankruptcy petition preparer is not authorized to give, in addition to any advice that the preparer may not give by reason of subsection (e)(2); and

(iii) shall—

(I) be signed by the debtor and, under penalty of perjury, by the bankruptcy petition preparer; and

(II) be filed with any document for filing.

(c)

(1) A bankruptcy petition preparer who prepares a document for filing shall place on the document, after the preparer's signature, an identifying number that identifies individuals who prepared the document.

(2)

(A) Subject to subparagraph (B), for purposes of this section, the identifying number of a bankruptcy petition preparer shall be the Social Security account number of each individual who prepared the document or assisted in its preparation.

(B) If a bankruptcy petition preparer is not an individual, the identifying number of the bankruptcy petition preparer shall be the Social Security account number of the officer, principal, responsible person, or partner of the bankruptcy petition preparer.

(d) A bankruptcy petition preparer shall, not later than the time at which a document for filing is presented for the debtor's signature, furnish to the debtor a copy of the document.

(e)

(1) A bankruptcy petition preparer shall not execute any document on behalf of a debtor.

(2)

(A) A bankruptcy petition preparer may not offer a potential bankruptcy debtor any legal advice, including any legal advice described in subparagraph (B).

(B) The legal advice referred to in subparagraph (A) includes advising the debtor—

(i) whether—

(I) to file a petition under this title; or

(II) commencing a case under chapter 7, 11, 12, or 13 is appropriate;

(ii) whether the debtor's debts will be discharged in a case under this title;

(iii) whether the debtor will be able to retain the debtor's home, car, or other property after commencing a case under this title;

(iv) concerning—

(I) the tax consequences of a case brought under this title; or

(II) the dischargeability of tax claims;

(v) whether the debtor may or should promise to repay debts to a creditor or enter into a reaffirmation agreement with a creditor to reaffirm a debt;

(vi) concerning how to characterize the nature of the debtor's interests in property or the debtor's debts; or

(vii) concerning bankruptcy procedures and rights.

(f) A bankruptcy petition preparer shall not use the word "legal" or any similar term in any advertisements, or advertise under any category that includes the word "legal" or any similar term.

(g) A bankruptcy petition preparer shall not collect or receive any payment from the debtor or on behalf of the debtor for the court fees in connection with filing the petition.

(h)

(1) The Supreme Court may promulgate rules under section 2075 of title 28, or the Judicial Conference of the United States may prescribe guidelines, for setting a maximum allowable fee chargeable by a bankruptcy petition preparer. A bankruptcy petition preparer shall notify the debtor of any such maximum amount before preparing any document for filing for the debtor or accepting any fee from or on behalf of the debtor.

(2) A declaration under penalty of perjury by the bankruptcy petition preparer shall be filed together with the petition, disclosing any fee received from or on behalf of the debtor within 12 months immediately prior to the filing of the case, and any unpaid fee charged to the debtor. If rules or guidelines setting a maximum fee for services have been promulgated or prescribed under paragraph (1), the declaration under this paragraph shall include a certification that the bankruptcy petition preparer complied with the notification requirement under paragraph (1).

(3)

(A) The court shall disallow and order the immediate turnover to the bankruptcy trustee any fee referred to in paragraph (2)—

(i) found to be in excess of the value of any services rendered by the bankruptcy petition preparer during the 12-month period immediately preceding the date of the filing of the petition; or

(ii) found to be in violation of any rule or guideline promulgated or prescribed under paragraph (1).

(B) All fees charged by a bankruptcy petition preparer may be forfeited in any case in which the bankruptcy petition preparer fails to comply with this subsection or subsection (b), (c), (d), (e), (f), or (g).

(C) An individual may exempt any funds recovered under this paragraph under *section 522(b)*.

(4) The debtor, the trustee, a creditor, the United States trustee (or the bankruptcy administrator, if any) or the court, on the initiative of the court, may file a motion for an order under paragraph (3).

(5) A bankruptcy petition preparer shall be fined not more than $500 for each failure to comply with a court order to turn over funds within 30 days of service of such order.

(i)

(1) If a bankruptcy petition preparer violates this section or commits any act that the court finds to be fraudulent, unfair, or deceptive, on the motion of the debtor, trustee, United States trustee (or the bankruptcy administrator, if any), and after notice and a hearing, the court shall order the bankruptcy petition preparer to pay to the debtor —

(A) the debtor's actual damages;

(B) the greater of—

(i) $2,000; or

(ii) twice the amount paid by the debtor to the bankruptcy petition preparer for the preparer's services; and

(C) reasonable attorneys' fees and costs in moving for damages under this subsection.

(2) If the trustee or creditor moves for damages on behalf of the debtor under this subsection, the bankruptcy petition preparer shall be ordered to pay the movant the additional amount of $1,000 plus reasonable attorneys' fees and costs incurred.

(j)

(1) A debtor for whom a bankruptcy petition preparer has prepared a document for filing, the trustee, a creditor, or the United States trustee in the district in which the bankruptcy petition preparer resides, has conducted business, or the United States trustee in any other district in which the debtor resides may bring a civil action to enjoin a bankruptcy petition preparer from engaging in any conduct in violation of this section or from further acting as a bankruptcy petition preparer.

(2)

(A) In an action under paragraph (1), if the court finds that—

(i) a bankruptcy petition preparer has—

(I) engaged in conduct in violation of this section or of any provision of this title;

(II) misrepresented the preparer's experience or education as a bankruptcy petition preparer; or

(III) engaged in any other fraudulent, unfair, or deceptive conduct; and

(ii) injunctive relief is appropriate to prevent the recurrence of such conduct,

the court may enjoin the bankruptcy petition preparer from engaging in such conduct.

(B) If the court finds that a bankruptcy petition preparer has continually engaged in conduct described in subclause (I), (II), or (III) of clause (i) and that an injunction prohibiting such conduct would not be sufficient to prevent such person's interference with the proper administration of this title, has not paid a penalty imposed under this section, or failed to disgorge all fees ordered by the court the court may enjoin the person from acting as a bankruptcy petition preparer.

(3) The court, as part of its contempt power, may enjoin a bankruptcy petition preparer that has failed to comply with a previous order issued under this section. The injunction under this paragraph may be issued on the motion of the court, the trustee, or the United States trustee (or the bankruptcy administrator, if any).

(4) The court shall award to a debtor, trustee, or creditor that brings a successful action under this subsection reasonable attorneys' fees and costs of the action, to be paid by the bankruptcy petition preparer.

(k) Nothing in this section shall be construed to permit activities that are otherwise prohibited by law, including rules and laws that prohibit the unauthorized practice of law.

(l)

(1) A bankruptcy petition preparer who fails to comply with any provision of subsection (b), (c), (d), (e), (f), (g), or (h) may be fined not more than $500 for each such failure.

(2) The court shall triple the amount of a fine assessed under paragraph (1) in any case in which the court finds that a bankruptcy petition preparer—

(A) advised the debtor to exclude assets or income that should have been included on applicable schedules;

(B) advised the debtor to use a false Social Security account number;

(C) failed to inform the debtor that the debtor was filing for relief under this title; or

(D) prepared a document for filing in a manner that failed to disclose the identity of the bankruptcy petition preparer.

(3) A debtor, trustee, creditor, or United States trustee (or the bankruptcy administrator, if any) may file a motion for an order imposing a fine on the bankruptcy petition preparer for any violation of this section.

(4)

(A) Fines imposed under this subsection in judicial districts served by United States trustees shall be paid to the United States trustees, who shall deposit an amount equal to such fines in the United States Trustee Fund.

(B) Fines imposed under this subsection in judicial districts served by bankruptcy administrators shall be deposited as offsetting receipts to the fund established under section 1931 of title 28, and shall remain available until expended to reimburse any appropriation for the amount paid out of such appropriation for expenses of the operation and maintenance of the courts of the United States.

(Added Pub. L. 103–394, title III, § 308(a), Oct. 22, 1994, 108 Stat. 4135; amended Pub. L. 109–8, title II, § 221, title XII, § 1205, Apr. 20, 2005, 119 Stat. 59, 194; Pub. L. 110–161, div. B, title II, § 212(b), Dec. 26, 2007, 121 Stat. 1914; Pub. L. 111–327, § 2(a)(7), Dec. 22, 2010, 124 Stat. 3558.)

Sections that reference this section: 101, 521

§111. Nonprofit budget and credit counseling agencies; financial management instructional courses

(a) The clerk shall maintain a publicly available list of—

(1) nonprofit budget and credit counseling agencies that provide 1 or more services described in *section 109(h)* currently approved by the United States trustee (or the bankruptcy administrator, if any); and

(2) instructional courses concerning personal financial management currently approved by the United States trustee (or the bankruptcy administrator, if any), as applicable.

(b) The United States trustee (or bankruptcy administrator, if any) shall only approve a nonprofit budget and credit counseling agency or an instructional course concerning personal financial management as follows:

(1) The United States trustee (or bankruptcy administrator, if any) shall have thoroughly reviewed the qualifications of the nonprofit budget and credit counseling agency or of the provider of the instructional course under the standards set forth in this section, and the services or instructional courses that will be offered by such agency or such provider, and may require such agency or such provider that has sought approval to provide information with respect to such review.

(2) The United States trustee (or bankruptcy administrator, if any) shall have determined that such agency or such instructional

course fully satisfies the applicable standards set forth in this section.

(3) If a nonprofit budget and credit counseling agency or instructional course did not appear on the approved list for the district under subsection (a) immediately before approval under this section, approval under this subsection of such agency or such instructional course shall be for a probationary period not to exceed 6 months.

(4) At the conclusion of the applicable probationary period under paragraph (3), the United States trustee (or bankruptcy administrator, if any) may only approve for an additional 1-year period, and for successive 1-year periods thereafter, an agency or instructional course that has demonstrated during the probationary or applicable subsequent period of approval that such agency or instructional course—

(A) has met the standards set forth under this section during such period; and

(B) can satisfy such standards in the future.

(5) Not later than 30 days after any final decision under paragraph (4), an interested person may seek judicial review of such decision in the appropriate district court of the United States.

(c)

(1) The United States trustee (or the bankruptcy administrator, if any) shall only approve a nonprofit budget and credit counseling agency that demonstrates that it will provide qualified counselors, maintain adequate provision for safekeeping and payment of client funds, provide adequate counseling with respect to client credit problems, and deal responsibly and effectively with other matters relating to the quality, effectiveness, and financial security of the services it provides.

(2) To be approved by the United States trustee (or the bankruptcy administrator, if any), a nonprofit budget and credit counseling agency shall, at a minimum—

(A) have a board of directors the majority of which—

(i) are not employed by such agency; and

(ii) will not directly or indirectly benefit financially from the outcome of the counseling services provided by such agency;

(B) if a fee is charged for counseling services, charge a reasonable fee, and provide services without regard to ability to pay the fee;

(C) provide for safekeeping and payment of client funds, including an annual audit of the trust accounts and appropriate employee bonding;

(D) provide full disclosures to a client, including funding sources, counselor qualifications, possible impact on credit reports, and any costs of such program that will be paid by such client and how such costs will be paid;

(E) provide adequate counseling with respect to a client's credit problems that includes an analysis of such client's current financial condition, factors that caused such financial condition, and how such client can develop a plan to respond to the problems without incurring negative amortization of debt;

(F) provide trained counselors who receive no commissions or bonuses based on the outcome of the counseling services provided by such agency, and who have adequate experience, and have been adequately trained to provide counseling services to individuals in financial difficulty, including the matters described in subparagraph (E);

(G) demonstrate adequate experience and background in providing credit counseling; and

(H) have adequate financial resources to provide continuing support services for budgeting plans over the life of any repayment plan.

(d) The United States trustee (or the bankruptcy administrator, if any) shall only approve an instructional course concerning personal financial management—

(1) for an initial probationary period under subsection (b)(3) if the course will provide at a minimum—

(A) trained personnel with adequate experience and training in providing effective instruction and services;

(B) learning materials and teaching methodologies designed to assist debtors in understanding personal financial management and that are consistent with stated objectives directly related to the goals of such instructional course;

(C) adequate facilities situated in reasonably convenient locations at which such instructional course is offered, except that such facilities may include the provision of such instructional course by telephone or through the Internet, if such instructional course is effective;

(D) the preparation and retention of reasonable records (which shall include the debtor's bankruptcy case number) to permit evaluation of the effectiveness of such instructional course, including any evaluation of satisfaction of instructional course requirements for each debtor attending such instructional course, which shall be available for inspection and evaluation by the Executive Office for United States Trustees, the United States trustee (or the bankruptcy administrator, if any), or the chief bankruptcy judge for the district in which such instructional course is offered; and

(E) if a fee is charged for the instructional course, charge a reasonable fee, and provide services without regard to ability to pay the fee; and

(2) for any 1-year period if the provider thereof has demonstrated that the course meets the standards of paragraph (1) and, in addition —

(A) has been effective in assisting a substantial number of debtors to understand personal financial management; and

(B) is otherwise likely to increase substantially the debtor's understanding of personal financial management.

(e) The district court may, at any time, investigate the qualifications of a nonprofit budget and credit counseling agency referred to in subsection (a), and request production of documents to ensure the integrity and effectiveness of such agency. The district court may, at any time, remove from the approved list under subsection (a) a nonprofit budget and credit counseling agency upon finding such agency does not meet the qualifications of subsection (b).

(f) The United States trustee (or the bankruptcy administrator, if any) shall notify the clerk that a nonprofit budget and credit counseling agency or an instructional course is no longer approved, in which case the clerk shall remove it from the list maintained under subsection (a).

(g)

(1) No nonprofit budget and credit counseling agency may provide to a credit reporting agency information concerning whether a debtor has received or sought instruction concerning personal financial management from such agency.

(2) A nonprofit budget and credit counseling agency that willfully or negligently fails to comply with any requirement under this title with respect to a debtor shall be liable for damages in an amount equal to the sum of—

(A) any actual damages sustained by the debtor as a result of the violation; and

(B) any court costs or reasonable attorneys' fees (as determined by the court) incurred in an action to recover those damages.

(Added Pub. L. 109–8, title I, § 106(e)(1), Apr. 20, 2005, 119 Stat. 38; amended Pub. L. 111–327, § 2(a)(8), Dec. 22, 2010, 124 Stat. 3558.)

Sections that reference this section: 109, 1328, 502, 727

§112. Prohibition on disclosure of name of minor children

The debtor may be required to provide information regarding a minor child involved in matters under this title but may not be required to disclose in the public records in the case the name of such minor child. The debtor may be required to disclose the name of such minor child in a nonpublic record that is maintained by the court and made available by the court for examination by the United States trustee, the trustee, and the auditor (if any) serving under section 586(f) of title 28, in the case. The court, the United States trustee, the trustee, and such auditor shall not disclose the name of such minor child maintained in such nonpublic record.

(Added Pub. L. 109–8, title II, § 233(a), Apr. 20, 2005, 119 Stat. 74.)

Sections that reference this section: 107

CHAPTER 3: CASE ADMINISTRATION

Subchapter I: Commencement of a Case

§301. Voluntary cases

(a) A voluntary case under a chapter of this title is commenced by the filing with the bankruptcy court of a petition under such chapter by an entity that may be a debtor under such chapter.

(b) The commencement of a voluntary case under a chapter of this title constitutes an order for relief under such chapter.

(Pub. L. 95–598, Nov. 6, 1978, 92 Stat. 2558; Pub. L. 109–8, title V, § 501(b), Apr. 20, 2005, 119 Stat. 118.)

Sections that reference this section: 101, 109, 1129, 1511, 362, 522, 541, 901, 921

§302. Joint cases

(a) A joint case under a chapter of this title is commenced by the filing with the bankruptcy court of a single petition under such chapter by an individual that may be a debtor under such chapter and such individual's spouse. The commencement of a joint case under a chapter of this title constitutes an order for relief under such chapter.

(b) After the commencement of a joint case, the court shall determine the extent, if any, to which the debtors' estates shall be consolidated.

(Pub. L. 95–598, Nov. 6, 1978, 92 Stat. 2558.)

Sections that reference this section: 522, 707

§303. Involuntary cases

(a) An involuntary case may be commenced only under chapter 7 or 11 of this title, and only against a person, except a farmer, family farmer, or a corporation that is not a moneyed, business, or commercial corporation, that may be a debtor under the chapter under which such case is commenced.

(b) An involuntary case against a person is commenced by the filing with the bankruptcy court of a petition under chapter 7 or 11 of this title—

(1) by three or more entities, each of which is either a holder of a claim against such person that is not contingent as to liability or the subject of a bona fide dispute as to liability or amount, or an indenture trustee representing such a holder, if such non-contingent, undisputed claims aggregate at least $21,050 more than the value of any lien on property of the debtor securing such claims held by the holders of such claims;

(2) if there are fewer than 12 such holders, excluding any employee or insider of such person and any transferee of a transfer that is voidable under *section 544, 545, 547, 548, 549,* or *724*(a) of this title, by one or more of such holders that hold in the aggregate at least $21,050 of such claims;

(3) if such person is a partnership—

(A) by fewer than all of the general partners in such partnership; or

(B) if relief has been ordered under this title with respect to all of the general partners in such partnership, by a general partner in such partnership, the trustee of such a general partner, or a holder of a claim against such partnership; or

(4) by a foreign representative of the estate in a foreign proceeding concerning such person.

(c) After the filing of a petition under this section but before the case is dismissed or relief is ordered, a creditor holding an unsecured claim that is not contingent, other than a creditor filing under subsection (b) of this section, may join in the petition with the same effect as if such joining creditor were a petitioning creditor under subsection (b) of this section.

(d) The debtor, or a general partner in a partnership debtor that did not join in the petition, may file an answer to a petition under this section.

(e) After notice and a hearing, and for cause, the court may require the petitioners under this section to file a bond to indemnify the debtor for such amounts as the court may later allow under subsection (i) of this section.

(f) Notwithstanding *section 363* of this title, except to the extent that the court orders otherwise, and until an order for relief in the case, any business of the debtor may continue to operate, and the debtor may continue to use, acquire, or dispose of property as if an involuntary case concerning the debtor had not been commenced.

(g) At any time after the commencement of an involuntary case under chapter 7 of this title but before an order for relief in the case, the court, on request of a party in interest, after notice to the debtor and a hearing, and if necessary to preserve the property of the estate or to prevent loss to the estate, may order the United States trustee to appoint an interim trustee under *section 701* of this title to take possession of the property of the estate and to operate any business of the debtor. Before an order for relief, the debtor may regain possession of property in the possession of a trustee ordered appointed under this subsection if the debtor files such bond as the court requires, conditioned on the debtor's accounting for and delivering to the trustee, if there is an order for relief in the case, such property, or the value, as of the date the debtor regains possession, of such property.

(h) If the petition is not timely controverted, the court shall order relief against the debtor in an involuntary case under the chapter under which the petition was filed. Otherwise, after trial, the court shall order relief against the debtor in an involuntary case under the chapter under which the petition was filed, only if—

(1) the debtor is generally not paying such debtor's debts as such debts become due unless such debts are the subject of a bona fide dispute as to liability or amount; or

(2) within 120 days before the date of the filing of the petition, a custodian, other than a trustee, receiver, or agent appointed or authorized to take charge of less than substantially all of the property of the debtor for the purpose of enforcing a lien against such property, was appointed or took possession.

(i) If the court dismisses a petition under this section other than on consent of all petitioners and the debtor, and if the debtor does not waive the right to judgment under this subsection, the court may grant judgment—

(1) against the petitioners and in favor of the debtor for—

(A) costs; or

(B) a reasonable attorney's fee; or

(2) against any petitioner that filed the petition in bad faith, for—

(A) any damages proximately caused by such filing; or

(B) punitive damages.

(j) Only after notice to all creditors and a hearing may the court dismiss a petition filed under this section—

(1) on the motion of a petitioner;

(2) on consent of all petitioners and the debtor; or

(3) for want of prosecution.

(k)

(1) If—

(A) the petition under this section is false or contains any materially false, fictitious, or fraudulent statement;

(B) the debtor is an individual; and

(C) the court dismisses such petition,

the court, upon the motion of the debtor, shall seal all the records of the court relating to such petition, and all references to such petition.

(2) If the debtor is an individual and the court dismisses a petition under this section, the court may enter an order prohibiting all consumer reporting agencies (as defined in section 603(f) of the Fair Credit Reporting Act (15 U.S.C. 1681a(f))) from making any consumer report (as defined in section 603(d) of that Act) that contains any information relating to such petition or to the case commenced by the filing of such petition.

(3) Upon the expiration of the statute of limitations described in section 3282 of title 18, for a violation of section 152 or 157 of such title, the court, upon the motion of the debtor and for good cause, may expunge any records relating to a petition filed under this section.

(Pub. L. 95–598, Nov. 6, 1978, 92 Stat. 2559; Pub. L. 98–353, title III, §§ 426, 427, July 10, 1984, 98 Stat. 369; Pub. L. 99–554, title II, §§ 204, 254, 283(b), Oct. 27, 1986, 100 Stat. 3097, 3105, 3116; Pub. L. 103–394, title I, § 108(b), Oct. 22, 1994, 108 Stat. 4112; Pub. L. 109–8, title III, § 332(b), title VIII, § 802(d)(2), title XII, § 1234(a), Apr. 20, 2005, 119 Stat. 103, 146, 204; Pub. L. 111–327, § 2(a)(9), Dec. 22, 2010, 124 Stat. 3558.)

Sections that reference this section: 1511, 1531, 306, 503, 504, 549

§304. Repealed. Pub. L. 109–8, title VIII, § 802(d)(3), Apr. 20, 2005, 119 Stat. 146

Sections that reference this section: None

§305. Abstention

(a) The court, after notice and a hearing, may dismiss a case under this title, or may suspend all proceedings in a case under this title, at any time if—

(1) the interests of creditors and the debtor would be better served by such dismissal or suspension; or

(2)

(A) a petition under *section 1515* for recognition of a foreign proceeding has been granted; and

(B) the purposes of chapter 15 of this title would be best served by such dismissal or suspension.

(b) A foreign representative may seek dismissal or suspension under subsection (a)(2) of this section.

(c) An order under subsection (a) of this section dismissing a case or suspending all proceedings in a case, or a decision not so to dismiss or suspend, is not reviewable by appeal or otherwise by the court of appeals under section 158(d), 1291, or 1292 of title 28 or by the Supreme Court of the United States under section 1254 of title 28.

(Pub. L. 95–598, Nov. 6, 1978, 92 Stat. 2561; Pub. L. 101–650, title III, § 309(a), Dec. 1, 1990, 104 Stat. 5113; Pub. L. 102–198, § 5, Dec. 9, 1991, 105 Stat. 1623; Pub. L. 109–8, title VIII, § 802(d)(6), Apr. 20, 2005, 119 Stat. 146.)

Sections that reference this section: 1529

§306. Limited appearance

An appearance in a bankruptcy court by a foreign representative in connection with a petition or request under *section 303* or *305* of this title does not submit such foreign representative to the jurisdiction of any court in the United States for any other purpose, but the bankruptcy court may condition any order under *section 303* or *305* of this title on compliance by such foreign representative with the orders of such bankruptcy court.

(Pub. L. 95–598, Nov. 6, 1978, 92 Stat. 2561; Pub. L. 109–8, title VIII, § 802(d)(5), Apr. 20, 2005, 119 Stat. 146.)

Sections that reference this section: 1509

§307. United States trustee

The United States trustee may raise and may appear and be heard on any issue in any case or proceeding under this title but may not file a plan pursuant to *section 1121(c)* of this title.

(Added Pub. L. 99–554, title II, § 205(a), Oct. 27, 1986, 100 Stat. 3098.)

Sections that reference this section: 103

§308. Debtor reporting requirements

(a) For purposes of this section, the term "profitability" means, with respect to a debtor, the amount of money that the debtor has earned or lost during current and recent fiscal periods.

(b) A debtor in a small business case shall file periodic financial and other reports containing information including—

(1) the debtor's profitability;

(2) reasonable approximations of the debtor's projected cash receipts and cash disbursements over a reasonable period;

(3) comparisons of actual cash receipts and disbursements with projections in prior reports;

(4) whether the debtor is—

(A) in compliance in all material respects with postpetition requirements imposed by this title and the Federal Rules of Bankruptcy Procedure; and

(B) timely filing tax returns and other required government filings and paying taxes and other administrative expenses when due;

(5) if the debtor is not in compliance with the requirements referred to in paragraph (4)(A) or filing tax returns and other required government filings and making the payments referred to in paragraph (4)(B), what the failures are and how, at what cost, and when the debtor intends to remedy such failures; and

(6) such other matters as are in the best interests of the debtor and creditors, and in the public interest in fair and efficient procedures under chapter 11 of this title.

(Added Pub. L. 109–8, title IV, § 434(a)(1), Apr. 20, 2005, 119 Stat. 111; amended Pub. L. 111–327, § 2(a)(10), Dec. 22, 2010, 124 Stat. 3558.)

Sections that reference this section: 1187

Subchapter II: Officers

§321. Eligibility to serve as trustee

(a) A person may serve as trustee in a case under this title only if such person is—

(1) an individual that is competent to perform the duties of trustee and, in a case under chapter 7, 12, or 13 of this title, resides or has an office in the judicial district within which the case is pending, or in any judicial district adjacent to such district; or

(2) a corporation authorized by such corporation's charter or bylaws to act as trustee, and, in a case under chapter 7, 12, or 13 of this title, having an office in at least one of such districts.

(b) A person that has served as an examiner in the case may not serve as trustee in the case.

(c) The United States trustee for the judicial district in which the case is pending is eligible to serve as trustee in the case if necessary.

(Pub. L. 95–598, Nov. 6, 1978, 92 Stat. 2561; Pub. L. 98–353, title III, § 428, July 10, 1984, 98 Stat. 369; Pub. L. 99–554, title II, §§ 206, 257(c), Oct. 27, 1986, 100 Stat. 3098, 3114.)

Sections that reference this section: None

§322. Qualification of trustee

(a) Except as provided in subsection (b)(1), a person selected under *section 701, 702, 703, 1104, 1163, 1183,* 1202, or 1302 of this title to serve as trustee in a case under this title qualifies if before seven days after such selection, and before beginning official duties, such person has filed with the court a bond in favor of the United States conditioned on the faithful performance of such official duties.

(b)

(1) The United States trustee qualifies wherever such trustee serves as trustee in a case under this title.

(2) The United States trustee shall determine—

(A) the amount of a bond required to be filed under subsection (a) of this section; and

(B) the sufficiency of the surety on such bond.

(c) A trustee is not liable personally or on such trustee's bond in favor of the United States for any penalty or forfeiture incurred by the debtor.

(d) A proceeding on a trustee's bond may not be commenced after two years after the date on which such trustee was discharged.

(Pub. L. 95–598, Nov. 6, 1978, 92 Stat. 2562; Pub. L. 98–353, title III, § 429, July 10, 1984, 98 Stat. 369; Pub. L. 99–554, title II, §§ 207, 257(d), Oct. 27, 1986, 100 Stat. 3098, 3114; Pub. L. 103–394, title V, § 501(d)(3), Oct. 22, 1994, 108 Stat. 4143; Pub. L. 111–16, § 2(2), May 7, 2009, 123 Stat. 1607; Pub. L. 116–54, § 4(a)(3), Aug. 23, 2019, 133 Stat. 1085.)

Sections that reference this section: 1101, 1104, 1183, 1202, 1302, 1522, 701, 703, 746

§323. Role and capacity of trustee

(a) The trustee in a case under this title is the representative of the estate.

(b) The trustee in a case under this title has capacity to sue and be sued.

(Pub. L. 95–598, Nov. 6, 1978, 92 Stat. 2562.)

Sections that reference this section: None

§324. Removal of trustee or examiner

(a) The court, after notice and a hearing, may remove a trustee, other than the United States trustee, or an examiner, for cause.

(b) Whenever the court removes a trustee or examiner under subsection (a) in a case under this title, such trustee or examiner shall thereby be removed in all other cases under this title in which such trustee or examiner is then serving unless the court orders otherwise.

(Pub. L. 95–598, Nov. 6, 1978, 92 Stat. 2562; Pub. L. 99–554, title II, § 208, Oct. 27, 1986, 100 Stat. 3098.)

Sections that reference this section: 1104, 703

§325. Effect of vacancy

A vacancy in the office of trustee during a case does not abate any pending action or proceeding, and the successor trustee shall be substituted as a party in such action or proceeding.

(Pub. L. 95–598, Nov. 6, 1978, 92 Stat. 2562.)

Sections that reference this section: None

§326. Limitation on compensation of trustee

(a) In a case under chapter 7 or 11, other than a case under subchapter V of chapter 11, the court may allow reasonable compensation under *section 330* of this title of the trustee for the trustee's services, payable after the trustee renders such services, not to exceed 25 percent on the first $5,000 or less, 10 percent on any amount in excess of $5,000 but not in excess of $50,000, 5 percent on any amount in excess of $50,000 but not in excess of $1,000,000, and reasonable compensation not to exceed 3 percent of such moneys in excess of $1,000,000, upon all moneys disbursed or turned over in the case by the trustee to parties in interest, excluding the debtor, but including holders of secured claims.

(b) In a case under subchapter V of chapter 11 or chapter 12 or 13 of this title, the court may not allow compensation for services or reimbursement of expenses of the United States trustee or of a standing trustee appointed under section 586(b) of title 28, but may allow reasonable compensation under *section 330* of this title of a trustee appointed under *section 1202(a)* or *1302*(a) of this title for the trustee's services, payable after the trustee renders such services, not to exceed five percent upon all payments under the plan.

(c) If more than one person serves as trustee in the case, the aggregate compensation of such persons for such service may not exceed the maximum compensation prescribed for a single trustee by subsection (a) or (b) of this section, as the case may be.

(d) The court may deny allowance of compensation for services or reimbursement of expenses of the trustee if the trustee failed to make diligent inquiry into facts that would permit denial of allowance under *section 328(c)* of this title or, with knowledge of such facts, employed a professional person under *section 327* of this title.

(Pub. L. 95–598, Nov. 6, 1978, 92 Stat. 2562; Pub. L. 98–353, title III, § 430(a), (b), July 10, 1984, 98 Stat. 369; Pub. L. 99–554, title II, § 209, Oct. 27, 1986, 100 Stat. 3098; Pub. L. 103–394, title I, § 107, Oct. 22, 1994, 108 Stat. 4111; Pub. L. 116–54, § 4(a)(4), Aug. 23, 2019, 133 Stat. 1085.)

Sections that reference this section: 330, 557

§327. Employment of professional persons

(a) Except as otherwise provided in this section, the trustee, with the court's approval, may employ one or more attorneys, accountants, appraisers, auctioneers, or other professional persons, that do not hold or represent an interest adverse to the estate, and that are disinterested persons, to represent or assist the trustee in carrying out the trustee's duties under this title.

(b) If the trustee is authorized to operate the business of the debtor under *section 721, 1202,* or *1108* of this title, and if the debtor has regularly employed attorneys, accountants, or other professional persons on salary, the trustee may retain or replace such professional persons if necessary in the operation of such business.

(c) In a case under chapter 7, 12, or 11 of this title, a person is not disqualified for employment under this section solely because of such person's employment by or representation of a creditor, unless there is objection by another creditor or the United States trustee, in which case the court shall disapprove such employment if there is an actual conflict of interest.

(d) The court may authorize the trustee to act as attorney or accountant for the estate if such authorization is in the best interest of the estate.

(e) The trustee, with the court's approval, may employ, for a specified special purpose, other than to represent the trustee in conducting the case, an attorney that has represented the debtor, if in the best interest of the estate, and if such attorney does not represent or hold any interest adverse to the debtor or to the estate with respect to the matter on which such attorney is to be employed.

(f) The trustee may not employ a person that has served as an examiner in the case.

(Pub. L. 95–598, Nov. 6, 1978, 92 Stat. 2563; Pub. L. 98–353, title III, § 430(c), July 10, 1984, 98 Stat. 370; Pub. L. 99–554, title II, §§ 210, 257(e), Oct. 27, 1986, 100 Stat. 3099, 3114.)

Sections that reference this section: 1107, 1195, 326, 328, 330, 331

§328. Limitation on compensation of professional persons

(a) The trustee, or a committee appointed under *section 1102* of this title, with the court's approval, may employ or authorize the employment of a professional person under *section 327* or *1103* of this title, as the case may be, on any reasonable terms and conditions of employment, including on a retainer, on an hourly basis, on a fixed or percentage fee basis, or on a contingent fee basis. Notwithstanding such terms and conditions, the court may allow compensation different from the compensation provided under such terms and conditions after the conclusion of such employment, if such terms and conditions prove to have been improvident in light of developments not capable of being anticipated at the time of the fixing of such terms and conditions.

(b) If the court has authorized a trustee to serve as an attorney or accountant for the estate under *section 327(d)* of this title, the court may allow compensation for the trustee's services as such attorney or accountant only to the extent that the trustee performed services as attorney or accountant for the estate and not for performance of any of the trustee's duties that are generally performed by a trustee without the assistance of an attorney or accountant for the estate.

(c) Except as provided in *section 327(c), 327*(e), or 1107(b) of this title, the court may deny allowance of compensation for services and reimbursement of expenses of a professional person employed under *section 327* or *1103* of this title if, at any time during such professional person's employment under *section 327* or *1103* of this title, such professional person is not a disinterested person, or represents or holds an interest adverse to the interest of the estate with respect to the matter on which such professional person is employed.

(Pub. L. 95–598, Nov. 6, 1978, 92 Stat. 2563; Pub. L. 98–353, title III, § 431, July 10, 1984, 98 Stat. 370; Pub. L. 109–8, title XII, § 1206, Apr. 20, 2005, 119 Stat. 194.)

Sections that reference this section: 326

§329. Debtor's transactions with attorneys

(a) Any attorney representing a debtor in a case under this title, or in connection with such a case, whether or not such attorney applies for compensation under this title, shall file with the court a statement of the compensation paid or agreed to be paid, if such payment or agreement was made after one year before the date of the filing of the petition, for services rendered or to be rendered in contemplation of or in connection with the case by such attorney, and the source of such compensation.

(b) If such compensation exceeds the reasonable value of any such services, the court may cancel any such agreement, or order the return of any such payment, to the extent excessive, to—

(1) the estate, if the property transferred—

(A) would have been property of the estate; or

(B) was to be paid by or on behalf of the debtor under a plan under chapter 11, 12, or 13 of this title; or

(2) the entity that made such payment.

(Pub. L. 95–598, Nov. 6, 1978, 92 Stat. 2564; Pub. L. 98–353, title III, § 432, July 10, 1984, 98 Stat. 370; Pub. L. 99–554, title II, § 257(c), Oct. 27, 1986, 100 Stat. 3114.)

Sections that reference this section: 541

§330. Compensation of officers

(a)

(1) After notice to the parties in interest and the United States Trustee and a hearing, and subject to *sections 326, 328,* and *329,* the court may award to a trustee, a consumer privacy ombudsman appointed under *section 332,* an examiner, an ombudsman appointed under *section 333,* or a professional person employed under *section 327* or *1103* —

(A) reasonable compensation for actual, necessary services rendered by the trustee, examiner, ombudsman, professional person, or attorney and by any paraprofessional person employed by any such person; and

(B) reimbursement for actual, necessary expenses.

(2) The court may, on its own motion or on the motion of the United States Trustee, the United States Trustee for the District or Region, the trustee for the estate, or any other party in interest, award compensation that is less than the amount of compensation that is requested.

(3) In determining the amount of reasonable compensation to be awarded to an examiner, trustee under chapter 11, or professional person, the court shall consider the nature, the extent, and the value of such services, taking into account all relevant factors, including—

(A) the time spent on such services;

(B) the rates charged for such services;

(C) whether the services were necessary to the administration of, or beneficial at the time at which the service was rendered toward the completion of, a case under this title;

(D) whether the services were performed within a reasonable amount of time commensurate with the complexity, importance, and nature of the problem, issue, or task addressed;

(E) with respect to a professional person, whether the person is board certified or otherwise has demonstrated skill and experience in the bankruptcy field; and

(F) whether the compensation is reasonable based on the customary compensation charged by comparably skilled practitioners in cases other than cases under this title.

(4)

(A) Except as provided in subparagraph (B), the court shall not allow compensation for—

(i) unnecessary duplication of services; or

(ii) services that were not—

(I) reasonably likely to benefit the debtor's estate; or

(II) necessary to the administration of the case.

(B) In a chapter 12 or chapter 13 case in which the debtor is an individual, the court may allow reasonable compensation to the debtor's attorney for representing the interests of the debtor in connection with the bankruptcy case based on a consideration of the benefit and necessity of such services to the debtor and the other factors set forth in this section.

(5) The court shall reduce the amount of compensation awarded under this section by the amount of any interim compensation awarded under *section 331*, and, if the amount of such interim compensation exceeds the amount of compensation awarded under this section, may order the return of the excess to the estate.

(6) Any compensation awarded for the preparation of a fee application shall be based on the level and skill reasonably required to prepare the application.

(7) In determining the amount of reasonable compensation to be awarded to a trustee, the court shall treat such compensation as a commission, based on *section 326*.

(b)

(1) There shall be paid from the filing fee in a case under chapter 7 of this title $105 to the trustee serving in such case, after such trustee's services are rendered.

(2) The Judicial Conference of the United States—

(A) shall prescribe additional fees of the same kind as prescribed under section 1914(b) of title 28; and

(B) may prescribe notice of appearance fees and fees charged against distributions in cases under this title;

to pay $15 to trustees serving in cases after such trustees' services are rendered. Beginning 1 year after the date of the enactment of the Bankruptcy Reform Act of 1994, such $15 shall be paid in addition to the amount paid under paragraph (1).

(c) Unless the court orders otherwise, in a case under chapter 12 or 13 of this title the compensation paid to the trustee serving in the case shall not be less than $5 per month from any distribution under the plan during the administration of the plan.

(d) In a case in which the United States trustee serves as trustee, the compensation of the trustee under this section shall be paid to the clerk of the bankruptcy court and deposited by the clerk into the United States Trustee System Fund established by section 589a of title 28.

(Pub. L. 95–598, Nov. 6, 1978, 92 Stat. 2564; Pub. L. 98–353, title III, §§ 433, 434, July 10, 1984, 98 Stat. 370; Pub. L. 99–554, title II, §§ 211, 257(f), Oct. 27, 1986, 100 Stat. 3099, 3114; Pub. L. 103–394, title I, § 117, title II, § 224(b), Oct. 22, 1994, 108 Stat. 4119, 4130; Pub. L. 109–8, title II, § 232(b), title IV, §§ 407, 415, title XI, § 1104(b), Apr. 20, 2005, 119 Stat. 74, 106, 107, 192; Pub. L. 116–325, § 3(c), Jan. 12, 2021, 134 Stat. 5087; Pub. L. 117–43, div. A, § 131, Sept. 30, 2021, 135 Stat. 351; Pub. L. 119–76, § 3(a), Feb. 6, 2026, 140 Stat. 741.)

Sections that reference this section: 1107, 1184, 1203, 326, 331, 503

§331. Interim compensation

A trustee, an examiner, a debtor's attorney, or any professional person employed under *section 327* or *1103* of this title may apply to the court not more than once every 120 days after an order for relief in a case under this title, or more often if the court permits, for such compensation for services rendered before the date of such an application or reimbursement for expenses incurred before such date as is provided under *section 330* of this title. After notice and a hearing, the court may allow and disburse to such applicant such compensation or reimbursement.

(Pub. L. 95–598, Nov. 6, 1978, 92 Stat. 2564.)

Sections that reference this section: 330

§332. Consumer privacy ombudsman

(a) If a hearing is required under *section 363(b)(1)(B)*, the court shall order the United States trustee to appoint, not later than 7 days before the commencement of the hearing, 1 disinterested person (other than the United States trustee) to serve as the consumer privacy ombudsman in the case and shall require that notice of such hearing be timely given to such ombudsman.

(b) The consumer privacy ombudsman may appear and be heard at such hearing and shall provide to the court information to assist the court in its consideration of the facts, circumstances, and conditions of the proposed sale or lease of personally identifiable information under *section 363(b)(1)(B)*. Such information may include presentation of—

(1) the debtor's privacy policy;

(2) the potential losses or gains of privacy to consumers if such sale or such lease is approved by the court;

(3) the potential costs or benefits to consumers if such sale or such lease is approved by the court; and

(4) the potential alternatives that would mitigate potential privacy losses or potential costs to consumers.

(c) A consumer privacy ombudsman shall not disclose any personally identifiable information obtained by the ombudsman under this title.

(Added Pub. L. 109–8, title II, § 232(a), Apr. 20, 2005, 119 Stat. 73; amended Pub. L. 111–16, § 2(3), May 7, 2009, 123 Stat. 1607.)

Sections that reference this section: 330, 363

§333. Appointment of patient care ombudsman

(a)

(1) If the debtor in a case under chapter 7, 9, or 11 is a health care business, the court shall order, not later than 30 days after the commencement of the case, the appointment of an ombudsman to monitor the quality of patient care and to represent the interests of the patients of the health care business unless the court finds that the appointment of such ombudsman is not necessary for the protection of patients under the specific facts of the case.

(2)

(A) If the court orders the appointment of an ombudsman under paragraph (1), the United States trustee shall appoint 1 disinterested person (other than the United States trustee) to serve as such ombudsman.

(B) If the debtor is a health care business that provides long-term care, then the United States trustee may appoint the State Long-Term Care Ombudsman appointed under the Older Americans Act of 1965 for the State in which the case is pending to serve as the ombudsman required by paragraph (1).

(C) If the United States trustee does not appoint a State Long-Term Care Ombudsman under subparagraph (B), the court shall notify the State Long-Term Care Ombudsman appointed under the Older Americans Act of 1965 for the State in which the case is pending, of the name and address of the person who is appointed under subparagraph (A).

(b) An ombudsman appointed under subsection (a) shall—

(1) monitor the quality of patient care provided to patients of the debtor, to the extent necessary under the circumstances, including interviewing patients and physicians;

(2) not later than 60 days after the date of appointment, and not less frequently than at 60-day intervals thereafter, report to the court after notice to the parties in interest, at a hearing or in writing, regarding the quality of patient care provided to patients of the debtor; and

(3) if such ombudsman determines that the quality of patient care provided to patients of the debtor is declining significantly or is otherwise being materially compromised, file with the court a motion or a written report, with notice to the parties in interest immediately upon making such determination.

(c)

(1) An ombudsman appointed under subsection (a) shall maintain any information obtained by such ombudsman under this section that relates to patients (including information relating to patient records) as confidential information. Such ombudsman may not review confidential patient records unless the court approves such review in advance and imposes restrictions on such ombudsman to protect the confidentiality of such records.

(2) An ombudsman appointed under subsection (a)(2)(B) shall have access to patient records consistent with authority of such ombudsman under the Older Americans Act of 1965 and under non-Federal laws governing the State Long-Term Care Ombudsman program.

(Added Pub. L. 109–8, title XI, § 1104(a)(1), Apr. 20, 2005, 119 Stat. 191.)

Sections that reference this section: 330

Subchapter III: Administration

§341. Meetings of creditors and equity security holders

(a) Within a reasonable time after the order for relief in a case under this title, the United States trustee shall convene and preside at a meeting of creditors.

(b) The United States trustee may convene a meeting of any equity security holders.

(c) The court may not preside at, and may not attend, any meeting under this section including any final meeting of creditors. Notwithstanding any local court rule, provision of a State constitution, any otherwise applicable nonbankruptcy law, or any other requirement that representation at the meeting of creditors under subsection (a) be by an attorney, a creditor holding a consumer debt or any representative of the creditor (which may include an entity or an employee of an entity and may be a representative for more than 1 creditor) shall be permitted to appear at and participate in the meeting of creditors in a case under chapter 7 or 13, either alone or in conjunction with an attorney for the creditor. Nothing in this subsection shall be construed to require any creditor to be represented by an attorney at any meeting of creditors.

(d) Prior to the conclusion of the meeting of creditors or equity security holders, the trustee shall orally examine the debtor to ensure that the debtor in a case under chapter 7 of this title is aware of—

(1) the potential consequences of seeking a discharge in bankruptcy, including the effects on credit history;

(2) the debtor's ability to file a petition under a different chapter of this title;

(3) the effect of receiving a discharge of debts under this title; and

(4) the effect of reaffirming a debt, including the debtor's knowledge of the provisions of *section 524(d)* of this title.

(e) Notwithstanding subsections (a) and (b), the court, on the request of a party in interest and after notice and a hearing, for cause may order that the United States trustee not convene a meeting of creditors or equity security holders if the debtor has filed a plan as to which the debtor solicited acceptances prior to the commencement of the case.

(Pub. L. 95–598, Nov. 6, 1978, 92 Stat. 2564; Pub. L. 99–554, title II, § 212, Oct. 27, 1986, 100 Stat. 3099; Pub. L. 103–394, title I, § 115, Oct. 22, 1994, 108 Stat. 4118; Pub. L. 109–8, title IV, §§ 402, 413, Apr. 20, 2005, 119 Stat. 104, 107.)

Sections that reference this section: 1112, 1116, 1161, 1308, 1324, 343, 521, 702, 705

§342. Notice

(a) There shall be given such notice as is appropriate, including notice to any holder of a community claim, of an order for relief in a case under this title.

(b) Before the commencement of a case under this title by an individual whose debts are primarily consumer debts, the clerk shall give to such individual written notice containing—

(1) a brief description of—

(A) chapters 7, 11, 12, and 13 and the general purpose, benefits, and costs of proceeding under each of those chapters; and

(B) the types of services available from credit counseling agencies; and

(2) statements specifying that—

(A) a person who knowingly and fraudulently conceals assets or makes a false oath or statement under penalty of perjury in connection with a case under this title shall be subject to fine, imprisonment, or both; and

(B) all information supplied by a debtor in connection with a case under this title is subject to examination by the Attorney General.

(c)

(1) If notice is required to be given by the debtor to a creditor under this title, any rule, any applicable law, or any order of the court, such notice shall contain the name, address, and last 4 digits of the taxpayer identification number of the debtor. If the notice concerns an amendment that adds a creditor to the schedules of assets and liabilities, the debtor shall include the full taxpayer identification number in the notice sent to that creditor, but the debtor shall include only the last 4 digits of the taxpayer identification number in the copy of the notice filed with the court.

(2)

(A) If, within the 90 days before the commencement of a voluntary case, a creditor supplies the debtor in at least 2 communications sent to the debtor with the current account number of the debtor and the address at which such creditor requests to receive correspondence, then any notice required by this title to be sent by the debtor to such creditor shall be sent to such address and shall include such account number.

(B) If a creditor would be in violation of applicable nonbankruptcy law by sending any such communication within such 90-day period and if such creditor supplies the debtor in the last 2 communications with the current account number of the debtor and the address at which such creditor requests to receive correspondence, then any notice required by this title to be sent by the debtor to such creditor shall be sent to such address and shall include such account number.

(d) In a case under chapter 7 of this title in which the debtor is an individual and in which the presumption of abuse arises under *section 707(b)*, the clerk shall give written notice to all creditors not later than 10 days after the date of the filing of the petition that the presumption of abuse has arisen.

(e)

(1) In a case under chapter 7 or 13 of this title of a debtor who is an individual, a creditor at any time may both file with the court and serve on the debtor a notice of address to be used to provide notice in such case to such creditor.

(2) Any notice in such case required to be provided to such creditor by the debtor or the court later than 7 days after the court and the debtor receive such creditor's notice of address, shall be provided to such address.

(f)

(1) An entity may file with any bankruptcy court a notice of address to be used by all the bankruptcy courts or by particular bankruptcy courts, as so specified by such entity at the time such notice is filed, to provide notice to such entity in all cases under chapters 7 and 13 pending in the courts with respect to which such notice is filed, in which such entity is a creditor.

(2) In any case filed under chapter 7 or 13, any notice required to be provided by a court with respect to which a notice is filed under paragraph (1), to such entity later than 30 days after the filing of such notice under paragraph (1) shall be provided to such address unless with respect to a particular case a different address is specified in a notice filed and served in accordance with subsection (e).

(3) A notice filed under paragraph (1) may be withdrawn by such entity.

(g)

(1) Notice provided to a creditor by the debtor or the court other than in accordance with this section (excluding this subsection) shall not be effective notice until such notice is brought to the attention of such creditor. If such creditor designates a person or an organizational subdivision of such creditor to be responsible for receiving notices under this title and establishes reasonable procedures so that such notices receivable

by such creditor are to be delivered to such person or such subdivision, then a notice provided to such creditor other than in accordance with this section (excluding this subsection) shall not be considered to have been brought to the attention of such creditor until such notice is received by such person or such subdivision.

(2) A monetary penalty may not be imposed on a creditor for a violation of a stay in effect under *section 362(a)* (including a monetary penalty imposed under *section 362(k)*) or for failure to comply with *section 542* or *543* unless the conduct that is the basis of such violation or of such failure occurs after such creditor receives notice effective under this section of the order for relief.

(Pub. L. 95–598, Nov. 6, 1978, 92 Stat. 2565; Pub. L. 98–353, title III, §§ 302, 435, July 10, 1984, 98 Stat. 352, 370; Pub. L. 103–394, title II, § 225, Oct. 22, 1994, 108 Stat. 4131; Pub. L. 109–8, title I, §§ 102(d), 104, title II, § 234(b), title III, § 315(a), Apr. 20, 2005, 119 Stat. 33, 35, 75, 88; Pub. L. 111–16, § 2(4), May 7, 2009, 123 Stat. 1607.)

Sections that reference this section: 348, 521, 527, 741, 743, 762, 765

§343. Examination of the debtor

The debtor shall appear and submit to examination under oath at the meeting of creditors under *section 341(a)* of this title. Creditors, any indenture trustee, any trustee or examiner in the case, or the United States trustee may examine the debtor. The United States trustee may administer the oath required under this section.

(Pub. L. 95–598, Nov. 6, 1978, 92 Stat. 2565; Pub. L. 98–353, title III, § 436, July 10, 1984, 98 Stat. 370; Pub. L. 99–554, title II, § 213, Oct. 27, 1986, 100 Stat. 3099.)

Sections that reference this section: None

§344. Self-incrimination; immunity

Immunity for persons required to submit to examination, to testify, or to provide information in a case under this title may be granted under part V of title 18.

(Pub. L. 95–598, Nov. 6, 1978, 92 Stat. 2565.)

Sections that reference this section: 521

§345. Money of estates

(a) A trustee in a case under this title may make such deposit or investment of the money of the estate for which such trustee serves as will yield the maximum reasonable net return on such money, taking into account the safety of such deposit or investment.

(b) Except with respect to a deposit or investment that is insured or guaranteed by the United States or by a department, agency, or instrumentality of the United States or backed by the full faith and credit of the United States, the trustee shall require from an entity with which such money is deposited or invested—

  (1) a bond—

    (A) in favor of the United States;

    (B) secured by the undertaking of a corporate surety approved by the United States trustee for the district in which the case is pending; and

    (C) conditioned on—

      (i) a proper accounting for all money so deposited or invested and for any return on such money;

      (ii) prompt repayment of such money and return; and

      (iii) faithful performance of duties as a depository; or

  (2) the deposit of securities of the kind specified in section 9303 of title 31;

unless the court for cause orders otherwise.

(c) An entity with which such moneys are deposited or invested is authorized to deposit or invest such moneys as may be required under this section.

(Pub. L. 95–598, Nov. 6, 1978, 92 Stat. 2565; Pub. L. 97–258, § 3(c), Sept. 13, 1982, 96 Stat. 1064; Pub. L. 98–353, title III, § 437, July 10, 1984, 98 Stat. 370; Pub. L. 99–554, title II, § 214, Oct. 27, 1986, 100 Stat. 3099; Pub. L. 103–394, title II, § 210, Oct. 22, 1994, 108 Stat. 4125.)

Sections that reference this section: None

§346. Special provisions related to the treatment of State and local taxes

(a) Whenever the Internal Revenue Code of 1986 provides that a separate taxable estate or entity is created in a case concerning a debtor under this title, and the income, gain, loss, deductions, and credits of such estate shall be taxed to or claimed by the estate, a separate taxable estate is also created for purposes of any State and local law imposing a tax on or measured by income and such income, gain, loss, deductions, and credits shall be taxed to or claimed by the estate and may not be taxed to or claimed by the debtor. The preceding sentence shall not apply if the case is dismissed. The trustee shall make tax returns of income required under any such State or local law.

(b) Whenever the Internal Revenue Code of 1986 provides that no separate taxable estate shall be created in a case concerning a debtor under this title, and the income, gain, loss, deductions, and credits of an estate shall be taxed to or claimed by the debtor, such income, gain, loss, deductions, and credits shall be taxed to or claimed by the debtor under a State or local law imposing a tax on or measured by income and may not be taxed to or claimed by the estate. The trustee shall make such tax returns of income of corporations and of partnerships as are required under any State or local law, but with respect to partnerships, shall make such returns only to the extent such returns are also required to be made under such Code. The estate shall be liable for any tax imposed on such corporation or partnership, but not for any tax imposed on partners or members.

(c) With respect to a partnership or any entity treated as a partnership under a State or local law imposing a tax on or measured by income that is a debtor in a case under this title, any gain or loss resulting from a distribution of property from such partnership, or any distributive share of any income, gain, loss, deduction, or credit of a partner or member that is distributed, or considered distributed, from such partnership, after the commencement of the case, is gain, loss, income, deduction, or credit, as the case may be, of the partner or member, and if such partner or member is a debtor in a case under this title, shall be subject to tax in accordance with subsection (a) or (b).

(d) For purposes of any State or local law imposing a tax on or measured by income, the taxable period of a debtor in a case under this title shall terminate only if and to the extent that the taxable period of such debtor terminates under the Internal Revenue Code of 1986.

(e) The estate in any case described in subsection (a) shall use the same accounting method as the debtor used immediately before the commencement of the case, if such method of accounting complies with applicable nonbankruptcy tax law.

(f) For purposes of any State or local law imposing a tax on or measured by income, a transfer of property from the debtor to the estate or from the estate to the debtor shall not be treated as a disposition for purposes of any provision assigning tax consequences to a disposition, except to the extent that such transfer is treated as a disposition under the Internal Revenue Code of 1986.

(g) Whenever a tax is imposed pursuant to a State or local law imposing a tax on or measured by income pursuant to subsection (a) or (b), such tax shall be imposed at rates generally applicable to the same types of entities under such State or local law.

(h) The trustee shall withhold from any payment of claims for wages, salaries, commissions, dividends, interest, or other payments, or collect, any amount required to be withheld or collected under applicable State or local tax law, and shall pay such withheld or collected amount to the appropriate governmental unit at the time and in the manner required by such tax law, and with the same priority as the claim from which such amount was withheld or collected was paid.

(i)

(1) To the extent that any State or local law imposing a tax on or measured by income provides for the carryover of any tax attribute from one taxable period to a subsequent taxable period, the estate shall succeed to such tax attribute in any case in which such estate is subject to tax under subsection (a).

(2) After such a case is closed or dismissed, the debtor shall succeed to any tax attribute to which the estate succeeded under paragraph (1) to the extent consistent with the Internal Revenue Code of 1986.

(3) The estate may carry back any loss or tax attribute to a taxable period of the debtor that ended before the date of the order for relief under this title to the extent that—

(A) applicable State or local tax law provides for a carryback in the case of the debtor; and

(B) the same or a similar tax attribute may be carried back by the estate to such a taxable period of the debtor under the Internal Revenue Code of 1986.

(j)

(1) For purposes of any State or local law imposing a tax on or measured by income,

income is not realized by the estate, the debtor, or a successor to the debtor by reason of discharge of indebtedness in a case under this title, except to the extent, if any, that such income is subject to tax under the Internal Revenue Code of 1986.

(2) Whenever the Internal Revenue Code of 1986 provides that the amount excluded from gross income in respect of the discharge of indebtedness in a case under this title shall be applied to reduce the tax attributes of the debtor or the estate, a similar reduction shall be made under any State or local law imposing a tax on or measured by income to the extent such State or local law recognizes such attributes. Such State or local law may also provide for the reduction of other attributes to the extent that the full amount of income from the discharge of indebtedness has not been applied.

(k)

(1) Except as provided in this section and *section 505*, the time and manner of filing tax returns and the items of income, gain, loss, deduction, and credit of any taxpayer shall be determined under applicable nonbankruptcy law.

(2) For Federal tax purposes, the provisions of this section are subject to the Internal Revenue Code of 1986 and other applicable Federal nonbankruptcy law.

(Pub. L. 95–598, Nov. 6, 1978, 92 Stat. 2565; Pub. L. 98–353, title III, § 438, July 10, 1984, 98 Stat. 370; Pub. L. 99–554, title II, §§ 257(g), 283(c), Oct. 27, 1986, 100 Stat. 3114, 3116; Pub. L. 103–394, title V, § 501(d)(4), Oct. 22, 1994, 108 Stat. 4143; Pub. L. 109–8, title VII, § 719(a)(1), Apr. 20, 2005, 119 Stat. 131.)

Sections that reference this section: 1146, 1231

§347. Unclaimed property

(a) Ninety days after the final distribution under *section 726, 1194, 1226,* or *1326* of this title in a case under chapter 7, subchapter V of chapter 11, 12, or 13 of this title, as the case may be, the trustee shall stop payment on any check remaining unpaid, and any remaining property of the estate shall be paid into the court and disposed of under chapter 129 of title 28.

(b) Any security, money, or other property remaining unclaimed at the expiration of the time allowed in a case under chapter 9, 11, or 12 of this title for the presentation of a security or the performance of any other act as a condition to participation in the distribution under any plan confirmed under *section 943(b), 1129, 1173, 1191,* or *1225* of this title, as the case may be, becomes the property of the debtor or of the entity acquiring the assets of the debtor under the plan, as the case may be.

(Pub. L. 95–598, Nov. 6, 1978, 92 Stat. 2568; Pub. L. 99–554, title II, § 257(h), Oct. 27, 1986, 100 Stat. 3114; Pub. L. 116–54, § 4(a)(5), Aug. 23, 2019, 133 Stat. 1086; Pub. L. 116–136, div. A, title I, § 1113(a)(4)(B), Mar. 27, 2020, 134 Stat. 311.)

Sections that reference this section: None

§348. Effect of conversion

(a) Conversion of a case from a case under one chapter of this title to a case under another chapter of this title constitutes an order for relief under the chapter to which the case is converted, but, except as provided in subsections (b) and (c) of this section, does not effect a change in the date of the filing of the petition, the commencement of the case, or the order for relief.

(b) Unless the court for cause orders otherwise, in *sections 701(a), 727*(a)(10), 727(b), 1102(a), 1110(a)(1), 1121(b), 1121(c), 1141(d)(4), 1201(a), 1221, 1228(a), 1301(a), and 1305(a) of this title, “the order for relief under this chapter” in a chapter to which a case has been converted under *section 706, 1112, 1208,* or *1307* of this title means the conversion of such case to such chapter.

(c) *Sections 342* and *365*(d) of this title apply in a case that has been converted under *section 706, 1112, 1208,* or *1307* of this title, as if the conversion order were the order for relief.

(d) A claim against the estate or the debtor that arises after the order for relief but before conversion in a case that is converted under *section 1112, 1208,* or *1307* of this title, other than a claim specified in *section 503(b)* of this title, shall be treated for all purposes as if such claim had arisen immediately before the date of the filing of the petition.

(e) Conversion of a case under *section 706, 1112, 1208,* or *1307* of this title terminates the service of any trustee or examiner that is serving in the case before such conversion.

(f)

(1) Except as provided in paragraph (2), when a case under chapter 13 of this title is converted to a case under another chapter under this title—

(A) property of the estate in the converted case shall consist of property of the estate, as of the date of filing of the petition, that remains in the possession of or is under the control of the debtor on the date of conversion;

(B) valuations of property and of allowed secured claims in the chapter 13 case shall apply only in a case converted to a case under chapter 11 or 12, but not in a case converted to a case under chapter 7, with allowed secured claims in cases under chapters 11 and 12 reduced to the extent that they have been paid in accordance with the chapter 13 plan; and

(C) with respect to cases converted from chapter 13—

(i) the claim of any creditor holding security as of the date of the filing of the petition shall continue to be secured by that security unless the full amount of such claim determined under applicable nonbankruptcy law has been paid in full as of the date of conversion, notwithstanding any valuation or determination of the amount of an allowed secured claim made for the purposes of the case under chapter 13; and

(ii) unless a prebankruptcy default has been fully cured under the plan at the time of conversion, in any proceeding under this title or otherwise, the default shall have the effect given under applicable nonbankruptcy law.

(2) If the debtor converts a case under chapter 13 of this title to a case under another chapter under this title in bad faith, the property of the estate in the converted case shall consist of the property of the estate as of the date of conversion.

(Pub. L. 95–598, Nov. 6, 1978, 92 Stat. 2568; Pub. L. 99–554, title II, § 257(i), Oct. 27, 1986, 100 Stat. 3115; Pub. L. 103–394, title III, § 311, title V, § 501(d)(5), Oct. 22, 1994, 108 Stat. 4138, 4144; Pub. L. 109–8, title III, § 309(a), title XII, § 1207, Apr. 20, 2005, 119 Stat. 82, 194; Pub. L. 111–327, § 2(a)(11), Dec. 22, 2010, 124 Stat. 3558.)

Sections that reference this section: 101

§349. Effect of dismissal

(a) Unless the court, for cause, orders otherwise, the dismissal of a case under this title does not bar the discharge, in a later case under this title, of debts that were dischargeable in the case dismissed; nor does the dismissal of a case under this title prejudice the debtor with regard to the filing of a subsequent petition under this title, except as provided in *section 109(g)* of this title.

(b) Unless the court, for cause, orders otherwise, a dismissal of a case other than under *section 742* of this title—

(1) reinstates—

(A) any proceeding or custodianship superseded under *section 543* of this title;

(B) any transfer avoided under *section 522, 544, 545, 547, 548, 549,* or 724(a) of this title, or preserved under *section 510(c)(2), 522*(i)(2), or 551 of this title; and

(C) any lien voided under *section 506(d)* of this title;

(2) vacates any order, judgment, or transfer ordered, under *section 522(i)(1), 542, 550,* or *553* of this title; and

(3) revests the property of the estate in the entity in which such property was vested immediately before the commencement of the case under this title.

(Pub. L. 95–598, Nov. 6, 1978, 92 Stat. 2569; Pub. L. 98–353, title III, § 303, July 10, 1984, 98 Stat. 352; Pub. L. 103–394, title V, § 501(d)(6), Oct. 22, 1994, 108 Stat. 4144.)

Sections that reference this section: None

§350. Closing and reopening cases

(a) After an estate is fully administered and the court has discharged the trustee, the court shall close the case.

(b) A case may be reopened in the court in which such case was closed to administer assets, to accord relief to the debtor, or for other cause.

(Pub. L. 95–598, Nov. 6, 1978, 92 Stat. 2569; Pub. L. 98–353, title III, § 439, July 10, 1984, 98 Stat. 370.)

Sections that reference this section: 1517, 554, 703

§351. Disposal of patient records

If a health care business commences a case under chapter 7, 9, or 11, and the trustee does not have a sufficient amount of funds to pay for the storage of patient records in the manner required under applicable Federal or State law, the following requirements shall apply:

(1) The trustee shall—

 (A) promptly publish notice, in 1 or more appropriate newspapers, that if patient records are not claimed by the patient or an insurance provider (if applicable law permits the insurance provider to make that claim) by the date that is 365 days after the date of that notification, the trustee will destroy the patient records; and

 (B) during the first 180 days of the 365-day period described in subparagraph (A), promptly attempt to notify directly each patient that is the subject of the patient records and appropriate insurance carrier concerning the patient records by mailing to the most recent known address of that patient, or a family member or contact person for that patient, and to the appropriate insurance carrier an appropriate notice regarding the claiming or disposing of patient records.

(2) If, after providing the notification under paragraph (1), patient records are not claimed during the 365-day period described under that paragraph, the trustee shall mail, by certified mail, at the end of such 365-day period a written request to each appropriate Federal agency to request permission from that agency to deposit the patient records with that agency, except that no Federal agency is required to accept patient records under this paragraph.

(3) If, following the 365-day period described in paragraph (2) and after providing the notification under paragraph (1), patient records are not claimed by a patient or insurance provider, or request is not granted by a Federal agency to deposit such records with that agency, the trustee shall destroy those records by—

 (A) if the records are written, shredding or burning the records; or

 (B) if the records are magnetic, optical, or other electronic records, by otherwise destroying those records so that those records cannot be retrieved.

(Added Pub. L. 109–8, title XI, § 1102(a), Apr. 20, 2005, 119 Stat. 189.)

Sections that reference this section: 109, 503

Subchapter IV: Administrative Powers

§361. Adequate protection

When adequate protection is required under *section 362, 363,* or *364* of this title of an interest of an entity in property, such adequate protection may be provided by—

(1) requiring the trustee to make a cash payment or periodic cash payments to such entity, to the extent that the stay under *section 362* of this title, use, sale, or lease under *section 363* of this title, or any grant of a lien under *section 364* of this title results in a decrease in the value of such entity's interest in such property;

(2) providing to such entity an additional or replacement lien to the extent that such stay, use, sale, lease, or grant results in a decrease in the value of such entity's interest in such property; or

(3) granting such other relief, other than entitling such entity to compensation allowable under *section 503(b)(1)* of this title as an administrative expense, as will result in the realization by such entity of the indubitable equivalent of such entity's interest in such property.

(Pub. L. 95–598, Nov. 6, 1978, 92 Stat. 2569; Pub. L. 98–353, title III, § 440, July 10, 1984, 98 Stat. 370.)

Sections that reference this section: 1205, 1520, 362

§362. Automatic stay

(a) Except as provided in subsection (b) of this section, a petition filed under *section 301, 302,* or *303* of this title, or an application filed under section 5(a)(3) of the Securities Investor Protection Act of 1970, operates as a stay, applicable to all entities, of—

 (1) the commencement or continuation, including the issuance or employment of process, of a judicial, administrative, or other action or proceeding against the debtor that was or could have been commenced before the commencement of the case under this title, or to recover a claim against the debtor that arose before the commencement of the case under this title;

(2) the enforcement, against the debtor or against property of the estate, of a judgment obtained before the commencement of the case under this title;

(3) any act to obtain possession of property of the estate or of property from the estate or to exercise control over property of the estate;

(4) any act to create, perfect, or enforce any lien against property of the estate;

(5) any act to create, perfect, or enforce against property of the debtor any lien to the extent that such lien secures a claim that arose before the commencement of the case under this title;

(6) any act to collect, assess, or recover a claim against the debtor that arose before the commencement of the case under this title;

(7) the setoff of any debt owing to the debtor that arose before the commencement of the case under this title against any claim against the debtor; and

(8) the commencement or continuation of a proceeding before the United States Tax Court concerning a tax liability of a debtor that is a corporation for a taxable period the bankruptcy court may determine or concerning the tax liability of a debtor who is an individual for a taxable period ending before the date of the order for relief under this title.

(b) The filing of a petition under *section 301, 302,* or *303* of this title, or of an application under section 5(a)(3) of the Securities Investor Protection Act of 1970, does not operate as a stay—

(1) under subsection (a) of this section, of the commencement or continuation of a criminal action or proceeding against the debtor;

(2) under subsection (a)—

(A) of the commencement or continuation of a civil action or proceeding—

(i) for the establishment of paternity;

(ii) for the establishment or modification of an order for domestic support obligations;

(iii) concerning child custody or visitation;

(iv) for the dissolution of a marriage, except to the extent that such proceeding seeks to determine the division of property that is property of the estate; or

(v) regarding domestic violence;

(B) of the collection of a domestic support obligation from property that is not property of the estate;

(C) with respect to the withholding of income that is property of the estate or property of the debtor for payment of a domestic support obligation under a judicial or administrative order or a statute;

(D) of the withholding, suspension, or restriction of a driver's license, a professional or occupational license, or a recreational license, under State law, as specified in section 466(a)(16) of the Social Security Act;

(E) of the reporting of overdue support owed by a parent to any consumer reporting agency as specified in section 466(a)(7) of the Social Security Act;

(F) of the interception of a tax refund, as specified in sections 464 and 466(a)(3) of the Social Security Act or under an analogous State law; or

(G) of the enforcement of a medical obligation, as specified under title IV of the Social Security Act;

(3) under subsection (a) of this section, of any act to perfect, or to maintain or continue the perfection of, an interest in property to the extent that the trustee's rights and powers are subject to such perfection under *section 546(b)* of this title or to the extent that such act is accomplished within the period provided under *section 547(e)(2)(A)* of this title;

(4) under paragraph (1), (2), (3), or (6) of subsection (a) of this section, of the commencement or continuation of an action or proceeding by a governmental unit or any organization exercising authority under the Convention on the Prohibition of the Development, Production, Stockpiling and Use of Chemical Weapons and on Their Destruction, opened for signature on January 13, 1993, to enforce such

governmental unit's or organization's police and regulatory power, including the enforcement of a judgment other than a money judgment, obtained in an action or proceeding by the governmental unit to enforce such governmental unit's or organization's police or regulatory power;

[(5) Repealed. Pub. L. 105–277, div. I, title VI, § 603(1), Oct. 21, 1998, 112 Stat. 2681–866;]

(6) under subsection (a) of this section, of the exercise by a commodity broker, forward contract merchant, stockbroker, financial institution, financial participant, or securities clearing agency of any contractual right (as defined in *section 555* or *556*) under any security agreement or arrangement or other credit enhancement forming a part of or related to any commodity contract, forward contract or securities contract, or of any contractual right (as defined in *section 555* or *556*) to offset or net out any termination value, payment amount, or other transfer obligation arising under or in connection with 1 or more such contracts, including any master agreement for such contracts;

(7) under subsection (a) of this section, of the exercise by a repo participant or financial participant of any contractual right (as defined in *section 559*) under any security agreement or arrangement or other credit enhancement forming a part of or related to any repurchase agreement, or of any contractual right (as defined in *section 559*) to offset or net out any termination value, payment amount, or other transfer obligation arising under or in connection with 1 or more such agreements, including any master agreement for such agreements;

(8) under subsection (a) of this section, of the commencement of any action by the Secretary of Housing and Urban Development to foreclose a mortgage or deed of trust in any case in which the mortgage or deed of trust held by the Secretary is insured or was formerly insured under the National Housing Act and covers property, or combinations of property, consisting of five or more living units;

(9) under subsection (a), of—

(A) an audit by a governmental unit to determine tax liability;

(B) the issuance to the debtor by a governmental unit of a notice of tax deficiency;

(C) a demand for tax returns; or

(D) the making of an assessment for any tax and issuance of a notice and demand for payment of such an assessment (but any tax lien that would otherwise attach to property of the estate by reason of such an assessment shall not take effect unless such tax is a debt of the debtor that will not be discharged in the case and such property or its proceeds are transferred out of the estate to, or otherwise revested in, the debtor).

(10) under subsection (a) of this section, of any act by a lessor to the debtor under a lease of nonresidential real property that has terminated by the expiration of the stated term of the lease before the commencement of or during a case under this title to obtain possession of such property;

(11) under subsection (a) of this section, of the presentment of a negotiable instrument and the giving of notice of and protesting dishonor of such an instrument;

(12) under subsection (a) of this section, after the date which is 90 days after the filing of such petition, of the commencement or continuation, and conclusion to the entry of final judgment, of an action which involves a debtor subject to reorganization pursuant to chapter 11 of this title and which was brought by the Secretary of Transportation under section 31325 of title 46 (including distribution of any proceeds of sale) to foreclose a preferred ship or fleet mortgage, or a security interest in or relating to a vessel or vessel under construction, held by the Secretary of Transportation under chapter 537 of title 46 or *section 109(h)* of title 49, or under applicable State law;

(13) under subsection (a) of this section, after the date which is 90 days after the filing of such petition, of the commencement or continuation, and conclusion to the entry of final judgment, of an action which involves a debtor subject to reorganization

pursuant to chapter 11 of this title and which was brought by the Secretary of Commerce under section 31325 of title 46 (including distribution of any proceeds of sale) to foreclose a preferred ship or fleet mortgage in a vessel or a mortgage, deed of trust, or other security interest in a fishing facility held by the Secretary of Commerce under chapter 537 of title 46;

(14) under subsection (a) of this section, of any action by an accrediting agency regarding the accreditation status of the debtor as an educational institution;

(15) under subsection (a) of this section, of any action by a State licensing body regarding the licensure of the debtor as an educational institution;

(16) under subsection (a) of this section, of any action by a guaranty agency, as defined in section 435(j) of the Higher Education Act of 1965 or the Secretary of Education regarding the eligibility of the debtor to participate in programs authorized under such Act;

(17) under subsection (a) of this section, of the exercise by a swap participant or financial participant of any contractual right (as defined in *section 560*) under any security agreement or arrangement or other credit enhancement forming a part of or related to any swap agreement, or of any contractual right (as defined in *section 560*) to offset or net out any termination value, payment amount, or other transfer obligation arising under or in connection with 1 or more such agreements, including any master agreement for such agreements;

(18) under subsection (a) of the creation or perfection of a statutory lien for an ad valorem property tax, or a special tax or special assessment on real property whether or not ad valorem, imposed by a governmental unit, if such tax or assessment comes due after the date of the filing of the petition;

(19) under subsection (a), of withholding of income from a debtor's wages and collection of amounts withheld, under the debtor's agreement authorizing that withholding and collection for the benefit of a pension, profit-sharing, stock bonus, or other plan established under section 401, 403, 408, 408A, 414, 457, or 501(c) of the Internal Revenue Code of 1986, that is sponsored by the employer of the debtor, or an affiliate, successor, or predecessor of such employer—

(A) to the extent that the amounts withheld and collected are used solely for payments relating to a loan from a plan under section 408(b)(1) of the Employee Retirement Income Security Act of 1974 or is subject to section 72(p) of the Internal Revenue Code of 1986; or

(B) a loan from a thrift savings plan permitted under subchapter III of chapter 84 of title 5, that satisfies the requirements of section 8433(g) of such title;

but nothing in this paragraph may be construed to provide that any loan made under a governmental plan under section 414(d), or a contract or account under section 403(b), of the Internal Revenue Code of 1986 constitutes a claim or a debt under this title;

(20) under subsection (a), of any act to enforce any lien against or security interest in real property following entry of the order under subsection (d)(4) as to such real property in any prior case under this title, for a period of 2 years after the date of the entry of such an order, except that the debtor, in a subsequent case under this title, may move for relief from such order based upon changed circumstances or for other good cause shown, after notice and a hearing;

(21) under subsection (a), of any act to enforce any lien against or security interest in real property—

(A) if the debtor is ineligible under *section 109(g)* to be a debtor in a case under this title; or

(B) if the case under this title was filed in violation of a bankruptcy court order in a prior case under this title prohibiting the debtor from being a debtor in another case under this title;

(22) subject to subsection (*l*), under subsection (a)(3), of the continuation of any eviction, unlawful detainer action, or similar proceeding by a lessor against a debtor involving residential property in which the

debtor resides as a tenant under a lease or rental agreement and with respect to which the lessor has obtained before the date of the filing of the bankruptcy petition, a judgment for possession of such property against the debtor;

(23) subject to subsection (m), under subsection (a)(3), of an eviction action that seeks possession of the residential property in which the debtor resides as a tenant under a lease or rental agreement based on endangerment of such property or the illegal use of controlled substances on such property, but only if the lessor files with the court, and serves upon the debtor, a certification under penalty of perjury that such an eviction action has been filed, or that the debtor, during the 30-day period preceding the date of the filing of the certification, has endangered property or illegally used or allowed to be used a controlled substance on the property;

(24) under subsection (a), of any transfer that is not avoidable under *section 544* and that is not avoidable under *section 549*;

(25) under subsection (a), of—

   (A) the commencement or continuation of an investigation or action by a securities self regulatory organization to enforce such organization's regulatory power;

   (B) the enforcement of an order or decision, other than for monetary sanctions, obtained in an action by such securities self regulatory organization to enforce such organization's regulatory power; or

   (C) any act taken by such securities self regulatory organization to delist, delete, or refuse to permit quotation of any stock that does not meet applicable regulatory requirements;

(26) under subsection (a), of the setoff under applicable nonbankruptcy law of an income tax refund, by a governmental unit, with respect to a taxable period that ended before the date of the order for relief against an income tax liability for a taxable period that also ended before the date of the order for relief, except that in any case in which the setoff of an income tax refund is not permitted under applicable nonbankruptcy law because of a pending action to determine the amount or legality of a tax liability, the governmental unit may hold the refund pending the resolution of the action, unless the court, on the motion of the trustee and after notice and a hearing, grants the taxing authority adequate protection (within the meaning of *section 361*) for the secured claim of such authority in the setoff under *section 506(a)*;

(27) under subsection (a) of this section, of the exercise by a master netting agreement participant of any contractual right (as defined in *section 555, 556, 559,* or *560*) under any security agreement or arrangement or other credit enhancement forming a part of or related to any master netting agreement, or of any contractual right (as defined in *section 555, 556, 559,* or *560*) to offset or net out any termination value, payment amount, or other transfer obligation arising under or in connection with 1 or more such master netting agreements to the extent that such participant is eligible to exercise such rights under paragraph (6), (7), or (17) for each individual contract covered by the master netting agreement in issue;

(28) under subsection (a), of the exclusion by the Secretary of Health and Human Services of the debtor from participation in the medicare program or any other Federal health care program (as defined in *section 1128B(f)* of the Social Security Act pursuant to title XI or XVIII of such Act); and

(29) under subsection (a)(1) of this section, of any action by—

   (A) an amateur sports organization, as defined in section 220501(b) of title 36, to replace a national governing body, as defined in that section, under section 220528 of that title; or

   (B) the corporation, as defined in section 220501(b) of title 36, to revoke the certification of a national governing body, as defined in that section, under section 220521 of that title.

The provisions of paragraphs (12) and (13) of this subsection shall apply with respect to any such petition filed on or before December 31, 1989.

(c) Except as provided in subsections (d), (e), (f), and (h) of this section—

(1) the stay of an act against property of the estate under subsection (a) of this section continues until such property is no longer property of the estate;

(2) the stay of any other act under subsection (a) of this section continues until the earliest of—

(A) the time the case is closed;

(B) the time the case is dismissed; or

(C) if the case is a case under chapter 7 of this title concerning an individual or a case under chapter 9, 11, 12, or 13 of this title, the time a discharge is granted or denied;

(3) if a single or joint case is filed by or against a debtor who is an individual in a case under chapter 7, 11, or 13, and if a single or joint case of the debtor was pending within the preceding 1-year period but was dismissed, other than a case refiled under a chapter other than chapter 7 after dismissal under *section 707(b)*—

(A) the stay under subsection (a) with respect to any action taken with respect to a debt or property securing such debt or with respect to any lease shall terminate with respect to the debtor on the 30th day after the filing of the later case;

(B) on the motion of a party in interest for continuation of the automatic stay and upon notice and a hearing, the court may extend the stay in particular cases as to any or all creditors (subject to such conditions or limitations as the court may then impose) after notice and a hearing completed before the expiration of the 30-day period only if the party in interest demonstrates that the filing of the later case is in good faith as to the creditors to be stayed; and

(C) for purposes of subparagraph (B), a case is presumptively filed not in good faith (but such presumption may be rebutted by clear and convincing evidence to the contrary)—

(i) as to all creditors, if—

(I) more than 1 previous case under any of chapters 7, 11, and 13 in which the individual was a debtor was pending within the preceding 1-year period;

(II) a previous case under any of chapters 7, 11, and 13 in which the individual was a debtor was dismissed within such 1-year period, after the debtor failed to —

(aa) file or amend the petition or other documents as required by this title or the court without substantial excuse (but mere inadvertence or negligence shall not be a substantial excuse unless the dismissal was caused by the negligence of the debtor's attorney);

(bb) provide adequate protection as ordered by the court; or

(cc) perform the terms of a plan confirmed by the court; or

(III) there has not been a substantial change in the financial or personal affairs of the debtor since the dismissal of the next most previous case under chapter 7, 11, or 13 or any other reason to conclude that the later case will be concluded—

(aa) if a case under chapter 7, with a discharge; or

(bb) if a case under chapter 11 or 13, with a confirmed plan that will be fully performed; and

(ii) as to any creditor that commenced an action under subsection (d) in a previous case in which the individual was a debtor if, as of the date of dismissal of such case, that action was still pending or had been resolved by terminating, conditioning, or limiting the stay as to actions of such creditor; and

(4)

(A)

(i) if a single or joint case is filed by or against a debtor who is an individual under this title, and if 2 or more single or joint cases of the debtor were pending within the previous year but were dismissed, other than a case refiled under a chapter other than chapter 7 after dismissal under *section 707(b)*, the stay under subsection (a) shall not go into effect upon the filing of the later case; and

(ii) on request of a party in interest, the court shall promptly enter an order confirming that no stay is in effect;

(B) if, within 30 days after the filing of the later case, a party in interest requests the court may order the stay to take effect in the case as to any or all creditors (subject to such conditions or limitations as the court may impose), after notice and a hearing, only if the party in interest demonstrates that the filing of the later case is in good faith as to the creditors to be stayed;

(C) a stay imposed under subparagraph (B) shall be effective on the date of the entry of the order allowing the stay to go into effect; and

(D) for purposes of subparagraph (B), a case is presumptively filed not in good faith (but such presumption may be rebutted by clear and convincing evidence to the contrary)—

(i) as to all creditors if—

(I) 2 or more previous cases under this title in which the individual was a debtor were pending within the 1-year period;

(II) a previous case under this title in which the individual was a debtor was dismissed within the time period stated in this paragraph after the debtor failed to file or amend the petition or other documents as required by this title or the court without substantial excuse (but mere inadvertence or negligence shall not be substantial excuse unless the dismissal was caused by the negligence of the debtor's attorney), failed to provide adequate protection as ordered by the court, or failed to perform the terms of a plan confirmed by the court; or

(III) there has not been a substantial change in the financial or personal affairs of the debtor since the dismissal of the next most previous case under this title, or any other reason to conclude that the later case will not be concluded, if a case under chapter 7, with a discharge, and if a case under chapter 11 or 13, with a confirmed plan that will be fully performed; or

(ii) as to any creditor that commenced an action under subsection (d) in a previous case in which the individual was a debtor if, as of the date of dismissal of such case, such action was still pending or had been resolved by terminating, conditioning, or limiting the stay as to such action of such creditor.

(d) On request of a party in interest and after notice and a hearing, the court shall grant relief from the stay provided under subsection (a) of this section, such as by terminating, annulling, modifying, or conditioning such stay—

(1) for cause, including the lack of adequate protection of an interest in property of such party in interest;

(2) with respect to a stay of an act against property under subsection (a) of this section, if—

(A) the debtor does not have an equity in such property; and

(B) such property is not necessary to an effective reorganization;

(3) with respect to a stay of an act against single asset real estate under subsection (a), by a creditor whose claim is secured by an interest in such real estate, unless, not later than the date that is 90 days after the entry of the order for relief (or such later date as the court may determine for cause by order entered within that 90-day period) or 30 days after the court determines that the debtor is subject to this paragraph, whichever is later—

(A) the debtor has filed a plan of reorganization that has a reasonable possibility of being confirmed within a reasonable time; or

(B) the debtor has commenced monthly payments that—

(i) may, in the debtor's sole discretion, notwithstanding *section 363(c)(2)*, be made from rents or other income generated before, on, or after the date of the commencement of the case by or from the property to each creditor whose claim is secured by such real estate (other than a claim secured by a judgment lien or by an unmatured statutory lien); and

(ii) are in an amount equal to interest at the then applicable nondefault contract rate of interest on the value of the creditor's interest in the real estate; or

(4) with respect to a stay of an act against real property under subsection (a), by a creditor whose claim is secured by an interest in such real property, if the court finds that the filing of the petition was part of a scheme to delay, hinder, or defraud creditors that involved either—

(A) transfer of all or part ownership of, or other interest in, such real property without the consent of the secured creditor or court approval; or

(B) multiple bankruptcy filings affecting such real property.

If recorded in compliance with applicable State laws governing notices of interests or liens in real property, an order entered under paragraph (4) shall be binding in any other case under this title purporting to affect such real property filed not later than 2 years after the date of the entry of such order by the court, except that a debtor in a subsequent case under this title may move for relief from such order based upon changed circumstances or for good cause shown, after notice and a hearing. Any Federal, State, or local governmental unit that accepts notices of interests or liens in real property shall accept any certified copy of an order described in this subsection for indexing and recording.

(e)

(1) Thirty days after a request under subsection (d) of this section for relief from the stay of any act against property of the estate under subsection (a) of this section,

such stay is terminated with respect to the party in interest making such request, unless the court, after notice and a hearing, orders such stay continued in effect pending the conclusion of, or as a result of, a final hearing and determination under subsection (d) of this section. A hearing under this subsection may be a preliminary hearing, or may be consolidated with the final hearing under subsection (d) of this section. The court shall order such stay continued in effect pending the conclusion of the final hearing under subsection (d) of this section if there is a reasonable likelihood that the party opposing relief from such stay will prevail at the conclusion of such final hearing. If the hearing under this subsection is a preliminary hearing, then such final hearing shall be concluded not later than thirty days after the conclusion of such preliminary hearing, unless the 30-day period is extended with the consent of the parties in interest or for a specific time which the court finds is required by compelling circumstances.

(2) Notwithstanding paragraph (1), in a case under chapter 7, 11, or 13 in which the debtor is an individual, the stay under subsection (a) shall terminate on the date that is 60 days after a request is made by a party in interest under subsection (d), unless—

(A) a final decision is rendered by the court during the 60-day period beginning on the date of the request; or

(B) such 60-day period is extended—

(i) by agreement of all parties in interest; or

(ii) by the court for such specific period of time as the court finds is required for good cause, as described in findings made by the court.

(f) Upon request of a party in interest, the court, with or without a hearing, shall grant such relief from the stay provided under subsection (a) of this section as is necessary to prevent irreparable damage to the interest of an entity in property, if such interest will suffer such damage before there is an opportunity for notice and a hearing under subsection (d) or (e) of this section.

(g) In any hearing under subsection (d) or (e) of this section concerning relief from the stay of any act under subsection (a) of this section—

(1) the party requesting such relief has the burden of proof on the issue of the debtor's equity in property; and

(2) the party opposing such relief has the burden of proof on all other issues.

(h)

(1) In a case in which the debtor is an individual, the stay provided by subsection (a) is terminated with respect to personal property of the estate or of the debtor securing in whole or in part a claim, or subject to an unexpired lease, and such personal property shall no longer be property of the estate if the debtor fails within the applicable time set by *section 521(a)(2)*—

(A) to file timely any statement of intention required under *section 521(a)(2)* with respect to such personal property or to indicate in such statement that the debtor will either surrender such personal property or retain it and, if retaining such personal property, either redeem such personal property pursuant to *section 722*, enter into an agreement of the kind specified in *section 524(c)* applicable to the debt secured by such personal property, or assume such unexpired lease pursuant to *section 365(p)* if the trustee does not do so, as applicable; and

(B) to take timely the action specified in such statement, as it may be amended before expiration of the period for taking action, unless such statement specifies the debtor's intention to reaffirm such debt on the original contract terms and the creditor refuses to agree to the reaffirmation on such terms.

(2) Paragraph (1) does not apply if the court determines, on the motion of the trustee filed before the expiration of the applicable time set by *section 521(a)(2)*, after notice and a hearing, that such personal property is of consequential value or benefit to the estate, and orders appropriate adequate protection of the creditor's interest, and orders the debtor to deliver any

collateral in the debtor's possession to the trustee. If the court does not so determine, the stay provided by subsection (a) shall terminate upon the conclusion of the hearing on the motion.

(i) If a case commenced under chapter 7, 11, or 13 is dismissed due to the creation of a debt repayment plan, for purposes of subsection (c)(3), any subsequent case commenced by the debtor under any such chapter shall not be presumed to be filed not in good faith.

(j) On request of a party in interest, the court shall issue an order under subsection (c) confirming that the automatic stay has been terminated.

(k)

(1) Except as provided in paragraph (2), an individual injured by any willful violation of a stay provided by this section shall recover actual damages, including costs and attorneys' fees, and, in appropriate circumstances, may recover punitive damages.

(2) If such violation is based on an action taken by an entity in the good faith belief that subsection (h) applies to the debtor, the recovery under paragraph (1) of this subsection against such entity shall be limited to actual damages.

(l)

(1) Except as otherwise provided in this subsection, subsection (b)(22) shall apply on the date that is 30 days after the date on which the bankruptcy petition is filed, if the debtor files with the petition and serves upon the lessor a certification under penalty of perjury that—

(A) under nonbankruptcy law applicable in the jurisdiction, there are circumstances under which the debtor would be permitted to cure the entire monetary default that gave rise to the judgment for possession, after that judgment for possession was entered; and

(B) the debtor (or an adult dependent of the debtor) has deposited with the clerk of the court, any rent that would become due during the 30-day period after the filing of the bankruptcy petition.

(2) If, within the 30-day period after the filing of the bankruptcy petition, the debtor (or an adult dependent of the debtor) complies with paragraph (1) and files with the court and serves upon the lessor a further certification under penalty of perjury that the debtor (or an adult dependent of the debtor) has cured, under nonbankruptcy law applicable in the jurisdiction, the entire monetary default that gave rise to the judgment under which possession is sought by the lessor, subsection (b)(22) shall not apply, unless ordered to apply by the court under paragraph (3).

(3)

(A) If the lessor files an objection to any certification filed by the debtor under paragraph (1) or (2), and serves such objection upon the debtor, the court shall hold a hearing within 10 days after the filing and service of such objection to determine if the certification filed by the debtor under paragraph (1) or (2) is true.

(B) If the court upholds the objection of the lessor filed under subparagraph (A)—

(i) subsection (b)(22) shall apply immediately and relief from the stay provided under subsection (a)(3) shall not be required to enable the lessor to complete the process to recover full possession of the property; and

(ii) the clerk of the court shall immediately serve upon the lessor and the debtor a certified copy of the court's order upholding the lessor's objection.

(4) If a debtor, in accordance with paragraph (5), indicates on the petition that there was a judgment for possession of the residential rental property in which the debtor resides and does not file a certification under paragraph (1) or (2)—

(A) subsection (b)(22) shall apply immediately upon failure to file such certification, and relief from the stay provided under subsection (a)(3) shall not be required to enable the lessor to complete the process to recover full possession of the property; and

(B) the clerk of the court shall immediately serve upon the lessor and the debtor a certified copy of the docket indicating the absence of a filed certification and the applicability of the exception to the stay under subsection (b)(22).

(5)

(A) Where a judgment for possession of residential property in which the debtor resides as a tenant under a lease or rental agreement has been obtained by the lessor, the debtor shall so indicate on the bankruptcy petition and shall provide the name and address of the lessor that obtained that pre-petition judgment on the petition and on any certification filed under this subsection.

(B) The form of certification filed with the petition, as specified in this subsection, shall provide for the debtor to certify, and the debtor shall certify—

(i) whether a judgment for possession of residential rental housing in which the debtor resides has been obtained against the debtor before the date of the filing of the petition; and

(ii) whether the debtor is claiming under paragraph (1) that under nonbankruptcy law applicable in the jurisdiction, there are circumstances under which the debtor would be permitted to cure the entire monetary default that gave rise to the judgment for possession, after that judgment of possession was entered, and has made the appropriate deposit with the court.

(C) The standard forms (electronic and otherwise) used in a bankruptcy proceeding shall be amended to reflect the requirements of this subsection.

(D) The clerk of the court shall arrange for the prompt transmittal of the rent deposited in accordance with paragraph (1)(B) to the lessor.

(m)

(1) Except as otherwise provided in this subsection, subsection (b)(23) shall apply on the date that is 15 days after the date on which the lessor files and serves a certification described in subsection (b)(23).

(2)

(A) If the debtor files with the court an objection to the truth or legal sufficiency of the certification described in subsection (b)(23) and serves such objection upon the lessor, subsection (b)(23) shall not apply, unless ordered to apply by the court under this subsection.

(B) If the debtor files and serves the objection under subparagraph (A), the court shall hold a hearing within 10 days after the filing and service of such objection to determine if the situation giving rise to the lessor's certification under paragraph (1) existed or has been remedied.

(C) If the debtor can demonstrate to the satisfaction of the court that the situation giving rise to the lessor's certification under paragraph (1) did not exist or has been remedied, the stay provided under subsection (a)(3) shall remain in effect until the termination of the stay under this section.

(D) If the debtor cannot demonstrate to the satisfaction of the court that the situation giving rise to the lessor's certification under paragraph (1) did not exist or has been remedied—

(i) relief from the stay provided under subsection (a)(3) shall not be required to enable the lessor to proceed with the eviction; and

(ii) the clerk of the court shall immediately serve upon the lessor and the debtor a certified copy of the court's order upholding the lessor's certification.

(3) If the debtor fails to file, within 15 days, an objection under paragraph (2)(A)—

(A) subsection (b)(23) shall apply immediately upon such failure and relief from the stay provided under subsection (a)(3) shall not be required to enable the lessor to complete the process to recover full possession of the property; and

(B) the clerk of the court shall immediately serve upon the lessor and the debtor a certified copy of the docket indicating such failure.

(n)

(1) Except as provided in paragraph (2), subsection (a) does not apply in a case in which the debtor—

(A) is a debtor in a small business case pending at the time the petition is filed;

(B) was a debtor in a small business case that was dismissed for any reason by an order that became final in the 2-year period ending on the date of the order for relief entered with respect to the petition;

(C) was a debtor in a small business case in which a plan was confirmed in the 2-year period ending on the date of the order for relief entered with respect to the petition; or

(D) is an entity that has acquired substantially all of the assets or business of a small business debtor described in subparagraph (A), (B), or (C), unless such entity establishes by a preponderance of the evidence that such entity acquired substantially all of the assets or business of such small business debtor in good faith and not for the purpose of evading this paragraph.

(2) Paragraph (1) does not apply—

(A) to an involuntary case involving no collusion by the debtor with creditors; or

(B) to the filing of a petition if—

(i) the debtor proves by a preponderance of the evidence that the filing of the petition resulted from circumstances beyond the control of the debtor not foreseeable at the time the case then pending was filed; and

(ii) it is more likely than not that the court will confirm a feasible plan, but not a liquidating plan, within a reasonable period of time.

(o) The exercise of rights not subject to the stay arising under subsection (a) pursuant to paragraph (6), (7), (17), or (27) of subsection (b) shall not be stayed by any order of a court or administrative agency in any proceeding under this title.

(Pub. L. 95–598, Nov. 6, 1978, 92 Stat. 2570; Pub. L. 97–222, § 3, July 27, 1982, 96 Stat. 235; Pub. L. 98–353, title III, §§ 304, 363(b), 392, 441, July 10, 1984, 98 Stat. 352, 363, 365, 371; Pub. L. 99–509, title V, § 5001(a), Oct. 21, 1986, 100 Stat. 1911; Pub. L. 99–554, title II, §§ 257(j), 283(d), Oct. 27, 1986, 100 Stat. 3115, 3116; Pub. L. 101–311, title I, § 102, title II, § 202, June 25, 1990, 104 Stat. 267, 269; Pub. L. 101–508, title III, § 3007(a)(1), Nov. 5, 1990, 104 Stat. 1388–28; Pub. L. 103–394, title I, §§ 101, 116, title II, §§ 204(a), 218(b), title III, § 304(b), title IV, § 401, title V, § 501(b)(2), (d)(7), Oct. 22, 1994, 108 Stat. 4107, 4119, 4122, 4128, 4132, 4141, 4142, 4144; Pub. L. 105–277, div. I, title VI, § 603, Oct. 21, 1998, 112 Stat. 2681–886; Pub. L. 109–8, title I, § 106(f), title II, §§ 214, 224(b), title III, §§ 302, 303, 305(1), 311, 320, title IV, §§ 401(b), 441, 444, title VII, §§ 709, 718, title IX, § 907(d), (o)(1), (2), title XI, § 1106, title XII, § 1225, Apr. 20, 2005, 119 Stat. 41, 54, 64, 75, 77, 79, 84, 94, 104, 114, 117, 127, 131, 176, 181, 182, 192, 199; Pub. L. 109–304, § 17(b)(1), Oct. 6, 2006, 120 Stat. 1706; Pub. L. 109–390, § 5(a)(2), Dec. 12, 2006, 120 Stat. 2696; Pub. L. 111–327, § 2(a)(12), Dec. 22, 2010, 124 Stat. 3558; Pub. L. 116–189, § 9, Oct. 30, 2020, 134 Stat. 970; Pub. L. 119–27, § 11(c), July 18, 2025, 139 Stat. 457.)

Sections that reference this section: 108, 109, 1110, 1168, 1205, 1322, 1519, 1521, 342, 361, 363, 365, 505, 507, 521, 542, 553, 557, 742, 922

§363. Use, sale, or lease of property

(a) In this section, "cash collateral" means cash, negotiable instruments, documents of title, securities, deposit accounts, or other cash equivalents whenever acquired in which the estate and an entity other than the estate have an interest and includes the proceeds, products, offspring, rents, or profits of property and the fees, charges, accounts or other payments for the use or occupancy of rooms and other public facilities in hotels, motels, or other lodging properties subject to a security interest as provided in *section 552(b)* of this title, whether existing before or after the commencement of a case under this title.

(b)

(1) The trustee, after notice and a hearing, may use, sell, or lease, other than in the ordinary course of business, property of the estate, except that if the debtor in connection with

offering a product or a service discloses to an individual a policy prohibiting the transfer of personally identifiable information about individuals to persons that are not affiliated with the debtor and if such policy is in effect on the date of the commencement of the case, then the trustee may not sell or lease personally identifiable information to any person unless—

(A) such sale or such lease is consistent with such policy; or

(B) after appointment of a consumer privacy ombudsman in accordance with *section 332,* and after notice and a hearing, the court approves such sale or such lease—

(i) giving due consideration to the facts, circumstances, and conditions of such sale or such lease; and

(ii) finding that no showing was made that such sale or such lease would violate applicable nonbankruptcy law.

(2) If notification is required under subsection (a) of section 7A of the Clayton Act in the case of a transaction under this subsection, then—

(A) notwithstanding subsection (a) of such section, the notification required by such subsection to be given by the debtor shall be given by the trustee; and

(B) notwithstanding subsection (b) of such section, the required waiting period shall end on the 15th day after the date of the receipt, by the Federal Trade Commission and the Assistant Attorney General in charge of the Antitrust Division of the Department of Justice, of the notification required under such subsection (a), unless such waiting period is extended—

(i) pursuant to subsection (e)(2) of such section, in the same manner as such subsection (e)(2) applies to a cash tender offer;

(ii) pursuant to subsection (g)(2) of such section; or

(iii) by the court after notice and a hearing.

(c)

(1) If the business of the debtor is authorized to be operated under *section 721, 1108, 1183, 1184, 1203, 1204,* or 1304 of this title and unless the court orders otherwise, the trustee may enter into transactions, including the sale or lease of property of the estate, in the ordinary course of business, without notice or a hearing, and may use property of the estate in the ordinary course of business without notice or a hearing.

(2) The trustee may not use, sell, or lease cash collateral under paragraph (1) of this subsection unless—

(A) each entity that has an interest in such cash collateral consents; or

(B) the court, after notice and a hearing, authorizes such use, sale, or lease in accordance with the provisions of this section.

(3) Any hearing under paragraph (2)(B) of this subsection may be a preliminary hearing or may be consolidated with a hearing under subsection (e) of this section, but shall be scheduled in accordance with the needs of the debtor. If the hearing under paragraph (2)(B) of this subsection is a preliminary hearing, the court may authorize such use, sale, or lease only if there is a reasonable likelihood that the trustee will prevail at the final hearing under subsection (e) of this section. The court shall act promptly on any request for authorization under paragraph (2)(B) of this subsection.

(4) Except as provided in paragraph (2) of this subsection, the trustee shall segregate and account for any cash collateral in the trustee's possession, custody, or control.

(d) The trustee may use, sell, or lease property under subsection (b) or (c) of this section—

(1) in the case of a debtor that is a corporation or trust that is not a moneyed business, commercial corporation, or trust, only in accordance with nonbankruptcy law applicable to the transfer of property by a debtor that is such a corporation or trust; and

(2) only to the extent not inconsistent with any relief granted under subsection (c), (d), (e), or (f) of *section 362.*

(e) Notwithstanding any other provision of this section, at any time, on request of an entity that has an interest in property used, sold, or leased, or proposed to be used, sold, or leased, by the trustee, the court, with or without a hearing, shall prohibit or condition such use, sale, or lease as is necessary to provide adequate protection of such interest. This subsection also applies to property that is subject to any unexpired lease of personal property (to the exclusion of such property being subject to an order to grant relief from the stay under *section 362*).

(f) The trustee may sell property under subsection (b) or (c) of this section free and clear of any interest in such property of an entity other than the estate, only if—

(1) applicable nonbankruptcy law permits sale of such property free and clear of such interest;

(2) such entity consents;

(3) such interest is a lien and the price at which such property is to be sold is greater than the aggregate value of all liens on such property;

(4) such interest is in bona fide dispute; or

(5) such entity could be compelled, in a legal or equitable proceeding, to accept a money satisfaction of such interest.

(g) Notwithstanding subsection (f) of this section, the trustee may sell property under subsection (b) or (c) of this section free and clear of any vested or contingent right in the nature of dower or curtesy.

(h) Notwithstanding subsection (f) of this section, the trustee may sell both the estate's interest, under subsection (b) or (c) of this section, and the interest of any co-owner in property in which the debtor had, at the time of the commencement of the case, an undivided interest as a tenant in common, joint tenant, or tenant by the entirety, only if—

(1) partition in kind of such property among the estate and such co-owners is impracticable;

(2) sale of the estate's undivided interest in such property would realize significantly less for the estate than sale of such property free of the interests of such co-owners;

(3) the benefit to the estate of a sale of such property free of the interests of co-owners outweighs the detriment, if any, to such co-owners; and

(4) such property is not used in the production, transmission, or distribution, for sale, of electric energy or of natural or synthetic gas for heat, light, or power.

(i) Before the consummation of a sale of property to which subsection (g) or (h) of this section applies, or of property of the estate that was community property of the debtor and the debtor's spouse immediately before the commencement of the case, the debtor's spouse, or a co-owner of such property, as the case may be, may purchase such property at the price at which such sale is to be consummated.

(j) After a sale of property to which subsection (g) or (h) of this section applies, the trustee shall distribute to the debtor's spouse or the co-owners of such property, as the case may be, and to the estate, the proceeds of such sale, less the costs and expenses, not including any compensation of the trustee, of such sale, according to the interests of such spouse or co-owners, and of the estate.

(k) At a sale under subsection (b) of this section of property that is subject to a lien that secures an allowed claim, unless the court for cause orders otherwise the holder of such claim may bid at such sale, and, if the holder of such claim purchases such property, such holder may offset such claim against the purchase price of such property.

(l) Subject to the provisions of *section 365*, the trustee may use, sell, or lease property under subsection (b) or (c) of this section, or a plan under chapter 11, 12, or 13 of this title may provide for the use, sale, or lease of property, notwithstanding any provision in a contract, a lease, or applicable law that is conditioned on the insolvency or financial condition of the debtor, on the commencement of a case under this title concerning the debtor, or on the appointment of or the taking possession by a trustee in a case under this title or a custodian, and that effects, or gives an option to effect, a forfeiture, modification, or termination of the debtor's interest in such property.

(m) The reversal or modification on appeal of an authorization under subsection (b) or (c) of this section of a sale or lease of property does not affect the validity of a sale or lease under such authorization to an entity that purchased or leased such property in good faith, whether or not such entity knew of the pendency of the appeal, unless such authorization and such sale or lease were stayed pending appeal.

(n) The trustee may avoid a sale under this section if the sale price was controlled by an agreement among potential bidders at such sale, or may recover from a party to such agreement any amount by which the value of the property sold exceeds the price at which such sale was consummated, and may recover any costs, attorneys' fees, or expenses incurred in avoiding such sale or recovering such amount. In addition to any recovery under the preceding sentence, the court may grant judgment for punitive damages in favor of the estate and against any such party that entered into such an agreement in willful disregard of this subsection.

(o) Notwithstanding subsection (f), if a person purchases any interest in a consumer credit transaction that is subject to the Truth in Lending Act or any interest in a consumer credit contract (as defined in section 433.1 of title 16 of the Code of Federal Regulations (January 1, 2004), as amended from time to time), and if such interest is purchased through a sale under this section, then such person shall remain subject to all claims and defenses that are related to such consumer credit transaction or such consumer credit contract, to the same extent as such person would be subject to such claims and defenses of the consumer had such interest been purchased at a sale not under this section.

(p) In any hearing under this section—

(1) the trustee has the burden of proof on the issue of adequate protection; and

(2) the entity asserting an interest in property has the burden of proof on the issue of the validity, priority, or extent of such interest.

(Pub. L. 95–598, Nov. 6, 1978, 92 Stat. 2572; Pub. L. 98–353, title III, § 442, July 10, 1984, 98 Stat. 371; Pub. L. 99–554, title II, § 257(k), Oct. 27, 1986, 100 Stat. 3115; Pub. L. 103–394, title I, § 109, title II, §§ 214(b), 219(c), title V, § 501(d)(8), Oct. 22, 1994, 108 Stat. 4113, 4126, 4129, 4144; Pub. L. 109–8, title II, §§ 204, 231(a), title XII, § 1221(a), Apr. 20, 2005, 119 Stat. 49, 72, 195; Pub. L. 111–327, § 2(a)(13), Dec. 22, 2010, 124 Stat. 3559; Pub. L. 116–54, § 4(a)(6), Aug. 23, 2019, 133 Stat. 1086.)

Sections that reference this section: 1111, 1116, 1129, 1205, 1206, 1303, 1304, 1326, 1520, 303, 332, 361, 362, 507, 542, 552

§364. Obtaining credit

(a) If the trustee is authorized to operate the business of the debtor under *section 721, 1108, 1183, 1184, 1203, 1204,* or 1304 of this title, unless the court orders otherwise, the trustee may obtain unsecured credit and incur unsecured debt in the ordinary course of business allowable under *section 503(b)(1)* of this title as an administrative expense.

(b) The court, after notice and a hearing, may authorize the trustee to obtain unsecured credit or to incur unsecured debt other than under subsection (a) of this section, allowable under *section 503(b)(1)* of this title as an administrative expense.

(c) If the trustee is unable to obtain unsecured credit allowable under *section 503(b)(1)* of this title as an administrative expense, the court, after notice and a hearing, may authorize the obtaining of credit or the incurring of debt—

(1) with priority over any or all administrative expenses of the kind specified in *section 503(b)* or *507*(b) of this title;

(2) secured by a lien on property of the estate that is not otherwise subject to a lien; or

(3) secured by a junior lien on property of the estate that is subject to a lien.

(d)

(1) The court, after notice and a hearing, may authorize the obtaining of credit or the incurring of debt secured by a senior or equal lien on property of the estate that is subject to a lien only if—

(A) the trustee is unable to obtain such credit otherwise; and

(B) there is adequate protection of the interest of the holder of the lien on the property of the estate on which such senior or equal lien is proposed to be granted.

(2) In any hearing under this subsection, the trustee has the burden of proof on the issue of adequate protection.

(e) The reversal or modification on appeal of an authorization under this section to obtain credit or incur debt, or of a grant under this section of a priority or a lien, does not affect the validity of any debt so incurred, or any priority or lien so granted, to an entity that extended such credit in good faith, whether or not such entity knew of the pendency of the appeal, unless such authorization and the incurring of such debt, or the granting of such priority or lien, were stayed pending appeal.

(f) Except with respect to an entity that is an underwriter as defined in *section 1145(b)* of this title, section 5 of the Securities Act of 1933, the Trust Indenture Act of 1939, and any State or local law requiring registration for offer or sale of a security or registration or licensing of an issuer of, underwriter of, or broker or dealer in, a security does not apply to the offer or sale under this section of a security that is not an equity security.

(Pub. L. 95–598, Nov. 6, 1978, 92 Stat. 2574; Pub. L. 99–554, title II, § 257(l), Oct. 27, 1986, 100 Stat. 3115; Pub. L. 103–394, title V, § 501(d)(9), Oct. 22, 1994, 108 Stat. 4144; Pub. L. 116–54, § 4(a)(7), Aug. 23, 2019, 133 Stat. 1086; Pub. L. 116–260, div. N, title III, § 320(a), (f)(2)(A)(i), Dec. 27, 2020, 134 Stat. 2015, 2016.)

Sections that reference this section: 1205, 361, 507, 921, 922

§365. Executory contracts and unexpired leases

(a) Except as provided in *sections 765* and *766* of this title and in subsections (b), (c), and (d) of this section, the trustee, subject to the court's approval, may assume or reject any executory contract or unexpired lease of the debtor.

(b)

(1) If there has been a default in an executory contract or unexpired lease of the debtor, the trustee may not assume such contract or lease unless, at the time of assumption of such contract or lease, the trustee—

(A) cures, or provides adequate assurance that the trustee will promptly cure, such default other than a default that is a breach of a provision relating to the satisfaction of any provision (other than a penalty rate or penalty provision) relating to a default arising from any failure to perform nonmonetary obligations under an unexpired lease of real property, if it is impossible for the trustee to cure such default by performing nonmonetary acts at and after the time of assumption, except that if such default arises from a failure to operate in accordance with a nonresidential real property lease, then such default shall be cured by performance at and after the time of assumption in accordance with such lease, and pecuniary losses resulting from such default shall be compensated in accordance with the provisions of this paragraph;

(B) compensates, or provides adequate assurance that the trustee will promptly compensate, a party other than the debtor to such contract or lease, for any actual pecuniary loss to such party resulting from such default; and

(C) provides adequate assurance of future performance under such contract or lease.

(2) Paragraph (1) of this subsection does not apply to a default that is a breach of a provision relating to—

(A) the insolvency or financial condition of the debtor at any time before the closing of the case;

(B) the commencement of a case under this title;

(C) the appointment of or taking possession by a trustee in a case under this title or a custodian before such commencement; or

(D) the satisfaction of any penalty rate or penalty provision relating to a default arising from any failure by the debtor to perform nonmonetary obligations under the executory contract or unexpired lease.

(3) For the purposes of paragraph (1) of this subsection and paragraph (2)(B) of subsection (f), adequate assurance of future performance of a lease of real property in a shopping center includes adequate assurance—

(A) of the source of rent and other consideration due under such lease, and in the case of an assignment, that the financial condition and operating performance of the proposed assignee and its guarantors, if any, shall be similar to the financial condition and operating performance of the debtor and its guarantors, if any, as of the time the debtor became the lessee under the lease;

(B) that any percentage rent due under such lease will not decline substantially;

(C) that assumption or assignment of such lease is subject to all the provisions thereof, including (but not limited to) provisions such as a radius, location, use, or exclusivity provision, and will not breach any such provision contained in any other lease, financing agreement, or master agreement relating to such shopping center; and

(D) that assumption or assignment of such lease will not disrupt any tenant mix or balance in such shopping center.

(4) Notwithstanding any other provision of this section, if there has been a default in an unexpired lease of the debtor, other than a default of a kind specified in paragraph (2) of this subsection, the trustee may not require a lessor to provide services or supplies incidental to such lease before assumption of such lease unless the lessor is compensated under the terms of such lease for any services and supplies provided under such lease before assumption of such lease.

(c) The trustee may not assume or assign any executory contract or unexpired lease of the debtor, whether or not such contract or lease prohibits or restricts assignment of rights or delegation of duties, if—

(1)

(A) applicable law excuses a party, other than the debtor, to such contract or lease from accepting performance from or rendering performance to an entity other than the debtor or the debtor in possession, whether or not such contract or lease prohibits or restricts assignment of rights or delegation of duties; and

(B) such party does not consent to such assumption or assignment; or

(2) such contract is a contract to make a loan, or extend other debt financing or financial accommodations, to or for the benefit of the debtor, or to issue a security of the debtor; or

(3) such lease is of nonresidential real property and has been terminated under applicable nonbankruptcy law prior to the order for relief.

(d)

(1) In a case under chapter 7 of this title, if the trustee does not assume or reject an executory contract or unexpired lease of residential real property or of personal property of the debtor within 60 days after the order for relief, or within such additional time as the court, for cause, within such 60-day period, fixes, then such contract or lease is deemed rejected.

(2) In a case under chapter 9, 11, 12, or 13 of this title, the trustee may assume or reject an executory contract or unexpired lease of residential real property or of personal property of the debtor at any time before the confirmation of a plan but the court, on the request of any party to such contract or lease, may order the trustee to determine within a specified period of time whether to assume or reject such contract or lease.

(3) The trustee shall timely perform all the obligations of the debtor, except those specified in section 365(b)(2), arising from and after the order for relief under any unexpired lease of nonresidential real property, until such lease is assumed or rejected, notwithstanding *section 503(b)(1)* of this title. The court may extend, for cause, the time for performance of any such obligation that arises within 60 days after the date of the order for relief, but the time for performance shall not be extended beyond such 60-day period. This subsection shall not be deemed to affect the trustee's obligations under the provisions of subsection (b) or (f) of this section. Acceptance of any such performance does not constitute waiver or relinquishment of the lessor's rights under such lease or under this title.

(4)

(A) Subject to subparagraph (B), an unexpired lease of nonresidential real property under which the debtor is the lessee shall be deemed rejected, and the trustee shall immediately surrender that nonresidential real property to the lessor, if the trustee does not assume or reject the unexpired lease by the earlier of—

(i) the date that is 120 days after the date of the order for relief; or

(ii) the date of the entry of an order confirming a plan.

(B)

(i) The court may extend the period determined under subparagraph (A), prior to the expiration of the 120-day period, for 90 days on the motion of the trustee or lessor for cause.

(ii) If the court grants an extension under clause (i), the court may grant a subsequent extension only upon prior written consent of the lessor in each instance.

(5) The trustee shall timely perform all of the obligations of the debtor, except those specified in section 365(b)(2), first arising from or after 60 days after the order for relief in a case under chapter 11 of this title under an unexpired lease of personal property (other than personal property leased to an individual primarily for personal, family, or household purposes), until such lease is assumed or rejected notwithstanding *section 503(b)(1)* of this title, unless the court, after notice and a hearing and based on the equities of the case, orders otherwise with respect to the obligations or timely performance thereof. This subsection shall not be deemed to affect the trustee's obligations under the provisions of subsection (b) or (f). Acceptance of any such performance does not constitute waiver or relinquishment of the lessor's rights under such lease or under this title.

(e)

(1) Notwithstanding a provision in an executory contract or unexpired lease, or in applicable law, an executory contract or unexpired lease of the debtor may not be terminated or modified, and any right or obligation under such contract or lease may not be terminated or modified, at any time after the commencement of the case solely because of a provision in such contract or lease that is conditioned on—

(A) the insolvency or financial condition of the debtor at any time before the closing of the case;

(B) the commencement of a case under this title; or

(C) the appointment of or taking possession by a trustee in a case under this title or a custodian before such commencement.

(2) Paragraph (1) of this subsection does not apply to an executory contract or unexpired lease of the debtor, whether or not such contract or lease prohibits or restricts assignment of rights or delegation of duties, if—

(A)

(i) applicable law excuses a party, other than the debtor, to such contract or lease from accepting performance from or rendering performance to the trustee or to an assignee of such contract or lease, whether or not such contract or lease prohibits or restricts assignment of rights or delegation of duties; and

(ii) such party does not consent to such assumption or assignment; or

(B) such contract is a contract to make a loan, or extend other debt financing or financial accommodations, to or for the benefit of the debtor, or to issue a security of the debtor.

(f)

(1) Except as provided in subsections (b) and (c) of this section, notwithstanding a provision in an executory contract or unexpired lease of the debtor, or in applicable law, that prohibits, restricts, or conditions the assignment of such contract or lease, the trustee may assign such contract or lease under paragraph (2) of this subsection.

(2) The trustee may assign an executory contract or unexpired lease of the debtor only if—

(A) the trustee assumes such contract or lease in accordance with the provisions of this section; and

(B) adequate assurance of future performance by the assignee of such contract or lease is provided, whether or not there has been a default in such contract or lease.

(3) Notwithstanding a provision in an executory contract or unexpired lease of the debtor, or in applicable law that terminates or modifies, or permits a party other than the debtor to terminate or modify, such contract or lease or a right or obligation under such contract or lease on account of an assignment of such contract or lease, such contract, lease, right, or obligation

may not be terminated or modified under such provision because of the assumption or assignment of such contract or lease by the trustee.

(g) Except as provided in subsections (h)(2) and (i)(2) of this section, the rejection of an executory contract or unexpired lease of the debtor constitutes a breach of such contract or lease—

(1) if such contract or lease has not been assumed under this section or under a plan confirmed under chapter 9, 11, 12, or 13 of this title, immediately before the date of the filing of the petition; or

(2) if such contract or lease has been assumed under this section or under a plan confirmed under chapter 9, 11, 12, or 13 of this title—

(A) if before such rejection the case has not been converted under *section 1112, 1208,* or *1307* of this title, at the time of such rejection; or

(B) if before such rejection the case has been converted under *section 1112, 1208,* or *1307* of this title—

(i) immediately before the date of such conversion, if such contract or lease was assumed before such conversion; or

(ii) at the time of such rejection, if such contract or lease was assumed after such conversion.

(h)

(1)

(A) If the trustee rejects an unexpired lease of real property under which the debtor is the lessor and—

(i) if the rejection by the trustee amounts to such a breach as would entitle the lessee to treat such lease as terminated by virtue of its terms, applicable nonbankruptcy law, or any agreement made by the lessee, then the lessee under such lease may treat such lease as terminated by the rejection; or

(ii) if the term of such lease has commenced, the lessee may retain its rights under such lease (including rights such as those relating to the amount and timing of payment of rent and other amounts payable by the lessee and any right of use, possession, quiet enjoyment, subletting, assignment, or hypothecation) that are in or appurtenant to the real property for the balance of the term of such lease and for any renewal or extension of such rights to the extent that such rights are enforceable under applicable nonbankruptcy law.

(B) If the lessee retains its rights under subparagraph (A)(ii), the lessee may offset against the rent reserved under such lease for the balance of the term after the date of the rejection of such lease and for the term of any renewal or extension of such lease, the value of any damage caused by the nonperformance after the date of such rejection, of any obligation of the debtor under such lease, but the lessee shall not have any other right against the estate or the debtor on account of any damage occurring after such date caused by such nonperformance.

(C) The rejection of a lease of real property in a shopping center with respect to which the lessee elects to retain its rights under subparagraph (A)(ii) does not affect the enforceability under applicable nonbankruptcy law of any provision in the lease pertaining to radius, location, use, exclusivity, or tenant mix or balance.

(D) In this paragraph, "lessee" includes any successor, assign, or mortgagee permitted under the terms of such lease.

(2)

(A) If the trustee rejects a timeshare interest under a timeshare plan under which the debtor is the timeshare interest seller and—

(i) if the rejection amounts to such a breach as would entitle the timeshare interest purchaser to treat the timeshare plan as terminated under its terms, applicable nonbankruptcy law, or any agreement made by timeshare interest purchaser, the timeshare interest purchaser under the timeshare plan may treat the timeshare plan as terminated by such rejection; or

(ii) if the term of such timeshare interest has commenced, then the timeshare interest purchaser may retain its rights in such timeshare interest for the balance of such term and for any term of renewal or extension of such timeshare interest to the extent that such rights are enforceable under applicable nonbankruptcy law.

(B) If the timeshare interest purchaser retains its rights under subparagraph (A), such timeshare interest purchaser may offset against the moneys due for such timeshare interest for the balance of the term after the date of the rejection of such timeshare interest, and the term of any renewal or extension of such timeshare interest, the value of any damage caused by the nonperformance after the date of such rejection, of any obligation of the debtor under such timeshare plan, but the timeshare interest purchaser shall not have any right against the estate or the debtor on account of any damage occurring after such date caused by such nonperformance.

(i)

(1) If the trustee rejects an executory contract of the debtor for the sale of real property or for the sale of a timeshare interest under a timeshare plan, under which the purchaser is in possession, such purchaser may treat such contract as terminated, or, in the alternative, may remain in possession of such real property or timeshare interest.

(2) If such purchaser remains in possession—

(A) such purchaser shall continue to make all payments due under such contract, but may, offset against such payments any damages occurring after the date of the rejection of such contract caused by the nonperformance of any obligation of the debtor after such date, but such purchaser does not have any rights against the estate on account of any damages arising after such date from such rejection, other than such offset; and

(B) the trustee shall deliver title to such purchaser in accordance with the provisions of such contract, but is relieved of all other obligations to perform under such contract.

(j) A purchaser that treats an executory contract as terminated under subsection (i) of this section, or a party whose executory contract to purchase real property from the debtor is rejected and under which such party is not in possession, has a lien on the interest of the debtor in such property for the recovery of any portion of the purchase price that such purchaser or party has paid.

(k) Assignment by the trustee to an entity of a contract or lease assumed under this section relieves the trustee and the estate from any liability for any breach of such contract or lease occurring after such assignment.

(l) If an unexpired lease under which the debtor is the lessee is assigned pursuant to this section, the lessor of the property may require a deposit or other security for the performance of the debtor's obligations under the lease substantially the same as would have been required by the landlord upon the initial leasing to a similar tenant.

(m) For purposes of this section 365 and *sections 541(b)(2)* and *362*(b)(10), leases of real property shall include any rental agreement to use real property.

(n)

(1) If the trustee rejects an executory contract under which the debtor is a licensor of a right to intellectual property, the licensee under such contract may elect—

(A) to treat such contract as terminated by such rejection if such rejection by the trustee amounts to such a breach as would entitle the licensee to treat such contract as terminated by virtue of its own terms, applicable nonbankruptcy law, or an agreement made by the licensee with another entity; or

(B) to retain its rights (including a right to enforce any exclusivity provision of such contract, but excluding any other right under applicable nonbankruptcy law to specific performance of such contract) under such contract and under any agreement supplementary to such contract, to such intellectual property (including any embodiment of such intellectual property to the extent protected by applicable nonbankruptcy law), as such rights existed immediately before the case commenced, for—

(i) the duration of such contract; and

(ii) any period for which such contract may be extended by the licensee as of right under applicable nonbankruptcy law.

(2) If the licensee elects to retain its rights, as described in paragraph (1)(B) of this subsection, under such contract—

(A) the trustee shall allow the licensee to exercise such rights;

(B) the licensee shall make all royalty payments due under such contract for the duration of such contract and for any period described in paragraph (1)(B) of this subsection for which the licensee extends such contract; and

(C) the licensee shall be deemed to waive —

(i) any right of setoff it may have with respect to such contract under this title or applicable nonbankruptcy law; and

(ii) any claim allowable under *section 503(b)* of this title arising from the performance of such contract.

(3) If the licensee elects to retain its rights, as described in paragraph (1)(B) of this subsection, then on the written request of the licensee the trustee shall—

(A) to the extent provided in such contract, or any agreement supplementary to such contract, provide to the licensee any intellectual property (including such embodiment) held by the trustee; and

(B) not interfere with the rights of the licensee as provided in such contract, or any agreement supplementary to such contract, to such intellectual property (including such embodiment) including any right to obtain such intellectual property (or such embodiment) from another entity.

(4) Unless and until the trustee rejects such contract, on the written request of the licensee the trustee shall—

(A) to the extent provided in such contract or any agreement supplementary to such contract—

(i) perform such contract; or

(ii) provide to the licensee such intellectual property (including any embodiment of such intellectual property to the extent protected by applicable nonbankruptcy law) held by the trustee; and

(B) not interfere with the rights of the licensee as provided in such contract, or any agreement supplementary to such contract, to such intellectual property (including such embodiment), including any right to obtain such intellectual property (or such embodiment) from another entity.

(o) In a case under chapter 11 of this title, the trustee shall be deemed to have assumed (consistent with the debtor's other obligations under *section 507*), and shall immediately cure any deficit under, any commitment by the debtor to a Federal depository institutions regulatory agency (or predecessor to such agency) to maintain the capital of an insured depository institution, and any claim for a subsequent breach of the obligations thereunder shall be entitled to priority under *section 507*. This subsection shall not extend any commitment that would otherwise be terminated by any act of such an agency.

(p)

(1) If a lease of personal property is rejected or not timely assumed by the trustee under subsection (d), the leased property is no longer property of the estate and the stay under *section 362(a)* is automatically terminated.

(2)

(A) If the debtor in a case under chapter 7 is an individual, the debtor may notify the creditor in writing that the debtor desires to assume the lease. Upon being so notified, the creditor may, at its option, notify the debtor that it is willing to have the lease assumed by the debtor and may condition such assumption on cure of any outstanding default on terms set by the contract.

(B) If, not later than 30 days after notice is provided under subparagraph (A), the debtor notifies the lessor in writing that the lease is assumed, the liability under the lease will be assumed by the debtor and not by the estate.

(C) The stay under *section 362* and the injunction under *section 524(a)(2)* shall not be violated by notification of the debtor and negotiation of cure under this subsection.

(3) In a case under chapter 11 in which the debtor is an individual and in a case under chapter 13, if the debtor is the lessee with respect to personal property and the lease is not assumed in the plan confirmed by the court, the lease is deemed rejected as of the conclusion of the hearing on confirmation. If the lease is rejected, the stay under *section 362* and any stay under *section 1301* is automatically terminated with respect to the property subject to the lease.

(Pub. L. 95–598, Nov. 6, 1978, 92 Stat. 2574; Pub. L. 98–353, title III, §§ 362, 402–404, July 10, 1984, 98 Stat. 361, 367; Pub. L. 99–554, title II, §§ 257(j), (m), 283(e), Oct. 27, 1986, 100 Stat. 3115, 3117; Pub. L. 100–506, § 1(b), Oct. 18, 1988, 102 Stat. 2538; Pub. L. 101–647, title XXV, § 2522(c), Nov. 29, 1990, 104 Stat. 4866; Pub. L. 102–365, § 19(b)–(e), Sept. 3, 1992, 106 Stat. 982–984; Pub. L. 103–394, title II, §§ 205(a), 219(a), (b), title V, § 501(d)(10), Oct. 22, 1994, 108 Stat. 4122, 4128, 4145; Pub. L. 103–429, § 1, Oct. 31, 1994, 108 Stat. 4377; Pub. L. 109–8, title III, §§ 309(b), 328(a), title IV, § 404, Apr. 20, 2005, 119 Stat. 82, 100, 104; Pub. L. 116–260, div. FF, title X, § 1001(f)(1), (2)(A), Dec. 27, 2020, 134 Stat. 3219.)

Sections that reference this section: 1110, 1123, 1124, 1167, 1168, 1169, 1222, 1322, 362, 363, 502, 503, 541, 555, 556, 559, 560, 561, 562, 744, 929

§366. Utility service

(a) Except as provided in subsections (b) and (c) of this section, a utility may not alter, refuse, or discontinue service to, or discriminate against, the trustee or the debtor solely on the basis of the commencement of a case under this title or that a debt owed by the debtor to such utility for service rendered before the order for relief was not paid when due.

(b) Such utility may alter, refuse, or discontinue service if neither the trustee nor the debtor, within 20 days after the date of the order for relief, furnishes adequate assurance of payment, in the form of a deposit or other security, for service after such date. On request of a party in interest and after notice and a hearing, the court may order reasonable modification of the amount of the deposit or other security necessary to provide adequate assurance of payment.

(c)

(1)

(A) For purposes of this subsection, the term "assurance of payment" means—

(i) a cash deposit;

(ii) a letter of credit;

(iii) a certificate of deposit;

(iv) a surety bond;

(v) a prepayment of utility consumption; or

(vi) another form of security that is mutually agreed on between the utility and the debtor or the trustee.

(B) For purposes of this subsection an administrative expense priority shall not constitute an assurance of payment.

(2) Subject to paragraphs (3) and (4), with respect to a case filed under chapter 11, a utility referred to in subsection (a) may alter, refuse, or discontinue utility service, if during the 30-day period beginning on the date of the filing of the petition, the utility does not receive from the debtor or the trustee adequate assurance of payment for utility service that is satisfactory to the utility.

(3)

(A) On request of a party in interest and after notice and a hearing, the court may order modification of the amount of an assurance of payment under paragraph (2).

(B) In making a determination under this paragraph whether an assurance of payment is adequate, the court may not consider—

(i) the absence of security before the date of the filing of the petition;

(ii) the payment by the debtor of charges for utility service in a timely manner before the date of the filing of the petition; or

(iii) the availability of an administrative expense priority.

(4) Notwithstanding any other provision of law, with respect to a case subject to this subsection, a utility may recover or set off against a security deposit provided to the utility by the debtor before the date of the filing of the petition without notice or order of the court.

(Pub. L. 95–598, Nov. 6, 1978, 92 Stat. 2578; Pub. L. 98–353, title III, § 443, July 10, 1984, 98 Stat. 373; Pub. L. 109–8, title IV, § 417, Apr. 20, 2005, 119 Stat. 108; Pub. L. 116–260, div. FF, title X, § 1001(h), Dec. 27, 2020, 134 Stat. 3221.)

Sections that reference this section: None

CHAPTER 5: CREDITORS, THE DEBTOR, AND THE ESTATE

Subchapter I: Creditors and Claims

§501. Filing of proofs of claims or interests

(a) A creditor or an indenture trustee may file a proof of claim. An equity security holder may file a proof of interest.

(b) If a creditor does not timely file a proof of such creditor's claim, an entity that is liable to such creditor with the debtor, or that has secured such creditor, may file a proof of such claim.

(c) If a creditor does not timely file a proof of such creditor's claim, the debtor or the trustee may file a proof of such claim.

(d) A claim of a kind specified in *section 502(e)(2), 502*(f), 502(g), 502(h) or 502(i) of this title may be filed under subsection (a), (b), or (c) of this section the same as if such claim were a claim against the debtor and had arisen before the date of the filing of the petition.

(e) A claim arising from the liability of a debtor for fuel use tax assessed consistent with the requirements of section 31705 of title 49 may be filed by the base jurisdiction designated pursuant to the International Fuel Tax Agreement (as defined in section 31701 of title 49) and, if so filed, shall be allowed as a single claim.

(Pub. L. 95–598, Nov. 6, 1978, 92 Stat. 2578; Pub. L. 98–353, title III, § 444, July 10, 1984, 98 Stat. 373; Pub. L. 109–8, title VII, § 702, Apr. 20, 2005, 119 Stat. 125; Pub. L. 116–260, div. FF, title X, § 1001(d)(1), (3)(A), Dec. 27, 2020, 134 Stat. 3217, 3218.)

Sections that reference this section: 101, 1111, 1141, 502, 506, 541, 726, 727, 925, 944

§502. Allowance of claims or interests

(a) A claim or interest, proof of which is filed under *section 501* of this title, is deemed allowed, unless a party in interest, including a creditor of a general partner in a partnership that is a debtor in a case under chapter 7 of this title, objects.

(b) Except as provided in subsections (e)(2), (f), (g), (h) and (i) of this section, if such objection to a claim is made, the court, after notice and a hearing, shall determine the amount of such claim in lawful currency of the United States as of the date of the filing of the petition, and shall allow such claim in such amount, except to the extent that—

(1) such claim is unenforceable against the debtor and property of the debtor, under any agreement or applicable law for a reason other than because such claim is contingent or unmatured;

(2) such claim is for unmatured interest;

(3) if such claim is for a tax assessed against property of the estate, such claim exceeds the value of the interest of the estate in such property;

(4) if such claim is for services of an insider or attorney of the debtor, such claim exceeds the reasonable value of such services;

(5) such claim is for a debt that is unmatured on the date of the filing of the petition and that is excepted from discharge under *section 523(a)(5)* of this title;

(6) if such claim is the claim of a lessor for damages resulting from the termination of a lease of real property, such claim exceeds —

(A) the rent reserved by such lease, without acceleration, for the greater of one year, or 15 percent, not to exceed three years, of the remaining term of such lease, following the earlier of—

(i) the date of the filing of the petition; and

(ii) the date on which such lessor repossessed, or the lessee surrendered, the leased property; plus

(B) any unpaid rent due under such lease, without acceleration, on the earlier of such dates;

(7) if such claim is the claim of an employee for damages resulting from the termination of an employment contract, such claim exceeds—

(A) the compensation provided by such contract, without acceleration, for one year following the earlier of—

(i) the date of the filing of the petition; or

(ii) the date on which the employer directed the employee to terminate, or such employee terminated, performance under such contract; plus

(B) any unpaid compensation due under such contract, without acceleration, on the earlier of such dates;

(8) such claim results from a reduction, due to late payment, in the amount of an otherwise applicable credit available to the debtor in connection with an employment tax on wages, salaries, or commissions earned from the debtor; or

(9) proof of such claim is not timely filed, except to the extent tardily filed as permitted under paragraph (1), (2), or (3) of *section 726(a)* or under the Federal Rules of Bankruptcy Procedure, except that—

(A) a claim of a governmental unit shall be timely filed if it is filed before 180 days after the date of the order for relief or such later time as the Federal Rules of Bankruptcy Procedure may provide; and

(B) in a case under chapter 13, a claim of a governmental unit for a tax with respect to a return filed under *section 1308* shall be timely if the claim is filed on or before the date that is 60 days after the date on which such return was filed as required.

(c) There shall be estimated for purpose of allowance under this section—

(1) any contingent or unliquidated claim, the fixing or liquidation of which, as the case may be, would unduly delay the administration of the case; or

(2) any right to payment arising from a right to an equitable remedy for breach of performance.

(d) Notwithstanding subsections (a) and (b) of this section, the court shall disallow any claim of any entity from which property is recoverable under *section 542, 543, 550,* or *553* of this title or that is a transferee of a transfer avoidable under *section 522(f), 522*(h), 544, 545, 547, 548, 549, or 724(a) of this title, unless such entity or transferee has paid the amount, or turned over any such property, for which such entity or transferee is liable under *section 522(i), 542, 543, 550,* or *553* of this title.

(e)

(1) Notwithstanding subsections (a), (b), and (c) of this section and paragraph (2) of this subsection, the court shall disallow any

claim for reimbursement or contribution of an entity that is liable with the debtor on or has secured the claim of a creditor, to the extent that—

(A) such creditor's claim against the estate is disallowed;

(B) such claim for reimbursement or contribution is contingent as of the time of allowance or disallowance of such claim for reimbursement or contribution; or

(C) such entity asserts a right of subrogation to the rights of such creditor under *section 509* of this title.

(2) A claim for reimbursement or contribution of such an entity that becomes fixed after the commencement of the case shall be determined, and shall be allowed under subsection (a), (b), or (c) of this section, or disallowed under subsection (d) of this section, the same as if such claim had become fixed before the date of the filing of the petition.

(f) In an involuntary case, a claim arising in the ordinary course of the debtor's business or financial affairs after the commencement of the case but before the earlier of the appointment of a trustee and the order for relief shall be determined as of the date such claim arises, and shall be allowed under subsection (a), (b), or (c) of this section or disallowed under subsection (d) or (e) of this section, the same as if such claim had arisen before the date of the filing of the petition.

(g)

(1) A claim arising from the rejection, under *section 365* of this title or under a plan under chapter 9, 11, 12, or 13 of this title, of an executory contract or unexpired lease of the debtor that has not been assumed shall be determined, and shall be allowed under subsection (a), (b), or (c) of this section or disallowed under subsection (d) or (e) of this section, the same as if such claim had arisen before the date of the filing of the petition.

(2) A claim for damages calculated in accordance with *section 562* shall be allowed under subsection (a), (b), or (c), or disallowed under subsection (d) or (e), as if such claim had arisen before the date of the filing of the petition.

(h) A claim arising from the recovery of property under *section 522, 550,* or *553* of this title shall be determined, and shall be allowed under subsection (a), (b), or (c) of this section, or disallowed under subsection (d) or (e) of this section, the same as if such claim had arisen before the date of the filing of the petition.

(i) A claim that does not arise until after the commencement of the case for a tax entitled to priority under *section 507(a)(8)* of this title shall be determined, and shall be allowed under subsection (a), (b), or (c) of this section, or disallowed under subsection (d) or (e) of this section, the same as if such claim had arisen before the date of the filing of the petition.

(j) A claim that has been allowed or disallowed may be reconsidered for cause. A reconsidered claim may be allowed or disallowed according to the equities of the case. Reconsideration of a claim under this subsection does not affect the validity of any payment or transfer from the estate made to a holder of an allowed claim on account of such allowed claim that is not reconsidered, but if a reconsidered claim is allowed and is of the same class as such holder's claim, such holder may not receive any additional payment or transfer from the estate on account of such holder's allowed claim until the holder of such reconsidered and allowed claim receives payment on account of such claim proportionate in value to that already received by such other holder. This subsection does not alter or modify the trustee's right to recover from a creditor any excess payment or transfer made to such creditor.

(k)

(1) The court, on the motion of the debtor and after a hearing, may reduce a claim filed under this section based in whole on an unsecured consumer debt by not more than 20 percent of the claim, if—

(A) the claim was filed by a creditor who unreasonably refused to negotiate a reasonable alternative repayment schedule proposed on behalf of the debtor by an approved nonprofit budget and credit counseling agency described in *section 111*;

(B) the offer of the debtor under subparagraph (A)—

(i) was made at least 60 days before the date of the filing of the petition; and

(ii) provided for payment of at least 60 percent of the amount of the debt over a period not to exceed the repayment period of the loan, or a reasonable extension thereof; and

(C) no part of the debt under the alternative repayment schedule is nondischargeable.

(2) The debtor shall have the burden of proving, by clear and convincing evidence, that —

(A) the creditor unreasonably refused to consider the debtor's proposal; and

(B) the proposed alternative repayment schedule was made prior to expiration of the 60-day period specified in paragraph (1)(B)(i).

(Pub. L. 95–598, Nov. 6, 1978, 92 Stat. 2579; Pub. L. 98–353, title III, § 445, July 10, 1984, 98 Stat. 373; Pub. L. 99–554, title II, §§ 257(j), 283(f), Oct. 27, 1986, 100 Stat. 3115, 3117; Pub. L. 103–394, title II, § 213(a), title III, § 304(h)(1), Oct. 22, 1994, 108 Stat. 4125, 4134; Pub. L. 109–8, title II, § 201(a), title VII, § 716(d), title IX, § 910(b), Apr. 20, 2005, 119 Stat. 42, 130, 184; Pub. L. 116–260, div. FF, title X, § 1001(d)(2), (3)(B), Dec. 27, 2020, 134 Stat. 3218.)

Sections that reference this section: 1111, 1114, 1126, 1141, 1228, 1232, 1305, 1328, 501, 503, 506, 507, 509, 510, 522, 544, 723, 727, 944

§503. Allowance of administrative expenses

(a) An entity may timely file a request for payment of an administrative expense, or may tardily file such request if permitted by the court for cause.

(b) After notice and a hearing, there shall be allowed administrative expenses, other than claims allowed under *section 502(f)* of this title, including—

(1)

(A) the actual, necessary costs and expenses of preserving the estate including—

(i) wages, salaries, and commissions for services rendered after the commencement of the case; and

(ii) wages and benefits awarded pursuant to a judicial proceeding or a proceeding of the National Labor Relations Board as back pay attributable to any period of time occurring after commencement of the case under this title, as a result of a violation of Federal or State law by the debtor, without regard to the time of the occurrence of unlawful conduct on which such award is based or to whether any services were rendered, if the court determines that payment of wages and benefits by reason of the operation of this clause will not substantially increase the probability of layoff or termination of current employees, or of nonpayment of domestic support obligations, during the case under this title;

(B) any tax—

(i) incurred by the estate, whether secured or unsecured, including property taxes for which liability is in rem, in personam, or both, except a tax of a kind specified in *section 507(a)(8)* of this title; or

(ii) attributable to an excessive allowance of a tentative carryback adjustment that the estate received, whether the taxable year to which such adjustment relates ended before or after the commencement of the case;

(C) any fine, penalty, or reduction in credit relating to a tax of a kind specified in subparagraph (B) of this paragraph; and

(D) notwithstanding the requirements of subsection (a), a governmental unit shall not be required to file a request for the payment of an expense described in subparagraph (B) or (C), as a condition of its being an allowed administrative expense;

(2) compensation and reimbursement awarded under *section 330(a)* of this title;

(3) the actual, necessary expenses, other than compensation and reimbursement specified in paragraph (4) of this subsection, incurred by—

(A) a creditor that files a petition under *section 303* of this title;

(B) a creditor that recovers, after the court's approval, for the benefit of the estate any property transferred or concealed by the debtor;

(C) a creditor in connection with the prosecution of a criminal offense relating to the case or to the business or property of the debtor;

(D) a creditor, an indenture trustee, an equity security holder, or a committee representing creditors or equity security holders other than a committee appointed under *section 1102* of this title, in making a substantial contribution in a case under chapter 9 or 11 of this title;

(E) a custodian superseded under *section 543* of this title, and compensation for the services of such custodian; or

(F) a member of a committee appointed under *section 1102* of this title, if such expenses are incurred in the performance of the duties of such committee;

(4) reasonable compensation for professional services rendered by an attorney or an accountant of an entity whose expense is allowable under subparagraph (A), (B), (C), (D), or (E) of paragraph (3) of this subsection, based on the time, the nature, the extent, and the value of such services, and the cost of comparable services other than in a case under this title, and reimbursement for actual, necessary expenses incurred by such attorney or accountant;

(5) reasonable compensation for services rendered by an indenture trustee in making a substantial contribution in a case under chapter 9 or 11 of this title, based on the time, the nature, the extent, and the value of such services, and the cost of comparable services other than in a case under this title;

(6) the fees and mileage payable under chapter 119 of title 28;

(7) with respect to a nonresidential real property lease previously assumed under *section 365*, and subsequently rejected, a sum equal to all monetary obligations due, excluding those arising from or relating to a failure to operate or a penalty provision, for the period of 2 years following the later of the rejection date or the date of actual turnover of the premises, without reduction or setoff for any reason whatsoever except for sums actually received or to be received from an entity other than the debtor, and the claim for remaining sums due for the balance of the term of the lease shall be a claim under *section 502(b)(6)*;

(8) the actual, necessary costs and expenses of closing a health care business incurred by a trustee or by a Federal agency (as defined in *section 551(1)* of title 5) or a department or agency of a State or political subdivision thereof, including any cost or expense incurred—

(A) in disposing of patient records in accordance with *section 351*; or

(B) in connection with transferring patients from the health care business that is in the process of being closed to another health care business; and

(9) the value of any goods received by the debtor within 20 days before the date of commencement of a case under this title in which the goods have been sold to the debtor in the ordinary course of such debtor's business.

(c) Notwithstanding subsection (b), there shall neither be allowed, nor paid—

(1) a transfer made to, or an obligation incurred for the benefit of, an insider of the debtor for the purpose of inducing such person to remain with the debtor's business, absent a finding by the court based on evidence in the record that—

(A) the transfer or obligation is essential to retention of the person because the individual has a bona fide job offer from another business at the same or greater rate of compensation;

(B) the services provided by the person are essential to the survival of the business; and

(C) either—

(i) the amount of the transfer made to, or obligation incurred for the benefit of, the person is not greater than an amount equal to 10 times the amount of the mean transfer or obligation of a similar kind given to nonmanagement employees for any purpose during the calendar year in which the transfer is made or the obligation is incurred; or

(ii) if no such similar transfers were made to, or obligations were incurred for the benefit of, such nonmanagement employees during such calendar year, the amount of the transfer or obligation is not greater than an amount equal to 25 percent of the amount of any similar transfer or obligation made to or incurred for the benefit of such insider for any purpose during the calendar year before the year in which such transfer is made or obligation is incurred;

(2) a severance payment to an insider of the debtor, unless—

(A) the payment is part of a program that is generally applicable to all full-time employees; and

(B) the amount of the payment is not greater than 10 times the amount of the mean severance pay given to nonmanagement employees during the calendar year in which the payment is made; or

(3) other transfers or obligations that are outside the ordinary course of business and not justified by the facts and circumstances of the case, including transfers made to, or obligations incurred for the benefit of, officers, managers, or consultants hired after the date of the filing of the petition.

(Pub. L. 95–598, Nov. 6, 1978, 92 Stat. 2581; Pub. L. 98–353, title III, § 446, July 10, 1984, 98 Stat. 374; Pub. L. 99–554, title II, § 283(g), Oct. 27, 1986, 100 Stat. 3117; Pub. L. 103–394, title I, § 110, title II, § 213(c), title III, § 304(h)(2), Oct. 22, 1994, 108 Stat. 4113, 4126, 4134; Pub. L. 109–8, title III, §§ 329, 331, title IV, § 445, title VII, § 712(b), (c), title XI, § 1103, title XII, §§ 1208, 1227(b), Apr. 20, 2005, 119 Stat. 101, 102, 117, 128, 190, 194, 200; Pub. L. 116–260, div. N, title III, § 320(b), (f)(2)(A)(ii), Dec. 27, 2020, 134 Stat. 2015, 2016.)

Sections that reference this section: 1114, 1192, 1194, 1205, 1226, 1228, 1326, 348, 361, 364, 365, 504, 507, 546, 557, 726, 922

§504. Sharing of compensation

(a) Except as provided in subsection (b) of this section, a person receiving compensation or reimbursement under *section 503(b)(2)* or *503*(b)(4) of this title may not share or agree to share—

(1) any such compensation or reimbursement with another person; or

(2) any compensation or reimbursement received by another person under such sections.

(b)

(1) A member, partner, or regular associate in a professional association, corporation, or partnership may share compensation or reimbursement received under *section 503(b)(2)* or *503*(b)(4) of this title with another member, partner, or regular associate in such association, corporation, or partnership, and may share in any compensation or reimbursement received under such sections by another member, partner, or regular associate in such association, corporation, or partnership.

(2) An attorney for a creditor that files a petition under *section 303* of this title may share compensation and reimbursement received under *section 503(b)(4)* of this title with any other attorney contributing to the services rendered or expenses incurred by such creditor's attorney.

(c) This section shall not apply with respect to sharing, or agreeing to share, compensation with a bona fide public service attorney referral program that operates in accordance with non-Federal law regulating attorney referral services and with rules of professional responsibility applicable to attorney acceptance of referrals.

(Pub. L. 95–598, Nov. 6, 1978, 92 Stat. 2582; Pub. L. 109–8, title III, § 326, Apr. 20, 2005, 119 Stat. 99.)

Sections that reference this section: None

§505. Determination of tax liability

(a)

(1) Except as provided in paragraph (2) of this subsection, the court may determine the amount or legality of any tax, any fine or penalty relating to a tax, or any addition to tax, whether or not previously assessed, whether or not paid, and whether or not contested before and adjudicated by a judicial or administrative tribunal of competent jurisdiction.

(2) The court may not so determine—

(A) the amount or legality of a tax, fine, penalty, or addition to tax if such amount or legality was contested before and adjudicated by a judicial or administrative tribunal of competent jurisdiction before the commencement of the case under this title;

(B) any right of the estate to a tax refund, before the earlier of—

(i) 120 days after the trustee properly requests such refund from the governmental unit from which such refund is claimed; or

(ii) a determination by such governmental unit of such request; or

(C) the amount or legality of any amount arising in connection with an ad valorem tax on real or personal property of the estate, if the applicable period for contesting or redetermining that amount under applicable nonbankruptcy law has expired.

(b)

(1)

(A) The clerk shall maintain a list under which a Federal, State, or local governmental unit responsible for the collection of taxes within the district may —

(i) designate an address for service of requests under this subsection; and

(ii) describe where further information concerning additional requirements for filing such requests may be found.

(B) If such governmental unit does not designate an address and provide such address to the clerk under subparagraph (A), any request made under this subsection may be served at the address for the filing of a tax return or protest with the appropriate taxing authority of such governmental unit.

(2) A trustee may request a determination of any unpaid liability of the estate for any tax incurred during the administration of the case by submitting a tax return for such tax and a request for such a determination to the governmental unit charged with responsibility for collection or determination of such tax at the address and in the manner designated in paragraph (1). Unless such return is fraudulent, or contains a material misrepresentation, the estate, the trustee, the debtor, and any successor to the debtor are discharged from any liability for such tax—

(A) upon payment of the tax shown on such return, if—

(i) such governmental unit does not notify the trustee, within 60 days after such request, that such return has been selected for examination; or

(ii) such governmental unit does not complete such an examination and notify the trustee of any tax due, within 180 days after such request or within such additional time as the court, for cause, permits;

(B) upon payment of the tax determined by the court, after notice and a hearing, after completion by such governmental unit of such examination; or

(C) upon payment of the tax determined by such governmental unit to be due.

(c) Notwithstanding *section 362* of this title, after determination by the court of a tax under this section, the governmental unit charged with responsibility for collection of such tax may assess such tax against the estate, the debtor, or a successor to the debtor, as the case may be, subject to any otherwise applicable law.

(Pub. L. 95–598, Nov. 6, 1978, 92 Stat. 2582; Pub. L. 98–353, title III, § 447, July 10, 1984, 98 Stat. 374; Pub. L. 109–8, title VII, §§ 701(b), 703, 715, Apr. 20, 2005, 119 Stat. 124, 125, 129; Pub. L. 111–327, § 2(a)(14), Dec. 22, 2010, 124 Stat. 3559.)

Sections that reference this section: 1232, 346

§506. Determination of secured status

(a)

(1) An allowed claim of a creditor secured by a lien on property in which the estate has an interest, or that is subject to setoff under *section 553* of this title, is a secured claim to the extent of the value of such creditor's interest in the estate's interest in such property, or to the extent of the amount subject to setoff, as the case may be, and is an unsecured claim to the extent that the value of such creditor's interest or the amount so subject to setoff is less than the amount

of such allowed claim. Such value shall be determined in light of the purpose of the valuation and of the proposed disposition or use of such property, and in conjunction with any hearing on such disposition or use or on a plan affecting such creditor's interest.

(2) If the debtor is an individual in a case under chapter 7 or 13, such value with respect to personal property securing an allowed claim shall be determined based on the replacement value of such property as of the date of the filing of the petition without deduction for costs of sale or marketing. With respect to property acquired for personal, family, or household purposes, replacement value shall mean the price a retail merchant would charge for property of that kind considering the age and condition of the property at the time value is determined.

(b) To the extent that an allowed secured claim is secured by property the value of which, after any recovery under subsection (c) of this section, is greater than the amount of such claim, there shall be allowed to the holder of such claim, interest on such claim, and any reasonable fees, costs, or charges provided for under the agreement or State statute under which such claim arose.

(c) The trustee may recover from property securing an allowed secured claim the reasonable, necessary costs and expenses of preserving, or disposing of, such property to the extent of any benefit to the holder of such claim, including the payment of all ad valorem property taxes with respect to the property.

(d) To the extent that a lien secures a claim against the debtor that is not an allowed secured claim, such lien is void, unless—

(1) such claim was disallowed only under *section 502(b)(5)* or *502*(e) of this title; or

(2) such claim is not an allowed secured claim due only to the failure of any entity to file a proof of such claim under *section 501* of this title.

(Pub. L. 95–598, Nov. 6, 1978, 92 Stat. 2583; Pub. L. 98–353, title III, § 448, July 10, 1984, 98 Stat. 374; Pub. L. 109–8, title III, § 327, title VII, § 712(d), Apr. 20, 2005, 119 Stat. 99, 128.)

Sections that reference this section: 1111, 1123, 1222, 1322, 1325, 349, 362, 522, 527, 551, 724

§507. Priorities

(a) The following expenses and claims have priority in the following order:

(1) First:

(A) Allowed unsecured claims for domestic support obligations that, as of the date of the filing of the petition in a case under this title, are owed to or recoverable by a spouse, former spouse, or child of the debtor, or such child's parent, legal guardian, or responsible relative, without regard to whether the claim is filed by such person or is filed by a governmental unit on behalf of such person, on the condition that funds received under this paragraph by a governmental unit under this title after the date of the filing of the petition shall be applied and distributed in accordance with applicable nonbankruptcy law.

(B) Subject to claims under subparagraph (A), allowed unsecured claims for domestic support obligations that, as of the date of the filing of the petition, are assigned by a spouse, former spouse, child of the debtor, or such child's parent, legal guardian, or responsible relative to a governmental unit (unless such obligation is assigned voluntarily by the spouse, former spouse, child, parent, legal guardian, or responsible relative of the child for the purpose of collecting the debt) or are owed directly to or recoverable by a governmental unit under applicable nonbankruptcy law, on the condition that funds received under this paragraph by a governmental unit under this title after the date of the filing of the petition be applied and distributed in accordance with applicable nonbankruptcy law.

(C) If a trustee is appointed or elected under *section 701, 702, 703, 1104, 1202,* or *1302,* the administrative expenses of the trustee allowed under paragraphs (1)(A), (2), and (6) of *section 503(b)* shall be paid before payment of claims under subparagraphs (A) and (B), to the extent that the trustee administers assets that are otherwise available for the payment of such claims.

(2) Second, administrative expenses allowed under *section 503(b)* of this title, unsecured claims of any Federal reserve bank related to loans made through programs or facilities authorized under section 13(3) of the Federal Reserve Act (12 U.S.C. 343), and any fees and charges assessed against the estate under chapter 123 of title 28.

(3) Third, unsecured claims allowed under *section 502(f)* of this title.

(4) Fourth, allowed unsecured claims, but only to the extent of $17,150 for each individual or corporation, as the case may be, earned within 180 days before the date of the filing of the petition or the date of the cessation of the debtor's business, whichever occurs first, for—

(A) wages, salaries, or commissions, including vacation, severance, and sick leave pay earned by an individual; or

(B) sales commissions earned by an individual or by a corporation with only 1 employee, acting as an independent contractor in the sale of goods or services for the debtor in the ordinary course of the debtor's business if, and only if, during the 12 months preceding that date, at least 75 percent of the amount that the individual or corporation earned by acting as an independent contractor in the sale of goods or services was earned from the debtor.

(5) Fifth, allowed unsecured claims for contributions to an employee benefit plan—

(A) arising from services rendered within 180 days before the date of the filing of the petition or the date of the cessation of the debtor's business, whichever occurs first; but only

(B) for each such plan, to the extent of—

(i) the number of employees covered by each such plan multiplied by $17,150; less

(ii) the aggregate amount paid to such employees under paragraph (4) of this subsection, plus the aggregate amount paid by the estate on behalf of such employees to any other employee benefit plan.

(6) Sixth, allowed unsecured claims of persons—

(A) engaged in the production or raising of grain, as defined in *section 557(b)* of this title, against a debtor who owns or operates a grain storage facility, as defined in *section 557(b)* of this title, for grain or the proceeds of grain, or

(B) engaged as a United States fisherman against a debtor who has acquired fish or fish produce from a fisherman through a sale or conversion, and who is engaged in operating a fish produce storage or processing facility—

but only to the extent of $8,450 for each such individual.

(7) Seventh, allowed unsecured claims of individuals, to the extent of $3,800 for each such individual, arising from the deposit, before the commencement of the case, of money in connection with the purchase, lease, or rental of property, or the purchase of services, for the personal, family, or household use of such individuals, that were not delivered or provided.

(8) Eighth, allowed unsecured claims of governmental units, only to the extent that such claims are for—

(A) a tax on or measured by income or gross receipts for a taxable year ending on or before the date of the filing of the petition—

(i) for which a return, if required, is last due, including extensions, after three years before the date of the filing of the petition;

(ii) assessed within 240 days before the date of the filing of the petition, exclusive of—

(I) any time during which an offer in compromise with respect to that tax was pending or in effect during that 240-day period, plus 30 days; and

(II) any time during which a stay of proceedings

against collections was in effect in a prior case under this title during that 240-day period, plus 90 days; or

(iii) other than a tax of a kind specified in *section 523(a)(1)(B)* or *523*(a)(1)(C) of this title, not assessed before, but assessable, under applicable law or by agreement, after, the commencement of the case;

(B) a property tax incurred before the commencement of the case and last payable without penalty after one year before the date of the filing of the petition;

(C) a tax required to be collected or withheld and for which the debtor is liable in whatever capacity;

(D) an employment tax on a wage, salary, or commission of a kind specified in paragraph (4) of this subsection earned from the debtor before the date of the filing of the petition, whether or not actually paid before such date, for which a return is last due, under applicable law or under any extension, after three years before the date of the filing of the petition;

(E) an excise tax on—

(i) a transaction occurring before the date of the filing of the petition for which a return, if required, is last due, under applicable law or under any extension, after three years before the date of the filing of the petition; or

(ii) if a return is not required, a transaction occurring during the three years immediately preceding the date of the filing of the petition;

(F) a customs duty arising out of the importation of merchandise—

(i) entered for consumption within one year before the date of the filing of the petition;

(ii) covered by an entry liquidated or reliquidated within one year before the date of the filing of the petition; or

(iii) entered for consumption within four years before the date of the filing of the petition but unliquidated on such date, if the Secretary of the Treasury certifies that failure to liquidate such entry was due to an investigation pending on such date into assessment of antidumping or countervailing duties or fraud, or if information needed for the proper appraisement or classification of such merchandise was not available to the appropriate customs officer before such date; or

(G) a penalty related to a claim of a kind specified in this paragraph and in compensation for actual pecuniary loss.

An otherwise applicable time period specified in this paragraph shall be suspended for any period during which a governmental unit is prohibited under applicable nonbankruptcy law from collecting a tax as a result of a request by the debtor for a hearing and an appeal of any collection action taken or proposed against the debtor, plus 90 days; plus any time during which the stay of proceedings was in effect in a prior case under this title or during which collection was precluded by the existence of 1 or more confirmed plans under this title, plus 90 days.

(9) Ninth, allowed unsecured claims based upon any commitment by the debtor to a Federal depository institutions regulatory agency (or predecessor to such agency) to maintain the capital of an insured depository institution.

(10) Tenth, allowed claims for death or personal injury resulting from the operation of a motor vehicle or vessel if such operation was unlawful because the debtor was intoxicated from using alcohol, a drug, or another substance.

(b) If the trustee, under *section 362, 363,* or *364* of this title, provides adequate protection of the interest of a holder of a claim secured by a lien on property of the debtor and if, notwithstanding such protection, such creditor has a claim allowable under subsection (a)(2) of this section arising from the stay of action against such property under *section 362* of this title, from the use, sale, or lease of such property under *section 363* of this title, or from the granting of a lien under *section 364(d)* of this title, then such creditor's claim under such subsection shall have priority over every other claim allowable under such subsection.

(c) For the purpose of subsection (a) of this section, a claim of a governmental unit arising from an erroneous refund or credit of a tax has the same priority as a claim for the tax to which such refund or credit relates.

(d) An entity that is subrogated to the rights of a holder of a claim of a kind specified in subsection (a)(1), (a)(4), (a)(5), (a)(6), (a)(7), (a)(8) excluding subparagraph (F), or (a)(9) of this section is not subrogated to the right of the holder of such claim to priority under such subsection.

(Pub. L. 95–598, Nov. 6, 1978, 92 Stat. 2583; Pub. L. 98–353, title III, §§ 350, 449, July 10, 1984, 98 Stat. 358, 374; Pub. L. 101–647, title XXV, § 2522(d), Nov. 29, 1990, 104 Stat. 4867; Pub. L. 103–394, title I, § 108(c), title II, § 207, title III, § 304(c), title V, § 501(b)(3), (d)(11), Oct. 22, 1994, 108 Stat. 4112, 4123, 4132, 4142, 4145; Pub. L. 109–8, title II, §§ 212, 223, title VII, §§ 705, 706, title XIV, § 1401, title XV, § 1502(a)(1), Apr. 20, 2005, 119 Stat. 51, 62, 126, 214, 216; Pub. L. 111–203, title XI, § 1101(b), July 21, 2010, 124 Stat. 2115; Pub. L. 111–327, § 2(a)(15), Dec. 22, 2010, 124 Stat. 3559; Pub. L. 116–260, div. FF, title X, § 1001(i), Dec. 27, 2020, 134 Stat. 3221; Pub. L. 118–42, div. C, title V, § 544(a), Mar. 9, 2024, 138 Stat. 178; Pub. L. 119–27, § 11(d), July 18, 2025, 139 Stat. 458.)

Sections that reference this section: 1123, 1129, 1191, 1222, 1226, 1232, 1322, 1326, 1328, 1513, 365, 502, 503, 523, 546, 724, 726, 752, 766, 943

§508. Effect of distribution other than under this title

If a creditor of a partnership debtor receives, from a general partner that is not a debtor in a case under chapter 7 of this title, payment of, or a transfer of property on account of, a claim that is allowed under this title and that is not secured by a lien on property of such partner, such creditor may not receive any payment under this title on account of such claim until each of the other holders of claims on account of which such holders are entitled to share equally with such creditor under this title has received payment under this title equal in value to the consideration received by such creditor from such general partner.

(Pub. L. 95–598, Nov. 6, 1978, 92 Stat. 2585; Pub. L. 109–8, title VIII, § 802(d)(7), Apr. 20, 2005, 119 Stat. 146.)

Sections that reference this section: None

§509. Claims of codebtors

(a) Except as provided in subsection (b) or (c) of this section, an entity that is liable with the debtor on, or that has secured, a claim of a creditor against the debtor, and that pays such claim, is subrogated to the rights of such creditor to the extent of such payment.

(b) Such entity is not subrogated to the rights of such creditor to the extent that—

 (1) a claim of such entity for reimbursement or contribution on account of such payment of such creditor's claim is—

  (A) allowed under *section 502* of this title;

  (B) disallowed other than under *section 502(e)* of this title; or

  (C) subordinated under *section 510* of this title; or

 (2) as between the debtor and such entity, such entity received the consideration for the claim held by such creditor.

(c) The court shall subordinate to the claim of a creditor and for the benefit of such creditor an allowed claim, by way of subrogation under this section, or for reimbursement or contribution, of an entity that is liable with the debtor on, or that has secured, such creditor's claim, until such creditor's claim is paid in full, either through payments under this title or otherwise.

(Pub. L. 95–598, Nov. 6, 1978, 92 Stat. 2585; Pub. L. 98–353, title III, § 450, July 10, 1984, 98 Stat. 375.)

Sections that reference this section: 502

§510. Subordination

(a) A subordination agreement is enforceable in a case under this title to the same extent that such agreement is enforceable under applicable nonbankruptcy law.

(b) For the purpose of distribution under this title, a claim arising from rescission of a purchase or sale of a security of the debtor or of an affiliate of the debtor, for damages arising from the purchase or sale of such a security, or for reimbursement or contribution allowed under *section 502* on account of such a claim, shall be subordinated to all claims or interests that are senior to or equal the claim or interest represented by such security, except that if such security is common stock, such claim has the same priority as common stock.

(c) Notwithstanding subsections (a) and (b) of this section, after notice and a hearing, the court may —

(1) under principles of equitable subordination, subordinate for purposes of distribution all or part of an allowed claim to all or part of another allowed claim or all or part of an allowed interest to all or part of another allowed interest; or

(2) order that any lien securing such a subordinated claim be transferred to the estate.

(Pub. L. 95–598, Nov. 6, 1978, 92 Stat. 2586; Pub. L. 98–353, title III, § 451, July 10, 1984, 98 Stat. 375.)

Sections that reference this section: 1129, 1191, 349, 509, 522, 541, 726, 747, 752, 766

§511. Rate of interest on tax claims

(a) If any provision of this title requires the payment of interest on a tax claim or on an administrative expense tax, or the payment of interest to enable a creditor to receive the present value of the allowed amount of a tax claim, the rate of interest shall be the rate determined under applicable nonbankruptcy law.

(b) In the case of taxes paid under a confirmed plan under this title, the rate of interest shall be determined as of the calendar month in which the plan is confirmed.

(Added Pub. L. 109–8, title VII, § 704(a), Apr. 20, 2005, 119 Stat. 125.)

Sections that reference this section: None

Subchapter II: Debtor's Duties and Benefits

§521. Debtor's duties

(a) The debtor shall—

(1) file—

(A) a list of creditors; and

(B) unless the court orders otherwise—

(i) a schedule of assets and liabilities;

(ii) a schedule of current income and current expenditures;

(iii) a statement of the debtor's financial affairs and, if *section 342(b)* applies, a certificate—

(I) of an attorney whose name is indicated on the petition as the attorney for the debtor, or a bankruptcy petition preparer signing the petition under *section 110(b)(1)*, indicating that such attorney or the bankruptcy petition preparer delivered to the debtor the notice required by *section 342(b)*; or

(II) if no attorney is so indicated, and no bankruptcy petition preparer signed the petition, of the debtor that such notice was received and read by the debtor;

(iv) copies of all payment advices or other evidence of payment received within 60 days before the date of the filing of the petition, by the debtor from any employer of the debtor;

(v) a statement of the amount of monthly net income, itemized to show how the amount is calculated; and

(vi) a statement disclosing any reasonably anticipated increase in income or expenditures over the 12-month period following the date of the filing of the petition;

(2) if an individual debtor's schedule of assets and liabilities includes debts which are secured by property of the estate—

(A) within thirty days after the date of the filing of a petition under chapter 7 of this title or on or before the date of the meeting of creditors, whichever is earlier, or within such additional time as the court, for cause, within such period fixes, file with the clerk a statement of his intention with respect to the retention or surrender of such property and, if applicable, specifying that such property is claimed as exempt, that the debtor intends to redeem such property, or that the debtor intends to reaffirm debts secured by such property; and

(B) within 30 days after the first date set for the meeting of creditors under *section 341(a)*, or within such additional time as the court, for cause, within such 30-day period fixes, perform his intention with respect to such property, as specified by subparagraph (A) of this paragraph;

except that nothing in subparagraphs (A) and (B) of this paragraph shall alter the debtor's or the trustee's rights with regard to such property under this title, except as provided in *section 362(h)*;

(3) if a trustee is serving in the case or an auditor is serving under section 586(f) of title 28, cooperate with the trustee as necessary to enable the trustee to perform the trustee's duties under this title;

(4) if a trustee is serving in the case or an auditor is serving under section 586(f) of title 28, surrender to the trustee all property of the estate and any recorded information, including books, documents, records, and papers, relating to property of the estate, whether or not immunity is granted under *section 344* of this title;

(5) appear at the hearing required under *section 524(d)* of this title;

(6) in a case under chapter 7 of this title in which the debtor is an individual, not retain possession of personal property as to which a creditor has an allowed claim for the purchase price secured in whole or in part by an interest in such personal property unless the debtor, not later than 45 days after the first meeting of creditors under *section 341(a)*, either—

(A) enters into an agreement with the creditor pursuant to *section 524(c)* with respect to the claim secured by such property; or

(B) redeems such property from the security interest pursuant to *section 722*; and

(7) unless a trustee is serving in the case, continue to perform the obligations required of the administrator (as defined in section 3 of the Employee Retirement Income Security Act of 1974) of an employee benefit plan if at the time of the commencement of the case the debtor (or any entity designated by the debtor) served as such administrator.

If the debtor fails to so act within the 45-day period referred to in paragraph (6), the stay under *section 362(a)* is terminated with respect to the personal property of the estate or of the debtor which is affected, such property shall no longer be property of the estate, and the creditor may take whatever action as to such property as is permitted by applicable nonbankruptcy law, unless the court determines on the motion of the trustee filed before the expiration of such 45-day period, and after notice and a hearing, that such property is of consequential value or benefit to the estate, orders appropriate adequate protection of the creditor's interest, and orders the debtor to deliver any collateral in the debtor's possession to the trustee.

(b) In addition to the requirements under subsection (a), a debtor who is an individual shall file with the court—

(1) a certificate from the approved nonprofit budget and credit counseling agency that provided the debtor services under *section 109(h)* describing the services provided to the debtor; and

(2) a copy of the debt repayment plan, if any, developed under *section 109(h)* through the approved nonprofit budget and credit counseling agency referred to in paragraph (1).

(c) In addition to meeting the requirements under subsection (a), a debtor shall file with the court a record of any interest that a debtor has in an education individual retirement account (as defined in section 530(b)(1) of the Internal Revenue Code of 1986), an interest in an account in a qualified ABLE program (as defined in section 529A(b) of such Code, or under a qualified State tuition program (as defined in section 529(b)(1) of such Code).

(d) If the debtor fails timely to take the action specified in subsection (a)(6) of this section, or in paragraphs (1) and (2) of *section 362(h)*, with respect to property which a lessor or bailor owns and has leased, rented, or bailed to the debtor or as to which a creditor holds a security interest not otherwise voidable under *section 522(f), 544, 545, 547, 548*, or *549*, nothing in this title shall prevent or limit the operation of a provision in the underlying lease or agreement that has the effect of placing the debtor in default under such lease or agreement by reason of the occurrence, pendency, or existence of a proceeding under this title or the insolvency of the debtor. Nothing in this subsection shall be deemed to justify limiting such a provision in any other circumstance.

(e)

(1) If the debtor in a case under chapter 7 or 13 is an individual and if a creditor files with the court at any time a request to receive a copy of the petition, schedules, and statement of financial affairs filed by the debtor, then the court shall make such petition, such schedules, and such statement available to such creditor.

(2)

(A) The debtor shall provide—

(i) not later than 7 days before the date first set for the first meeting of creditors, to the trustee a copy of the Federal income tax return required under applicable law (or at the election of the debtor, a transcript of such return) for the most recent tax year ending immediately before the commencement of the case and for which a Federal income tax return was filed; and

(ii) at the same time the debtor complies with clause (i), a copy of such return (or if elected under clause (i), such transcript) to any creditor that timely requests such copy.

(B) If the debtor fails to comply with clause (i) or (ii) of subparagraph (A), the court shall dismiss the case unless the debtor demonstrates that the failure to so comply is due to circumstances beyond the control of the debtor.

(C) If a creditor requests a copy of such tax return or such transcript and if the debtor fails to provide a copy of such tax return or such transcript to such creditor at the time the debtor provides such tax return or such transcript to the trustee, then the court shall dismiss the case unless the debtor demonstrates that the failure to provide a copy of such tax return or such transcript is due to circumstances beyond the control of the debtor.

(3) If a creditor in a case under chapter 13 files with the court at any time a request to receive a copy of the plan filed by the debtor, then the court shall make available to such creditor a copy of the plan—

(A) at a reasonable cost; and

(B) not later than 7 days after such request is filed.

(f) At the request of the court, the United States trustee, or any party in interest in a case under chapter 7, 11, or 13, a debtor who is an individual shall file with the court—

(1) at the same time filed with the taxing authority, a copy of each Federal income tax return required under applicable law (or at the election of the debtor, a transcript of such tax return) with respect to each tax year of the debtor ending while the case is pending under such chapter;

(2) at the same time filed with the taxing authority, each Federal income tax return required under applicable law (or at the election of the debtor, a transcript of such tax return) that had not been filed with such authority as of the date of the commencement of the case and that was subsequently filed for any tax year of the debtor ending in the 3-year period ending on the date of the commencement of the case;

(3) a copy of each amendment to any Federal income tax return or transcript filed with the court under paragraph (1) or (2); and

(4) in a case under chapter 13—

(A) on the date that is either 90 days after the end of such tax year or 1 year after the date of the commencement of the case, whichever is later, if a plan is not confirmed before such later date; and

(B) annually after the plan is confirmed and until the case is closed, not later than the date that is 45 days before the anniversary of the confirmation of the plan;

a statement, under penalty of perjury, of the income and expenditures of the debtor during the tax year of the debtor most recently concluded before such statement is filed under this paragraph, and of the monthly income of the debtor, that shows how income, expenditures, and monthly income are calculated.

(g)

(1) A statement referred to in subsection (f)(4) shall disclose—

(A) the amount and sources of the income of the debtor;

(B) the identity of any person responsible with the debtor for the support of any dependent of the debtor; and

(C) the identity of any person who contributed, and the amount contributed, to the household in which the debtor resides.

(2) The tax returns, amendments, and statement of income and expenditures described in subsections (e)(2)(A) and (f) shall be available to the United States trustee (or the bankruptcy administrator, if any), the trustee, and any party in interest for inspection and copying, subject to the requirements of section 315(c) of the Bankruptcy Abuse Prevention and Consumer Protection Act of 2005.

(h) If requested by the United States trustee or by the trustee, the debtor shall provide—

(1) a document that establishes the identity of the debtor, including a driver's license, passport, or other document that contains a photograph of the debtor; or

(2) such other personal identifying information relating to the debtor that establishes the identity of the debtor.

(i)

(1) Subject to paragraphs (2) and (4) and notwithstanding *section 707(a)*, if an individual debtor in a voluntary case under chapter 7 or 13 fails to file all of the information required under subsection (a)(1) within 45 days after the date of the filing of the petition, the case shall be automatically dismissed effective on the 46th day after the date of the filing of the petition.

(2) Subject to paragraph (4) and with respect to a case described in paragraph (1), any party in interest may request the court to enter an order dismissing the case. If requested, the court shall enter an order of dismissal not later than 7 days after such request.

(3) Subject to paragraph (4) and upon request of the debtor made within 45 days after the date of the filing of the petition described in paragraph (1), the court may allow the debtor an additional period of not to exceed 45 days to file the information required under subsection (a)(1) if the court finds justification for extending the period for the filing.

(4) Notwithstanding any other provision of this subsection, on the motion of the trustee filed before the expiration of the applicable period of time specified in paragraph (1), (2), or (3), and after notice and a hearing, the court may decline to dismiss the case if the court finds that the debtor attempted in good faith to file all the information required by subsection (a)(1)(B)(iv) and that the best interests of creditors would be served by administration of the case.

(j)

(1) Notwithstanding any other provision of this title, if the debtor fails to file a tax return that becomes due after the commencement of the case or to properly obtain an extension of the due date for filing such return, the taxing authority may request that the court enter an order converting or dismissing the case.

(2) If the debtor does not file the required return or obtain the extension referred to in paragraph (1) within 90 days after a request is filed by the taxing authority under that paragraph, the court shall convert or dismiss the case, whichever is in the best interests of creditors and the estate.

(Pub. L. 95–598, Nov. 6, 1978, 92 Stat. 2586; Pub. L. 98–353, title III, §§ 305, 452, July 10, 1984, 98 Stat. 352, 375; Pub. L. 99–554, title II, § 283(h), Oct. 27, 1986, 100 Stat. 3117; Pub. L. 109–8, title I, § 106(d), title II, § 225(b), title III, §§ 304(1), 305(2), 315(b), 316, title IV, § 446(a), title VI, § 603(c), title VII, § 720, Apr. 20, 2005, 119 Stat. 38, 66, 78, 80, 89, 92, 118, 123, 133; Pub. L. 111–16, § 2(5), (6), May 7, 2009, 123 Stat. 1607; Pub. L. 111–327, § 2(a)(16), Dec. 22, 2010, 124 Stat. 3559; Pub. L. 113–295, div. B, title I, § 104(c), Dec. 19, 2014, 128 Stat. 4064.)

Sections that reference this section: 101, 1106, 1111, 1112, 1307, 362, 523, 526, 527, 554, 704, 707

§522. Exemptions

(a) In this section—

(1) "dependent" includes spouse, whether or not actually dependent; and

(2) "value" means fair market value as of the date of the filing of the petition or, with respect to property that becomes property of the estate after such date, as of the date such property becomes property of the estate.

(b)

(1) Notwithstanding *section 541* of this title, an individual debtor may exempt from property of the estate the property listed in either paragraph (2) or, in the alternative, paragraph (3) of this subsection. In joint cases filed under *section 302* of this title and individual cases filed under *section 301* or *303* of this title by or against debtors who are husband and wife, and whose estates are ordered to be jointly administered under Rule 1015(b) of the Federal Rules of Bankruptcy Procedure, one debtor may not elect to exempt property listed in paragraph (2) and the other debtor elect to exempt property listed in paragraph (3) of this subsection. If the parties cannot agree on the alternative to be elected, they shall be deemed to elect paragraph (2), where such election is permitted under the law of the jurisdiction where the case is filed.

(2) Property listed in this paragraph is property that is specified under subsection (d), unless the State law that is applicable to the debtor under paragraph (3)(A) specifically does not so authorize.

(3) Property listed in this paragraph is—

(A) subject to subsections (*o*) and (p), any property that is exempt under Federal law, other than subsection (d) of this section, or State or local law that is applicable on the date of the filing of the petition to the place in which the debtor's domicile has been located for the 730 days immediately preceding the date of the filing of the petition or if the debtor's domicile has not been located in a single State for such 730-day period, the place in which the debtor's domicile was located for 180 days immediately preceding the 730-day period or for a longer portion of such 180-day period than in any other place;

(B) any interest in property in which the debtor had, immediately before the commencement of the case, an interest as a tenant by the entirety or joint tenant to the extent that such interest as a tenant by the entirety or joint tenant is exempt from process under applicable nonbankruptcy law; and

(C) retirement funds to the extent that those funds are in a fund or account that is exempt from taxation under section 401, 403, 408, 408A, 414, 457, or 501(a) of the Internal Revenue Code of 1986.

If the effect of the domiciliary requirement under subparagraph (A) is to render the debtor ineligible for any exemption, the debtor may elect to exempt property that is specified under subsection (d).

(4) For purposes of paragraph (3)(C) and subsection (d)(12), the following shall apply:

(A) If the retirement funds are in a retirement fund that has received a favorable determination under section 7805 of the Internal Revenue Code of 1986, and that determination is in effect as of the date of the filing of the petition in a case under this title, those funds shall be presumed to be exempt from the estate.

(B) If the retirement funds are in a retirement fund that has not received a favorable determination under such section 7805, those funds are exempt from the estate if the debtor demonstrates that—

(i) no prior determination to the contrary has been made by a court or the Internal Revenue Service; and

(ii)

(I) the retirement fund is in substantial compliance with the applicable requirements of the Internal Revenue Code of 1986; or

(II) the retirement fund fails to be in substantial compliance with the applicable requirements of the Internal Revenue Code of 1986 and the debtor is not materially responsible for that failure.

(C) A direct transfer of retirement funds from 1 fund or account that is exempt from taxation under section 401, 403, 408, 408A, 414, 457, or 501(a) of the Internal Revenue Code of 1986, under section 401(a)(31) of the Internal Revenue Code of 1986, or otherwise, shall not cease to qualify for exemption under paragraph (3)(C) or subsection (d)(12) by reason of such direct transfer.

(D)

(i) Any distribution that qualifies as an eligible rollover distribution within the meaning of section 402(c) of the Internal Revenue Code of 1986 or that is described in clause (ii) shall not cease to qualify for exemption under paragraph (3)(C) or subsection (d)(12) by reason of such distribution.

(ii) A distribution described in this clause is an amount that—

(I) has been distributed from a fund or account that is exempt from taxation under section 401, 403, 408, 408A, 414, 457, or 501(a) of the Internal Revenue Code of 1986; and

(II) to the extent allowed by law, is deposited in such a fund or account not later than 60 days after the distribution of such amount.

(c) Unless the case is dismissed, property exempted under this section is not liable during or after the case for any debt of the debtor that arose, or that is determined under *section 502* of this title as if such debt had arisen, before the commencement of the case, except—

(1) a debt of a kind specified in paragraph (1) or (5) of *section 523(a)* (in which case, notwithstanding any provision of applicable nonbankruptcy law to the contrary, such property shall be liable for a debt of a kind specified in such paragraph);

(2) a debt secured by a lien that is—

(A)

(i) not avoided under subsection (f) or (g) of this section or under *section 544, 545, 547, 548, 549,* or *724*(a) of this title; and

(ii) not void under *section 506(d)* of this title; or

(B) a tax lien, notice of which is properly filed;

(3) a debt of a kind specified in *section 523(a)(4)* or *523*(a)(6) of this title owed by an institution-affiliated party of an insured depository institution to a Federal depository institutions regulatory agency acting in its capacity as conservator, receiver, or liquidating agent for such institution; or

(4) a debt in connection with fraud in the obtaining or providing of any scholarship, grant, loan, tuition, discount, award, or other financial assistance for purposes of financing an education at an institution of higher education (as that term is defined in *section 101* of the Higher Education Act of 1965 (20 U.S.C. 1001)).

(d) The following property may be exempted under subsection (b)(2) of this section:

(1) The debtor's aggregate interest, not to exceed $31,575 in value, in real property or personal property that the debtor or a dependent of the debtor uses as a residence, in a cooperative that owns property that the debtor or a dependent of the debtor uses as a residence, or in a burial plot for the debtor or a dependent of the debtor.

(2) The debtor's interest, not to exceed $5,025 in value, in one motor vehicle.

(3) The debtor's interest, not to exceed $800 in value in any particular item or $16,850 in aggregate value, in household furnishings, household goods, wearing apparel, appliances, books, animals, crops, or musical instruments, that are held primarily for the personal, family, or household use of the debtor or a dependent of the debtor.

(4) The debtor's aggregate interest, not to exceed $2,125 in value, in jewelry held primarily for the personal, family, or

household use of the debtor or a dependent of the debtor.

(5) The debtor's aggregate interest in any property, not to exceed in value $1,675 plus up to $15,800 of any unused amount of the exemption provided under paragraph (1) of this subsection.

(6) The debtor's aggregate interest, not to exceed $3,175 in value, in any implements, professional books, or tools, of the trade of the debtor or the trade of a dependent of the debtor.

(7) Any unmatured life insurance contract owned by the debtor, other than a credit life insurance contract.

(8) The debtor's aggregate interest, not to exceed in value $16,850 less any amount of property of the estate transferred in the manner specified in *section 542(d)* of this title, in any accrued dividend or interest under, or loan value of, any unmatured life insurance contract owned by the debtor under which the insured is the debtor or an individual of whom the debtor is a dependent.

(9) Professionally prescribed health aids for the debtor or a dependent of the debtor.

(10) The debtor's right to receive—

(A) a social security benefit, unemployment compensation, or a local public assistance benefit;

(B) a veterans' benefit;

(C) a disability, illness, or unemployment benefit;

(D) alimony, support, or separate maintenance, to the extent reasonably necessary for the support of the debtor and any dependent of the debtor;

(E) a payment under a stock bonus, pension, profitsharing, annuity, or similar plan or contract on account of illness, disability, death, age, or length of service, to the extent reasonably necessary for the support of the debtor and any dependent of the debtor, unless—

(i) such plan or contract was established by or under the auspices of an insider that employed the debtor at the time the debtor's rights under such plan or contract arose;

(ii) such payment is on account of age or length of service; and

(iii) such plan or contract does not qualify under section 401(a), 403(a), 403(b), or 408 of the Internal Revenue Code of 1986.

(11) The debtor's right to receive, or property that is traceable to—

(A) an award under a crime victim's reparation law;

(B) a payment on account of the wrongful death of an individual of whom the debtor was a dependent, to the extent reasonably necessary for the support of the debtor and any dependent of the debtor;

(C) a payment under a life insurance contract that insured the life of an individual of whom the debtor was a dependent on the date of such individual's death, to the extent reasonably necessary for the support of the debtor and any dependent of the debtor;

(D) a payment, not to exceed $31,575 on account of personal bodily injury, not including pain and suffering or compensation for actual pecuniary loss, of the debtor or an individual of whom the debtor is a dependent; or

(E) a payment in compensation of loss of future earnings of the debtor or an individual of whom the debtor is or was a dependent, to the extent reasonably necessary for the support of the debtor and any dependent of the debtor.

(12) Retirement funds to the extent that those funds are in a fund or account that is exempt from taxation under section 401, 403, 408, 408A, 414, 457, or 501(a) of the Internal Revenue Code of 1986.

(e) A waiver of an exemption executed in favor of a creditor that holds an unsecured claim against the debtor is unenforceable in a case under this title with respect to such claim against property that the debtor may exempt under subsection

(b) of this section. A waiver by the debtor of a power under subsection (f) or (h) of this section to avoid a transfer, under subsection (g) or (i) of this section to exempt property, or under subsection (i) of this section to recover property or to preserve a transfer, is unenforceable in a case under this title.

(f)

(1) Notwithstanding any waiver of exemptions but subject to paragraph (3), the debtor may avoid the fixing of a lien on an interest of the debtor in property to the extent that such lien impairs an exemption to which the debtor would have been entitled under subsection (b) of this section, if such lien is—

(A) a judicial lien, other than a judicial lien that secures a debt of a kind that is specified in *section 523(a)(5)*; or

(B) a nonpossessory, nonpurchase-money security interest in any—

(i) household furnishings, household goods, wearing apparel, appliances, books, animals, crops, musical instruments, or jewelry that are held primarily for the personal, family, or household use of the debtor or a dependent of the debtor;

(ii) implements, professional books, or tools, of the trade of the debtor or the trade of a dependent of the debtor; or

(iii) professionally prescribed health aids for the debtor or a dependent of the debtor.

(2)

(A) For the purposes of this subsection, a lien shall be considered to impair an exemption to the extent that the sum of—

(i) the lien;

(ii) all other liens on the property; and

(iii) the amount of the exemption that the debtor could claim if there were no liens on the property;

exceeds the value that the debtor's interest in the property would have in the absence of any liens.

(B) In the case of a property subject to more than 1 lien, a lien that has been avoided shall not be considered in making the calculation under subparagraph (A) with respect to other liens.

(C) This paragraph shall not apply with respect to a judgment arising out of a mortgage foreclosure.

(3) In a case in which State law that is applicable to the debtor—

(A) permits a person to voluntarily waive a right to claim exemptions under subsection (d) or prohibits a debtor from claiming exemptions under subsection (d); and

(B) either permits the debtor to claim exemptions under State law without limitation in amount, except to the extent that the debtor has permitted the fixing of a consensual lien on any property or prohibits avoidance of a consensual lien on property otherwise eligible to be claimed as exempt property;

the debtor may not avoid the fixing of a lien on an interest of the debtor or a dependent of the debtor in property if the lien is a nonpossessory, nonpurchase-money security interest in implements, professional books, or tools of the trade of the debtor or a dependent of the debtor or farm animals or crops of the debtor or a dependent of the debtor to the extent the value of such implements, professional books, tools of the trade, animals, and crops exceeds $8,575.

(4)

(A) Subject to subparagraph (B), for purposes of paragraph (1)(B), the term "household goods" means—

(i) clothing;

(ii) furniture;

(iii) appliances;

(iv) 1 radio;

(v) 1 television;

(vi) 1 VCR;

(vii) linens;

(viii) china;

(ix) crockery;

(x) kitchenware;

(xi) educational materials and educational equipment primarily for the use of minor dependent children of the debtor;

(xii) medical equipment and supplies;

(xiii) furniture exclusively for the use of minor children, or elderly or disabled dependents of the debtor;

(xiv) personal effects (including the toys and hobby equipment of minor dependent children and wedding rings) of the debtor and the dependents of the debtor; and

(xv) 1 personal computer and related equipment.

(B) The term "household goods" does not include—

(i) works of art (unless by or of the debtor, or any relative of the debtor);

(ii) electronic entertainment equipment with a fair market value of more than $900 in the aggregate (except 1 television, 1 radio, and 1 VCR);

(iii) items acquired as antiques with a fair market value of more than $900 in the aggregate;

(iv) jewelry with a fair market value of more than $900 in the aggregate (except wedding rings); and

(v) a computer (except as otherwise provided for in this section), motor vehicle (including a tractor or lawn tractor), boat, or a motorized recreational device, conveyance, vehicle, watercraft, or aircraft.

(g) Notwithstanding *sections 550* and *551* of this title, the debtor may exempt under subsection (b) of this section property that the trustee recovers under *section 510(c)(2), 542, 543, 550, 551,* or *553* of this title, to the extent that the debtor could have exempted such property under subsection (b) of this section if such property had not been transferred, if—

(1)

(A) such transfer was not a voluntary transfer of such property by the debtor; and

(B) the debtor did not conceal such property; or

(2) the debtor could have avoided such transfer under subsection (f)(1)(B) of this section.

(h) The debtor may avoid a transfer of property of the debtor or recover a setoff to the extent that the debtor could have exempted such property under subsection (g)(1) of this section if the trustee had avoided such transfer, if—

(1) such transfer is avoidable by the trustee under *section 544, 545, 547, 548, 549,* or *724*(a) of this title or recoverable by the trustee under *section 553* of this title; and

(2) the trustee does not attempt to avoid such transfer.

(i)

(1) If the debtor avoids a transfer or recovers a setoff under subsection (f) or (h) of this section, the debtor may recover in the manner prescribed by, and subject to the limitations of, *section 550* of this title, the same as if the trustee had avoided such transfer, and may exempt any property so recovered under subsection (b) of this section.

(2) Notwithstanding *section 551* of this title, a transfer avoided under *section 544, 545, 547, 548, 549,* or *724*(a) of this title, under subsection (f) or (h) of this section, or property recovered under *section 553* of this title, may be preserved for the benefit of the debtor to the extent that the debtor may exempt such property under subsection (g) of this section or paragraph (1) of this subsection.

(j) Notwithstanding subsections (g) and (i) of this section, the debtor may exempt a particular kind of property under subsections (g) and (i) of this section only to the extent that the debtor has exempted less property in value of such kind than that to which the debtor is entitled under subsection (b) of this section.

(k) Property that the debtor exempts under this section is not liable for payment of any administrative expense except—

(1) the aliquot share of the costs and expenses of avoiding a transfer of property that the debtor exempts under subsection (g) of this section, or of recovery of such property, that is attributable to the value of the portion of such property exempted in relation to the value of the property recovered; and

(2) any costs and expenses of avoiding a transfer under subsection (f) or (h) of this section, or of recovery of property under subsection (i)(1) of this section, that the debtor has not paid.

(l) The debtor shall file a list of property that the debtor claims as exempt under subsection (b) of this section. If the debtor does not file such a list, a dependent of the debtor may file such a list, or may claim property as exempt from property of the estate on behalf of the debtor. Unless a party in interest objects, the property claimed as exempt on such list is exempt.

(m) Subject to the limitation in subsection (b), this section shall apply separately with respect to each debtor in a joint case.

(n) For assets in individual retirement accounts described in section 408 or 408A of the Internal Revenue Code of 1986, other than a simplified employee pension under section 408(k) of such Code or a simple retirement account under section 408(p) of such Code, the aggregate value of such assets exempted under this section, without regard to amounts attributable to rollover contributions under section 402(c), 402(e)(6), 403(a)(4), 403(a)(5), and 403(b)(8) of the Internal Revenue Code of 1986, and earnings thereon, shall not exceed $1,711,975 in a case filed by a debtor who is an individual, except that such amount may be increased if the interests of justice so require.

(o) For purposes of subsection (b)(3)(A), and notwithstanding subsection (a), the value of an interest in—

(1) real or personal property that the debtor or a dependent of the debtor uses as a residence;

(2) a cooperative that owns property that the debtor or a dependent of the debtor uses as a residence;

(3) a burial plot for the debtor or a dependent of the debtor; or

(4) real or personal property that the debtor or a dependent of the debtor claims as a homestead;

shall be reduced to the extent that such value is attributable to any portion of any property that the debtor disposed of in the 10-year period ending on the date of the filing of the petition with the intent to hinder, delay, or defraud a creditor and that the debtor could not exempt, or that portion that the debtor could not exempt, under subsection (b), if on such date the debtor had held the property so disposed of.

(p)

(1) Except as provided in paragraph (2) of this subsection and *sections 544* and *548*, as a result of electing under subsection (b)(3)(A) to exempt property under State or local law, a debtor may not exempt any amount of interest that was acquired by the debtor during the 1215-day period preceding the date of the filing of the petition that exceeds in the aggregate $214,000 in value in—

(A) real or personal property that the debtor or a dependent of the debtor uses as a residence;

(B) a cooperative that owns property that the debtor or a dependent of the debtor uses as a residence;

(C) a burial plot for the debtor or a dependent of the debtor; or

(D) real or personal property that the debtor or dependent of the debtor claims as a homestead.

(2)

(A) The limitation under paragraph (1) shall not apply to an exemption claimed under subsection (b)(3)(A) by a family farmer for the principal residence of such farmer.

(B) For purposes of paragraph (1), any amount of such interest does not include any interest transferred from a debtor's previous principal residence (which was acquired prior to the beginning of such 1215-day period) into the debtor's current principal residence, if the debtor's previous and current residences are located in the same State.

(q)

(1) As a result of electing under subsection (b)(3)(A) to exempt property under State or local law, a debtor may not exempt any amount of an interest in property described in subparagraphs (A), (B), (C), and (D) of subsection (p)(1) which exceeds in the aggregate $214,000 if—

(A) the court determines, after notice and a hearing, that the debtor has been convicted of a felony (as defined in section 3156 of title 18), which under the circumstances, demonstrates that the filing of the case was an abuse of the provisions of this title; or

(B) the debtor owes a debt arising from—

(i) any violation of the Federal securities laws (as defined in section 3(a)(47) of the Securities Exchange Act of 1934), any State securities laws, or any regulation or order issued under Federal securities laws or State securities laws;

(ii) fraud, deceit, or manipulation in a fiduciary capacity or in connection with the purchase or sale of any security registered under section 12 or 15(d) of the Securities Exchange Act of 1934 or under section 6 of the Securities Act of 1933;

(iii) any civil remedy under section 1964 of title 18; or

(iv) any criminal act, intentional tort, or willful or reckless misconduct that caused serious physical injury or death to another individual in the preceding 5 years.

(2) Paragraph (1) shall not apply to the extent the amount of an interest in property described in subparagraphs (A), (B), (C), and (D) of subsection (p)(1) is reasonably necessary for the support of the debtor and any dependent of the debtor.

(Pub. L. 95–598, Nov. 6, 1978, 92 Stat. 2586; Pub. L. 98–353, title III, §§ 306, 453, July 10, 1984, 98 Stat. 353, 375; Pub. L. 99–554, title II, § 283(i), Oct. 27, 1986, 100 Stat. 3117; Pub. L. 101–647, title XXV, § 2522(b), Nov. 29, 1990, 104 Stat. 4866; Pub. L. 103–394, title I, § 108(d), title III, §§ 303, 304(d), 310, title V, § 501(d)(12), Oct. 22, 1994, 108 Stat. 4112, 4132, 4133, 4137, 4145; Pub. L. 106–420, § 4, Nov. 1, 2000, 114 Stat. 1868; Pub. L. 109–8, title II, §§ 216, 224(a), (e)(1), title III, §§ 307, 308, 313(a), 322(a), Apr. 20, 2005, 119 Stat. 55, 62, 65, 81, 87, 96; Pub. L. 111–327, § 2(a)(17), Dec. 22, 2010, 124 Stat. 3559.)

Sections that reference this section: 101, 110, 1123, 1141, 1228, 1328, 1521, 1523, 349, 502, 521, 542, 551, 722, 727

§523. Exceptions to discharge

(a) A discharge under *section 727, 1141, 1192* 1228(a), 1228(b), or 1328(b) of this title does not discharge an individual debtor from any debt —

(1) for a tax or a customs duty—

(A) of the kind and for the periods specified in *section 507(a)(3)* or *507*(a)(8) of this title, whether or not a claim for such tax was filed or allowed;

(B) with respect to which a return, or equivalent report or notice, if required—

(i) was not filed or given; or

(ii) was filed or given after the date on which such return, report, or notice was last due, under applicable law or under any extension, and after two years before the date of the filing of the petition; or

(C) with respect to which the debtor made a fraudulent return or willfully attempted in any manner to evade or defeat such tax;

(2) for money, property, services, or an extension, renewal, or refinancing of credit, to the extent obtained by—

(A) false pretenses, a false representation, or actual fraud, other than a statement respecting the debtor's or an insider's financial condition;

(B) use of a statement in writing—

(i) that is materially false;

(ii) respecting the debtor's or an insider's financial condition;

(iii) on which the creditor to whom the debtor is liable for such money, property, services, or credit reasonably relied; and

(iv) that the debtor caused to be made or published with intent to deceive; or

(C)

(i) for purposes of subparagraph (A)—

(I) consumer debts owed to a single creditor and aggregating more than $900 for luxury goods or services incurred by an individual debtor on or within 90 days before the order for relief under this title are presumed to be nondischargeable; and

(II) cash advances aggregating more than $1,250 that are extensions of consumer credit under an open end credit plan obtained by an individual debtor on or within 70 days before the order for relief under this title, are presumed to be nondischargeable; and

(ii) for purposes of this subparagraph—

(I) the terms “consumer”, “credit”, and “open end credit plan” have the same meanings as in *section 103* of the Truth in Lending Act; and

(II) the term “luxury goods or services” does not include goods or services reasonably necessary for the support or maintenance of the debtor or a dependent of the debtor;

(3) neither listed nor scheduled under *section 521(a)(1)* of this title, with the name, if known to the debtor, of the creditor to whom such debt is owed, in time to permit—

(A) if such debt is not of a kind specified in paragraph (2), (4), or (6) of this subsection, timely filing of a proof of claim, unless such creditor had notice or actual knowledge of the case in time for such timely filing; or

(B) if such debt is of a kind specified in paragraph (2), (4), or (6) of this subsection, timely filing of a proof of claim and timely request for a determination of dischargeability of such debt under one of such paragraphs, unless such creditor had notice or actual knowledge of the case in time for such timely filing and request;

(4) for fraud or defalcation while acting in a fiduciary capacity, embezzlement, or larceny;

(5) for a domestic support obligation;

(6) for willful and malicious injury by the debtor to another entity or to the property of another entity;

(7) to the extent such debt is for a fine, penalty, or forfeiture payable to and for the benefit of a governmental unit, and is not compensation for actual pecuniary loss, other than a tax penalty—

(A) relating to a tax of a kind not specified in paragraph (1) of this subsection; or

(B) imposed with respect to a transaction or event that occurred before three years before the date of the filing of the petition;

(8) unless excepting such debt from discharge under this paragraph would impose an undue hardship on the debtor and the debtor’s dependents, for—

(A)

(i) an educational benefit overpayment or loan made, insured, or guaranteed by a governmental unit, or made under any program funded in whole or in part by a governmental unit or nonprofit institution; or

(ii) an obligation to repay funds received as an educational benefit, scholarship, or stipend; or

(B) any other educational loan that is a qualified education loan, as defined in section 221(d)(1) of the Internal Revenue Code of 1986, incurred by a debtor who is an individual;

(9) for death or personal injury caused by the debtor's operation of a motor vehicle, vessel, or aircraft if such operation was unlawful because the debtor was intoxicated from using alcohol, a drug, or another substance;

(10) that was or could have been listed or scheduled by the debtor in a prior case concerning the debtor under this title or under the Bankruptcy Act in which the debtor waived discharge, or was denied a discharge under *section 727(a)(2)*, (3), (4), (5), (6), or (7) of this title, or under section 14c(1), (2), (3), (4), (6), or (7) of such Act;

(11) provided in any final judgment, unreviewable order, or consent order or decree entered in any court of the United States or of any State, issued by a Federal depository institutions regulatory agency, or contained in any settlement agreement entered into by the debtor, arising from any act of fraud or defalcation while acting in a fiduciary capacity committed with respect to any depository institution or insured credit union;

(12) for malicious or reckless failure to fulfill any commitment by the debtor to a Federal depository institutions regulatory agency to maintain the capital of an insured depository institution, except that this paragraph shall not extend any such commitment which would otherwise be terminated due to any act of such agency;

(13) for any payment of an order of restitution issued under title 18, United States Code;

(14) incurred to pay a tax to the United States that would be nondischargeable pursuant to paragraph (1);

(14A) incurred to pay a tax to a governmental unit, other than the United States, that would be nondischargeable under paragraph (1);

(14B) incurred to pay fines or penalties imposed under Federal election law;

(15) to a spouse, former spouse, or child of the debtor and not of the kind described in paragraph (5) that is incurred by the debtor in the course of a divorce or separation or in connection with a separation agreement, divorce decree or other order of a court of record, or a determination made in accordance with State or territorial law by a governmental unit;

(16) for a fee or assessment that becomes due and payable after the order for relief to a membership association with respect to the debtor's interest in a unit that has condominium ownership, in a share of a cooperative corporation, or a lot in a homeowners association, for as long as the debtor or the trustee has a legal, equitable, or possessory ownership interest in such unit, such corporation, or such lot, but nothing in this paragraph shall except from discharge the debt of a debtor for a membership association fee or assessment for a period arising before entry of the order for relief in a pending or subsequent bankruptcy case;

(17) for a fee imposed on a prisoner by any court for the filing of a case, motion, complaint, or appeal, or for other costs and expenses assessed with respect to such filing, regardless of an assertion of poverty by the debtor under subsection (b) or (f)(2) of section 1915 of title 28 (or a similar non-Federal law), or the debtor's status as a prisoner, as defined in section 1915(h) of title 28 (or a similar non-Federal law);

(18) owed to a pension, profit-sharing, stock bonus, or other plan established under section 401, 403, 408, 408A, 414, 457, or 501(c) of the Internal Revenue Code of 1986, under—

(A) a loan permitted under section 408(b)(1) of the Employee Retirement Income Security Act of 1974, or subject to section 72(p) of the Internal Revenue Code of 1986; or

(B) a loan from a thrift savings plan permitted under subchapter III of chapter 84 of title 5, that satisfies the requirements of section 8433(g) of such title;

but nothing in this paragraph may be construed to provide that any loan made under a governmental plan under section 414(d), or a contract or account under section 403(b), of the Internal Revenue Code of 1986 constitutes a claim or a debt under this title;

(19) that—

(A) is for—

(i) the violation of any of the Federal securities laws (as that term is defined in section 3(a)(47) of the Securities Exchange Act of 1934), any of the State securities laws, or any regulation or order issued under such Federal or State securities laws; or

(ii) common law fraud, deceit, or manipulation in connection with the purchase or sale of any security; and

(B) results, before, on, or after the date on which the petition was filed, from—

(i) any judgment, order, consent order, or decree entered in any Federal or State judicial or administrative proceeding;

(ii) any settlement agreement entered into by the debtor; or

(iii) any court or administrative order for any damages, fine, penalty, citation, restitutionary payment, disgorgement payment, attorney fee, cost, or other payment owed by the debtor; or

(20) for injury to an individual by the debtor relating to a violation of chapter 77 of title 18, including injury caused by an instance in which the debtor knowingly benefitted financially, or by receiving anything of value, from participation in a venture that the debtor knew or should have known engaged in an act in violation of chapter 77 of title 18.

For purposes of this subsection, the term "return" means a return that satisfies the requirements of applicable nonbankruptcy law (including applicable filing requirements). Such term includes a return prepared pursuant to section 6020(a) of the Internal Revenue Code of 1986, or similar State or local law, or a written stipulation to a judgment or a final order entered by a nonbankruptcy tribunal, but does not include a return made pursuant to section 6020(b) of the Internal Revenue Code of 1986, or a similar State or local law.

(b) Notwithstanding subsection (a) of this section, a debt that was excepted from discharge under subsection (a)(1), (a)(3), or (a)(8) of this section, under section 17a(1), 17a(3), or 17a(5) of the Bankruptcy Act, under section 439A of the Higher Education Act of 1965, or under section 733(g) of the Public Health Service Act in a prior case concerning the debtor under this title, or under the Bankruptcy Act, is dischargeable in a case under this title unless, by the terms of subsection (a) of this section, such debt is not dischargeable in the case under this title.

(c)

(1) Except as provided in subsection (a)(3)(B) of this section, the debtor shall be discharged from a debt of a kind specified in paragraph (2), (4), or (6) of subsection (a) of this section, unless, on request of the creditor to whom such debt is owed, and after notice and a hearing, the court determines such debt to be excepted from discharge under paragraph (2), (4), or (6), as the case may be, of subsection (a) of this section.

(2) Paragraph (1) shall not apply in the case of a Federal depository institutions regulatory agency seeking, in its capacity as conservator, receiver, or liquidating agent for an insured depository institution, to recover a debt described in subsection (a)(2), (a)(4), (a)(6), or (a)(11) owed to such institution by an institution-affiliated party unless the receiver, conservator, or liquidating agent was appointed in time to reasonably comply,

or for a Federal depository institutions regulatory agency acting in its corporate capacity as a successor to such receiver, conservator, or liquidating agent to reasonably comply, with subsection (a)(3)(B) as a creditor of such institution-affiliated party with respect to such debt.

(d) If a creditor requests a determination of dischargeability of a consumer debt under subsection (a)(2) of this section, and such debt is discharged, the court shall grant judgment in favor of the debtor for the costs of, and a reasonable attorney's fee for, the proceeding if the court finds that the position of the creditor was not substantially justified, except that the court shall not award such costs and fees if special circumstances would make the award unjust.

(e) Any institution-affiliated party of an insured depository institution shall be considered to be acting in a fiduciary capacity with respect to the purposes of subsection (a)(4) or (11).

(Pub. L. 95–598, Nov. 6, 1978, 92 Stat. 2590; Pub. L. 96–56, § 3, Aug. 14, 1979, 93 Stat. 387; Pub. L. 97–35, title XXIII, § 2334(b), Aug. 13, 1981, 95 Stat. 863; Pub. L. 98–353, title III, §§ 307, 371, 454, July 10, 1984, 98 Stat. 353, 364, 375; Pub. L. 99–554, title II, §§ 257(n), 281, 283(j), Oct. 27, 1986, 100 Stat. 3115–3117; Pub. L. 101–581, § 2(a), Nov. 15, 1990, 104 Stat. 2865; Pub. L. 101–647, title XXV, § 2522(a), title XXXI, § 3102(a), title XXXVI, § 3621, Nov. 29, 1990, 104 Stat. 4865, 4916, 4964; Pub. L. 103–322, title XXXII, § 320934, Sept. 13, 1994, 108 Stat. 2135; Pub. L. 103–394, title II, § 221, title III, §§ 304(e), (h)(3), 306, 309, title V, § 501(d)(13), Oct. 22, 1994, 108 Stat. 4129, 4133–4135, 4137, 4145; Pub. L. 104–134, title I, § 101[(a)] [title VIII, § 804(b)], Apr. 26, 1996, 110 Stat. 1321, 1321–74; renumbered title I, Pub. L. 104–140, § 1(a), May 2, 1996, 110 Stat. 1327; Pub. L. 104–193, title III, § 374(a), Aug. 22, 1996, 110 Stat. 2255; Pub. L. 105–244, title IX, § 971(a), Oct. 7, 1998, 112 Stat. 1837; Pub. L. 107–204, title VIII, § 803, July 30, 2002, 116 Stat. 801; Pub. L. 109–8, title II, §§ 215, 220, 224(c), title III, §§ 301, 310, 314(a), title IV, § 412, title VII, § 714, title XII, §§ 1209, 1235, title XIV, § 1404(a), title XV, § 1502(a)(2), Apr. 20, 2005, 119 Stat. 54, 59, 64, 75, 84, 88, 107, 128, 194, 204, 215, 216; Pub. L. 111–327, § 2(a)(18), Dec. 22, 2010, 124 Stat. 3559; Pub. L. 116–54, § 4(a)(8), Aug. 23, 2019, 133 Stat. 1086; Pub. L. 117–347, title II, § 201, Jan. 5, 2023, 136 Stat. 6205.)

Sections that reference this section: 1106, 1141, 1192, 1202, 1228, 1232, 1302, 1328, 502, 507, 522, 524, 704, 727

§524. Effect of discharge

(a) A discharge in a case under this title—

(1) voids any judgment at any time obtained, to the extent that such judgment is a determination of the personal liability of the debtor with respect to any debt discharged under *section 727, 944, 1141, 1192, 1228,* or *1328* of this title, whether or not discharge of such debt is waived;

(2) operates as an injunction against the commencement or continuation of an action, the employment of process, or an act, to collect, recover or offset any such debt as a personal liability of the debtor, whether or not discharge of such debt is waived; and

(3) operates as an injunction against the commencement or continuation of an action, the employment of process, or an act, to collect or recover from, or offset against, property of the debtor of the kind specified in *section 541(a)(2)* of this title that is acquired after the commencement of the case, on account of any allowable community claim, except a community claim that is excepted from discharge under *section 523, 1192, 1228*(a)(1), or 1328(a)(1), or that would be so excepted, determined in accordance with the provisions of *sections 523(c)* and *523*(d) of this title, in a case concerning the debtor's spouse commenced on the date of the filing of the petition in the case concerning the debtor, whether or not discharge of the debt based on such community claim is waived.

(b) Subsection (a)(3) of this section does not apply if—

(1)

(A) the debtor's spouse is a debtor in a case under this title, or a bankrupt or a debtor in a case under the Bankruptcy Act, commenced within six years of the date of the filing of the petition in the case concerning the debtor; and

(B) the court does not grant the debtor's spouse a discharge in such case concerning the debtor's spouse; or

(2)

(A) the court would not grant the debtor's spouse a discharge in a case under chapter 7 of this title concerning such spouse commenced on the date of the filing of the petition in the case concerning the debtor; and

(B) a determination that the court would not so grant such discharge is made by the bankruptcy court within the time and in the manner provided for a determination under *section 727* of this title of whether a debtor is granted a discharge.

(c) An agreement between a holder of a claim and the debtor, the consideration for which, in whole or in part, is based on a debt that is dischargeable in a case under this title is enforceable only to any extent enforceable under applicable nonbankruptcy law, whether or not discharge of such debt is waived, only if—

(1) such agreement was made before the granting of the discharge under *section 727, 1141, 1192, 1228,* or *1328* of this title;

(2) the debtor received the disclosures described in subsection (k) at or before the time at which the debtor signed the agreement;

(3) such agreement has been filed with the court and, if applicable, accompanied by a declaration or an affidavit of the attorney that represented the debtor during the course of negotiating an agreement under this subsection, which states that—

(A) such agreement represents a fully informed and voluntary agreement by the debtor;

(B) such agreement does not impose an undue hardship on the debtor or a dependent of the debtor; and

(C) the attorney fully advised the debtor of the legal effect and consequences of—

(i) an agreement of the kind specified in this subsection; and

(ii) any default under such an agreement;

(4) the debtor has not rescinded such agreement at any time prior to discharge or within sixty days after such agreement is filed with the court, whichever occurs later, by giving notice of rescission to the holder of such claim;

(5) the provisions of subsection (d) of this section have been complied with; and

(6)

(A) in a case concerning an individual who was not represented by an attorney during the course of negotiating an agreement under this subsection, the court approves such agreement as—

(i) not imposing an undue hardship on the debtor or a dependent of the debtor; and

(ii) in the best interest of the debtor.

(B) Subparagraph (A) shall not apply to the extent that such debt is a consumer debt secured by real property.

(d) In a case concerning an individual, when the court has determined whether to grant or not to grant a discharge under *section 727, 1141, 1192, 1228,* or *1328* of this title, the court may hold a hearing at which the debtor shall appear in person. At any such hearing, the court shall inform the debtor that a discharge has been granted or the reason why a discharge has not been granted. If a discharge has been granted and if the debtor desires to make an agreement of the kind specified in subsection (c) of this section and was not represented by an attorney during the course of negotiating such agreement, then the court shall hold a hearing at which the debtor shall appear in person and at such hearing the court shall—

(1) inform the debtor—

(A) that such an agreement is not required under this title, under nonbankruptcy law, or under any agreement not made in accordance with the provisions of subsection (c) of this section; and

(B) of the legal effect and consequences of —

(i) an agreement of the kind specified in subsection (c) of this section; and

(ii) a default under such an agreement; and

(2) determine whether the agreement that the debtor desires to make complies with the requirements of subsection (c)(6) of this section, if the consideration for such agreement is based in whole or in part on a consumer debt that is not secured by real property of the debtor.

(e) Except as provided in subsection (a)(3) of this section, discharge of a debt of the debtor does not affect the liability of any other entity on, or the property of any other entity for, such debt.

(f) Nothing contained in subsection (c) or (d) of this section prevents a debtor from voluntarily repaying any debt.

(g)

(1)

(A) After notice and hearing, a court that enters an order confirming a plan of reorganization under chapter 11 may issue, in connection with such order, an injunction in accordance with this subsection to supplement the injunctive effect of a discharge under this section.

(B) An injunction may be issued under subparagraph (A) to enjoin entities from taking legal action for the purpose of directly or indirectly collecting, recovering, or receiving payment or recovery with respect to any claim or demand that, under a plan of reorganization, is to be paid in whole or in part by a trust described in paragraph (2)(B)(i), except such legal actions as are expressly allowed by the injunction, the confirmation order, or the plan of reorganization.

(2)

(A) Subject to subsection (h), if the requirements of subparagraph (B) are met at the time an injunction described in paragraph (1) is entered, then after entry of such injunction, any proceeding that involves the validity, application, construction, or modification of such injunction, or of this subsection with respect to such injunction, may be commenced only in the district court in which such injunction was entered, and such court shall have exclusive jurisdiction over any such proceeding without regard to the amount in controversy.

(B) The requirements of this subparagraph are that—

(i) the injunction is to be implemented in connection with a trust that, pursuant to the plan of reorganization—

(I) is to assume the liabilities of a debtor which at the time of entry of the order for relief has been named as a defendant in personal injury, wrongful death, or property-damage actions seeking recovery for damages allegedly caused by the presence of, or exposure to, asbestos or asbestos-containing products;

(II) is to be funded in whole or in part by the securities of 1 or more debtors involved in such plan and by the obligation of such debtor or debtors to make future payments, including dividends;

(III) is to own, or by the exercise of rights granted under such plan would be entitled to own if specified contingencies occur, a majority of the voting shares of—

(aa) each such debtor;

(bb) the parent corporation of each such debtor; or

(cc) a subsidiary of each such debtor that is also a debtor; and

(IV) is to use its assets or income to pay claims and demands; and

(ii) subject to subsection (h), the court determines that—

(I) the debtor is likely to be subject to substantial future demands for payment arising out of the same or similar conduct or events that gave rise to the claims that are addressed by the injunction;

(II) the actual amounts, numbers, and timing of such future demands cannot be determined;

(III) pursuit of such demands outside the procedures prescribed by such plan is likely to threaten the plan's purpose to deal equitably with claims and future demands;

(IV) as part of the process of seeking confirmation of such plan—

(aa) the terms of the injunction proposed to be issued under paragraph (1)(A), including any provisions barring actions against third parties pursuant to paragraph (4)(A), are set out in such plan and in any disclosure statement supporting the plan; and

(bb) a separate class or classes of the claimants whose claims are to be addressed by a trust described in clause (i) is established and votes, by at least 75 percent of those voting, in favor of the plan; and

(V) subject to subsection (h), pursuant to court orders or otherwise, the trust will operate through mechanisms such as structured, periodic, or supplemental payments, pro rata distributions, matrices, or periodic review of estimates of the numbers and values of present claims and future demands, or other comparable mechanisms, that provide reasonable assurance that the trust will value, and be in a financial position to pay, present claims and future demands that involve similar claims in substantially the same manner.

(3)

(A) If the requirements of paragraph (2)(B) are met and the order confirming the plan of reorganization was issued or affirmed by the district court that has jurisdiction over the reorganization case, then after the time for appeal of the order that issues or affirms the plan—

(i) the injunction shall be valid and enforceable and may not be revoked or modified by any court except through appeal in accordance with paragraph (6);

(ii) no entity that pursuant to such plan or thereafter becomes a direct or indirect transferee of, or successor to any assets of, a debtor or trust that is the subject of the injunction shall be liable with respect to any claim or demand made against such entity by reason of its becoming such a transferee or successor; and

(iii) no entity that pursuant to such plan or thereafter makes a loan to such a debtor or trust or to such a successor or transferee shall, by reason of making the loan, be liable with respect to any claim or demand made against such entity, nor shall any pledge of assets made in connection with such a loan be upset or impaired for that reason;

(B) Subparagraph (A) shall not be construed to—

(i) imply that an entity described in subparagraph (A)(ii) or (iii) would, if this paragraph were not applicable, necessarily be liable to any entity by reason of any of the acts described in subparagraph (A);

(ii) relieve any such entity of the duty to comply with, or of liability under, any Federal or State law regarding the making of a fraudulent conveyance in a transaction described in subparagraph (A)(ii) or (iii); or

(iii) relieve a debtor of the debtor's obligation to comply with the terms of the plan of reorganization, or affect the power of the court to exercise its authority under *sections 1141* and *1142* to compel the debtor to do so.

(4)

(A)

(i) Subject to subparagraph (B), an injunction described in paragraph (1) shall be valid and enforceable against all entities that it addresses.

(ii) Notwithstanding the provisions of section 524(e), such an injunction may bar any action directed against a third party who is identifiable from the terms of such injunction (by name or as part of an identifiable group) and is alleged to be directly or indirectly liable for the conduct of, claims against, or demands on the debtor to the extent such alleged liability of such third party arises by reason of—

(I) the third party's ownership of a financial interest in the debtor, a past or present affiliate of the debtor, or a predecessor in interest of the debtor;

(II) the third party's involvement in the management of the debtor or a predecessor in interest of the debtor, or service as an officer, director or employee of the debtor or a related party;

(III) the third party's provision of insurance to the debtor or a related party; or

(IV) the third party's involvement in a transaction changing the corporate structure, or in a loan or other financial transaction affecting the financial condition, of the debtor or a related party, including but not limited to—

(aa) involvement in providing financing (debt or equity), or advice to an entity involved in such a transaction; or

(bb) acquiring or selling a financial interest in an entity as part of such a transaction.

(iii) As used in this subparagraph, the term "related party" means —

(I) a past or present affiliate of the debtor;

(II) a predecessor in interest of the debtor; or

(III) any entity that owned a financial interest in—

(aa) the debtor;

(bb) a past or present affiliate of the debtor; or

(cc) a predecessor in interest of the debtor.

(B) Subject to subsection (h), if, under a plan of reorganization, a kind of demand described in such plan is to be paid in whole or in part by a trust described in paragraph (2)(B)(i) in connection with which an injunction described in paragraph (1) is to be implemented, then such injunction shall be valid and enforceable with respect to a demand of such kind made, after such plan is confirmed, against the debtor or debtors involved, or against a third party described in subparagraph (A)(ii), if—

(i) as part of the proceedings leading to issuance of such injunction, the court appoints a legal representative for the purpose of protecting the rights of persons that might subsequently assert demands of such kind, and

(ii) the court determines, before entering the order confirming such plan, that identifying such debtor or debtors, or such third party (by name or as part of an identifiable group), in such injunction with respect to such demands for purposes of this subparagraph is fair and equitable with respect to the persons that might subsequently assert such demands, in light of the benefits provided, or to be provided, to such trust on behalf of such debtor or debtors or such third party.

(5) In this subsection, the term "demand" means a demand for payment, present or future, that—

(A) was not a claim during the proceedings leading to the confirmation of a plan of reorganization;

(B) arises out of the same or similar conduct or events that gave rise to the claims addressed by the injunction issued under paragraph (1); and

(C) pursuant to the plan, is to be paid by a trust described in paragraph (2)(B)(i).

(6) Paragraph (3)(A)(i) does not bar an action taken by or at the direction of an appellate court on appeal of an injunction issued under paragraph (1) or of the order of confirmation that relates to the injunction.

(7) This subsection does not affect the operation of *section 1144* or the power of the district court to refer a proceeding under section 157 of title 28 or any reference of a proceeding made prior to the date of the enactment of this subsection.

(h) Application to Existing Injunctions.—

For purposes of subsection (g)—

(1) subject to paragraph (2), if an injunction of the kind described in subsection (g)(1)(B) was issued before the date of the enactment of this Act, as part of a plan of reorganization confirmed by an order entered before such date, then the injunction shall be considered to meet the requirements of subsection (g)(2)(B) for purposes of subsection (g)(2)(A), and to satisfy subsection (g)(4)(A)(ii), if—

(A) the court determined at the time the plan was confirmed that the plan was fair and equitable in accordance with the requirements of *section 1129(b)*;

(B) as part of the proceedings leading to issuance of such injunction and confirmation of such plan, the court had appointed a legal representative for the purpose of protecting the rights of persons that might subsequently assert demands described in subsection (g)(4)(B) with respect to such plan; and

(C) such legal representative did not object to confirmation of such plan or issuance of such injunction; and

(2) for purposes of paragraph (1), if a trust described in subsection (g)(2)(B)(i) is subject to a court order on the date of the enactment of this Act staying such trust from settling or paying further claims—

(A) the requirements of subsection (g)(2)(B)(ii)(V) shall not apply with respect to such trust until such stay is lifted or dissolved; and

(B) if such trust meets such requirements on the date such stay is lifted or dissolved, such trust shall be considered to have met such requirements continuously from the date of the enactment of this Act.

(i) The willful failure of a creditor to credit payments received under a plan confirmed under this title, unless the order confirming the plan is revoked, the plan is in default, or the creditor has not received payments required to be made under the plan in the manner required by the plan (including crediting the amounts required under the plan), shall constitute a violation of an injunction under subsection (a)(2) if the act of the creditor to collect and failure to credit payments in the manner required by the plan caused material injury to the debtor.

(j) Subsection (a)(2) does not operate as an injunction against an act by a creditor that is the holder of a secured claim, if—

(1) such creditor retains a security interest in real property that is the principal residence of the debtor;

(2) such act is in the ordinary course of business between the creditor and the debtor; and

(3) such act is limited to seeking or obtaining periodic payments associated with a valid security interest in lieu of pursuit of in rem relief to enforce the lien.

(k)

(1) The disclosures required under subsection (c)(2) shall consist of the disclosure statement described in paragraph (3), completed as required in that paragraph, together with the agreement specified in subsection (c), statement, declaration, motion and order described, respectively, in paragraphs (4) through (8), and shall be the only disclosures required in connection with entering into such agreement.

(2) Disclosures made under paragraph (1) shall be made clearly and conspicuously and in writing. The terms "Amount Reaffirmed" and "Annual Percentage Rate" shall be disclosed more conspicuously than other terms, data or information provided in connection with this disclosure, except that the phrases "Before agreeing to reaffirm a debt, review these important disclosures" and "Summary of Reaffirmation Agreement" may be equally conspicuous. Disclosures may be made in a different order and may use terminology different from that set forth in paragraphs (2) through (8), except that the terms "Amount Reaffirmed" and "Annual Percentage Rate" must be used where indicated.

(3) The disclosure statement required under this paragraph shall consist of the following:

(A) The statement: "Part A: Before agreeing to reaffirm a debt, review these important disclosures:";

(B) Under the heading "Summary of Reaffirmation Agreement", the statement: "This Summary is made pursuant to the requirements of the Bankruptcy Code";

(C) The "Amount Reaffirmed", using that term, which shall be—

(i) the total amount of debt that the debtor agrees to reaffirm by entering into an agreement of the kind specified in subsection (c), and

(ii) the total of any fees and costs accrued as of the date of the disclosure statement, related to such total amount.

(D) In conjunction with the disclosure of the "Amount Reaffirmed", the statements—

(i) "The amount of debt you have agreed to reaffirm"; and

(ii) "Your credit agreement may obligate you to pay additional amounts which may come due after the date of this disclosure. Consult your credit agreement.".

(E) The "Annual Percentage Rate", using that term, which shall be disclosed as —

(i) if, at the time the petition is filed, the debt is an extension of credit under an open end credit plan, as the terms "credit" and "open end credit plan" are defined in *section 103* of the Truth in Lending Act, then—

(I) the annual percentage rate determined under paragraphs (5) and (6) of section 127(b) of the Truth in Lending Act, as applicable, as disclosed to the debtor in the most recent periodic statement prior to entering into an agreement of the kind specified in subsection (c) or, if no such periodic statement has been given to the debtor during the prior 6 months, the annual percentage rate as it would have been so disclosed at the time the disclosure statement is given to the debtor, or to the extent this annual percentage rate is not readily available or not applicable, then

(II) the simple interest rate applicable to the amount reaffirmed as of the date the disclosure statement is given to the debtor, or if different simple interest rates apply to different balances, the simple interest rate applicable to each such balance, identifying the amount of each such balance included in the amount reaffirmed, or

(III) if the entity making the disclosure elects, to disclose the annual percentage rate under subclause (I) and the simple interest rate under subclause (II); or

(ii) if, at the time the petition is filed, the debt is an extension of credit other than under an open end credit plan, as the terms "credit" and "open end credit plan" are defined in *section 103* of the Truth in Lending Act, then—

(I) the annual percentage rate under section 128(a)(4) of the Truth in Lending Act, as disclosed to the debtor in the most recent disclosure statement given to the debtor prior to the entering into an agreement of the kind specified in subsection (c) with respect to the debt, or, if no such disclosure statement was given to the debtor, the annual percentage rate as it would have been so disclosed at the time the disclosure statement is given to the debtor, or to the extent this annual percentage rate is not readily available or not applicable, then

(II) the simple interest rate applicable to the amount reaffirmed as of the date the disclosure statement is given to the debtor, or if different simple interest rates apply to different balances, the simple interest rate applicable to each such balance, identifying the amount of such balance included in the amount reaffirmed, or

(III) if the entity making the disclosure elects, to disclose the annual percentage rate under (I) and the simple interest rate under (II).

(F) If the underlying debt transaction was disclosed as a variable rate transaction on the most recent disclosure given under the Truth in Lending Act, by stating "The interest rate on your loan may be a variable interest rate which changes from time to time, so that the annual percentage rate disclosed here may be higher or lower.".

(G) If the debt is secured by a security interest which has not been waived in whole or in part or determined to be void by a final order of the court at the time of the disclosure, by disclosing that a security interest or lien in goods or property is asserted over some or all of the debts the debtor is reaffirming and listing the items and their original purchase price that are subject to the asserted security interest, or if not a purchase-money security interest then listing by items or types and the original amount of the loan.

(H) At the election of the creditor, a statement of the repayment schedule using 1 or a combination of the following—

(i) by making the statement: "Your first payment in the amount of $___ is due on ___ but the future payment amount may be different. Consult your reaffirmation agreement or credit agreement, as applicable.", and stating the amount of the first payment and the due date of that payment in the places provided;

(ii) by making the statement: "Your payment schedule will be:", and describing the repayment schedule with the number, amount, and due dates or period of payments scheduled to repay the debts reaffirmed to the extent then known by the disclosing party; or

(iii) by describing the debtor's repayment obligations with reasonable specificity to the extent then known by the disclosing party.

(I) The following statement: "Note: When this disclosure refers to what a creditor 'may' do, it does not use the word 'may' to give the creditor specific permission. The word 'may' is used to tell you what might occur if the law permits the creditor to take the action. If you have questions about your reaffirming a debt or what the law requires, consult with the attorney who helped you negotiate this agreement reaffirming a debt. If you don't have an attorney helping you, the judge will explain the effect of your reaffirming a debt when the hearing on the reaffirmation agreement is held.".

(J)

(i) The following additional statements:

"Reaffirming a debt is a serious financial decision. The law requires you to take certain steps to make sure the decision is in your best interest. If these steps are not completed, the reaffirmation agreement is not effective, even though you have signed it.

"1. Read the disclosures in this Part A carefully. Consider the decision to reaffirm carefully. Then, if you want to reaffirm, sign the reaffirmation agreement in Part B (or you may use a separate agreement you and your creditor agree on).

"2. Complete and sign Part D and be sure you can afford to make the payments you are agreeing to make and have received a copy of the disclosure statement and a completed and signed reaffirmation agreement.

"3. If you were represented by an attorney during the negotiation of your reaffirmation agreement, the attorney must have signed the certification in Part C.

"4. If you were not represented by an attorney during the negotiation of your reaffirmation agreement, you must have completed and signed Part E.

"5. The original of this disclosure must be filed with the court by you or your creditor. If a separate reaffirmation agreement (other than the one in Part B) has been signed, it must be attached.

"6. If you were represented by an attorney during the negotiation of your reaffirmation agreement, your reaffirmation agreement becomes effective upon filing with the court unless the reaffirmation is presumed to be an undue hardship as explained in Part D.

"7. If you were not represented by an attorney during the negotiation of your reaffirmation agreement, it will not be effective unless the court approves it. The court will notify you of the hearing on your reaffirmation agreement. You must attend this hearing in bankruptcy court where the judge will review your reaffirmation agreement. The bankruptcy court must approve your reaffirmation agreement as consistent with your best interests, except that no court approval is required if your reaffirmation agreement is for a consumer debt secured by a mortgage, deed of trust, security deed, or other lien on your real property, like your home.

"Your right to rescind (cancel) your reaffirmation agreement. You may rescind (cancel) your reaffirmation agreement at any time before the bankruptcy court enters a discharge order, or before the expiration of the 60-day period that begins on the date your reaffirmation agreement is filed with the court, whichever occurs later. To rescind (cancel) your reaffirmation agreement, you must notify the creditor that your reaffirmation agreement is rescinded (or canceled).

"What are your obligations if you reaffirm the debt? A reaffirmed debt remains your personal legal obligation. It is not discharged in your bankruptcy case. That means that if you default on your reaffirmed debt after your bankruptcy case is over, your creditor may be able to take your property or your wages. Otherwise, your obligations will be determined by the reaffirmation agreement which may have changed the terms of the original agreement. For example, if you are reaffirming an open end credit agreement, the creditor may be permitted by that agreement or applicable law to change the terms of that agreement in the future under certain conditions.

"Are you required to enter into a reaffirmation agreement by any law? No, you are not required to reaffirm a debt by any law. Only agree to reaffirm a debt if it is in your best interest. Be sure you can afford the payments you agree to make.

"What if your creditor has a security interest or lien? Your bankruptcy discharge does not eliminate any lien on your property. A 'lien' is often referred to as a security interest, deed of trust, mortgage or security deed. Even if you do not reaffirm and your personal liability on the debt is discharged, because of the lien your creditor may still have the right to take the property securing the lien if you do not pay the debt or default on it. If the lien is on an item of personal property that is exempt under your State's law or that the trustee has abandoned, you may be able to redeem the item rather than reaffirm the debt. To redeem, you must make a single payment to the creditor equal to the amount of the allowed secured claim, as agreed by the parties or determined by the court.".

(ii) In the case of a reaffirmation under subsection (m)(2), numbered paragraph 6 in the disclosures required by clause (i) of this subparagraph shall read as follows:

"6. If you were represented by an attorney during the negotiation of your reaffirmation agreement, your reaffirmation agreement becomes effective upon filing with the court.".

(4) The form of such agreement required under this paragraph shall consist of the following:

"Part B: Reaffirmation Agreement. I (we) agree to reaffirm the debts arising under the credit agreement described below.

"Brief description of credit agreement:

"Description of any changes to the credit agreement made as part of this reaffirmation agreement:

"Signature: Date:

"Borrower:

"Co-borrower, if also reaffirming these debts:

"Accepted by creditor:

"Date of creditor acceptance:".

(5) The declaration shall consist of the following:

(A) The following certification:

"Part C: Certification by Debtor's Attorney (If Any).

"I hereby certify that (1) this agreement represents a fully informed and voluntary agreement by the debtor; (2) this agreement does not impose an undue hardship on the debtor or any dependent of the debtor; and (3) I have fully advised the debtor of the legal effect and consequences of this agreement and any default under this agreement.

"Signature of Debtor's Attorney: Date:".

(B) If a presumption of undue hardship has been established with respect to such agreement, such certification shall state that, in the opinion of the attorney, the debtor is able to make the payment.

(C) In the case of a reaffirmation agreement under subsection (m)(2), subparagraph (B) is not applicable.

(6)

(A) The statement in support of such agreement, which the debtor shall sign and date prior to filing with the court, shall consist of the following:

"Part D: Debtor's Statement in Support of Reaffirmation Agreement.

"1. I believe this reaffirmation agreement will not impose an undue hardship on my dependents or me. I can afford to make the payments on the reaffirmed debt because my monthly income (take home pay plus any other income received) is $___, and my actual current monthly expenses including monthly payments on post-bankruptcy debt and other reaffirmation agreements total $___, leaving $___ to make the required payments on this reaffirmed debt. I understand that if my income less my monthly expenses does not leave enough to make the payments, this reaffirmation agreement is presumed to be an undue hardship on me and must be reviewed by the court. However, this presumption may be overcome if I explain to the satisfaction of the court how I can afford to make the payments here: ___.

"2. I received a copy of the Reaffirmation Disclosure Statement in Part A and a completed and signed reaffirmation agreement.".

(B) Where the debtor is represented by an attorney and is reaffirming a debt owed to a creditor defined in section 19(b)(1)(A)(iv) of the Federal Reserve Act, the statement of support of the reaffirmation agreement, which the debtor shall sign and date prior to filing with the court, shall consist of the following:

"I believe this reaffirmation agreement is in my financial interest. I can afford to make the payments on the reaffirmed debt. I received a copy of the Reaffirmation Disclosure Statement in Part A and a completed and signed reaffirmation agreement.".

(7) The motion that may be used if approval of such agreement by the court is required in order for it to be effective, shall be signed and dated by the movant and shall consist of the following:

"Part E: Motion for Court Approval (To be completed only if the debtor is not represented by an attorney.). I (we), the debtor(s), affirm the following to be true and correct:

"I am not represented by an attorney in connection with this reaffirmation agreement.

"I believe this reaffirmation agreement is in my best interest based on the income and expenses I have disclosed in my Statement in Support of this reaffirmation agreement, and because (provide any additional relevant reasons the court should consider):

"Therefore, I ask the court for an order approving this reaffirmation agreement.".

(8) The court order, which may be used to approve such agreement, shall consist of the following:

"Court Order: The court grants the debtor's motion and approves the reaffirmation agreement described above.".

(l) Notwithstanding any other provision of this title the following shall apply:

(1) A creditor may accept payments from a debtor before and after the filing of an agreement of the kind specified in subsection (c) with the court.

(2) A creditor may accept payments from a debtor under such agreement that the creditor believes in good faith to be effective.

(3) The requirements of subsections (c)(2) and (k) shall be satisfied if disclosures required under those subsections are given in good faith.

(m)

(1) Until 60 days after an agreement of the kind specified in subsection (c) is filed with the court (or such additional period as the court, after notice and a hearing and for cause, orders before the expiration of such period), it shall be presumed that such agreement is an undue hardship on the debtor if the debtor's monthly income less the debtor's monthly expenses as shown on the debtor's completed and signed statement in support of such agreement required under subsection (k)(6)(A) is less than the scheduled payments on the reaffirmed debt. This presumption shall be reviewed by the court. The presumption may be rebutted in writing by the debtor if the statement includes an explanation that identifies additional sources of funds to make the payments as agreed upon under the terms of such agreement. If the presumption is not rebutted to the satisfaction of the court, the court may disapprove such agreement. No agreement shall be disapproved without notice and a hearing to the debtor and creditor, and such hearing shall be concluded before the entry of the debtor's discharge.

(2) This subsection does not apply to reaffirmation agreements where the creditor is a credit union, as defined in section 19(b)(1)(A)(iv) of the Federal Reserve Act.

(Pub. L. 95–598, Nov. 6, 1978, 92 Stat. 2592; Pub. L. 98–353, title III, §§ 308, 455, July 10, 1984, 98 Stat. 354, 376; Pub. L. 99–554, title II, §§ 257(o), 282, 283(k), Oct. 27, 1986, 100 Stat. 3115–3117; Pub. L. 103–394, title I, §§ 103, 111(a), title V, § 501(d)(14), Oct. 22, 1994, 108 Stat. 4108, 4113, 4145; Pub. L. 109–8, title II, §§ 202, 203(a), title XII, § 1210, Apr. 20, 2005, 119 Stat. 43, 194; Pub. L. 111–327, § 2(a)(19), Dec. 22, 2010, 124 Stat. 3559; Pub. L. 116–54, § 4(a)(9), Aug. 23, 2019, 133 Stat. 1086.)

Sections that reference this section: 108, 1106, 1202, 1302, 341, 362, 365, 521, 704

§525. Protection against discriminatory treatment

(a) Except as provided in the Perishable Agricultural Commodities Act, 1930, the Packers and Stockyards Act, 1921, and section 1 of the Act entitled "An Act making appropriations for the Department of Agriculture for the fiscal year ending June 30, 1944, and for other purposes," approved July 12, 1943, a governmental unit may not deny, revoke, suspend, or refuse to renew a license, permit, charter, franchise, or other similar grant to, condition such a grant to, discriminate with respect to such a grant against, deny employment to, terminate the employment of, or discriminate with respect to employment against, a person that is or has been a debtor under this title or a bankrupt or a debtor under the Bankruptcy Act, or another person with whom such bankrupt or debtor has been associated, solely because such bankrupt or debtor is or has been a debtor under this title or a bankrupt or debtor under the Bankruptcy Act, has been insolvent before the commencement of the case under this title, or during the case but before the debtor is granted or denied a discharge, or has not paid a debt that is dischargeable in the case under this title or that was discharged under the Bankruptcy Act.

(b) No private employer may terminate the employment of, or discriminate with respect to employment against, an individual who is or has been a debtor under this title, a debtor or bankrupt under the Bankruptcy Act, or an individual associated with such debtor or bankrupt, solely because such debtor or bankrupt—

(1) is or has been a debtor under this title or a debtor or bankrupt under the Bankruptcy Act;

(2) has been insolvent before the commencement of a case under this title or during the case but before the grant or denial of a discharge; or

(3) has not paid a debt that is dischargeable in a case under this title or that was discharged under the Bankruptcy Act.

(c)

(1) A governmental unit that operates a student grant or loan program and a person engaged in a business that includes the making of loans guaranteed or insured under a student loan program may not deny a student grant, loan, loan guarantee, or loan insurance to a person that is or has been a debtor under this title or a bankrupt or debtor under the Bankruptcy Act, or another person with whom the debtor or bankrupt has been associated, because the debtor or bankrupt is or has been a debtor under this title or a bankrupt or debtor under the Bankruptcy Act, has been insolvent before the commencement of a case under this title or during the pendency of the case but before the debtor is granted or denied a discharge, or has not paid a debt that is dischargeable in the case under this title or that was discharged under the Bankruptcy Act.

(2) In this section, "student loan program" means any program operated under title IV of the Higher Education Act of 1965 or a similar program operated under State or local law.

(Pub. L. 95–598, Nov. 6, 1978, 92 Stat. 2593; Pub. L. 98–353, title III, § 309, July 10, 1984, 98 Stat. 354; Pub. L. 103–394, title III, § 313, title V, § 501(d)(15), Oct. 22, 1994, 108 Stat. 4140, 4145; Pub. L. 109–8, title XII, § 1211, Apr. 20, 2005, 119 Stat. 194; Pub. L. 116–260, div. FF, title X, § 1001(c), Dec. 27, 2020, 134 Stat. 3217.)

Sections that reference this section: None

§526. Restrictions on debt relief agencies

(a) A debt relief agency shall not—

(1) fail to perform any service that such agency informed an assisted person or prospective assisted person it would provide in connection with a case or proceeding under this title;

(2) make any statement, or counsel or advise any assisted person or prospective assisted person to make a statement in a document filed in a case or proceeding under this title, that is untrue or misleading, or that upon the exercise of reasonable care, should have been known by such agency to be untrue or misleading;

(3) misrepresent to any assisted person or prospective assisted person, directly or indirectly, affirmatively or by material omission, with respect to—

(A) the services that such agency will provide to such person; or

(B) the benefits and risks that may result if such person becomes a debtor in a case under this title; or

(4) advise an assisted person or prospective assisted person to incur more debt in contemplation of such person filing a case under this title or to pay an attorney or bankruptcy petition preparer a fee or charge for services performed as part of preparing for or representing a debtor in a case under this title.

(b) Any waiver by any assisted person of any protection or right provided under this section shall not be enforceable against the debtor by any Federal or State court or any other person, but may be enforced against a debt relief agency.

(c)

(1) Any contract for bankruptcy assistance between a debt relief agency and an assisted person that does not comply with the material requirements of this section, *section 527*, or *section 528* shall be void and may not be enforced by any Federal or State court or by any other person, other than such assisted person.

(2) Any debt relief agency shall be liable to an assisted person in the amount of any fees or charges in connection with providing bankruptcy assistance to such person that such debt relief agency has received, for actual damages, and for reasonable attorneys' fees and costs if such agency is found, after notice and a hearing, to have—

(A) intentionally or negligently failed to comply with any provision of this section, *section 527*, or *section 528* with respect to a case or proceeding under this title for such assisted person;

(B) provided bankruptcy assistance to an assisted person in a case or proceeding under this title that is dismissed or converted to a case under another chapter of this title because of such agency's intentional or negligent failure to file any required document including those specified in *section 521*; or

(C) intentionally or negligently disregarded the material requirements of this title or the Federal Rules of Bankruptcy Procedure applicable to such agency.

(3) In addition to such other remedies as are provided under State law, whenever the chief law enforcement officer of a State, or an official or agency designated by a State, has reason to believe that any person has violated or is violating this section, the State—

(A) may bring an action to enjoin such violation;

(B) may bring an action on behalf of its residents to recover the actual damages of assisted persons arising from such violation, including any liability under paragraph (2); and

(C) in the case of any successful action under subparagraph (A) or (B), shall be awarded the costs of the action and reasonable attorneys' fees as determined by the court.

(4) The district courts of the United States for districts located in the State shall have concurrent jurisdiction of any action under subparagraph (A) or (B) of paragraph (3).

(5) Notwithstanding any other provision of Federal law and in addition to any other remedy provided under Federal or State law, if the court, on its own motion or on the motion of the United States trustee or the debtor, finds that a person intentionally violated this section, or engaged in a clear and consistent pattern or practice of violating this section, the court may—

(A) enjoin the violation of such section; or

(B) impose an appropriate civil penalty against such person.

(d) No provision of this section, *section 527*, or *section 528* shall—

(1) annul, alter, affect, or exempt any person subject to such sections from complying with any law of any State except to the extent that such law is inconsistent with those sections, and then only to the extent of the inconsistency; or

(2) be deemed to limit or curtail the authority or ability—

(A) of a State or subdivision or instrumentality thereof, to determine and enforce qualifications for the practice of law under the laws of that State; or

(B) of a Federal court to determine and enforce the qualifications for the practice of law before that court.

(Added Pub. L. 109–8, title II, § 227(a), Apr. 20, 2005, 119 Stat. 67; amended Pub. L. 111–327, § 2(a)(20), Dec. 22, 2010, 124 Stat. 3560.)

Sections that reference this section: None

§527. Disclosures

(a) A debt relief agency providing bankruptcy assistance to an assisted person shall provide—

(1) the written notice required under *section 342(b)(1)*; and

(2) to the extent not covered in the written notice described in paragraph (1), and not later than 3 business days after the first date on which a debt relief agency first offers to provide any bankruptcy assistance services to an assisted person, a clear and conspicuous written notice advising assisted persons that—

(A) all information that the assisted person is required to provide with a petition and thereafter during a case under this title is required to be complete, accurate, and truthful;

(B) all assets and all liabilities are required to be completely and accurately disclosed in the documents filed to commence the case, and the replacement value of each asset as defined in *section 506* must be stated in those documents where requested after reasonable inquiry to establish such value;

(C) current monthly income, the amounts specified in *section 707(b)(2)*, and, in a case under chapter 13 of this title, disposable income (determined in accordance with *section 707(b)(2)*), are required to be stated after reasonable inquiry; and

(D) information that an assisted person provides during their case may be audited pursuant to this title, and that failure to provide such information may result in dismissal of the case under this title or other sanction, including a criminal sanction.

(b) A debt relief agency providing bankruptcy assistance to an assisted person shall provide each assisted person at the same time as the notices required under subsection (a)(1) the following statement, to the extent applicable, or one substantially similar. The statement shall be clear and conspicuous and shall be in a single document separate from other documents or notices provided to the assisted person:

"IMPORTANT INFORMATION ABOUT BANKRUPTCY ASSISTANCE SERVICES FROM AN ATTORNEY OR BANKRUPTCY PETITION PREPARER.

"If you decide to seek bankruptcy relief, you can represent yourself, you can hire an attorney to represent you, or you can get help in some localities from a bankruptcy petition preparer who is not an attorney. THE LAW REQUIRES AN ATTORNEY OR BANKRUPTCY PETITION PREPARER TO GIVE YOU A WRITTEN CONTRACT SPECIFYING WHAT THE ATTORNEY OR BANKRUPTCY PETITION PREPARER WILL DO FOR YOU AND HOW MUCH IT WILL COST. Ask to see the contract before you hire anyone.

"The following information helps you understand what must be done in a routine bankruptcy case to help you evaluate how much service you need. Although bankruptcy can be complex, many cases are routine.

"Before filing a bankruptcy case, either you or your attorney should analyze your eligibility for different forms of debt relief available under the Bankruptcy Code and which form of relief is most likely to be beneficial for you. Be sure you understand the relief you can obtain and its limitations. To file a bankruptcy case, documents called a Petition, Schedules, and Statement of Financial Affairs, and in some cases a Statement of Intention, need to be prepared correctly and filed with the bankruptcy court. You will have to pay a filing fee to the bankruptcy court. Once your case starts, you will have to attend the required first meeting of creditors where you may be questioned by a court official called a 'trustee' and by creditors.

"If you choose to file a chapter 7 case, you may be asked by a creditor to reaffirm a debt. You may want help deciding whether to do so. A creditor is not permitted to coerce you into reaffirming your debts.

"If you choose to file a chapter 13 case in which you repay your creditors what you can afford over 3 to 5 years, you may also want help with preparing your chapter 13 plan and with the confirmation hearing on your plan which will be before a bankruptcy judge.

"If you select another type of relief under the Bankruptcy Code other than chapter 7 or chapter 13, you will want to find out what should be done from someone familiar with that type of relief.

"Your bankruptcy case may also involve litigation. You are generally permitted to represent yourself in litigation in bankruptcy court, but only attorneys, not bankruptcy petition preparers, can give you legal advice.".

(c) Except to the extent the debt relief agency provides the required information itself after reasonably diligent inquiry of the assisted person or others so as to obtain such information reasonably accurately for inclusion on the petition, schedules or statement of financial affairs, a debt relief agency providing bankruptcy assistance to an assisted person, to the extent permitted by nonbankruptcy law, shall provide each assisted person at the time required for the notice required under subsection (a)(1) reasonably sufficient information (which shall be provided in a clear and conspicuous writing) to the assisted person on how to provide all the information the assisted person is required to provide under this title pursuant to *section 521*, including—

(1) how to value assets at replacement value, determine current monthly income, the amounts specified in *section 707(b)(2)* and, in a chapter 13 case, how to determine disposable income in accordance with *section 707(b)(2)* and related calculations;

(2) how to complete the list of creditors, including how to determine what amount is owed and what address for the creditor should be shown; and

(3) how to determine what property is exempt and how to value exempt property at replacement value as defined in *section 506*.

(d) A debt relief agency shall maintain a copy of the notices required under subsection (a) of this section for 2 years after the date on which the notice is given the assisted person.

(Added Pub. L. 109–8, title II, § 228(a), Apr. 20, 2005, 119 Stat. 69; amended Pub. L. 111–327, § 2(a)(21), Dec. 22, 2010, 124 Stat. 3560.)

Sections that reference this section: 526

§528. Requirements for debt relief agencies

(a) A debt relief agency shall—

(1) not later than 5 business days after the first date on which such agency provides any bankruptcy assistance services to an assisted person, but prior to such assisted person's petition under this title being filed, execute a written contract with such assisted person that explains clearly and conspicuously—

(A) the services such agency will provide to such assisted person; and

(B) the fees or charges for such services, and the terms of payment;

(2) provide the assisted person with a copy of the fully executed and completed contract;

(3) clearly and conspicuously disclose in any advertisement of bankruptcy assistance services or of the benefits of bankruptcy directed to the general public (whether in general media, seminars or specific mailings, telephonic or electronic messages, or otherwise) that the services or benefits are with respect to bankruptcy relief under this title; and

(4) clearly and conspicuously use the following statement in such advertisement: "We are a debt relief agency. We help people file for bankruptcy relief under the Bankruptcy Code." or a substantially similar statement.

(b)

(1) An advertisement of bankruptcy assistance services or of the benefits of bankruptcy directed to the general public includes—

(A) descriptions of bankruptcy assistance in connection with a chapter 13 plan whether or not chapter 13 is specifically mentioned in such advertisement; and

(B) statements such as "federally supervised repayment plan" or "Federal debt restructuring help" or other similar statements that could lead a reasonable consumer to believe that debt counseling was being offered when in fact the services were directed to providing bankruptcy assistance with a chapter 13 plan or other form of bankruptcy relief under this title.

(2) An advertisement, directed to the general public, indicating that the debt relief agency provides assistance with respect to credit defaults, mortgage foreclosures, eviction proceedings, excessive debt, debt collection pressure, or inability to pay any consumer debt shall—

(A) disclose clearly and conspicuously in such advertisement that the assistance may involve bankruptcy relief under this title; and

(B) include the following statement: "We are a debt relief agency. We help people file for bankruptcy relief under the Bankruptcy Code." or a substantially similar statement.

(Added Pub. L. 109–8, title II, § 229(a), Apr. 20, 2005, 119 Stat. 71.)

Sections that reference this section: 526

Subchapter III: The Estate

§541. Property of the estate

(a) The commencement of a case under *section 301*, *302*, or *303* of this title creates an estate. Such estate is comprised of all the following property, wherever located and by whomever held:

(1) Except as provided in subsections (b) and (c)(2) of this section, all legal or equitable interests of the debtor in property as of the commencement of the case.

(2) All interests of the debtor and the debtor's spouse in community property as of the commencement of the case that is—

(A) under the sole, equal, or joint management and control of the debtor; or

(B) liable for an allowable claim against the debtor, or for both an allowable claim against the debtor and an allowable claim against the debtor's spouse, to the extent that such interest is so liable.

(3) Any interest in property that the trustee recovers under *section 329(b)*, *363*(n), 543, 550, 553, or 723 of this title.

(4) Any interest in property preserved for the benefit of or ordered transferred to the estate under *section 510(c)* or *551* of this title.

(5) Any interest in property that would have been property of the estate if such interest had been an interest of the debtor on the date of the filing of the petition, and that the debtor acquires or becomes entitled to acquire within 180 days after such date—

(A) by bequest, devise, or inheritance;

(B) as a result of a property settlement agreement with the debtor's spouse, or of an interlocutory or final divorce decree; or

(C) as a beneficiary of a life insurance policy or of a death benefit plan.

(6) Proceeds, product, offspring, rents, or profits of or from property of the estate, except such as are earnings from services performed by an individual debtor after the commencement of the case.

(7) Any interest in property that the estate acquires after the commencement of the case.

(b) Property of the estate does not include—

(1) any power that the debtor may exercise solely for the benefit of an entity other than the debtor;

(2) any interest of the debtor as a lessee under a lease of nonresidential real property that has terminated at the expiration of the stated term of such lease before the commencement of the case under this title, and ceases to include any interest of the debtor as a lessee under a lease of nonresidential real property that has terminated at the expiration of the stated term of such lease during the case;

(3) any eligibility of the debtor to participate in programs authorized under the Higher Education Act of 1965 (20 U.S.C. 1001 et seq.; 42 U.S.C. 2751 et seq.), or any accreditation status or State licensure of the debtor as an educational institution;

(4) any interest of the debtor in liquid or gaseous hydrocarbons to the extent that—

(A)

(i) the debtor has transferred or has agreed to transfer such interest pursuant to a farmout agreement or any written agreement directly related to a farmout agreement; and

(ii) but for the operation of this paragraph, the estate could include the interest referred to in clause (i) only by virtue of *section 365* or *544*(a)(3) of this title; or

(B)

(i) the debtor has transferred such interest pursuant to a written conveyance of a production payment to an entity that does not participate in the operation of the property from which such production payment is transferred; and

(ii) but for the operation of this paragraph, the estate could include the interest referred to in clause (i) only by virtue of *section 365* or *542* of this title;

(5) funds placed in an education individual retirement account (as defined in section 530(b)(1) of the Internal Revenue Code of 1986) not later than 365 days before the date of the filing of the petition in a case under this title, but—

(A) only if the designated beneficiary of such account was a child, stepchild, grandchild, or stepgrandchild of the debtor for the taxable year for which funds were placed in such account;

(B) only to the extent that such funds—

(i) are not pledged or promised to any entity in connection with any extension of credit; and

(ii) are not excess contributions (as described in section 4973(e) of the Internal Revenue Code of 1986); and

(C) in the case of funds placed in all such accounts having the same designated beneficiary not earlier than 720 days nor later than 365 days before such date, only so much of such funds as does not exceed $8,575;

(6) funds used to purchase a tuition credit or certificate or contributed to an account in accordance with section 529(b)(1)(A) of the Internal Revenue Code of 1986 under a qualified State tuition program (as defined in section 529(b)(1) of such Code) not later than 365 days before the date of the filing of the petition in a case under this title, but—

(A) only if the designated beneficiary of the amounts paid or contributed to such tuition program was a child, stepchild, grandchild, or stepgrandchild of the debtor for the taxable year for which funds were paid or contributed;

(B) with respect to the aggregate amount paid or contributed to such program having the same designated beneficiary, only so much of such amount as does not exceed the total contributions permitted under section 529(b)(6) of such Code with respect to such beneficiary, as adjusted beginning on the date of the filing of the petition in a case under this title by the annual increase or decrease (rounded to the nearest tenth of 1 percent) in the education expenditure category of the Consumer Price Index prepared by the Department of Labor; and

(C) in the case of funds paid or contributed to such program having the same designated beneficiary not earlier than 720 days nor later than 365 days before such date, only so much of such funds as does not exceed $8,575;

(7) any amount—

(A) withheld by an employer from the wages of employees for payment as contributions—

(i) to—

(I) an employee benefit plan that is subject to title I of the Employee Retirement Income Security Act of 1974 or under an employee benefit plan which is a governmental plan under section 414(d) of the Internal Revenue Code of 1986;

(II) a deferred compensation plan under section 457 of the Internal Revenue Code of 1986; or

(III) a tax-deferred annuity under section 403(b) of the Internal Revenue Code of 1986;

except that such amount under this subparagraph shall not constitute disposable income as defined in *section 1325(b)(2)*; or

(ii) to a health insurance plan regulated by State law whether or not subject to such title; or

(B) received by an employer from employees for payment as contributions —

(i) to—

(I) an employee benefit plan that is subject to title I of the Employee Retirement Income Security Act of 1974 or under an employee benefit plan which is a governmental plan under section 414(d) of the Internal Revenue Code of 1986;

(II) a deferred compensation plan under section 457 of the Internal Revenue Code of 1986; or

(III) a tax-deferred annuity under section 403(b) of the Internal Revenue Code of 1986;

except that such amount under this subparagraph shall not constitute disposable income, as defined in *section 1325(b)(2)*; or

(ii) to a health insurance plan regulated by State law whether or not subject to such title;

(8) subject to subchapter III of chapter 5, any interest of the debtor in property where the

debtor pledged or sold tangible personal property (other than securities or written or printed evidences of indebtedness or title) as collateral for a loan or advance of money given by a person licensed under law to make such loans or advances, where—

(A) the tangible personal property is in the possession of the pledgee or transferee;

(B) the debtor has no obligation to repay the money, redeem the collateral, or buy back the property at a stipulated price; and

(C) neither the debtor nor the trustee have exercised any right to redeem provided under the contract or State law, in a timely manner as provided under State law and *section 108(b)*;

(9) any interest in cash or cash equivalents that constitute proceeds of a sale by the debtor of a money order that is made—

(A) on or after the date that is 14 days prior to the date on which the petition is filed; and

(B) under an agreement with a money order issuer that prohibits the commingling of such proceeds with property of the debtor (notwithstanding that, contrary to the agreement, the proceeds may have been commingled with property of the debtor),

unless the money order issuer had not taken action, prior to the filing of the petition, to require compliance with the prohibition; or

(10) funds placed in an account of a qualified ABLE program (as defined in section 529A(b) of the Internal Revenue Code of 1986) not later than 365 days before the date of the filing of the petition in a case under this title, but—

(A) only if the designated beneficiary of such account was a child, stepchild, grandchild, or stepgrandchild of the debtor for the taxable year for which funds were placed in such account;

(B) only to the extent that such funds—

(i) are not pledged or promised to any entity in connection with any extension of credit; and

(ii) are not excess contributions (as described in section 4973(h) of the Internal Revenue Code of 1986); and

(C) in the case of funds placed in all such accounts having the same designated beneficiary not earlier than 720 days nor later than 365 days before such date, only so much of such funds as does not exceed $8,575.

Paragraph (4) shall not be construed to exclude from the estate any consideration the debtor retains, receives, or is entitled to receive for transferring an interest in liquid or gaseous hydrocarbons pursuant to a farmout agreement.

(c)

(1) Except as provided in paragraph (2) of this subsection, an interest of the debtor in property becomes property of the estate under subsection (a)(1), (a)(2), or (a)(5) of this section notwithstanding any provision in an agreement, transfer instrument, or applicable nonbankruptcy law—

(A) that restricts or conditions transfer of such interest by the debtor; or

(B) that is conditioned on the insolvency or financial condition of the debtor, on the commencement of a case under this title, or on the appointment of or taking possession by a trustee in a case under this title or a custodian before such commencement, and that effects or gives an option to effect a forfeiture, modification, or termination of the debtor's interest in property.

(2) A restriction on the transfer of a beneficial interest of the debtor in a trust that is enforceable under applicable nonbankruptcy law is enforceable in a case under this title.

(d) Property in which the debtor holds, as of the commencement of the case, only legal title and not an equitable interest, such as a mortgage secured by real property, or an interest in such a mortgage, sold by the debtor but as to which the debtor retains legal title to service or supervise the servicing of such mortgage or interest, becomes property of the estate under subsection (a)(1) or (2) of this section only to the extent of the debtor's legal title to such property, but not to the extent of any equitable interest in such property that the debtor does not hold.

(e) In determining whether any of the relationships specified in paragraph (5)(A) or (6)(A) of subsection (b) exists, a legally adopted child of an individual (and a child who is a member of an individual's household, if placed with such individual by an authorized placement agency for legal adoption by such individual), or a foster child of an individual (if such child has as the child's principal place of abode the home of the debtor and is a member of the debtor's household) shall be treated as a child of such individual by blood.

(f) Notwithstanding any other provision of this title, property that is held by a debtor that is a corporation described in *section 501(c)(3)* of the Internal Revenue Code of 1986 and exempt from tax under *section 501(a)* of such Code may be transferred to an entity that is not such a corporation, but only under the same conditions as would apply if the debtor had not filed a case under this title.

(Pub. L. 95–598, Nov. 6, 1978, 92 Stat. 2594; Pub. L. 98–353, title III, §§ 363(a), 456, July 10, 1984, 98 Stat. 363, 376; Pub. L. 101–508, title III, § 3007(a)(2), Nov. 5, 1990, 104 Stat. 1388–28; Pub. L. 102–486, title XXX, § 3017(b), Oct. 24, 1992, 106 Stat. 3130; Pub. L. 103–394, title II, §§ 208(b), 223, Oct. 22, 1994, 108 Stat. 4124, 4129; Pub. L. 109–8, title II, § 225(a), title III, § 323, title XII, §§ 1212, 1221(c), 1230, Apr. 20, 2005, 119 Stat. 65, 97, 194, 196, 201; Pub. L. 111–327, § 2(a)(22), Dec. 22, 2010, 124 Stat. 3560; Pub. L. 113–295, div. B, title I, § 104(a), Dec. 19, 2014, 128 Stat. 4063; Pub. L. 116–260, div. FF, title X, § 1001(a), Dec. 27, 2020, 134 Stat. 3216; Pub. L. 119–27, § 11(e), July 18, 2025, 139 Stat. 458.)

Sections that reference this section: 101, 1115, 1186, 1207, 1306, 1505, 1528, 365, 522, 524, 726

§542. Turnover of property to the estate

(a) Except as provided in subsection (c) or (d) of this section, an entity, other than a custodian, in possession, custody, or control, during the case, of property that the trustee may use, sell, or lease under *section 363* of this title, or that the debtor may exempt under *section 522* of this title, shall deliver to the trustee, and account for, such property or the value of such property, unless such property is of inconsequential value or benefit to the estate.

(b) Except as provided in subsection (c) or (d) of this section, an entity that owes a debt that is property of the estate and that is matured, payable on demand, or payable on order, shall pay such debt to, or on the order of, the trustee, except to the extent that such debt may be offset under *section 553* of this title against a claim against the debtor.

(c) Except as provided in *section 362(a)(7)* of this title, an entity that has neither actual notice nor actual knowledge of the commencement of the case concerning the debtor may transfer property of the estate, or pay a debt owing to the debtor, in good faith and other than in the manner specified in subsection (d) of this section, to an entity other than the trustee, with the same effect as to the entity making such transfer or payment as if the case under this title concerning the debtor had not been commenced.

(d) A life insurance company may transfer property of the estate or property of the debtor to such company in good faith, with the same effect with respect to such company as if the case under this title concerning the debtor had not been commenced, if such transfer is to pay a premium or to carry out a nonforfeiture insurance option, and is required to be made automatically, under a life insurance contract with such company that was entered into before the date of the filing of the petition and that is property of the estate.

(e) Subject to any applicable privilege, after notice and a hearing, the court may order an attorney, accountant, or other person that holds recorded information, including books, documents, records, and papers, relating to the debtor's property or financial affairs, to turn over or disclose such recorded information to the trustee.

(Pub. L. 95–598, Nov. 6, 1978, 92 Stat. 2595; Pub. L. 98–353, title III, § 457, July 10, 1984, 98 Stat. 376; Pub. L. 103–394, title V, § 501(d)(16), Oct. 22, 1994, 108 Stat. 4146.)

Sections that reference this section: 342, 502, 522

§543. Turnover of property by a custodian

(a) A custodian with knowledge of the commencement of a case under this title concerning the debtor may not make any disbursement from, or take any action in the administration of, property of the debtor, proceeds, product, offspring, rents, or profits of such property, or property of the estate, in the possession, custody, or control of such custodian, except such action as is necessary to preserve such property.

(b) A custodian shall—

(1) deliver to the trustee any property of the debtor held by or transferred to such custodian, or proceeds, product, offspring, rents, or profits of such property, that is in such custodian's possession, custody, or control on the date that such custodian acquires

knowledge of the commencement of the case; and

(2) file an accounting of any property of the debtor, or proceeds, product, offspring, rents, or profits of such property, that, at any time, came into the possession, custody, or control of such custodian.

(c) The court, after notice and a hearing, shall—

(1) protect all entities to which a custodian has become obligated with respect to such property or proceeds, product, offspring, rents, or profits of such property;

(2) provide for the payment of reasonable compensation for services rendered and costs and expenses incurred by such custodian; and

(3) surcharge such custodian, other than an assignee for the benefit of the debtor's creditors that was appointed or took possession more than 120 days before the date of the filing of the petition, for any improper or excessive disbursement, other than a disbursement that has been made in accordance with applicable law or that has been approved, after notice and a hearing, by a court of competent jurisdiction before the commencement of the case under this title.

(d) After notice and hearing, the bankruptcy court —

(1) may excuse compliance with subsection (a), (b), or (c) of this section if the interests of creditors and, if the debtor is not insolvent, of equity security holders would be better served by permitting a custodian to continue in possession, custody, or control of such property, and

(2) shall excuse compliance with subsections (a) and (b)(1) of this section if the custodian is an assignee for the benefit of the debtor's creditors that was appointed or took possession more than 120 days before the date of the filing of the petition, unless compliance with such subsections is necessary to prevent fraud or injustice.

(Pub. L. 95–598, Nov. 6, 1978, 92 Stat. 2595; Pub. L. 98–353, title III, § 458, July 10, 1984, 98 Stat. 376; Pub. L. 103–394, title V, § 501(d)(17), Oct. 22, 1994, 108 Stat. 4146.)

Sections that reference this section: 349, 503, 726

§544. Trustee as lien creditor and as successor to certain creditors and purchasers

(a) The trustee shall have, as of the commencement of the case, and without regard to any knowledge of the trustee or of any creditor, the rights and powers of, or may avoid any transfer of property of the debtor or any obligation incurred by the debtor that is voidable by—

(1) a creditor that extends credit to the debtor at the time of the commencement of the case, and that obtains, at such time and with respect to such credit, a judicial lien on all property on which a creditor on a simple contract could have obtained such a judicial lien, whether or not such a creditor exists;

(2) a creditor that extends credit to the debtor at the time of the commencement of the case, and obtains, at such time and with respect to such credit, an execution against the debtor that is returned unsatisfied at such time, whether or not such a creditor exists; or

(3) a bona fide purchaser of real property, other than fixtures, from the debtor, against whom applicable law permits such transfer to be perfected, that obtains the status of a bona fide purchaser and has perfected such transfer at the time of the commencement of the case, whether or not such a purchaser exists.

(b)

(1) Except as provided in paragraph (2), the trustee may avoid any transfer of an interest of the debtor in property or any obligation incurred by the debtor that is voidable under applicable law by a creditor holding an unsecured claim that is allowable under *section 502* of this title or that is not allowable only under *section 502(e)* of this title.

(2) Paragraph (1) shall not apply to a transfer of a charitable contribution (as that term is defined in *section 548(d)(3)*) that is not covered under *section 548(a)(1)(B)*, by reason of *section 548(a)(2)*. Any claim by any person to recover a transferred contribution described in the preceding sentence under Federal or State law in a Federal or State court shall be preempted by the commencement of the case.

(Pub. L. 95–598, Nov. 6, 1978, 92 Stat. 2596; Pub. L. 98–353, title III, § 459, July 10, 1984, 98 Stat. 377; Pub. L. 105–183, § 3(b), June 19, 1998, 112 Stat. 518.)

Sections that reference this section: 303, 362, 522, 546, 548, 550, 749, 764, 926

§545. Statutory liens

The trustee may avoid the fixing of a statutory lien on property of the debtor to the extent that such lien—

(1) first becomes effective against the debtor—

(A) when a case under this title concerning the debtor is commenced;

(B) when an insolvency proceeding other than under this title concerning the debtor is commenced;

(C) when a custodian is appointed or authorized to take or takes possession;

(D) when the debtor becomes insolvent;

(E) when the debtor's financial condition fails to meet a specified standard; or

(F) at the time of an execution against property of the debtor levied at the instance of an entity other than the holder of such statutory lien;

(2) is not perfected or enforceable at the time of the commencement of the case against a bona fide purchaser that purchases such property at the time of the commencement of the case, whether or not such a purchaser exists, except in any case in which a purchaser is a purchaser described in section 6323 of the Internal Revenue Code of 1986, or in any other similar provision of State or local law;

(3) is for rent; or

(4) is a lien of distress for rent.

(Pub. L. 95–598, Nov. 6, 1978, 92 Stat. 2597; Pub. L. 98–353, title III, § 460, July 10, 1984, 98 Stat. 377; Pub. L. 109–8, title VII, § 711, Apr. 20, 2005, 119 Stat. 127.)

Sections that reference this section: 546, 547

§546. Limitations on avoiding powers

(a) An action or proceeding under *section 544, 545, 547, 548,* or *553* of this title may not be commenced after the earlier of—

(1) the later of—

(A) 2 years after the entry of the order for relief; or

(B) 1 year after the appointment or election of the first trustee under *section 702, 1104, 1163, 1202,* or *1302* of this title if such appointment or such election occurs before the expiration of the period specified in subparagraph (A); or

(2) the time the case is closed or dismissed.

(b)

(1) The rights and powers of a trustee under *sections 544, 545,* and *549* of this title are subject to any generally applicable law that —

(A) permits perfection of an interest in property to be effective against an entity that acquires rights in such property before the date of perfection; or

(B) provides for the maintenance or continuation of perfection of an interest in property to be effective against an entity that acquires rights in such property before the date on which action is taken to effect such maintenance or continuation.

(2) If—

(A) a law described in paragraph (1) requires seizure of such property or commencement of an action to accomplish such perfection, or maintenance or continuation of perfection of an interest in property; and

(B) such property has not been seized or such an action has not been commenced before the date of the filing of the petition;

such interest in such property shall be perfected, or perfection of such interest shall be maintained or continued, by giving notice within the time fixed by such law for such seizure or such commencement.

(c)

(1) Except as provided in subsection (d) of this section and in *section 507(c),* and subject to the prior rights of a holder of a security interest in such goods or the proceeds thereof, the rights and powers of the trustee under *sections 544(a), 545, 547,* and *549* are subject to the right of a seller of goods that has sold goods to the debtor, in the ordinary course of such seller's business, to reclaim such goods if the debtor has received such goods while insolvent, within 45 days before the date of the commencement of a case under this title, but such seller may not reclaim such goods unless such seller

demands in writing reclamation of such goods—

(A) not later than 45 days after the date of receipt of such goods by the debtor; or

(B) not later than 20 days after the date of commencement of the case, if the 45-day period expires after the commencement of the case.

(2) If a seller of goods fails to provide notice in the manner described in paragraph (1), the seller still may assert the rights contained in *section 503(b)(9)*.

(d) In the case of a seller who is a producer of grain sold to a grain storage facility, owned or operated by the debtor, in the ordinary course of such seller's business (as such terms are defined in *section 557* of this title) or in the case of a United States fisherman who has caught fish sold to a fish processing facility owned or operated by the debtor in the ordinary course of such fisherman's business, the rights and powers of the trustee under *sections 544(a), 545, 547,* and *549* of this title are subject to any statutory or common law right of such producer or fisherman to reclaim such grain or fish if the debtor has received such grain or fish while insolvent, but—

(1) such producer or fisherman may not reclaim any grain or fish unless such producer or fisherman demands, in writing, reclamation of such grain or fish before ten days after receipt thereof by the debtor; and

(2) the court may deny reclamation to such a producer or fisherman with a right of reclamation that has made such a demand only if the court secures such claim by a lien.

(e) Notwithstanding *sections 544, 545, 547, 548*(a)(1)(B), and 548(b) of this title, the trustee may not avoid a transfer that is a margin payment, as defined in *section 101, 741,* or *761* of this title, or settlement payment, as defined in *section 101* or *741* of this title, made by or to (or for the benefit of) a commodity broker, forward contract merchant, stockbroker, financial institution, financial participant, or securities clearing agency, or that is a transfer made by or to (or for the benefit of) a commodity broker, forward contract merchant, stockbroker, financial institution, financial participant, or securities clearing agency, in connection with a securities contract, as defined in *section 741(7)*, commodity contract, as defined in *section 761(4)*, or forward contract, that is made before the commencement of the case, except under *section 548(a)(1)(A)* of this title.

(f) Notwithstanding *sections 544, 545, 547, 548*(a)(1)(B), and 548(b) of this title, the trustee may not avoid a transfer made by or to (or for the benefit of) a repo participant or financial participant, in connection with a repurchase agreement and that is made before the commencement of the case, except under *section 548(a)(1)(A)* of this title.

(g) Notwithstanding *sections 544, 545, 547, 548*(a)(1)(B) and 548(b) of this title, the trustee may not avoid a transfer, made by or to (or for the benefit of) a swap participant or financial participant, under or in connection with any swap agreement and that is made before the commencement of the case, except under *section 548(a)(1)(A)* of this title.

(h) Notwithstanding the rights and powers of a trustee under *sections 544(a), 545, 547, 549,* and *553,* if the court determines on a motion by the trustee made not later than 120 days after the date of the order for relief in a case under chapter 11 of this title and after notice and a hearing, that a return is in the best interests of the estate, the debtor, with the consent of a creditor and subject to the prior rights of holders of security interests in such goods or the proceeds of such goods, may return goods shipped to the debtor by the creditor before the commencement of the case, and the creditor may offset the purchase price of such goods against any claim of the creditor against the debtor that arose before the commencement of the case.

(i)

(1) Notwithstanding paragraphs (2) and (3) of *section 545*, the trustee may not avoid a warehouseman's lien for storage, transportation, or other costs incidental to the storage and handling of goods.

(2) The prohibition under paragraph (1) shall be applied in a manner consistent with any State statute applicable to such lien that is similar to section 7–209 of the Uniform Commercial Code, as in effect on the date of enactment of the Bankruptcy Abuse Prevention and Consumer Protection Act of 2005, or any successor to such section 7–209.

(j) Notwithstanding *sections 544, 545, 547, 548*(a)(1)(B), and 548(b) the trustee may not avoid a transfer made by or to (or for the benefit of) a master netting agreement participant under or in connection with any master netting agreement or any individual contract covered thereby that is made before the commencement of the case, except under *section 548(a)(1)(A)* and except to the extent that the trustee could otherwise avoid such a transfer made under an individual contract covered by such master netting agreement.

(Pub. L. 95–598, Nov. 6, 1978, 92 Stat. 2597; Pub. L. 97–222, § 4, July 27, 1982, 96 Stat. 236; Pub. L. 98–353, title III, §§ 351, 393, 461, July 10, 1984, 98 Stat. 358, 365, 377; Pub. L. 99–554, title II, §§ 257(d), 283(l), Oct. 27, 1986, 100 Stat. 3114, 3117; Pub. L. 101–311, title I, § 103, title II, § 203, June 25, 1990, 104 Stat. 268, 269; Pub. L. 103–394, title II, §§ 204(b), 209, 216, 222(a), title V, § 501(b)(4), Oct. 22, 1994, 108 Stat. 4122, 4125, 4126, 4129, 4142; Pub. L. 105–183, § 3(c), June 19, 1998, 112 Stat. 518; Pub. L. 109–8, title IV, § 406, title IX, § 907(e), (o)(2), (3), title XII, § 1227(a), Apr. 20, 2005, 119 Stat. 105, 177, 182, 199; Pub. L. 109–390, § 5(b), Dec. 12, 2006, 120 Stat. 2697.)

Sections that reference this section: 362, 552

§547. Preferences

(a) In this section—

(1) "inventory" means personal property leased or furnished, held for sale or lease, or to be furnished under a contract for service, raw materials, work in process, or materials used or consumed in a business, including farm products such as crops or livestock, held for sale or lease;

(2) "new value" means money or money's worth in goods, services, or new credit, or release by a transferee of property previously transferred to such transferee in a transaction that is neither void nor voidable by the debtor or the trustee under any applicable law, including proceeds of such property, but does not include an obligation substituted for an existing obligation;

(3) "receivable" means right to payment, whether or not such right has been earned by performance; and

(4) a debt for a tax is incurred on the day when such tax is last payable without penalty, including any extension.

(b) Except as provided in subsections (c) and (i) of this section, the trustee may, based on reasonable due diligence in the circumstances of the case and taking into account a party's known or reasonably knowable affirmative defenses under subsection (c), avoid any transfer of an interest of the debtor in property—

(1) to or for the benefit of a creditor;

(2) for or on account of an antecedent debt owed by the debtor before such transfer was made;

(3) made while the debtor was insolvent;

(4) made—

(A) on or within 90 days before the date of the filing of the petition; or

(B) between ninety days and one year before the date of the filing of the petition, if such creditor at the time of such transfer was an insider; and

(5) that enables such creditor to receive more than such creditor would receive if—

(A) the case were a case under chapter 7 of this title;

(B) the transfer had not been made; and

(C) such creditor received payment of such debt to the extent provided by the provisions of this title.

(c) The trustee may not avoid under this section a transfer—

(1) to the extent that such transfer was—

(A) intended by the debtor and the creditor to or for whose benefit such transfer was made to be a contemporaneous exchange for new value given to the debtor; and

(B) in fact a substantially contemporaneous exchange;

(2) to the extent that such transfer was in payment of a debt incurred by the debtor in the ordinary course of business or financial affairs of the debtor and the transferee, and such transfer was—

(A) made in the ordinary course of business or financial affairs of the debtor and the transferee; or

(B) made according to ordinary business terms;

(3) that creates a security interest in property acquired by the debtor—

(A) to the extent such security interest secures new value that was—

(i) given at or after the signing of a security agreement that contains a description of such property as collateral;

(ii) given by or on behalf of the secured party under such agreement;

(iii) given to enable the debtor to acquire such property; and

(iv) in fact used by the debtor to acquire such property; and

(B) that is perfected on or before 30 days after the debtor receives possession of such property;

(4) to or for the benefit of a creditor, to the extent that, after such transfer, such creditor gave new value to or for the benefit of the debtor—

(A) not secured by an otherwise unavoidable security interest; and

(B) on account of which new value the debtor did not make an otherwise unavoidable transfer to or for the benefit of such creditor;

(5) that creates a perfected security interest in inventory or a receivable or the proceeds of either, except to the extent that the aggregate of all such transfers to the transferee caused a reduction, as of the date of the filing of the petition and to the prejudice of other creditors holding unsecured claims, of any amount by which the debt secured by such security interest exceeded the value of all security interests for such debt on the later of—

(A)

(i) with respect to a transfer to which subsection (b)(4)(A) of this section applies, 90 days before the date of the filing of the petition; or

(ii) with respect to a transfer to which subsection (b)(4)(B) of this section applies, one year before the date of the filing of the petition; or

(B) the date on which new value was first given under the security agreement creating such security interest;

(6) that is the fixing of a statutory lien that is not avoidable under *section 545* of this title;

(7) to the extent such transfer was a bona fide payment of a debt for a domestic support obligation;

(8) if, in a case filed by an individual debtor whose debts are primarily consumer debts, the aggregate value of all property that constitutes or is affected by such transfer is less than $600; or

(9) if, in a case filed by a debtor whose debts are not primarily consumer debts, the aggregate value of all property that constitutes or is affected by such transfer is less than $8,575.

(d) The trustee may avoid a transfer of an interest in property of the debtor transferred to or for the benefit of a surety to secure reimbursement of such a surety that furnished a bond or other obligation to dissolve a judicial lien that would have been avoidable by the trustee under subsection (b) of this section. The liability of such surety under such bond or obligation shall be discharged to the extent of the value of such property recovered by the trustee or the amount paid to the trustee.

(e)

(1) For the purposes of this section—

(A) a transfer of real property other than fixtures, but including the interest of a seller or purchaser under a contract for the sale of real property, is perfected when a bona fide purchaser of such property from the debtor against whom applicable law permits such transfer to be perfected cannot acquire an interest that is superior to the interest of the transferee; and

(B) a transfer of a fixture or property other than real property is perfected when a creditor on a simple contract cannot acquire a judicial lien that is superior to the interest of the transferee.

(2) For the purposes of this section, except as provided in paragraph (3) of this subsection, a transfer is made—

(A) at the time such transfer takes effect between the transferor and the transferee, if such transfer is perfected at, or within 30 days after, such time, except as provided in subsection (c)(3)(B);

(B) at the time such transfer is perfected, if such transfer is perfected after such 30 days; or

(C) immediately before the date of the filing of the petition, if such transfer is not perfected at the later of—

(i) the commencement of the case; or

(ii) 30 days after such transfer takes effect between the transferor and the transferee.

(3) For the purposes of this section, a transfer is not made until the debtor has acquired rights in the property transferred.

(f) For the purposes of this section, the debtor is presumed to have been insolvent on and during the 90 days immediately preceding the date of the filing of the petition.

(g) For the purposes of this section, the trustee has the burden of proving the avoidability of a transfer under subsection (b) of this section, and the creditor or party in interest against whom recovery or avoidance is sought has the burden of proving the nonavoidability of a transfer under subsection (c) of this section.

(h) The trustee may not avoid a transfer if such transfer was made as a part of an alternative repayment schedule between the debtor and any creditor of the debtor created by an approved nonprofit budget and credit counseling agency.

(i) If the trustee avoids under subsection (b) a transfer made between 90 days and 1 year before the date of the filing of the petition, by the debtor to an entity that is not an insider for the benefit of a creditor that is an insider, such transfer shall be considered to be avoided under this section only with respect to the creditor that is an insider.

(Pub. L. 95–598, Nov. 6, 1978, 92 Stat. 2597; Pub. L. 98–353, title III, §§ 310, 462, July 10, 1984, 98 Stat. 355, 377; Pub. L. 99–554, title II, § 283(m), Oct. 27, 1986, 100 Stat. 3117; Pub. L. 103–394, title II, § 203, title III, § 304(f), Oct. 22, 1994, 108 Stat. 4121, 4133; Pub. L. 109–8, title II, §§ 201(b), 217, title IV, §§ 403, 409, title XII, §§ 1213(a), 1222, Apr. 20, 2005, 119 Stat. 42, 55, 104, 106, 194, 196; Pub. L. 116–54, § 3(a), Aug. 23, 2019, 133 Stat. 1085; Pub. L. 116–260, div. FF, title X, § 1001(g)(1), (2)(A), Dec. 27, 2020, 134 Stat. 3219, 3220.)

Sections that reference this section: 109, 362, 550, 926

§548. Fraudulent transfers and obligations

(a)

(1) The trustee may avoid any transfer (including any transfer to or for the benefit of an insider under an employment contract) of an interest of the debtor in property, or any obligation (including any obligation to or for the benefit of an insider under an employment contract) incurred by the debtor, that was made or incurred on or within 2 years before the date of the filing of the petition, if the debtor voluntarily or involuntarily—

(A) made such transfer or incurred such obligation with actual intent to hinder, delay, or defraud any entity to which the debtor was or became, on or after the date that such transfer was made or such obligation was incurred, indebted; or

(B)

(i) received less than a reasonably equivalent value in exchange for such transfer or obligation; and

(ii)

(I) was insolvent on the date that such transfer was made or such obligation was incurred, or became insolvent as a result of such transfer or obligation;

(II) was engaged in business or a transaction, or was about to engage in business or a transaction, for which any property remaining with the debtor was an unreasonably small capital;

(III) intended to incur, or believed that the debtor would incur, debts that would be beyond the debtor's ability to pay as such debts matured; or

(IV) made such transfer to or for the benefit of an insider, or incurred such obligation to or for the benefit of an insider, under an employment contract and not in the ordinary course of business.

(2) A transfer of a charitable contribution to a qualified religious or charitable entity or organization shall not be considered to be a transfer covered under paragraph (1)(B) in any case in which—

(A) the amount of that contribution does not exceed 15 percent of the gross annual income of the debtor for the year in which the transfer of the contribution is made; or

(B) the contribution made by a debtor exceeded the percentage amount of gross annual income specified in subparagraph (A), if the transfer was consistent with the practices of the debtor in making charitable contributions.

(b) The trustee of a partnership debtor may avoid any transfer of an interest of the debtor in property, or any obligation incurred by the debtor, that was made or incurred on or within 2 years before the date of the filing of the petition, to a general partner in the debtor, if the debtor was insolvent on the date such transfer was made or such obligation was incurred, or became insolvent as a result of such transfer or obligation.

(c) Except to the extent that a transfer or obligation voidable under this section is voidable under *section 544, 545,* or *547* of this title, a transferee or obligee of such a transfer or obligation that takes for value and in good faith has a lien on or may retain any interest transferred or may enforce any obligation incurred, as the case may be, to the extent that such transferee or obligee gave value to the debtor in exchange for such transfer or obligation.

(d)

(1) For the purposes of this section, a transfer is made when such transfer is so perfected that a bona fide purchaser from the debtor against whom applicable law permits such transfer to be perfected cannot acquire an interest in the property transferred that is superior to the interest in such property of the transferee, but if such transfer is not so perfected before the commencement of the case, such transfer is made immediately before the date of the filing of the petition.

(2) In this section—

(A) "value" means property, or satisfaction or securing of a present or antecedent debt of the debtor, but does not include an unperformed promise to furnish support to the debtor or to a relative of the debtor;

(B) a commodity broker, forward contract merchant, stockbroker, financial institution, financial participant, or securities clearing agency that receives a margin payment, as defined in *section 101, 741,* or *761* of this title, or settlement payment, as defined in *section 101* or *741* of this title, takes for value to the extent of such payment;

(C) a repo participant or financial participant that receives a margin payment, as defined in *section 741* or *761* of this title, or settlement payment, as defined in *section 741* of this title, in connection with a repurchase agreement, takes for value to the extent of such payment;

(D) a swap participant or financial participant that receives a transfer in connection with a swap agreement takes for value to the extent of such transfer; and

(E) a master netting agreement participant that receives a transfer in connection with a master netting agreement or any individual contract covered thereby takes for value to the extent of such transfer, except that, with respect to a transfer under any individual contract covered thereby, to the extent that such master netting agreement participant otherwise did not take (or is otherwise not deemed to have taken) such transfer for value.

(3) In this section, the term "charitable contribution" means a charitable contribution, as that term is defined in section 170(c) of the Internal Revenue Code of 1986, if that contribution—

(A) is made by a natural person; and

(B) consists of—

(i) a financial instrument (as that term is defined in section 731(c)(2)(C) of the Internal Revenue Code of 1986); or

(ii) cash.

(4) In this section, the term "qualified religious or charitable entity or organization" means —

(A) an entity described in section 170(c)(1) of the Internal Revenue Code of 1986; or

(B) an entity or organization described in section 170(c)(2) of the Internal Revenue Code of 1986.

(e)

(1) In addition to any transfer that the trustee may otherwise avoid, the trustee may avoid any transfer of an interest of the debtor in property that was made on or within 10 years before the date of the filing of the petition, if—

(A) such transfer was made to a self-settled trust or similar device;

(B) such transfer was by the debtor;

(C) the debtor is a beneficiary of such trust or similar device; and

(D) the debtor made such transfer with actual intent to hinder, delay, or defraud any entity to which the debtor was or became, on or after the date that such transfer was made, indebted.

(2) For the purposes of this subsection, a transfer includes a transfer made in anticipation of any money judgment, settlement, civil penalty, equitable order, or criminal fine incurred by, or which the debtor believed would be incurred by—

(A) any violation of the securities laws (as defined in section 3(a)(47) of the Securities Exchange Act of 1934 (15 U.S.C. 78c(a)(47))), any State securities laws, or any regulation or order issued under Federal securities laws or State securities laws; or

(B) fraud, deceit, or manipulation in a fiduciary capacity or in connection with the purchase or sale of any security registered under section 12 or 15(d) of the Securities Exchange Act of 1934 (15 U.S.C. 78_l *and 78_o*(d)) or under section 6 of the Securities Act of 1933 (15 U.S.C. 77f).

(Pub. L. 95–598, Nov. 6, 1978, 92 Stat. 2600; Pub. L. 97–222, § 5, July 27, 1982, 96 Stat. 236; Pub. L. 98–353, title III, §§ 394, 463, July 10, 1984, 98 Stat. 365, 378; Pub. L. 99–554, title II, § 283(n), Oct. 27, 1986, 100 Stat. 3117; Pub. L. 101–311, title I, § 104, title II, § 204, June 25, 1990, 104 Stat. 268, 269; Pub. L. 103–394, title V, § 501(b)(5), Oct. 22, 1994, 108 Stat. 4142; Pub. L. 105–183, §§ 2, 3(a), June 19, 1998, 112 Stat. 517; Pub. L. 109–8, title IX, § 907(f), (o)(4)–(6), title XIV, § 1402, Apr. 20, 2005, 119 Stat. 177, 182, 214.)

Sections that reference this section: 1325, 544, 546, 707

§549. Postpetition transactions

(a) Except as provided in subsection (b) or (c) of this section, the trustee may avoid a transfer of property of the estate—

(1) that occurs after the commencement of the case; and

(2)

(A) that is authorized only under *section 303(f)* or *542*(c) of this title; or

(B) that is not authorized under this title or by the court.

(b) In an involuntary case, the trustee may not avoid under subsection (a) of this section a transfer made after the commencement of such case but before the order for relief to the extent any value, including services, but not including satisfaction or securing of a debt that arose before the commencement of the case, is given after the commencement of the case in exchange for such transfer, notwithstanding any notice or knowledge of the case that the transferee has.

(c) The trustee may not avoid under subsection (a) of this section a transfer of an interest in real property to a good faith purchaser without knowledge of the commencement of the case and for present fair equivalent value unless a copy or notice of the petition was filed, where a transfer of an interest in such real property may be recorded to perfect such transfer, before such transfer is so perfected that a bona fide purchaser of such real property, against whom applicable law permits such transfer to be perfected, could not acquire an interest that is superior to such interest of such good faith purchaser. A good faith purchaser without knowledge of the commencement of the case and for less than present fair equivalent value has a lien on the property transferred to the extent of any present value given, unless a copy or notice of the petition was so filed before such transfer was so perfected.

(d) An action or proceeding under this section may not be commenced after the earlier of—

(1) two years after the date of the transfer sought to be avoided; or

(2) the time the case is closed or dismissed.

(Pub. L. 95–598, Nov. 6, 1978, 92 Stat. 2601; Pub. L. 98–353, title III, § 464, July 10, 1984, 98 Stat. 379; Pub. L. 99–554, title II, § 283(o), Oct. 27, 1986, 100 Stat. 3117; Pub. L. 103–394, title V, § 501(d)(18), Oct. 22, 1994, 108 Stat. 4146; Pub. L. 109–8, title XII, § 1214, Apr. 20, 2005, 119 Stat. 195.)

Sections that reference this section: 362

§550. Liability of transferee of avoided transfer

(a) Except as otherwise provided in this section, to the extent that a transfer is avoided under *section 544, 545, 547, 548, 549, 553*(b), or 724(a) of this title, the trustee may recover, for the benefit of the estate, the property transferred, or, if the court so orders, the value of such property, from —

(1) the initial transferee of such transfer or the entity for whose benefit such transfer was made; or

(2) any immediate or mediate transferee of such initial transferee.

(b) The trustee may not recover under section (a)(2) of this section from—

(1) a transferee that takes for value, including satisfaction or securing of a present or antecedent debt, in good faith, and without knowledge of the voidability of the transfer avoided; or

(2) any immediate or mediate good faith transferee of such transferee.

(c) If a transfer made between 90 days and one year before the filing of the petition—

(1) is avoided under *section 547(b)* of this title; and

(2) was made for the benefit of a creditor that at the time of such transfer was an insider;

the trustee may not recover under subsection (a) from a transferee that is not an insider.

(d) The trustee is entitled to only a single satisfaction under subsection (a) of this section.

(e)

(1) A good faith transferee from whom the trustee may recover under subsection (a) of this section has a lien on the property recovered to secure the lesser of—

(A) the cost, to such transferee, of any improvement made after the transfer, less the amount of any profit realized by or accruing to such transferee from such property; and

(B) any increase in the value of such property as a result of such improvement, of the property transferred.

(2) In this subsection, "improvement" includes —

(A) physical additions or changes to the property transferred;

(B) repairs to such property;

(C) payment of any tax on such property;

(D) payment of any debt secured by a lien on such property that is superior or equal to the rights of the trustee; and

(E) preservation of such property.

(f) An action or proceeding under this section may not be commenced after the earlier of—

(1) one year after the avoidance of the transfer on account of which recovery under this section is sought; or

(2) the time the case is closed or dismissed.

(Pub. L. 95–598, Nov. 6, 1978, 92 Stat. 2601; Pub. L. 98–353, title III, § 465, July 10, 1984, 98 Stat. 379; Pub. L. 103–394, title II, § 202, Oct. 22, 1994, 108 Stat. 4121.)

Sections that reference this section: 522

§551. Automatic preservation of avoided transfer

Any transfer avoided under *section 522, 544, 545, 547, 548, 549*, or 724(a) of this title, or any lien void under *section 506(d)* of this title, is preserved for the benefit of the estate but only with respect to property of the estate.

(Pub. L. 95–598, Nov. 6, 1978, 92 Stat. 2602.)

Sections that reference this section: 503, 522

§552. Postpetition effect of security interest

(a) Except as provided in subsection (b) of this section, property acquired by the estate or by the debtor after the commencement of the case is not subject to any lien resulting from any security agreement entered into by the debtor before the commencement of the case.

(b)

(1) Except as provided in *sections 363, 506*(c), 522, 544, 545, 547, and 548 of this title, if the debtor and an entity entered into a security agreement before the commencement of the case and if the security interest created by such security agreement extends to property of the debtor acquired before the commencement of the case and to proceeds, products, offspring, or profits of such property, then such security interest extends to such proceeds, products, offspring, or

profits acquired by the estate after the commencement of the case to the extent provided by such security agreement and by applicable nonbankruptcy law, except to any extent that the court, after notice and a hearing and based on the equities of the case, orders otherwise.

(2) Except as provided in *sections 363, 506*(c), 522, 544, 545, 547, and 548 of this title, and notwithstanding *section 546(b)* of this title, if the debtor and an entity entered into a security agreement before the commencement of the case and if the security interest created by such security agreement extends to property of the debtor acquired before the commencement of the case and to amounts paid as rents of such property or the fees, charges, accounts, or other payments for the use or occupancy of rooms and other public facilities in hotels, motels, or other lodging properties, then such security interest extends to such rents and such fees, charges, accounts, or other payments acquired by the estate after the commencement of the case to the extent provided in such security agreement, except to any extent that the court, after notice and a hearing and based on the equities of the case, orders otherwise.

(Pub. L. 95–598, Nov. 6, 1978, 92 Stat. 2602; Pub. L. 98–353, title III, § 466, July 10, 1984, 98 Stat. 380; Pub. L. 103–394, title II, § 214(a), Oct. 22, 1994, 108 Stat. 4126; Pub. L. 109–8, title XII, § 1204(2), Apr. 20, 2005, 119 Stat. 194.)

Sections that reference this section: 1520, 363, 928

§553. Setoff

(a) Except as otherwise provided in this section and in *sections 362* and *363* of this title, this title does not affect any right of a creditor to offset a mutual debt owing by such creditor to the debtor that arose before the commencement of the case under this title against a claim of such creditor against the debtor that arose before the commencement of the case, except to the extent that—

(1) the claim of such creditor against the debtor is disallowed;

(2) such claim was transferred, by an entity other than the debtor, to such creditor—

(A) after the commencement of the case; or

(B)

(i) after 90 days before the date of the filing of the petition; and

(ii) while the debtor was insolvent (except for a setoff of a kind described in *section 362(b)(6), 362*(b)(7), 362(b)(17), 362(b)(27), 555, 556, 559, 560, or 561); or

(3) the debt owed to the debtor by such creditor was incurred by such creditor—

(A) after 90 days before the date of the filing of the petition;

(B) while the debtor was insolvent; and

(C) for the purpose of obtaining a right of setoff against the debtor (except for a setoff of a kind described in *section 362(b)(6), 362*(b)(7), 362(b)(17), 362(b)(27), 555, 556, 559, 560, or 561).

(b)

(1) Except with respect to a setoff of a kind described in *section 362(b)(6), 362*(b)(7), 362(b)(17), 362(b)(27), 555, 556, 559, 560, 561, 365(h), 546(h), or 365(i)(2) of this title, if a creditor offsets a mutual debt owing to the debtor against a claim against the debtor on or within 90 days before the date of the filing of the petition, then the trustee may recover from such creditor the amount so offset to the extent that any insufficiency on the date of such setoff is less than the insufficiency on the later of—

(A) 90 days before the date of the filing of the petition; and

(B) the first date during the 90 days immediately preceding the date of the filing of the petition on which there is an insufficiency.

(2) In this subsection, "insufficiency" means amount, if any, by which a claim against the debtor exceeds a mutual debt owing to the debtor by the holder of such claim.

(c) For the purposes of this section, the debtor is presumed to have been insolvent on and during the 90 days immediately preceding the date of the filing of the petition.

(Pub. L. 95–598, Nov. 6, 1978, 92 Stat. 2602; Pub. L. 98–353, title III, §§ 395, 467, July 10, 1984, 98 Stat. 365, 380; Pub. L. 101–311, title I, § 105, June 25, 1990, 104 Stat. 268; Pub. L. 103–394, title II, §§ 205(b), 222(b), title V, § 501(d)(19), Oct. 22, 1994, 108 Stat. 4123, 4129, 4146; Pub. L. 109–8, title IX, § 907(n), Apr. 20, 2005, 119 Stat. 181.)

Sections that reference this section: 506, 522, 542

§554. Abandonment of property of the estate

(a) After notice and a hearing, the trustee may abandon any property of the estate that is burdensome to the estate or that is of inconsequential value and benefit to the estate.

(b) On request of a party in interest and after notice and a hearing, the court may order the trustee to abandon any property of the estate that is burdensome to the estate or that is of inconsequential value and benefit to the estate.

(c) Unless the court orders otherwise, any property scheduled under *section 521(a)(1)* of this title not otherwise administered at the time of the closing of a case is abandoned to the debtor and administered for purposes of *section 350* of this title.

(d) Unless the court orders otherwise, property of the estate that is not abandoned under this section and that is not administered in the case remains property of the estate.

(Pub. L. 95–598, Nov. 6, 1978, 92 Stat. 2603; Pub. L. 98–353, title III, § 468, July 10, 1984, 98 Stat. 380; Pub. L. 99–554, title II, § 283(p), Oct. 27, 1986, 100 Stat. 3118; Pub. L. 111–327, § 2(a)(23), Dec. 22, 2010, 124 Stat. 3560.)

Sections that reference this section: 722

§555. Contractual right to liquidate, terminate, or accelerate a securities contract

The exercise of a contractual right of a stockbroker, financial institution, financial participant, or securities clearing agency to cause the liquidation, termination, or acceleration of a securities contract, as defined in *section 741* of this title, because of a condition of the kind specified in *section 365(e)(1)* of this title shall not be stayed, avoided, or otherwise limited by operation of any provision of this title or by order of a court or administrative agency in any proceeding under this title unless such order is authorized under the provisions of the Securities Investor Protection Act of 1970 or any statute administered by the Securities and Exchange Commission. As used in this section, the term "contractual right" includes a right set forth in a rule or bylaw of a derivatives clearing organization (as defined in the Commodity Exchange Act), a multilateral clearing organization (as defined in the Federal Deposit Insurance Corporation Improvement Act of 1991), a national securities exchange, a national securities association, a securities clearing agency, a contract market designated under the Commodity Exchange Act, a derivatives transaction execution facility registered under the Commodity Exchange Act, or a board of trade (as defined in the Commodity Exchange Act), or in a resolution of the governing board thereof, and a right, whether or not in writing, arising under common law, under law merchant, or by reason of normal business practice.

(Added Pub. L. 97–222, § 6(a), July 27, 1982, 96 Stat. 236; amended Pub. L. 98–353, title III, § 469, July 10, 1984, 98 Stat. 380; Pub. L. 103–394, title V, § 501(b)(6), (d)(20), Oct. 22, 1994, 108 Stat. 4143, 4146; Pub. L. 109–8, title IX, § 907(g), (o)(7), Apr. 20, 2005, 119 Stat. 177, 182.)

Sections that reference this section: 362, 561

§556. Contractual right to liquidate, terminate, or accelerate a commodities contract or forward contract

The contractual right of a commodity broker, financial participant, or forward contract merchant to cause the liquidation, termination, or acceleration of a commodity contract, as defined in *section 761* of this title, or forward contract because of a condition of the kind specified in *section 365(e)(1)* of this title, and the right to a variation or maintenance margin payment received from a trustee with respect to open commodity contracts or forward contracts, shall not be stayed, avoided, or otherwise limited by operation of any provision of this title or by the order of a court in any proceeding under this title. As used in this section, the term "contractual right" includes a right set forth in a rule or bylaw of a derivatives clearing organization (as defined in the Commodity Exchange Act), a multilateral clearing organization (as defined in the Federal Deposit Insurance Corporation Improvement Act of 1991), a national securities exchange, a national securities association, a securities clearing agency, a contract market designated under the Commodity Exchange Act, a derivatives transaction execution facility registered under the Commodity Exchange Act, or a board of trade (as defined in the Commodity Exchange Act) or in a resolution of the governing board thereof and a right, whether or not evidenced in writing, arising under common law, under law merchant or by reason of normal business practice.

(Added Pub. L. 97–222, § 6(a), July 27, 1982, 96 Stat. 236; amended Pub. L. 101–311, title II, § 205, June 25, 1990, 104 Stat. 270; Pub. L. 103–394, title V, § 501(b)(7), Oct. 22, 1994, 108 Stat. 4143; Pub. L. 109–8, title IX, §§ 907(h), (o)(8), Apr. 20, 2005, 119 Stat. 178, 182.)

Sections that reference this section: None

§557. Expedited determination of interests in, and abandonment or other disposition of grain assets

(a) This section applies only in a case concerning a debtor that owns or operates a grain storage facility and only with respect to grain and the proceeds of grain. This section does not affect the application of any other section of this title to property other than grain and proceeds of grain.

(b) In this section—

(1) "grain" means wheat, corn, flaxseed, grain sorghum, barley, oats, rye, soybeans, other dry edible beans, or rice;

(2) "grain storage facility" means a site or physical structure regularly used to store grain for producers, or to store grain acquired from producers for resale; and

(3) "producer" means an entity which engages in the growing of grain.

(c)

(1) Notwithstanding *sections 362, 363, 365,* and *554* of this title, on the court's own motion the court may, and on the request of the trustee or an entity that claims an interest in grain or the proceeds of grain the court shall, expedite the procedures for the determination of interests in and the disposition of grain and the proceeds of grain, by shortening to the greatest extent feasible such time periods as are otherwise applicable for such procedures and by establishing, by order, a timetable having a duration of not to exceed 120 days for the completion of the applicable procedure specified in subsection (d) of this section. Such time periods and such timetable may be modified by the court, for cause, in accordance with subsection (f) of this section.

(2) The court shall determine the extent to which such time periods shall be shortened, based upon—

(A) any need of an entity claiming an interest in such grain or the proceeds of grain for a prompt determination of such interest;

(B) any need of such entity for a prompt disposition of such grain;

(C) the market for such grain;

(D) the conditions under which such grain is stored;

(E) the costs of continued storage or disposition of such grain;

(F) the orderly administration of the estate;

(G) the appropriate opportunity for an entity to assert an interest in such grain; and

(H) such other considerations as are relevant to the need to expedite such procedures in the case.

(d) The procedures that may be expedited under subsection (c) of this section include—

(1) the filing of and response to—

(A) a claim of ownership;

(B) a proof of claim;

(C) a request for abandonment;

(D) a request for relief from the stay of action against property under *section 362(a)* of this title;

(E) a request for determination of secured status;

(F) a request for determination of whether such grain or the proceeds of grain—

(i) is property of the estate;

(ii) must be turned over to the estate; or

(iii) may be used, sold, or leased; and

(G) any other request for determination of an interest in such grain or the proceeds of grain;

(2) the disposition of such grain or the proceeds of grain, before or after determination of interests in such grain or the proceeds of grain, by way of—

(A) sale of such grain;

(B) abandonment;

(C) distribution; or

(D) such other method as is equitable in the case;

(3) subject to *sections 701, 702, 703, 1104, 1183, 1202,* and 1302 of this title, the appointment of a trustee or examiner and the retention and compensation of any professional person required to assist with respect to matters relevant to the determination of interests in or disposition of such grain or the proceeds of grain; and

(4) the determination of any dispute concerning a matter specified in paragraph (1), (2), or (3) of this subsection.

(e)

(1) Any governmental unit that has regulatory jurisdiction over the operation or liquidation of the debtor or the debtor's business shall be given notice of any request made or order entered under subsection (c) of this section.

(2) Any such governmental unit may raise, and may appear and be heard on, any issue relating to grain or the proceeds of grain in a case in which a request is made, or an order is entered, under subsection (c) of this section.

(3) The trustee shall consult with such governmental unit before taking any action relating to the disposition of grain in the possession, custody, or control of the debtor or the estate.

(f) The court may extend the period for final disposition of grain or the proceeds of grain under this section beyond 120 days if the court finds that—

(1) the interests of justice so require in light of the complexity of the case; and

(2) the interests of those claimants entitled to distribution of grain or the proceeds of grain will not be materially injured by such additional delay.

(g) Unless an order establishing an expedited procedure under subsection (c) of this section, or determining any interest in or approving any disposition of grain or the proceeds of grain, is stayed pending appeal—

(1) the reversal or modification of such order on appeal does not affect the validity of any procedure, determination, or disposition that occurs before such reversal or modification, whether or not any entity knew of the pendency of the appeal; and

(2) neither the court nor the trustee may delay, due to the appeal of such order, any proceeding in the case in which such order is issued.

(h)

(1) The trustee may recover from grain and the proceeds of grain the reasonable and necessary costs and expenses allowable under *section 503(b)* of this title attributable to preserving or disposing of grain or the proceeds of grain, but may not recover from such grain or the proceeds of grain any other costs or expenses.

(2) Notwithstanding *section 326(a)* of this title, the dollar amounts of money specified in such section include the value, as of the date of disposition, of any grain that the trustee distributes in kind.

(i) In all cases where the quantity of a specific type of grain held by a debtor operating a grain storage facility exceeds ten thousand bushels, such grain shall be sold by the trustee and the assets thereof distributed in accordance with the provisions of this section.

(Added Pub. L. 98–353, title III, § 352(a), July 10, 1984, 98 Stat. 359; amended Pub. L. 99–554, title II, § 257(p), Oct. 27, 1986, 100 Stat. 3115; Pub. L. 116–54, § 4(a)(10), Aug. 23, 2019, 133 Stat. 1086.)

Sections that reference this section: 507, 546

§558. Defenses of the estate

The estate shall have the benefit of any defense available to the debtor as against any entity other than the estate, including statutes of limitation, statutes of frauds, usury, and other personal defenses. A waiver of any such defense by the debtor after the commencement of the case does not bind the estate.

(Added Pub. L. 98–353, title III, § 470(a), July 10, 1984, 98 Stat. 380.)

Sections that reference this section: None

§559. Contractual right to liquidate, terminate, or accelerate a repurchase agreement

The exercise of a contractual right of a repo participant or financial participant to cause the liquidation, termination, or acceleration of a repurchase agreement because of a condition of the kind specified in *section 365(e)(1)* of this title shall not be stayed, avoided, or otherwise limited by operation of any provision of this title or by order of a court or administrative agency in any proceeding under this title, unless, where the debtor is a stockbroker or securities clearing agency, such order is authorized under the provisions of the Securities Investor Protection Act of 1970 or any statute administered by the Securities and Exchange Commission. In the event that a repo participant or financial participant liquidates one or more repurchase agreements with a debtor and under the terms of one or more such agreements has agreed to deliver assets subject to repurchase agreements to the debtor, any excess of the market prices received on liquidation of such assets (or if any such assets are not disposed of on the date of liquidation of such repurchase agreements, at the prices available at the time of liquidation of such repurchase agreements from a generally recognized source or the most recent closing bid quotation from such a source) over the sum of the stated repurchase prices and all expenses in connection with the liquidation of such repurchase agreements shall be deemed property of the estate, subject to the available rights of setoff. As used in this section, the term "contractual right" includes a right set forth in a rule or bylaw of a derivatives clearing organization (as defined in the Commodity Exchange Act), a multilateral clearing organization (as defined in the Federal Deposit Insurance Corporation Improvement Act of 1991), a national securities exchange, a national securities association, a securities clearing agency, a contract market designated under the Commodity Exchange Act, a derivatives transaction execution facility registered under the Commodity Exchange Act, or a board of trade (as defined in the Commodity Exchange Act) or in a resolution of the governing board thereof and a right, whether or not evidenced in writing, arising under common law, under law merchant or by reason of normal business practice.

(Added Pub. L. 98–353, title III, § 396(a), July 10, 1984, 98 Stat. 366; amended Pub. L. 103–394, title V, § 501(d)(21), Oct. 22, 1994, 108 Stat. 4146; Pub. L. 109–8, title IX, § 907(i), (o)(9), Apr. 20, 2005, 119 Stat. 178, 182.)

Sections that reference this section: 362

§560. Contractual right to liquidate, terminate, or accelerate a swap agreement

The exercise of any contractual right of any swap participant or financial participant to cause the liquidation, termination, or acceleration of one or more swap agreements because of a condition of the kind specified in *section 365(e)(1)* of this title or to offset or net out any termination values or payment amounts arising under or in connection with the termination, liquidation, or acceleration of one or more swap agreements shall not be stayed, avoided, or otherwise limited by operation of any provision of this title or by order of a court or administrative agency in any proceeding under this title. As used in this section, the term "contractual right" includes a right set forth in a rule or bylaw of a derivatives clearing organization (as defined in the Commodity Exchange Act), a multilateral clearing organization (as defined in the Federal Deposit Insurance Corporation Improvement Act of 1991), a national securities exchange, a national securities association, a securities clearing agency, a contract market designated under the Commodity Exchange Act, a derivatives transaction execution facility registered under the Commodity Exchange Act, or a board of trade (as defined in the Commodity Exchange Act) or in a resolution of the governing board thereof and a right, whether or not evidenced in writing, arising under common law, under law merchant, or by reason of normal business practice.

(Added Pub. L. 101–311, title I, § 106(a), June 25, 1990, 104 Stat. 268; amended Pub. L. 109–8, title IX, § 907(j), (o)(10), Apr. 20, 2005, 119 Stat. 178, 182.)

Sections that reference this section: 362

§561. Contractual right to terminate, liquidate, accelerate, or offset under a master netting agreement and across contracts; proceedings under chapter 15

(a) Subject to subsection (b), the exercise of any contractual right, because of a condition of the kind specified in *section 365(e)(1)*, to cause the termination, liquidation, or acceleration of or to offset or net termination values, payment amounts, or other transfer obligations arising under or in connection with one or more (or the termination, liquidation, or acceleration of one or more)—

(1) securities contracts, as defined in *section 741(7)*;

(2) commodity contracts, as defined in *section 761(4)*;

(3) forward contracts;

(4) repurchase agreements;

(5) swap agreements; or

(6) master netting agreements,

shall not be stayed, avoided, or otherwise limited by operation of any provision of this title or by any order of a court or administrative agency in any proceeding under this title.

(b)

(1) A party may exercise a contractual right described in subsection (a) to terminate, liquidate, or accelerate only to the extent that such party could exercise such a right under *section 555*, *556*, *559*, or *560* for each individual contract covered by the master netting agreement in issue.

(2) If a debtor is a commodity broker subject to subchapter IV of chapter 7—

(A) a party may not net or offset an obligation to the debtor arising under, or in connection with, a commodity contract traded on or subject to the rules of a contract market designated under the Commodity Exchange Act or a derivatives transaction execution facility registered under the Commodity Exchange Act against any claim arising under, or in connection with, other instruments, contracts, or agreements listed in subsection (a) except to the extent that the party has positive net equity in the commodity accounts at the debtor, as calculated under such subchapter; and

(B) another commodity broker may not net or offset an obligation to the debtor arising under, or in connection with, a commodity contract entered into or held on behalf of a customer of the debtor and traded on or subject to the rules of a contract market designated under the Commodity Exchange Act or a derivatives transaction execution facility registered under the Commodity Exchange Act against any claim arising under, or in connection with, other instruments, contracts, or agreements listed in subsection (a).

(3) No provision of subparagraph (A) or (B) of paragraph (2) shall prohibit the offset of claims and obligations that arise under—

(A) a cross-margining agreement or similar arrangement that has been approved by the Commodity Futures Trading Commission or submitted to the Commodity Futures Trading Commission under paragraph (1) or (2) of section 5c(c) of the Commodity Exchange Act and has not been abrogated or rendered ineffective by the Commodity Futures Trading Commission; or

(B) any other netting agreement between a clearing organization (as defined in *section 761*) and another entity that has been approved by the Commodity Futures Trading Commission.

(c) As used in this section, the term “contractual right” includes a right set forth in a rule or bylaw of a derivatives clearing organization (as defined in the Commodity Exchange Act), a multilateral clearing organization (as defined in the Federal Deposit Insurance Corporation Improvement Act of 1991), a national securities exchange, a national securities association, a securities clearing agency, a contract market designated under the Commodity Exchange Act, a derivatives transaction execution facility registered under the Commodity Exchange Act, or a board of trade (as defined in the Commodity Exchange Act) or in a resolution of the governing board thereof, and a right, whether or not evidenced in writing, arising under common law, under law merchant, or by reason of normal business practice.

(d) Any provisions of this title relating to securities contracts, commodity contracts, forward contracts, repurchase agreements, swap agreements, or master netting agreements shall apply in a case under chapter 15, so that enforcement of contractual provisions of such contracts and agreements in accordance with their terms will not be stayed or otherwise limited by operation of any provision of this title or by order of a court in any case under this title, and to limit avoidance powers to the same extent as in a proceeding under chapter 7 or 11 of this title (such enforcement not to be limited based on the presence or absence of assets of the debtor in the United States).

(Added Pub. L. 109–8, title IX, § 907(k)(1), Apr. 20, 2005, 119 Stat. 179.)

Sections that reference this section: 101

§562. Timing of damage measurement in connection with swap agreements, securities contracts, forward contracts, commodity contracts, repurchase agreements, and master netting agreements

(a) If the trustee rejects a swap agreement, securities contract (as defined in *section 741*), forward contract, commodity contract (as defined in *section 761*), repurchase agreement, or master netting agreement pursuant to *section 365(a)*, or if a forward contract merchant, stockbroker, financial institution, securities clearing agency, repo participant, financial participant, master netting agreement participant, or swap participant liquidates, terminates, or accelerates such contract or agreement, damages shall be measured as of the earlier of—

(1) the date of such rejection; or

(2) the date or dates of such liquidation, termination, or acceleration.

(b) If there are not any commercially reasonable determinants of value as of any date referred to in paragraph (1) or (2) of subsection (a), damages shall be measured as of the earliest subsequent date or dates on which there are commercially reasonable determinants of value.

(c) For the purposes of subsection (b), if damages are not measured as of the date or dates of rejection, liquidation, termination, or acceleration, and the forward contract merchant, stockbroker, financial institution, securities clearing agency, repo participant, financial participant, master netting agreement participant, or swap participant or the trustee objects to the timing of the measurement of damages—

(1) the trustee, in the case of an objection by a forward contract merchant, stockbroker, financial institution, securities clearing agency, repo participant, financial participant, master netting agreement participant, or swap participant; or

(2) the forward contract merchant, stockbroker, financial institution, securities clearing agency, repo participant, financial participant, master netting agreement participant, or swap participant, in the case of an objection by the trustee,

has the burden of proving that there were no commercially reasonable determinants of value as of such date or dates.

(Added Pub. L. 109–8, title IX, § 910(a)(1), Apr. 20, 2005, 119 Stat. 184.)

Sections that reference this section: 101, 502, 741, 761

CHAPTER 7: LIQUIDATION

Subchapter I: Officers and Administration

§701. Interim trustee

(a)

(1) Promptly after the order for relief under this chapter, the United States trustee shall appoint one disinterested person that is a member of the panel of private trustees established under section 586(a)(1) of title 28 or that is serving as trustee in the case immediately before the order for relief under this chapter to serve as interim trustee in the case.

(2) If none of the members of such panel is willing to serve as interim trustee in the case, then the United States trustee may serve as interim trustee in the case.

(b) The service of an interim trustee under this section terminates when a trustee elected or designated under *section 702* of this title to serve as trustee in the case qualifies under *section 322* of this title.

(c) An interim trustee serving under this section is a trustee in a case under this title.

(Pub. L. 95–598, Nov. 6, 1978, 92 Stat. 2604; Pub. L. 99–554, title II, § 215, Oct. 27, 1986, 100 Stat. 3100.)

Sections that reference this section: 303, 322, 348, 507, 557, 703

§702. Election of trustee

(a) A creditor may vote for a candidate for trustee only if such creditor—

(1) holds an allowable, undisputed, fixed, liquidated, unsecured claim of a kind entitled to distribution under *section 726(a)(2), 726*(a)(3), 726(a)(4), 752(a), 766(h), or 766(i) of this title;

(2) does not have an interest materially adverse, other than an equity interest that is not substantial in relation to such creditor's interest as a creditor, to the interest of creditors entitled to such distribution; and

(3) is not an insider.

(b) At the meeting of creditors held under *section 341* of this title, creditors may elect one person to serve as trustee in the case if election of a trustee is requested by creditors that may vote under subsection (a) of this section, and that hold at least 20 percent in amount of the claims specified in subsection (a)(1) of this section that are held by creditors that may vote under subsection (a) of this section.

(c) A candidate for trustee is elected trustee if—

(1) creditors holding at least 20 percent in amount of the claims of a kind specified in subsection (a)(1) of this section that are held by creditors that may vote under subsection (a) of this section vote; and

(2) such candidate receives the votes of creditors holding a majority in amount of claims specified in subsection (a)(1) of this section that are held by creditors that vote for a trustee.

(d) If a trustee is not elected under this section, then the interim trustee shall serve as trustee in the case.

(Pub. L. 95–598, Nov. 6, 1978, 92 Stat. 2604; Pub. L. 97–222, § 7, July 27, 1982, 96 Stat. 237; Pub. L. 98–353, title III, § 472, July 10, 1984, 98 Stat. 380.)

Sections that reference this section: 1104, 546, 701, 703, 705

§703. Successor trustee

(a) If a trustee dies or resigns during a case, fails to qualify under *section 322* of this title, or is removed under *section 324* of this title, creditors may elect, in the manner specified in *section 702* of this title, a person to fill the vacancy in the office of trustee.

(b) Pending election of a trustee under subsection (a) of this section, if necessary to preserve or prevent loss to the estate, the United States trustee may appoint an interim trustee in the manner specified in *section 701(a)*.

(c) If creditors do not elect a successor trustee under subsection (a) of this section or if a trustee is needed in a case reopened under *section 350* of this title, then the United States trustee—

(1) shall appoint one disinterested person that is a member of the panel of private trustees established under section 586(a)(1) of title 28 to serve as trustee in the case; or

(2) may, if none of the disinterested members of such panel is willing to serve as trustee, serve as trustee in the case.

(Pub. L. 95–598, Nov. 6, 1978, 92 Stat. 2605; Pub. L. 98–353, title III, § 473, July 10, 1984, 98 Stat. 381; Pub. L. 99–554, title II, § 216, Oct. 27, 1986, 100 Stat. 3100.)

Sections that reference this section: None

§704. Duties of trustee

(a) The trustee shall—

(1) collect and reduce to money the property of the estate for which such trustee serves, and close such estate as expeditiously as is compatible with the best interests of parties in interest;

(2) be accountable for all property received;

(3) ensure that the debtor shall perform his intention as specified in *section 521(a)(2)(B)* of this title;

(4) investigate the financial affairs of the debtor;

(5) if a purpose would be served, examine proofs of claims and object to the allowance of any claim that is improper;

(6) if advisable, oppose the discharge of the debtor;

(7) unless the court orders otherwise, furnish such information concerning the estate and the estate's administration as is requested by a party in interest;

(8) if the business of the debtor is authorized to be operated, file with the court, with the United States trustee, and with any governmental unit charged with responsibility for collection or determination of any tax arising out of such operation, periodic reports and summaries of the operation of such business, including a statement of receipts and disbursements, and such other information as the United States trustee or the court requires;

(9) make a final report and file a final account of the administration of the estate with the court and with the United States trustee;

(10) if with respect to the debtor there is a claim for a domestic support obligation, provide the applicable notice specified in subsection (c);

(11) if, at the time of the commencement of the case, the debtor (or any entity designated by the debtor) served as the administrator (as defined in section 3 of the Employee Retirement Income Security Act of 1974)

of an employee benefit plan, continue to perform the obligations required of the administrator; and

(12) use all reasonable and best efforts to transfer patients from a health care business that is in the process of being closed to an appropriate health care business that—

(A) is in the vicinity of the health care business that is closing;

(B) provides the patient with services that are substantially similar to those provided by the health care business that is in the process of being closed; and

(C) maintains a reasonable quality of care.

(b)

(1) With respect to a debtor who is an individual in a case under this chapter—

(A) the United States trustee (or the bankruptcy administrator, if any) shall review all materials filed by the debtor and, not later than 10 days after the date of the first meeting of creditors, file with the court a statement as to whether the debtor's case would be presumed to be an abuse under *section 707(b)*; and

(B) not later than 7 days after receiving a statement under subparagraph (A), the court shall provide a copy of the statement to all creditors.

(2) The United States trustee (or bankruptcy administrator, if any) shall, not later than 30 days after the date of filing a statement under paragraph (1), either file a motion to dismiss or convert under *section 707(b)* or file a statement setting forth the reasons the United States trustee (or the bankruptcy administrator, if any) does not consider such a motion to be appropriate, if the United States trustee (or the bankruptcy administrator, if any) determines that the debtor's case should be presumed to be an abuse under *section 707(b)* and the product of the debtor's current monthly income, multiplied by 12 is not less than—

(A) in the case of a debtor in a household of 1 person, the median family income of the applicable State for 1 earner; or

(B) in the case of a debtor in a household of 2 or more individuals, the highest median family income of the applicable State for a family of the same number or fewer individuals.

(c)

(1) In a case described in subsection (a)(10) to which subsection (a)(10) applies, the trustee shall—

(A)

(i) provide written notice to the holder of the claim described in subsection (a)(10) of such claim and of the right of such holder to use the services of the State child support enforcement agency established under sections 464 and 466 of the Social Security Act for the State in which such holder resides, for assistance in collecting child support during and after the case under this title;

(ii) include in the notice provided under clause (i) the address and telephone number of such State child support enforcement agency; and

(iii) include in the notice provided under clause (i) an explanation of the rights of such holder to payment of such claim under this chapter;

(B)

(i) provide written notice to such State child support enforcement agency of such claim; and

(ii) include in the notice provided under clause (i) the name, address, and telephone number of such holder; and

(C) at such time as the debtor is granted a discharge under *section 727*, provide written notice to such holder and to such State child support enforcement agency of—

(i) the granting of the discharge;

(ii) the last recent known address of the debtor;

(iii) the last recent known name and address of the debtor's employer; and

(iv) the name of each creditor that holds a claim that—

(I) is not discharged under paragraph (2), (4), or (14A) of *section 523(a)*; or

(II) was reaffirmed by the debtor under *section 524(c)*.

(2)

(A) The holder of a claim described in subsection (a)(10) or the State child support enforcement agency of the State in which such holder resides may request from a creditor described in paragraph (1)(C)(iv) the last known address of the debtor.

(B) Notwithstanding any other provision of law, a creditor that makes a disclosure of a last known address of a debtor in connection with a request made under subparagraph (A) shall not be liable by reason of making such disclosure.

(Pub. L. 95–598, Nov. 6, 1978, 92 Stat. 2605; Pub. L. 98–353, title III, §§ 311(a), 474, July 10, 1984, 98 Stat. 355, 381; Pub. L. 99–554, title II, § 217, Oct. 27, 1986, 100 Stat. 3100; Pub. L. 109–8, title I, § 102(c), title II, § 219(a), title IV, § 446(b), title XI, § 1105(a), Apr. 20, 2005, 119 Stat. 32, 55, 118, 192; Pub. L. 111–16, § 2(7), May 7, 2009, 123 Stat. 1607; Pub. L. 111–327, § 2(a)(24), Dec. 22, 2010, 124 Stat. 3560.)

Sections that reference this section: 1106, 1183, 1202, 1302, 1304, 782

§705. Creditors' committee

(a) At the meeting under *section 341(a)* of this title, creditors that may vote for a trustee under *section 702(a)* of this title may elect a committee of not fewer than three, and not more than eleven, creditors, each of whom holds an allowable unsecured claim of a kind entitled to distribution under *section 726(a)(2)* of this title.

(b) A committee elected under subsection (a) of this section may consult with the trustee or the United States trustee in connection with the administration of the estate, make recommendations to the trustee or the United States trustee respecting the performance of the trustee's duties, and submit to the court or the United States trustee any question affecting the administration of the estate.

(Pub. L. 95–598, Nov. 6, 1978, 92 Stat. 2605; Pub. L. 99–554, title II, § 218, Oct. 27, 1986, 100 Stat. 3100.)

Sections that reference this section: None

§706. Conversion

(a) The debtor may convert a case under this chapter to a case under chapter 11, 12, or 13 of this title at any time, if the case has not been converted under *section 1112, 1208,* or *1307* of this title. Any waiver of the right to convert a case under this subsection is unenforceable.

(b) On request of a party in interest and after notice and a hearing, the court may convert a case under this chapter to a case under chapter 11 of this title at any time.

(c) The court may not convert a case under this chapter to a case under chapter 12 or 13 of this title unless the debtor requests or consents to such conversion.

(d) Notwithstanding any other provision of this section, a case may not be converted to a case under another chapter of this title unless the debtor may be a debtor under such chapter.

(Pub. L. 95–598, Nov. 6, 1978, 92 Stat. 2606; Pub. L. 99–554, title II, § 257(q), Oct. 27, 1986, 100 Stat. 3115; Pub. L. 103–394, title V, § 501(d)(22), Oct. 22, 1994, 108 Stat. 4146; Pub. L. 109–8, title I, § 101, Apr. 20, 2005, 119 Stat. 27.)

Sections that reference this section: 1172, 1208, 1307, 348

§707. Dismissal of a case or conversion to a case under chapter 11 or 13

(a) The court may dismiss a case under this chapter only after notice and a hearing and only for cause, including—

(1) unreasonable delay by the debtor that is prejudicial to creditors;

(2) nonpayment of any fees or charges required under chapter 123 of title 28; and

(3) failure of the debtor in a voluntary case to file, within fifteen days or such additional time as the court may allow after the filing of the petition commencing such case, the information required by paragraph (1) of *section 521(a)*, but only on a motion by the United States trustee.

(b)

(1) After notice and a hearing, the court, on its own motion or on a motion by the United States trustee, trustee (or bankruptcy administrator, if any), or any party in interest, may dismiss a case filed by an individual debtor under this chapter whose debts are primarily consumer debts, or, with the debtor's consent, convert such a case to a case under chapter 11 or 13 of this title, if it finds that the granting of relief would be an abuse of the provisions of this chapter. In making a determination whether to dismiss a case under this section, the court may not take into consideration whether a debtor has made, or continues to make, charitable contributions (that meet the definition of "charitable contribution" under *section 548(d)(3)*) to any qualified religious or charitable entity or organization (as that term is defined in *section 548(d)(4)*).

(2)

(A)

(i) In considering under paragraph (1) whether the granting of relief would be an abuse of the provisions of this chapter, the court shall presume abuse exists if the debtor's current monthly income reduced by the amounts determined under clauses (ii), (iii), and (iv), and multiplied by 60 is not less than the lesser of—

(I) 25 percent of the debtor's nonpriority unsecured claims in the case, or $10,275, whichever is greater; or

(II) $17,150.

(ii)

(I) The debtor's monthly expenses shall be the debtor's applicable monthly expense amounts specified under the National Standards and Local Standards, and the debtor's actual monthly expenses for the categories specified as Other Necessary Expenses issued by the Internal Revenue Service for the area in which the debtor resides, as in effect on the date of the order for relief, for the debtor, the dependents of the debtor, and the spouse of the debtor in a joint case, if the spouse is not otherwise a dependent. Such expenses shall include reasonably necessary health insurance, disability insurance, and health savings account expenses for the debtor, the spouse of the debtor, or the dependents of the debtor. Notwithstanding any other provision of this clause, the monthly expenses of the debtor shall not include any payments for debts. In addition, the debtor's monthly expenses shall include the debtor's reasonably necessary expenses incurred to maintain the safety of the debtor and the family of the debtor from family violence as identified under *section 302* of the Family Violence Prevention and Services Act, or other applicable Federal law. The expenses included in the debtor's monthly expenses described in the preceding sentence shall be kept confidential by the court. In addition, if it is demonstrated that it is reasonable and necessary, the debtor's monthly expenses may also include an additional allowance for food and clothing of up to 5 percent of the food and clothing categories as specified by the National Standards issued by the Internal Revenue Service.

(II) In addition, the debtor's monthly expenses may include, if applicable, the continuation of actual expenses paid by the debtor that are reasonable and necessary for care and support of an elderly, chronically ill, or disabled household member or member of the debtor's immediate family (including parents, grandparents, siblings, children, and grandchildren of the debtor, the dependents of the debtor, and the spouse of the debtor in a joint case who is not a dependent) and who is unable to pay for such reasonable and necessary expenses. Such monthly expenses may include, if applicable, contributions to an account of a qualified ABLE program to the extent such contributions are not excess contributions (as described in section 4973(h) of the Internal Revenue Code of 1986) and if the designated beneficiary of such account is a child, stepchild, grandchild, or stepgrandchild of the debtor.

(III) In addition, for a debtor eligible for chapter 13, the debtor's monthly expenses may include the actual administrative expenses of administering a chapter 13 plan for the district in which the debtor resides, up to an amount of 10 percent of the projected plan payments, as determined under schedules issued by the Executive Office for United States Trustees.

(IV) In addition, the debtor's monthly expenses may include the actual expenses for each dependent child less than 18 years of age, not to exceed $2,575 per year per child, to attend a private or public elementary or secondary school if the debtor provides documentation of such expenses and a detailed explanation of why such expenses are reasonable and necessary, and why such expenses are not already accounted for in the National Standards, Local Standards, or Other Necessary Expenses referred to in subclause (I).

(V) In addition, the debtor's monthly expenses may include an allowance for housing and utilities, in excess of the allowance specified by the Local Standards for housing and utilities issued by the Internal Revenue Service, based on the actual expenses for home energy costs if the debtor provides documentation of such actual expenses and demonstrates that such actual expenses are reasonable and necessary.

(iii) The debtor's average monthly payments on account of secured debts shall be calculated as the sum of—

(I) the total of all amounts scheduled as contractually due to secured creditors in each month of the 60 months following the date of the filing of the petition; and

(II) any additional payments to secured creditors necessary for the debtor, in filing a plan under chapter 13 of this title, to maintain possession of the debtor's primary residence, motor vehicle, or other property necessary for the support of the debtor and the debtor's dependents, that serves as collateral for secured debts;

divided by 60.

(iv) The debtor's expenses for payment of all priority claims (including priority child support and alimony claims) shall be calculated as the total amount of debts entitled to priority, divided by 60.

(B)

(i) In any proceeding brought under this subsection, the presumption of abuse may only be rebutted by demonstrating special circumstances, such as a serious medical condition or a call or order to active duty in the Armed Forces, to the extent such special circumstances that justify additional expenses or adjustments of current monthly income for which there is no reasonable alternative.

(ii) In order to establish special circumstances, the debtor shall be required to itemize each additional expense or adjustment of income and to provide—

(I) documentation for such expense or adjustment to income; and

(II) a detailed explanation of the special circumstances that make such expenses or adjustment to income necessary and reasonable.

(iii) The debtor shall attest under oath to the accuracy of any information provided to demonstrate that additional expenses or adjustments to income are required.

(iv) The presumption of abuse may only be rebutted if the additional expenses or adjustments to income referred to in clause (i) cause the product of the debtor's current monthly income reduced by the amounts determined under clauses (ii), (iii), and (iv) of subparagraph (A) when multiplied by 60 to be less than the lesser of—

(I) 25 percent of the debtor's nonpriority unsecured claims, or $10,275 whichever is greater; or

(II) $17,150.

(C) As part of the schedule of current income and expenditures required under *section 521*, the debtor shall include a statement of the debtor's current monthly income, and the calculations that determine whether a presumption arises under subparagraph (A)(i), that show how each such amount is calculated.

(D) Subparagraphs (A) through (C) shall not apply, and the court may not dismiss or convert a case based on any form of means testing—

(i) if the debtor is a disabled veteran (as defined in section 3741(1) of title 38), and the indebtedness occurred primarily during a period during which he or she was—

(I) on active duty (as defined in *section 101(d)(1)* of title 10); or

(II) performing a homeland defense activity (as defined in *section 901(1)* of title 32); or

(ii) with respect to the debtor, while the debtor is—

(I) on, and during the 540-day period beginning immediately after the debtor is released from, a period of active duty (as defined in *section 101(d)(1)* of title 10) of not less than 90 days; or

(II) performing, and during the 540-day period beginning immediately after the debtor is no longer performing, a homeland defense activity (as defined in *section 901(1)* of title 32) performed for a period of not less than 90 days;

if after September 11, 2001, the debtor while a member of a reserve component of the Armed Forces or a member of the National Guard, was called to such active duty or performed such homeland defense activity.

(3) In considering under paragraph (1) whether the granting of relief would be an abuse of the provisions of this chapter in a case in which the presumption in paragraph (2)(A)(i) does not arise or is rebutted, the court shall consider—

(A) whether the debtor filed the petition in bad faith; or

(B) the totality of the circumstances (including whether the debtor seeks to reject a personal services contract and the financial need for such rejection as sought by the debtor) of the debtor's financial situation demonstrates abuse.

(4)

(A) The court, on its own initiative or on the motion of a party in interest, in accordance with the procedures described in rule 9011 of the Federal Rules of Bankruptcy Procedure, may order the attorney for the debtor to reimburse the trustee for all reasonable costs in prosecuting a motion filed under section 707(b), including reasonable attorneys' fees, if—

(i) a trustee files a motion for dismissal or conversion under this subsection; and

(ii) the court—

(I) grants such motion; and

(II) finds that the action of the attorney for the debtor in filing a case under this chapter violated rule 9011 of the Federal Rules of Bankruptcy Procedure.

(B) If the court finds that the attorney for the debtor violated rule 9011 of the Federal Rules of Bankruptcy Procedure, the court, on its own initiative or on the motion of a party in interest, in accordance with such procedures, may order—

(i) the assessment of an appropriate civil penalty against the attorney for the debtor; and

(ii) the payment of such civil penalty to the trustee, the United States trustee (or the bankruptcy administrator, if any).

(C) The signature of an attorney on a petition, pleading, or written motion shall constitute a certification that the attorney has—

(i) performed a reasonable investigation into the circumstances that gave rise to the petition, pleading, or written motion; and

(ii) determined that the petition, pleading, or written motion—

(I) is well grounded in fact; and

(II) is warranted by existing law or a good faith argument for the extension, modification, or reversal of existing law and does not constitute an abuse under paragraph (1).

(D) The signature of an attorney on the petition shall constitute a certification that the attorney has no knowledge after an inquiry that the information in the schedules filed with such petition is incorrect.

(5)

(A) Except as provided in subparagraph (B) and subject to paragraph (6), the court, on its own initiative or on the motion of a party in interest, in accordance with the procedures described in rule 9011 of the Federal Rules of Bankruptcy Procedure, may award a debtor all reasonable costs (including reasonable attorneys' fees) in contesting a motion filed by a party in interest (other than a trustee or United States trustee (or bankruptcy administrator, if any)) under this subsection if—

(i) the court does not grant the motion; and

(ii) the court finds that—

(I) the position of the party that filed the motion violated rule 9011 of the Federal Rules of Bankruptcy Procedure; or

(II) the attorney (if any) who filed the motion did not comply with the requirements of clauses (i) and (ii) of paragraph (4)(C), and the motion was made solely for the purpose of coercing a debtor into waiving a right guaranteed to the debtor under this title.

(B) A small business that has a claim of an aggregate amount less than $1,725 shall not be subject to subparagraph (A)(ii)(I).

(C) For purposes of this paragraph—

(i) the term "small business" means an unincorporated business, partnership, corporation, association, or organization that—

(I) has fewer than 25 full-time employees as determined on the date on which the motion is filed; and

(II) is engaged in commercial or business activity; and

(ii) the number of employees of a wholly owned subsidiary of a corporation includes the employees of—

(I) a parent corporation; and

(II) any other subsidiary corporation of the parent corporation.

(6) Only the judge or United States trustee (or bankruptcy administrator, if any) may file a motion under section 707(b), if the current monthly income of the debtor, or in a joint case, the debtor and the debtor's spouse, as of the date of the order for relief, when multiplied by 12, is equal to or less than—

(A) in the case of a debtor in a household of 1 person, the median family income of the applicable State for 1 earner;

(B) in the case of a debtor in a household of 2, 3, or 4 individuals, the highest median family income of the applicable State for a family of the same number or fewer individuals; or

(C) in the case of a debtor in a household exceeding 4 individuals, the highest median family income of the applicable State for a family of 4 or fewer individuals, plus $925 per month for each individual in excess of 4.

(7)

(A) No judge, United States trustee (or bankruptcy administrator, if any), trustee, or other party in interest may file a motion under paragraph (2) if the current monthly income of the debtor, including a veteran (as that term is defined in *section 101* of title 38), and the debtor's spouse combined, as of the date of the order for relief when multiplied by 12, is equal to or less than—

(i) in the case of a debtor in a household of 1 person, the median family income of the applicable State for 1 earner;

(ii) in the case of a debtor in a household of 2, 3, or 4 individuals, the highest median family income of the applicable State for a family of the same number or fewer individuals; or

(iii) in the case of a debtor in a household exceeding 4 individuals, the highest median family income of the applicable State for a family of 4 or fewer individuals, plus $925 per month for each individual in excess of 4.

(B) In a case that is not a joint case, current monthly income of the debtor's spouse shall not be considered for purposes of subparagraph (A) if—

(i)

(I) the debtor and the debtor's spouse are separated under applicable nonbankruptcy law; or

(II) the debtor and the debtor's spouse are living separate and apart, other than for the purpose of evading subparagraph (A); and

(ii) the debtor files a statement under penalty of perjury—

(I) specifying that the debtor meets the requirement of subclause (I) or (II) of clause (i); and

(II) disclosing the aggregate, or best estimate of the aggregate, amount of any cash or money payments received from the debtor's spouse attributed to the debtor's current monthly income.

(c)

(1) In this subsection—

(A) the term "crime of violence" has the meaning given such term in section 16 of title 18; and

(B) the term "drug trafficking crime" has the meaning given such term in *section 924(c)(2)* of title 18.

(2) Except as provided in paragraph (3), after notice and a hearing, the court, on a motion by the victim of a crime of violence or a drug trafficking crime, may when it is in the best interest of the victim dismiss a voluntary case filed under this chapter by a debtor who is an individual if such individual was convicted of such crime.

(3) The court may not dismiss a case under paragraph (2) if the debtor establishes by a preponderance of the evidence that the filing of a case under this chapter is necessary to satisfy a claim for a domestic support obligation.

(Pub. L. 95–598, Nov. 6, 1978, 92 Stat. 2606; Pub. L. 98–353, title III, §§ 312, 475, July 10, 1984, 98 Stat. 355, 381; Pub. L. 99–554, title II, § 219, Oct. 27, 1986, 100 Stat. 3100; Pub. L. 105–183, § 4(b), June 19, 1998, 112 Stat. 518; Pub. L. 109–8, title I, § 102(a), (f), Apr. 20, 2005, 119 Stat. 27, 33; Pub. L. 110–438, § 2, Oct. 20, 2008, 122 Stat. 5000; Pub. L. 111–320, title II, § 202(a), Dec. 20, 2010, 124 Stat. 3509; Pub. L. 111–327, § 2(a)(25), Dec. 22, 2010, 124 Stat. 3560; Pub. L. 113–295, div. B, title I, § 104(b), Dec. 19, 2014, 128 Stat. 4064.)

Sections that reference this section: 1325, 1326, 342, 362, 521, 527, 704

Subchapter II: Collection, Liquidation, and Distribution of the Estate

§721. Authorization to operate business

The court may authorize the trustee to operate the business of the debtor for a limited period, if such operation is in the best interest of the estate and consistent with the orderly liquidation of the estate.

(Pub. L. 95–598, Nov. 6, 1978, 92 Stat. 2606.)

Sections that reference this section: 327, 363, 364

§722. Redemption

An individual debtor may, whether or not the debtor has waived the right to redeem under this section, redeem tangible personal property intended primarily for personal, family, or household use, from a lien securing a dischargeable consumer debt, if such property is exempted under *section 522* of this title or has been abandoned under *section 554* of this title, by paying the holder of such lien the amount of the allowed secured claim of such holder that is secured by such lien in full at the time of redemption.

(Pub. L. 95–598, Nov. 6, 1978, 92 Stat. 2606; Pub. L. 109–8, title III, § 304(2), Apr. 20, 2005, 119 Stat. 79.)

Sections that reference this section: 362, 521

§723. Rights of partnership trustee against general partners

(a) If there is a deficiency of property of the estate to pay in full all claims which are allowed in a case under this chapter concerning a partnership and with respect to which a general partner of the partnership is personally liable, the trustee shall have a claim against such general partner to the extent that under applicable nonbankruptcy law such general partner is personally liable for such deficiency.

(b) To the extent practicable, the trustee shall first seek recovery of such deficiency from any general partner in such partnership that is not a debtor in a case under this title. Pending determination of such deficiency, the court may order any such partner to provide the estate with indemnity for, or assurance of payment of, any deficiency recoverable from such partner, or not to dispose of property.

(c) The trustee has a claim against the estate of each general partner in such partnership that is a debtor in a case under this title for the full amount of all claims of creditors allowed in the case concerning such partnership. Notwithstanding *section 502* of this title, there shall not be allowed in such partner's case a claim against such partner on which both such partner and such partnership are liable, except to any extent that such claim is secured only by property of such partner and not by property of such partnership. The claim of the trustee under this subsection is entitled to distribution in such partner's case under *section 726(a)* of this title the same as any other claim of a kind specified in such section.

(d) If the aggregate that the trustee recovers from the estates of general partners under subsection (c) of this section is greater than any deficiency not recovered under subsection (b) of this section, the court, after notice and a hearing, shall determine an equitable distribution of the surplus so recovered, and the trustee shall distribute such surplus to the estates of the general partners in such partnership according to such determination.

(Pub. L. 95–598, Nov. 6, 1978, 92 Stat. 2606; Pub. L. 98–353, title III, § 476, July 10, 1984, 98 Stat. 381; Pub. L. 103–394, title II, § 212, Oct. 22, 1994, 108 Stat. 4125; Pub. L. 111–327, § 2(a)(26), Dec. 22, 2010, 124 Stat. 3560.)

Sections that reference this section: None

§724. Treatment of certain liens

(a) The trustee may avoid a lien that secures a claim of a kind specified in *section 726(a)(4)* of this title.

(b) Property in which the estate has an interest and that is subject to a lien that is not avoidable under this title (other than to the extent that there is a properly perfected unavoidable tax lien arising in connection with an ad valorem tax on real or personal property of the estate) and that secures an allowed claim for a tax, or proceeds of such property, shall be distributed—

  (1) first, to any holder of an allowed claim secured by a lien on such property that is not avoidable under this title and that is senior to such tax lien;

  (2) second, to any holder of a claim of a kind specified in *section 507(a)(1)(C)* or *507*(a)(2) (except that such expenses under each such section, other than claims for wages, salaries, or commissions that arise after the date of the filing of the petition, shall be limited to expenses incurred under this chapter and shall not include expenses incurred under chapter 11 of this title), 507(a)(1)(A), 507(a)(1)(B), 507(a)(3), 507(a)(4), 507(a)(5), 507(a)(6), or 507(a)(7) of this title, to the extent of the amount of such allowed tax claim that is secured by such tax lien;

  (3) third, to the holder of such tax lien, to any extent that such holder's allowed tax claim that is secured by such tax lien exceeds any amount distributed under paragraph (2) of this subsection;

(4) fourth, to any holder of an allowed claim secured by a lien on such property that is not avoidable under this title and that is junior to such tax lien;

(5) fifth, to the holder of such tax lien, to the extent that such holder's allowed claim secured by such tax lien is not paid under paragraph (3) of this subsection; and

(6) sixth, to the estate.

(c) If more than one holder of a claim is entitled to distribution under a particular paragraph of subsection (b) of this section, distribution to such holders under such paragraph shall be in the same order as distribution to such holders would have been other than under this section.

(d) A statutory lien the priority of which is determined in the same manner as the priority of a tax lien under section 6323 of the Internal Revenue Code of 1986 shall be treated under subsection (b) of this section the same as if such lien were a tax lien.

(e) Before subordinating a tax lien on real or personal property of the estate, the trustee shall—

(1) exhaust the unencumbered assets of the estate; and

(2) in a manner consistent with *section 506(c)*, recover from property securing an allowed secured claim the reasonable, necessary costs and expenses of preserving or disposing of such property.

(f) Notwithstanding the exclusion of ad valorem tax liens under this section and subject to the requirements of subsection (e), the following may be paid from property of the estate which secures a tax lien, or the proceeds of such property:

(1) Claims for wages, salaries, and commissions that are entitled to priority under *section 507(a)(4)*.

(2) Claims for contributions to an employee benefit plan entitled to priority under *section 507(a)(5)*.

(Pub. L. 95–598, Nov. 6, 1978, 92 Stat. 2607; Pub. L. 98–353, title III, § 477, July 10, 1984, 98 Stat. 381; Pub. L. 99–554, title II, § 283(r), Oct. 27, 1986, 100 Stat. 3118; Pub. L. 103–394, title III, § 304(h)(4), title V, § 501(d)(23), Oct. 22, 1994, 108 Stat. 4134, 4146; Pub. L. 109–8, title VII, § 701(a), Apr. 20, 2005, 119 Stat. 124; Pub. L. 111–327, § 2(a)(27), Dec. 22, 2010, 124 Stat. 3560.)

Sections that reference this section: None

§725. Disposition of certain property

After the commencement of a case under this chapter, but before final distribution of property of the estate under *section 726* of this title, the trustee, after notice and a hearing, shall dispose of any property in which an entity other than the estate has an interest, such as a lien, and that has not been disposed of under another section of this title.

(Pub. L. 95–598, Nov. 6, 1978, 92 Stat. 2607; Pub. L. 98–353, title III, § 478, July 10, 1984, 98 Stat. 381.)

Sections that reference this section: None

§726. Distribution of property of the estate

(a) Except as provided in *section 510* of this title, property of the estate shall be distributed—

(1) first, in payment of claims of the kind specified in, and in the order specified in, *section 507* of this title, proof of which is timely filed under *section 501* of this title or tardily filed on or before the earlier of—

(A) the date that is 10 days after the mailing to creditors of the summary of the trustee's final report; or

(B) the date on which the trustee commences final distribution under this section;

(2) second, in payment of any allowed unsecured claim, other than a claim of a kind specified in paragraph (1), (3), or (4) of this subsection, proof of which is—

(A) timely filed under *section 501(a)* of this title;

(B) timely filed under *section 501(b)* or *501*(c) of this title; or

(C) tardily filed under *section 501(a)* of this title, if—

(i) the creditor that holds such claim did not have notice or actual knowledge of the case in time for timely filing of a proof of such claim under *section 501(a)* of this title; and

(ii) proof of such claim is filed in time to permit payment of such claim;

(3) third, in payment of any allowed unsecured claim proof of which is tardily filed under *section 501(a)* of this title, other than a

claim of the kind specified in paragraph (2)(C) of this subsection;

(4) fourth, in payment of any allowed claim, whether secured or unsecured, for any fine, penalty, or forfeiture, or for multiple, exemplary, or punitive damages, arising before the earlier of the order for relief or the appointment of a trustee, to the extent that such fine, penalty, forfeiture, or damages are not compensation for actual pecuniary loss suffered by the holder of such claim;

(5) fifth, in payment of interest at the legal rate from the date of the filing of the petition, on any claim paid under paragraph (1), (2), (3), or (4) of this subsection; and

(6) sixth, to the debtor.

(b) Payment on claims of a kind specified in paragraph (1), (2), (3), (4), (5), (6), (7), (8), (9), or (10) of *section 507(a)* of this title, or in paragraph (2), (3), (4), or (5) of subsection (a) of this section, shall be made pro rata among claims of the kind specified in each such particular paragraph, except that in a case that has been converted to this chapter under *section 1112, 1208,* or *1307* of this title, a claim allowed under *section 503(b)* of this title incurred under this chapter after such conversion has priority over a claim allowed under *section 503(b)* of this title incurred under any other chapter of this title or under this chapter before such conversion and over any expenses of a custodian superseded under *section 543* of this title.

(c) Notwithstanding subsections (a) and (b) of this section, if there is property of the kind specified in *section 541(a)(2)* of this title, or proceeds of such property, in the estate, such property or proceeds shall be segregated from other property of the estate, and such property or proceeds and other property of the estate shall be distributed as follows:

(1) Claims allowed under *section 503* of this title shall be paid either from property of the kind specified in *section 541(a)(2)* of this title, or from other property of the estate, as the interest of justice requires.

(2) Allowed claims, other than claims allowed under *section 503* of this title, shall be paid in the order specified in subsection (a) of this section, and, with respect to claims of a kind specified in a particular paragraph of *section 507* of this title or subsection (a) of this section, in the following order and manner:

(A) First, community claims against the debtor or the debtor's spouse shall be paid from property of the kind specified in *section 541(a)(2)* of this title, except to the extent that such property is solely liable for debts of the debtor.

(B) Second, to the extent that community claims against the debtor are not paid under subparagraph (A) of this paragraph, such community claims shall be paid from property of the kind specified in *section 541(a)(2)* of this title that is solely liable for debts of the debtor.

(C) Third, to the extent that all claims against the debtor including community claims against the debtor are not paid under subparagraph (A) or (B) of this paragraph such claims shall be paid from property of the estate other than property of the kind specified in *section 541(a)(2)* of this title.

(D) Fourth, to the extent that community claims against the debtor or the debtor's spouse are not paid under subparagraph (A), (B), or (C) of this paragraph, such claims shall be paid from all remaining property of the estate.

(Pub. L. 95–598, Nov. 6, 1978, 92 Stat. 2608; Pub. L. 98–353, title III, § 479, July 10, 1984, 98 Stat. 381; Pub. L. 99–554, title II, §§ 257(r), 283(s), Oct. 27, 1986, 100 Stat. 3115, 3118; Pub. L. 103–394, title II, § 213(b), title III, § 304(h)(5), title V, § 501(d)(24), Oct. 22, 1994, 108 Stat. 4126, 4134, 4146; Pub. L. 109–8, title VII, § 713, title XII, § 1215, Apr. 20, 2005, 119 Stat. 128, 195; Pub. L. 111–327, § 2(a)(28), Dec. 22, 2010, 124 Stat. 3560.)

Sections that reference this section: 347, 502, 702, 705, 723, 724, 725, 752, 766

§727. Discharge

(a) The court shall grant the debtor a discharge, unless—

(1) the debtor is not an individual;

(2) the debtor, with intent to hinder, delay, or defraud a creditor or an officer of the estate charged with custody of property under this title, has transferred, removed, destroyed, mutilated, or concealed, or has permitted to be transferred, removed, destroyed, mutilated, or concealed—

(A) property of the debtor, within one year before the date of the filing of the petition; or

(B) property of the estate, after the date of the filing of the petition;

(3) the debtor has concealed, destroyed, mutilated, falsified, or failed to keep or preserve any recorded information, including books, documents, records, and papers, from which the debtor's financial condition or business transactions might be ascertained, unless such act or failure to act was justified under all of the circumstances of the case;

(4) the debtor knowingly and fraudulently, in or in connection with the case—

(A) made a false oath or account;

(B) presented or used a false claim;

(C) gave, offered, received, or attempted to obtain money, property, or advantage, or a promise of money, property, or advantage, for acting or forbearing to act; or

(D) withheld from an officer of the estate entitled to possession under this title, any recorded information, including books, documents, records, and papers, relating to the debtor's property or financial affairs;

(5) the debtor has failed to explain satisfactorily, before determination of denial of discharge under this paragraph, any loss of assets or deficiency of assets to meet the debtor's liabilities;

(6) the debtor has refused, in the case—

(A) to obey any lawful order of the court, other than an order to respond to a material question or to testify;

(B) on the ground of privilege against self-incrimination, to respond to a material question approved by the court or to testify, after the debtor has been granted immunity with respect to the matter concerning which such privilege was invoked; or

(C) on a ground other than the properly invoked privilege against self-incrimination, to respond to a material question approved by the court or to testify;

(7) the debtor has committed any act specified in paragraph (2), (3), (4), (5), or (6) of this subsection, on or within one year before the date of the filing of the petition, or during the case, in connection with another case, under this title or under the Bankruptcy Act, concerning an insider;

(8) the debtor has been granted a discharge under this section, under *section 1141* of this title, or under section 14, 371, or 476 of the Bankruptcy Act, in a case commenced within 8 years before the date of the filing of the petition;

(9) the debtor has been granted a discharge under *section 1228* or *1328* of this title, or under section 660 or 661 of the Bankruptcy Act, in a case commenced within six years before the date of the filing of the petition, unless payments under the plan in such case totaled at least—

(A) 100 percent of the allowed unsecured claims in such case; or

(B)

(i) 70 percent of such claims; and

(ii) the plan was proposed by the debtor in good faith, and was the debtor's best effort;

(10) the court approves a written waiver of discharge executed by the debtor after the order for relief under this chapter;

(11) after filing the petition, the debtor failed to complete an instructional course concerning personal financial management described in *section 111*, except that this paragraph shall not apply with respect to a debtor who is a person described in *section 109(h)(4)* or who resides in a district for which the United States trustee (or the bankruptcy administrator, if any) determines that the approved instructional courses are not adequate to service the additional individuals who would otherwise be required to complete such instructional courses under this section (The United States trustee (or the bankruptcy administrator, if any) who makes a determination described in this paragraph shall review such determination not later than 1 year after the date of such determination, and not less frequently than annually thereafter.); or

(12) the court after notice and a hearing held not more than 10 days before the date of the entry of the order granting the discharge finds that there is reasonable cause to believe that—

(A) *section 522(q)(1)* may be applicable to the debtor; and

(B) there is pending any proceeding in which the debtor may be found guilty of a felony of the kind described in *section 522(q)(1)(A)* or liable for a debt of the kind described in *section 522(q)(1)(B)*.

(b) Except as provided in *section 523* of this title, a discharge under subsection (a) of this section discharges the debtor from all debts that arose before the date of the order for relief under this chapter, and any liability on a claim that is determined under *section 502* of this title as if such claim had arisen before the commencement of the case, whether or not a proof of claim based on any such debt or liability is filed under *section 501* of this title, and whether or not a claim based on any such debt or liability is allowed under *section 502* of this title.

(c)

(1) The trustee, a creditor, or the United States trustee may object to the granting of a discharge under subsection (a) of this section.

(2) On request of a party in interest, the court may order the trustee to examine the acts and conduct of the debtor to determine whether a ground exists for denial of discharge.

(d) On request of the trustee, a creditor, or the United States trustee, and after notice and a hearing, the court shall revoke a discharge granted under subsection (a) of this section if—

(1) such discharge was obtained through the fraud of the debtor, and the requesting party did not know of such fraud until after the granting of such discharge;

(2) the debtor acquired property that is property of the estate, or became entitled to acquire property that would be property of the estate, and knowingly and fraudulently failed to report the acquisition of or entitlement to such property, or to deliver or surrender such property to the trustee;

(3) the debtor committed an act specified in subsection (a)(6) of this section; or

(4) the debtor has failed to explain satisfactorily—

(A) a material misstatement in an audit referred to in section 586(f) of title 28; or

(B) a failure to make available for inspection all necessary accounts, papers, documents, financial records, files, and all other papers, things, or property belonging to the debtor that are requested for an audit referred to in section 586(f) of title 28.

(e) The trustee, a creditor, or the United States trustee may request a revocation of a discharge —

(1) under subsection (d)(1) of this section within one year after such discharge is granted; or

(2) under subsection (d)(2) or (d)(3) of this section before the later of—

(A) one year after the granting of such discharge; and

(B) the date the case is closed.

(Pub. L. 95–598, Nov. 6, 1978, 92 Stat. 2609; Pub. L. 98–353, title III, § 480, July 10, 1984, 98 Stat. 382; Pub. L. 99–554, title II, §§ 220, 257(s), Oct. 27, 1986, 100 Stat. 3101, 3116; Pub. L. 109–8, title I, § 106(b), title III, §§ 312(1), 330(a), title VI, § 603(d), Apr. 20, 2005, 119 Stat. 38, 86, 101, 123.)

Sections that reference this section: 1141, 523, 524, 704

§728. Repealed. Pub. L. 109–8, title VII, § 719(b)(1), Apr. 20, 2005, 119 Stat. 133

Sections that reference this section: None

Subchapter III: Stockbroker Liquidation

§741. Definitions for this subchapter

In this subchapter—

(1) “Commission” means Securities and Exchange Commission;

(2) “customer” includes—

(A) entity with whom a person deals as principal or agent and that has a claim against such person on account of a security received, acquired, or held by such person in the ordinary course of such person’s business as a stockbroker, from or for the securities account or accounts of such entity—

(i) for safekeeping;

(ii) with a view to sale;

(iii) to cover a consummated sale;

(iv) pursuant to a purchase;

(v) as collateral under a security agreement; or

(vi) for the purpose of effecting registration of transfer; and

(B) entity that has a claim against a person arising out of—

(i) a sale or conversion of a security received, acquired, or held as specified in subparagraph (A) of this paragraph; or

(ii) a deposit of cash, a security, or other property with such person for the purpose of purchasing or selling a security;

(3) "customer name security" means security—

(A) held for the account of a customer on the date of the filing of the petition by or on behalf of the debtor;

(B) registered in such customer's name on such date or in the process of being so registered under instructions from the debtor; and

(C) not in a form transferable by delivery on such date;

(4) "customer property" means cash, security, or other property, and proceeds of such cash, security, or property, received, acquired, or held by or for the account of the debtor, from or for the securities account of a customer—

(A) including—

(i) property that was unlawfully converted from and that is the lawful property of the estate;

(ii) a security held as property of the debtor to the extent such security is necessary to meet a net equity claim of a customer based on a security of the same class and series of an issuer;

(iii) resources provided through the use or realization of a customer's debit cash balance or a debit item includible in the Formula for Determination of Reserve Requirement for Brokers and Dealers as promulgated by the Commission under the Securities Exchange Act of 1934; and

(iv) other property of the debtor that any applicable law, rule, or regulation requires to be set aside or held for the benefit of a customer, unless including such property as customer property would not significantly increase customer property; but

(B) not including—

(i) a customer name security delivered to or reclaimed by a customer under *section 751* of this title; or

(ii) property to the extent that a customer does not have a claim against the debtor based on such property;

(5) "margin payment" means payment or deposit of cash, a security, or other property, that is commonly known to the securities trade as original margin, initial margin, maintenance margin, or variation margin, or as a mark-to-market payment, or that secures an obligation of a participant in a securities clearing agency;

(6) "net equity" means, with respect to all accounts of a customer that such customer has in the same capacity—

(A)

(i) aggregate dollar balance that would remain in such accounts after the liquidation, by sale or purchase, at the time of the filing of the petition, of all securities positions in all such accounts, except any customer name securities of such customer; minus

(ii) any claim of the debtor against such customer in such capacity that would have been owing immediately after such liquidation; plus

(B) any payment by such customer to the trustee, within 60 days after notice under *section 342* of this title, of any business related claim of the debtor against such customer in such capacity;

(7) "securities contract"—

(A) means—

(i) a contract for the purchase, sale, or loan of a security, a certificate of deposit, a mortgage loan, any interest in a mortgage loan, a group or index of securities, certificates of deposit, or mortgage loans or interests therein (including an interest therein or based on the value thereof), or option on any of the foregoing, including an option to purchase or sell any such security, certificate of deposit, mortgage loan, interest, group or index, or option, and including any repurchase or reverse repurchase transaction on any such security, certificate of deposit, mortgage loan, interest, group or index, or option (whether or not such repurchase or reverse repurchase transaction is a "repurchase agreement", as defined in *section 101*);

(ii) any option entered into on a national securities exchange relating to foreign currencies;

(iii) the guarantee (including by novation) by or to any securities clearing agency of a settlement of cash, securities, certificates of deposit, mortgage loans or interests therein, group or index of securities, or mortgage loans or interests therein (including any interest therein or based on the value thereof), or option on any of the foregoing, including an option to purchase or sell any such security, certificate of deposit, mortgage loan, interest, group or index, or option (whether or not such settlement is in connection with any agreement or transaction referred to in clauses (i) through (xi));

(iv) any margin loan;

(v) any extension of credit for the clearance or settlement of securities transactions;

(vi) any loan transaction coupled with a securities collar transaction, any prepaid forward securities transaction, or any total return swap transaction coupled with a securities sale transaction;

(vii) any other agreement or transaction that is similar to an agreement or transaction referred to in this subparagraph;

(viii) any combination of the agreements or transactions referred to in this subparagraph;

(ix) any option to enter into any agreement or transaction referred to in this subparagraph;

(x) a master agreement that provides for an agreement or transaction referred to in clause (i), (ii), (iii), (iv), (v), (vi), (vii), (viii), or (ix), together with all supplements to any such master agreement, without regard to whether the master agreement provides for an agreement or transaction that is not a securities contract under this subparagraph, except that such master agreement shall be considered to be a securities contract under this subparagraph only with respect to each agreement or transaction under such master agreement that is referred to in clause (i), (ii), (iii), (iv), (v), (vi), (vii), (viii), or (ix); or

(xi) any security agreement or arrangement or other credit enhancement related to any agreement or transaction referred to in this subparagraph, including any guarantee or reimbursement obligation by or to a stockbroker, securities clearing agency, financial institution, or financial participant in connection with any agreement or transaction referred to in this subparagraph, but not to exceed the damages in connection with any such agreement or transaction, measured in accordance with *section 562*; and

(B) does not include any purchase, sale, or repurchase obligation under a participation in a commercial mortgage loan;

(8) "settlement payment" means a preliminary settlement payment, a partial settlement payment, an interim settlement payment, a settlement payment on account, a final settlement payment, or any other similar payment commonly used in the securities trade; and

(9) "SIPC" means Securities Investor Protection Corporation.

(Pub. L. 95–598, Nov. 6, 1978, 92 Stat. 2611; Pub. L. 97–222, § 8, July 27, 1982, 96 Stat. 237; Pub. L. 98–353, title III, § 482, July 10, 1984, 98 Stat. 382; Pub. L. 103–394, title V, § 501(d)(25), Oct. 22, 1994, 108 Stat. 4146; Pub. L. 109–8, title IX, § 907(a)(2), Apr. 20, 2005, 119 Stat. 173; Pub. L. 109–390, § 5(a)(3), Dec. 12, 2006, 120 Stat. 2697.)

Sections that reference this section: 101, 546, 548, 555, 561, 562, 752

§742. Effect of section 362 of this title in this subchapter

Notwithstanding *section 362* of this title, SIPC may file an application for a protective decree under the Securities Investor Protection Act of 1970. The filing of such application stays all proceedings in the case under this title unless and until such application is dismissed. If SIPC completes the liquidation of the debtor, then the court shall dismiss the case.

(Pub. L. 95–598, Nov. 6, 1978, 92 Stat. 2613; Pub. L. 97–222, § 9, July 27, 1982, 96 Stat. 237; Pub. L. 103–394, title V, § 501(d)(26), Oct. 22, 1994, 108 Stat. 4146.)

Sections that reference this section: 349

§743. Notice

The clerk shall give the notice required by *section 342* of this title to SIPC and to the Commission.

(Pub. L. 95–598, Nov. 6, 1978, 92 Stat. 2613; Pub. L. 99–554, title II, § 283(t), Oct. 27, 1986, 100 Stat. 3118; Pub. L. 103–394, title V, § 501(d)(27), Oct. 22, 1994, 108 Stat. 4146.)

Sections that reference this section: None

§744. Executory contracts

Notwithstanding *section 365(d)(1)* of this title, the trustee shall assume or reject, under *section 365* of this title, any executory contract of the debtor for the purchase or sale of a security in the ordinary course of the debtor's business, within a reasonable time after the date of the order for relief, but not to exceed 30 days. If the trustee does not assume such a contract within such time, such contract is rejected.

(Pub. L. 95–598, Nov. 6, 1978, 92 Stat. 2613; Pub. L. 97–222, § 10, July 27, 1982, 96 Stat. 238.)

Sections that reference this section: None

§745. Treatment of accounts

(a) Accounts held by the debtor for a particular customer in separate capacities shall be treated as accounts of separate customers.

(b) If a stockbroker or a bank holds a customer net equity claim against the debtor that arose out of a transaction for a customer of such stockbroker or bank, each such customer of such stockbroker or bank shall be treated as a separate customer of the debtor.

(c) Each trustee's account specified as such on the debtor's books, and supported by a trust deed filed with, and qualified as such by, the Internal Revenue Service, and under the Internal Revenue Code of 1986, shall be treated as a separate customer account for each beneficiary under such trustee account.

(Pub. L. 95–598, Nov. 6, 1978, 92 Stat. 2613; Pub. L. 97–222, § 11, July 27, 1982, 96 Stat. 238; Pub. L. 98–353, title III, § 483, July 10, 1984, 98 Stat. 383; Pub. L. 103–394, title V, § 501(d)(28), Oct. 22, 1994, 108 Stat. 4146.)

Sections that reference this section: None

§746. Extent of customer claims

(a) If, after the date of the filing of the petition, an entity enters into a transaction with the debtor, in a manner that would have made such entity a customer had such transaction occurred before the date of the filing of the petition, and such transaction was entered into by such entity in good faith and before the qualification under *section 322* of this title of a trustee, such entity shall be deemed a customer, and the date of such transaction shall be deemed to be the date of the filing of the petition for the purpose of determining such entity's net equity.

(b) An entity does not have a claim as a customer to the extent that such entity transferred to the debtor cash or a security that, by contract, agreement, understanding, or operation of law, is—

  (1) part of the capital of the debtor; or

  (2) subordinated to the claims of any or all creditors.

(Pub. L. 95–598, Nov. 6, 1978, 92 Stat. 2613; Pub. L. 97–222, § 12, July 27, 1982, 96 Stat. 238.)

Sections that reference this section: None

§747. Subordination of certain customer claims

Except as provided in *section 510* of this title, unless all other customer net equity claims have been paid in full, the trustee may not pay in full or pay in part, directly or indirectly, any net equity claim of a customer that was, on the date the transaction giving rise to such claim occurred—

(1) an insider;

(2) a beneficial owner of at least five percent of any class of equity securities of the debtor, other than —

  (A) nonconvertible stock having fixed preferential dividend and liquidation rights; or

  (B) interests of limited partners in a limited partnership;

(3) a limited partner with a participation of at least five percent in the net assets or net profits of the debtor; or

(4) an entity that, directly or indirectly, through agreement or otherwise, exercised or had the power to exercise control over the management or policies of the debtor.

(Pub. L. 95–598, Nov. 6, 1978, 92 Stat. 2613; Pub. L. 97–222, § 13, July 27, 1982, 96 Stat. 238.)

Sections that reference this section: None

§748. Reduction of securities to money

As soon as practicable after the date of the order for relief, the trustee shall reduce to money, consistent with good market practice, all securities held as property of the estate, except for customer name securities delivered or reclaimed under *section 751* of this title.

(Pub. L. 95–598, Nov. 6, 1978, 92 Stat. 2614.)

Sections that reference this section: None

§749. Voidable transfers

(a) Except as otherwise provided in this section, any transfer of property that, but for such transfer, would have been customer property, may be avoided by the trustee, and such property shall be treated as customer property, if and to the extent that the trustee avoids such transfer under *section 544, 545, 547, 548,* or *549* of this title. For the purpose of such sections, the property so transferred shall be deemed to have been property of the debtor and, if such transfer was made to a customer or for a customer's benefit, such customer shall be deemed, for the purposes of this section, to have been a creditor.

(b) Notwithstanding *sections 544, 545, 547, 548,* and *549* of this title, the trustee may not avoid a transfer made before seven days after the order for relief if such transfer is approved by the Commission by rule or order, either before or after such transfer, and if such transfer is—

  (1) a transfer of a securities contract entered into or carried by or through the debtor on behalf of a customer, and of any cash, security, or other property margining or securing such securities contract; or

  (2) the liquidation of a securities contract entered into or carried by or through the debtor on behalf of a customer.

(Pub. L. 95–598, Nov. 6, 1978, 92 Stat. 2614; Pub. L. 97–222, § 14, July 27, 1982, 96 Stat. 238; Pub. L. 111–16, § 2(8), May 7, 2009, 123 Stat. 1607.)

Sections that reference this section: None

§750. Distribution of securities

The trustee may not distribute a security except under *section 751* of this title.

(Pub. L. 95–598, Nov. 6, 1978, 92 Stat. 2614.)

Sections that reference this section: None

§751. Customer name securities

The trustee shall deliver any customer name security to or on behalf of the customer entitled to such security, unless such customer has a negative net equity. With the approval of the trustee, a customer may reclaim a customer name security after payment to the trustee, within such period as the trustee allows, of any claim of the debtor against such customer to the extent that such customer will not have a negative net equity after such payment.

(Pub. L. 95–598, Nov. 6, 1978, 92 Stat. 2614.)

Sections that reference this section: 741, 748, 750

§752. Customer property

(a) The trustee shall distribute customer property ratably to customers on the basis and to the extent of such customers' allowed net equity claims and in priority to all other claims, except claims of the kind specified in *section 507(a)(2)* of this title that are attributable to the administration of such customer property.

(b)

(1) The trustee shall distribute customer property in excess of that distributed under subsection (a) of this section in accordance with *section 726* of this title.

(2) Except as provided in *section 510* of this title, if a customer is not paid the full amount of such customer's allowed net equity claim from customer property, the unpaid portion of such claim is a claim entitled to distribution under *section 726* of this title.

(c) Any cash or security remaining after the liquidation of a security interest created under a security agreement made by the debtor, excluding property excluded under *section 741(4)(B)* of this title, shall be apportioned between the general estate and customer property in the same proportion as the general estate of the debtor and customer property were subject to such security interest.

(Pub. L. 95–598, Nov. 6, 1978, 92 Stat. 2614; Pub. L. 97–222, § 15, July 27, 1982, 96 Stat. 238; Pub. L. 98–353, title III, § 484, July 10, 1984, 98 Stat. 383; Pub. L. 109–8, title XV, § 1502(a)(3), Apr. 20, 2005, 119 Stat. 216.)

Sections that reference this section: None

§753. Stockbroker liquidation and forward contract merchants, commodity brokers, stockbrokers, financial institutions, financial participants, securities clearing agencies, swap participants, repo participants, and master netting agreement participants

Notwithstanding any other provision of this title, the exercise of rights by a forward contract merchant, commodity broker, stockbroker, financial institution, financial participant, securities clearing agency, swap participant, repo participant, or master netting agreement participant under this title shall not affect the priority of any unsecured claim it may have after the exercise of such rights.

(Added Pub. L. 109–8, title IX, § 907(m), Apr. 20, 2005, 119 Stat. 181.)

Sections that reference this section: None

Subchapter IV: Commodity Broker Liquidation

§761. Definitions for this subchapter

In this subchapter—

(1) "Act" means Commodity Exchange Act;

(2) "clearing organization" means a derivatives clearing organization registered under the Act;

(3) "Commission" means Commodity Futures Trading Commission;

(4) "commodity contract" means—

(A) with respect to a futures commission merchant, contract for the purchase or sale of a commodity for future delivery on, or subject to the rules of, a contract market or board of trade;

(B) with respect to a foreign futures commission merchant, foreign future;

(C) with respect to a leverage transaction merchant, leverage transaction;

(D) with respect to a clearing organization, contract for the purchase or sale of a commodity for future delivery on, or subject to the rules of, a contract market or board of trade that is cleared by such clearing organization, or commodity option traded on, or subject to the rules of, a contract market or board of trade that is cleared by such clearing organization;

(E) with respect to a commodity options dealer, commodity option;

(F)

(i) any other contract, option, agreement, or transaction that is similar to a contract, option, agreement, or transaction referred to in this paragraph; and

(ii) with respect to a futures commission merchant or a clearing organization, any other contract, option, agreement, or transaction, in each case, that is cleared by a clearing organization;

(G) any combination of the agreements or transactions referred to in this paragraph;

(H) any option to enter into an agreement or transaction referred to in this paragraph;

(I) a master agreement that provides for an agreement or transaction referred to in subparagraph (A), (B), (C), (D), (E), (F), (G), or (H), together with all supplements to such master agreement, without regard to whether the master agreement provides for an agreement or transaction that is not a commodity contract under this paragraph, except that the master agreement shall be considered to be a commodity contract under this paragraph only with respect to each agreement or transaction under the master agreement that is referred to in subparagraph (A), (B), (C), (D), (E), (F), (G), or (H); or

(J) any security agreement or arrangement or other credit enhancement related to any agreement or transaction referred to in this paragraph, including any guarantee or reimbursement obligation by or to a commodity broker or financial participant in connection with any agreement or transaction referred to in this paragraph, but not to exceed the damages in connection with any such agreement or transaction, measured in accordance with *section 562*;

(5) "commodity option" means agreement or transaction subject to regulation under section 4c(b) of the Act;

(6) "commodity options dealer" means person that extends credit to, or that accepts cash, a security, or other property from, a customer of such person for the purchase or sale of an interest in a commodity option;

(7) "contract market" means a registered entity;

(8) "contract of sale", "commodity", "derivatives clearing organization", "future delivery", "board of trade", "registered entity", and "futures commission merchant" have the meanings assigned to those terms in the Act;

(9) "customer" means—

(A) with respect to a futures commission merchant—

(i) entity for or with whom such futures commission merchant deals and that holds a claim against such futures commission merchant on account of a commodity contract made, received, acquired, or held by or through such futures commission merchant in the ordinary course of such futures commission merchant's business as a futures commission merchant from or for a commodity contract account of such entity; or

(ii) entity that holds a claim against such futures commission merchant arising out of—

(I) the making, liquidation, or change in the value of a commodity contract of a kind specified in clause (i) of this subparagraph;

(II) a deposit or payment of cash, a security, or other property with such futures commission merchant for the purpose of making or margining such a commodity contract; or

(III) the making or taking of delivery on such a commodity contract;

(B) with respect to a foreign futures commission merchant—

(i) entity for or with whom such foreign futures commission merchant deals and that holds a claim against such foreign futures commission merchant on account of a commodity contract made, received, acquired, or held by or through such foreign futures commission merchant in the ordinary course of such foreign futures commission merchant's business as a foreign futures commission merchant from or for the foreign futures account of such entity; or

(ii) entity that holds a claim against such foreign futures commission merchant arising out of—

(I) the making, liquidation, or change in value of a commodity contract of a kind specified in clause (i) of this subparagraph;

(II) a deposit or payment of cash, a security, or other property with such foreign futures commission merchant for the purpose of making or margining such a commodity contract; or

(III) the making or taking of delivery on such a commodity contract;

(C) with respect to a leverage transaction merchant—

(i) entity for or with whom such leverage transaction merchant deals and that holds a claim against such leverage transaction merchant on account of a commodity contract engaged in by or with such leverage transaction merchant in the ordinary course of such leverage transaction merchant's business as a leverage transaction merchant from or for the leverage account of such entity; or

(ii) entity that holds a claim against such leverage transaction merchant arising out of—

(I) the making, liquidation, or change in value of a commodity contract of a kind specified in clause (i) of this subparagraph;

(II) a deposit or payment of cash, a security, or other property with such leverage transaction merchant for the purpose of entering into or margining such a commodity contract; or

(III) the making or taking of delivery on such a commodity contract;

(D) with respect to a clearing organization, clearing member of such clearing organization with whom such clearing organization deals and that holds a claim against such clearing organization on account of cash, a security, or other property received by such clearing organization to margin, guarantee, or secure a commodity contract in such clearing member's proprietary account or customers' account; or

(E) with respect to a commodity options dealer—

(i) entity for or with whom such commodity options dealer deals and that holds a claim on account of a commodity contract made, received, acquired, or held by or through such commodity options dealer in the ordinary course of such commodity options dealer's business as a commodity options dealer from or for the commodity options account of such entity; or

(ii) entity that holds a claim against such commodity options dealer arising out of—

(I) the making of, liquidation of, exercise of, or a change in value of, a commodity contract of a kind specified in clause (i) of this subparagraph; or

(II) a deposit or payment of cash, a security, or other property with such commodity options dealer for the purpose of making, exercising, or margining such a commodity contract;

(10) "customer property" means cash, a security, or other property, or proceeds of such cash, security, or property, received, acquired, or held by or for the account of the debtor, from or for the account of a customer—

(A) including—

(i) property received, acquired, or held to margin, guarantee, secure, purchase, or sell a commodity contract;

(ii) profits or contractual or other rights accruing to a customer as a result of a commodity contract;

(iii) an open commodity contract;

(iv) specifically identifiable customer property;

(v) warehouse receipt or other document held by the debtor evidencing ownership of or title to property to be delivered to fulfill a commodity contract from or for the account of a customer;

(vi) cash, a security, or other property received by the debtor as payment for a commodity to be delivered to fulfill a commodity contract from or for the account of a customer;

(vii) a security held as property of the debtor to the extent such security is necessary to meet a net equity claim based on a security of the same class and series of an issuer;

(viii) property that was unlawfully converted from and that is the lawful property of the estate; and

(ix) other property of the debtor that any applicable law, rule, or regulation requires to be set aside or held for the benefit of a customer, unless including such property as customer property would not significantly increase customer property; but

(B) not including property to the extent that a customer does not have a claim against the debtor based on such property;

(11) "foreign future" means contract for the purchase or sale of a commodity for future delivery on, or subject to the rules of, a board of trade outside the United States;

(12) "foreign futures commission merchant" means entity engaged in soliciting or accepting orders for the purchase or sale of a foreign future or that, in connection with such a solicitation or acceptance, accepts cash, a security, or other property, or extends credit to margin, guarantee, or secure any trade or contract that results from such a solicitation or acceptance;

(13) "leverage transaction" means agreement that is subject to regulation under section 19 of the Commodity Exchange Act, and that is commonly known to the commodities trade as a margin account, margin contract, leverage account, or leverage contract;

(14) "leverage transaction merchant" means person in the business of engaging in leverage transactions;

(15) "margin payment" means payment or deposit of cash, a security, or other property, that is commonly known to the commodities trade as original margin, initial margin, maintenance margin, or variation margin, including mark-to-market payments, settlement payments, variation payments, daily settlement payments, and final settlement payments made as adjustments to settlement prices;

(16) "member property" means customer property received, acquired, or held by or for the account of a debtor that is a clearing organization, from or for the proprietary account of a customer that is a clearing member of the debtor; and

(17) "net equity" means, subject to such rules and regulations as the Commission promulgates under the Act, with respect to the aggregate of all of a customer's accounts that such customer has in the same capacity—

(A) the balance remaining in such customer's accounts immediately after—

(i) all commodity contracts of such customer have been transferred, liquidated, or become identified for delivery; and

(ii) all obligations of such customer in such capacity to the debtor have been offset; plus

(B) the value, as of the date of return under *section 766* of this title, of any specifically identifiable customer property actually returned to such customer before the date specified in subparagraph (A) of this paragraph; plus

(C) the value, as of the date of transfer, of—

(i) any commodity contract to which such customer is entitled that is transferred to another person under *section 766* of this title; and

(ii) any cash, security, or other property of such customer transferred to such other person under *section 766* of this title to margin or secure such transferred commodity contract.

(Pub. L. 95–598, Nov. 6, 1978, 92 Stat. 2615; Pub. L. 97–222, § 16, July 27, 1982, 96 Stat. 238; Pub. L. 98–353, title III, § 485, July 10, 1984, 98 Stat. 383; Pub. L. 103–394, title V, § 501(d)(29), Oct. 22, 1994, 108 Stat. 4146; Pub. L. 106–554, § 1(a)(5) [title I, § 112(c)(6)], Dec. 21, 2000, 114 Stat. 2763, 2763A–395; Pub. L. 109–8, title IX, § 907(a)(3), Apr. 20, 2005, 119 Stat. 174; Pub. L. 111–203, title VII, § 724(b), July 21, 2010, 124 Stat. 1684.)

Sections that reference this section: 101, 546, 556, 561, 562

§762. Notice to the Commission and right to be heard

(a) The clerk shall give the notice required by *section 342* of this title to the Commission.

(b) The Commission may raise and may appear and be heard on any issue in a case under this chapter.

(Pub. L. 95–598, Nov. 6, 1978, 92 Stat. 2618.)

Sections that reference this section: None

§763. Treatment of accounts

(a) Accounts held by the debtor for a particular customer in separate capacities shall be treated as accounts of separate customers.

(b) A member of a clearing organization shall be deemed to hold such member's proprietary account in a separate capacity from such member's customers' account.

(c) The net equity in a customer's account may not be offset against the net equity in the account of any other customer.

(Pub. L. 95–598, Nov. 6, 1978, 92 Stat. 2618; Pub. L. 98–353, title III, § 486, July 10, 1984, 98 Stat. 383.)

Sections that reference this section: None

§764. Voidable transfers

(a) Except as otherwise provided in this section, any transfer by the debtor of property that, but for such transfer, would have been customer property, may be avoided by the trustee, and such property shall be treated as customer property, if and to the extent that the trustee avoids such transfer under *section 544, 545, 547, 548, 549*, or *724*(a) of this title. For the purpose of such sections, the property so transferred shall be deemed to have been property of the debtor, and, if such transfer was made to a customer or for a customer's benefit, such customer shall be deemed, for the purposes of this section, to have been a creditor.

(b) Notwithstanding *sections 544, 545, 547, 548, 549*, and *724*(a) of this title, the trustee may not avoid a transfer made before seven days after the order for relief, if such transfer is approved by the Commission by rule or order, either before or after such transfer, and if such transfer is—

(1) a transfer of a commodity contract entered into or carried by or through the debtor on behalf of a customer, and of any cash, securities, or other property margining or securing such commodity contract; or

(2) the liquidation of a commodity contract entered into or carried by or through the debtor on behalf of a customer.

(Pub. L. 95–598, Nov. 6, 1978, 92 Stat. 2618; Pub. L. 97–222, § 17, July 27, 1982, 96 Stat. 240; Pub. L. 98–353, title III, § 487, July 10, 1984, 98 Stat. 383; Pub. L. 111–16, § 2(9), May 7, 2009, 123 Stat. 1607.)

Sections that reference this section: None

§765. Customer instructions

(a) The notice required by *section 342* of this title to customers shall instruct each customer—

(1) to file a proof of such customer's claim promptly, and to specify in such claim any specifically identifiable security, property, or commodity contract; and

(2) to instruct the trustee of such customer's desired disposition, including transfer under *section 766* of this title or liquidation, of any commodity contract specifically identified to such customer.

(b) The trustee shall comply, to the extent practicable, with any instruction received from a customer regarding such customer's desired disposition of any commodity contract specifically identified to such customer. If the trustee has transferred, under *section 766* of this title, such a commodity contract, the trustee shall transmit any such instruction to the commodity broker to whom such commodity contract was so transferred.

(Pub. L. 95–598, Nov. 6, 1978, 92 Stat. 2619; Pub. L. 97–222, § 18, July 27, 1982, 96 Stat. 240; Pub. L. 98–353, title III, § 488, July 10, 1984, 98 Stat. 383.)

Sections that reference this section: 365

§766. Treatment of customer property

(a) The trustee shall answer all margin calls with respect to a specifically identifiable commodity contract of a customer until such time as the trustee returns or transfers such commodity contract, but the trustee may not make a margin payment that has the effect of a distribution to such customer of more than that to which such customer is entitled under subsection (h) or (i) of this section.

(b) The trustee shall prevent any open commodity contract from remaining open after the last day of trading in such commodity contract, or into the first day on which notice of intent to deliver on such commodity contract may be tendered, whichever occurs first. With respect to any commodity contract that has remained open after the last day of trading in such commodity contract or with respect to which delivery must be made or accepted under the rules of the contract market on which such commodity contract was made, the trustee may operate the business of the debtor for the purpose of—

(1) accepting or making tender of notice of intent to deliver the physical commodity underlying such commodity contract;

(2) facilitating delivery of such commodity; or

(3) disposing of such commodity if a party to such commodity contract defaults.

(c) The trustee shall return promptly to a customer any specifically identifiable security, property, or commodity contract to which such customer is entitled, or shall transfer, on such customer's behalf, such security, property, or commodity contract to a commodity broker that is not a debtor under this title, subject to such rules or regulations as the Commission may prescribe, to the extent that the value of such security, property, or commodity contract does not exceed the amount to which such customer would be entitled under subsection (h) or (i) of this section if such security, property, or commodity contract were not returned or transferred under this subsection.

(d) If the value of a specifically identifiable security, property, or commodity contract exceeds the amount to which the customer of the debtor is entitled under subsection (h) or (i) of this section, then such customer to whom such security, property, or commodity contract is specifically identified may deposit cash with the trustee equal to the difference between the value of such security, property, or commodity contract and such amount, and the trustee then shall—

(1) return promptly such security, property, or commodity contract to such customer; or

(2) transfer, on such customer's behalf, such security, property, or commodity contract to a commodity broker that is not a debtor under this title, subject to such rules or regulations as the Commission may prescribe.

(e) Subject to subsection (b) of this section, the trustee shall liquidate any commodity contract that—

(1) is identified to a particular customer and with respect to which such customer has not timely instructed the trustee as to the desired disposition of such commodity contract;

(2) cannot be transferred under subsection (c) of this section; or

(3) cannot be identified to a particular customer.

(f) As soon as practicable after the commencement of the case, the trustee shall reduce to money, consistent with good market practice, all securities and other property, other than commodity contracts, held as property of the estate, except for specifically identifiable securities or property distributable under subsection (h) or (i) of this section.

(g) The trustee may not distribute a security or other property except under subsection (h) or (i) of this section.

(h) Except as provided in subsection (b) of this section, the trustee shall distribute customer property ratably to customers on the basis and to the extent of such customers' allowed net equity claims, and in priority to all other claims, except claims of a kind specified in *section 507(a)(2)* of this title that are attributable to the administration of customer property. Such distribution shall be in the form of—

(1) cash;

(2) the return or transfer, under subsection (c) or (d) of this section, of specifically identifiable customer securities, property, or commodity contracts; or

(3) payment of margin calls under subsection (a) of this section.

Notwithstanding any other provision of this subsection, a customer net equity claim based on a proprietary account, as defined by Commission rule, regulation, or order, may not be paid either in whole or in part, directly or indirectly, out of customer property unless all other customer net equity claims have been paid in full.

(i) If the debtor is a clearing organization, the trustee shall distribute—

(1) customer property, other than member property, ratably to customers on the basis and to the extent of such customers' allowed net equity claims based on such customers' accounts other than proprietary accounts, and in priority to all other claims, except claims of a kind specified in *section 507(a)(2)* of this title that are attributable to

the administration of such customer property; and

(2) member property ratably to customers on the basis and to the extent of such customers' allowed net equity claims based on such customers' proprietary accounts, and in priority to all other claims, except claims of a kind specified in *section 507(a)(2)* of this title that are attributable to the administration of member property or customer property.

(j)

(1) The trustee shall distribute customer property in excess of that distributed under subsection (h) or (i) of this section in accordance with *section 726* of this title.

(2) Except as provided in *section 510* of this title, if a customer is not paid the full amount of such customer's allowed net equity claim from customer property, the unpaid portion of such claim is a claim entitled to distribution under *section 726* of this title.

(Pub. L. 95–598, Nov. 6, 1978, 92 Stat. 2619; Pub. L. 97–222, § 19, July 27, 1982, 96 Stat. 240; Pub. L. 98–353, title III, § 489, July 10, 1984, 98 Stat. 383; Pub. L. 109–8, title XV, § 1502(a)(4), Apr. 20, 2005, 119 Stat. 216.)

Sections that reference this section: 761, 765

§767. Commodity broker liquidation and forward contract merchants, commodity brokers, stockbrokers, financial institutions, financial participants, securities clearing agencies, swap participants, repo participants, and master netting agreement participants

Notwithstanding any other provision of this title, the exercise of rights by a forward contract merchant, commodity broker, stockbroker, financial institution, financial participant, securities clearing agency, swap participant, repo participant, or master netting agreement participant under this title shall not affect the priority of any unsecured claim it may have after the exercise of such rights.

(Added Pub. L. 109–8, title IX, § 907(l), Apr. 20, 2005, 119 Stat. 181.)

Sections that reference this section: None

Subchapter V: Clearing Bank Liquidation

§781. Definitions

For purposes of this subchapter, the following definitions shall apply:

(1) Board.—

The term "Board" means the Board of Governors of the Federal Reserve System.

(2) Depository institution.—

The term "depository institution" has the same meaning as in section 3 of the Federal Deposit Insurance Act.

(3) Clearing bank.—

The term "clearing bank" means an uninsured State member bank, or a corporation organized under section 25A of the Federal Reserve Act, which operates, or operates as, a multilateral clearing organization pursuant to section 409 of the Federal Deposit Insurance Corporation Improvement Act of 1991.

(Added Pub. L. 106–554, § 1(a)(5) [title I, § 112(c)(5)(B)], Dec. 21, 2000, 114 Stat. 2763, 2763A–394.)

Sections that reference this section: None

§782. Selection of trustee

(a) In General.—

(1) Appointment.—

Notwithstanding any other provision of this title, the conservator or receiver who files the petition shall be the trustee under this chapter, unless the Board designates an alternative trustee.

(2) Successor.—

The Board may designate a successor trustee if required.

(b) Authority of Trustee.—

Whenever the Board appoints or designates a trustee, chapter 3 and *sections 704* and *705* of this title shall apply to the Board in the same way and to the same extent that they apply to a United States trustee.

(Added Pub. L. 106–554, § 1(a)(5) [title I, § 112(c)(5)(B)], Dec. 21, 2000, 114 Stat. 2763, 2763A–394.)

Sections that reference this section: None

§783. Additional powers of trustee

(a) Distribution of Property Not of the Estate.—

The trustee under this subchapter has power to distribute property not of the estate, including distributions to customers that are mandated by subchapters III and IV of this chapter.

(b) Disposition of Institution.—

The trustee under this subchapter may, after notice and a hearing—

(1) sell the clearing bank to a depository institution or consortium of depository institutions (which consortium may agree on the allocation of the clearing bank among the consortium);

(2) merge the clearing bank with a depository institution;

(3) transfer contracts to the same extent as could a receiver for a depository institution under paragraphs (9) and (10) of section 11(e) of the Federal Deposit Insurance Act;

(4) transfer assets or liabilities to a depository institution; and

(5) transfer assets and liabilities to a bridge depository institution as provided in paragraphs (1), (3)(A), (5), and (6) of section 11(n) of the Federal Deposit Insurance Act, paragraphs (9) through (13) of such section, and subparagraphs (A) through (H) and subparagraph (K) of paragraph (4) of such section 11(n), except that—

(A) the bridge depository institution to which such assets or liabilities are transferred shall be treated as a clearing bank for the purpose of this subsection; and

(B) any references in any such provision of law to the Federal Deposit Insurance Corporation shall be construed to be references to the appointing agency and that references to deposit insurance shall be omitted.

(c) Certain Transfers Included.—

Any reference in this section to transfers of liabilities includes a ratable transfer of liabilities within a priority class.

(Added Pub. L. 106–554, § 1(a)(5) [title I, § 112(c)(5)(B)], Dec. 21, 2000, 114 Stat. 2763, 2763A–395; amended Pub. L. 110–289, div. A, title VI, § 1604(b)(3), July 30, 2008, 122 Stat. 2829.)

Sections that reference this section: None

§784. Right to be heard

The Board or a Federal reserve bank (in the case of a clearing bank that is a member of that bank) may raise and may appear and be heard on any issue in a case under this subchapter.

(Added Pub. L. 106–554, § 1(a)(5) [title I, § 112(c)(5)(B)], Dec. 21, 2000, 114 Stat. 2763, 2763A–395.)

Sections that reference this section: None

CHAPTER 9: ADJUSTMENT OF DEBTS OF A MUNICIPALITY

Subchapter I: General Provisions

§901. Applicability of other sections of this title

(a) *Sections 301, 333, 344, 347*(b), 349, 350(b) 351,, 361, 362, 364(c), 364(d), 364(e), 364(f), 365, 366, 501, 502, 503, 504, 506, 507(a)(2), 509, 510, 524(a)(1), 524(a)(2), 544, 545, 546, 547, 548, 549(a), 549(c), 549(d), 550, 551, 552, 553, 555, 556, 557, 559, 560, 561, 562, 1102, 1103, 1109, 1111(b), 1122, 1123(a)(1), 1123(a)(2), 1123(a)(3), 1123(a)(4), 1123(a)(5), 1123(b), 1123(d), 1124, 1125, 1126(a), 1126(b), 1126(c), 1126(e), 1126(f), 1126(g), 1127(d), 1128, 1129(a)(2), 1129(a)(3), 1129(a)(6), 1129(a)(8), 1129(a)(10), 1129(b)(1), 1129(b)(2)(A), 1129(b)(2)(B), 1142(b), 1143, 1144, and 1145 of this title apply in a case under this chapter.

(b) A term used in a section of this title made applicable in a case under this chapter by subsection (a) of this section or *section 103(e)* of this title has the meaning defined for such term for the purpose of such applicable section, unless such term is otherwise defined in *section 902* of this title.

(c) A section made applicable in a case under this chapter by subsection (a) of this section that is operative if the business of the debtor is authorized to be operated is operative in a case under this chapter.

(Pub. L. 95–598, Nov. 6, 1978, 92 Stat. 2621; Pub. L. 98–353, title III, §§ 353, 490, July 10, 1984, 98 Stat. 361, 383; Pub. L. 100–597, § 3, Nov. 3, 1988, 102 Stat. 3028; Pub. L. 109–8, title V, § 502, title XII, § 1216, title XV, § 1502(a)(5), Apr. 20, 2005, 119 Stat. 118, 195, 216; Pub. L. 111–327, § 2(a)(29), Dec. 22, 2010, 124 Stat. 3560.)

Sections that reference this section: 101, 103, 707

§902. Definitions for this chapter

In this chapter—

(1) “property of the estate”, when used in a section that is made applicable in a case under this chapter by *section 103(e)* or 901 of this title, means property of the debtor;

(2) “special revenues” means—

(A) receipts derived from the ownership, operation, or disposition of projects or systems of the debtor that are primarily used or intended to be used primarily to provide transportation, utility, or other services, including the proceeds of borrowings to finance the projects or systems;

(B) special excise taxes imposed on particular activities or transactions;

(C) incremental tax receipts from the benefited area in the case of tax-increment financing;

(D) other revenues or receipts derived from particular functions of the debtor, whether or not the debtor has other functions; or

(E) taxes specifically levied to finance one or more projects or systems, excluding receipts from general property, sales, or income taxes (other than tax-increment financing) levied to finance the general purposes of the debtor;

(3) “special tax payer” means record owner or holder of legal or equitable title to real property against which a special assessment or special tax has been levied the proceeds of which are the sole source of payment of an obligation issued by the debtor to defray the cost of an improvement relating to such real property;

(4) “special tax payer affected by the plan” means special tax payer with respect to whose real property the plan proposes to increase the proportion of special assessments or special taxes referred to in paragraph (2) of this section assessed against such real property; and

(5) “trustee”, when used in a section that is made applicable in a case under this chapter by *section 103(e)* 1 or 901 of this title, means debtor, except as provided in *section 926* of this title.

(Pub. L. 95–598, Nov. 6, 1978, 92 Stat. 2622; Pub. L. 98–353, title III, § 491, July 10, 1984, 98 Stat. 383; Pub. L. 100–597, § 4, Nov. 3, 1988, 102 Stat. 3028.)

Sections that reference this section: 901

§903. Reservation of State power to control municipalities

This chapter does not limit or impair the power of a State to control, by legislation or otherwise, a municipality of or in such State in the exercise of the political or governmental powers of such municipality, including expenditures for such exercise, but —

(1) a State law prescribing a method of composition of indebtedness of such municipality may not bind any creditor that does not consent to such composition; and

(2) a judgment entered under such a law may not bind a creditor that does not consent to such composition.

(Pub. L. 95–598, Nov. 6, 1978, 92 Stat. 2622; Pub. L. 98–353, title III, § 492, July 10, 1984, 98 Stat. 383.)

Sections that reference this section: None

§904. Limitation on jurisdiction and powers of court

Notwithstanding any power of the court, unless the debtor consents or the plan so provides, the court may not, by any stay, order, or decree, in the case or otherwise, interfere with—

(1) any of the political or governmental powers of the debtor;

(2) any of the property or revenues of the debtor; or

(3) the debtor's use or enjoyment of any income-producing property.

(Pub. L. 95–598, Nov. 6, 1978, 92 Stat. 2622.)

Sections that reference this section: None

Subchapter II: Administration

§921. Petition and proceedings relating to petition

(a) Notwithstanding *sections 109(d)* and *301* of this title, a case under this chapter concerning an unincorporated tax or special assessment district that does not have such district's own officials is commenced by the filing under *section 301* of this title of a petition under this chapter by such district's governing authority or the board or body having authority to levy taxes or assessments to meet the obligations of such district.

(b) The chief judge of the court of appeals for the circuit embracing the district in which the case is commenced shall designate the bankruptcy judge to conduct the case.

(c) After any objection to the petition, the court, after notice and a hearing, may dismiss the petition if the debtor did not file the petition in good faith or if the petition does not meet the requirements of this title.

(d) If the petition is not dismissed under subsection (c) of this section, the court shall order relief under this chapter notwithstanding *section 301(b)*.

(e) The court may not, on account of an appeal from an order for relief, delay any proceeding under this chapter in the case in which the appeal is being taken; nor shall any court order a stay of such proceeding pending such appeal. The reversal on appeal of a finding of jurisdiction does not affect the validity of any debt incurred that is authorized by the court under *section 364(c)* or *364*(d) of this title.

(Pub. L. 95–598, Nov. 6, 1978, 92 Stat. 2622; Pub. L. 98–353, title III, § 494, July 10, 1984, 98 Stat. 383; Pub. L. 109–8, title V, § 501(a), Apr. 20, 2005, 119 Stat. 118.)

Sections that reference this section: None

§922. Automatic stay of enforcement of claims against the debtor

(a) A petition filed under this chapter operates as a stay, in addition to the stay provided by *section 362* of this title, applicable to all entities, of—

(1) the commencement or continuation, including the issuance or employment of process, of a judicial, administrative, or other action or proceeding against an officer or inhabitant of the debtor that seeks to enforce a claim against the debtor; and

(2) the enforcement of a lien on or arising out of taxes or assessments owed to the debtor.

(b) Subsections (c), (d), (e), (f), and (g) of *section 362* of this title apply to a stay under subsection (a) of this section the same as such subsections apply to a stay under *section 362(a)* of this title.

(c) If the debtor provides, under *section 362, 364,* or 922 of this title, adequate protection of the interest of the holder of a claim secured by a lien on property of the debtor and if, notwithstanding such protection such creditor has a claim arising from the stay of action against such property under *section 362* or 922 of this title or from the granting of a lien under *section 364(d)* of this title, then such claim shall be allowable as an administrative expense under *section 503(b)* of this title.

(d) Notwithstanding *section 362* of this title and subsection (a) of this section, a petition filed under this chapter does not operate as a stay of application of pledged special revenues in a manner consistent with *section 927* of this title to payment of indebtedness secured by such revenues.

(Pub. L. 95–598, Nov. 6, 1978, 92 Stat. 2623; Pub. L. 98–353, title III, § 495, July 10, 1984, 98 Stat. 384; Pub. L. 100–597, § 5, Nov. 3, 1988, 102 Stat. 3029.)

Sections that reference this section: None

§923. Notice

There shall be given notice of the commencement of a case under this chapter, notice of an order for relief under this chapter, and notice of the dismissal of a case under this chapter. Such notice shall also be published at least once a week for three successive weeks in at least one newspaper of general circulation published within the district in which the case is commenced, and in such other newspaper having a general circulation among bond dealers and bondholders as the court designates.

(Pub. L. 95–598, Nov. 6, 1978, 92 Stat. 2623.)

Sections that reference this section: None

§924. List of creditors

The debtor shall file a list of creditors.

(Pub. L. 95–598, Nov. 6, 1978, 92 Stat. 2623.)

Sections that reference this section: 707, 925

§925. Effect of list of claims

A proof of claim is deemed filed under *section 501* of this title for any claim that appears in the list filed under *section 924* of this title, except a claim that is listed as disputed, contingent, or unliquidated.

(Pub. L. 95–598, Nov. 6, 1978, 92 Stat. 2623.)

Sections that reference this section: None

§926. Avoiding powers

(a) If the debtor refuses to pursue a cause of action under *section 544, 545, 547, 548, 549*(a), or 550 of this title, then on request of a creditor, the court may appoint a trustee to pursue such cause of action.

(b) A transfer of property of the debtor to or for the benefit of any holder of a bond or note, on account of such bond or note, may not be avoided under *section 547* of this title.

(Pub. L. 95–598, Nov. 6, 1978, 92 Stat. 2623; Pub. L. 100–597, § 6, Nov. 3, 1988, 102 Stat. 3029.)

Sections that reference this section: 902

§927. Limitation on recourse

The holder of a claim payable solely from special revenues of the debtor under applicable nonbankruptcy law shall not be treated as having recourse against the debtor on account of such claim pursuant to *section 1111(b)* of this title.

(Added Pub. L. 100–597, § 7(2), Nov. 3, 1988, 102 Stat. 3029.)

Sections that reference this section: 922

§928. Post petition effect of security interest

(a) Notwithstanding *section 552(a)* of this title and subject to subsection (b) of this section, special revenues acquired by the debtor after the commencement of the case shall remain subject to any lien resulting from any security agreement entered into by the debtor before the commencement of the case.

(b) Any such lien on special revenues, other than municipal betterment assessments, derived from a project or system shall be subject to the necessary operating expenses of such project or system, as the case may be.

(Added Pub. L. 100–597, § 8, Nov. 3, 1988, 102 Stat. 3029.)

Sections that reference this section: None

§929. Municipal leases

A lease to a municipality shall not be treated as an executory contract or unexpired lease for the purposes of *section 365* or *502*(b)(6) of this title solely by reason of its being subject to termination in the event the debtor fails to appropriate rent.

(Added Pub. L. 100–597, § 9, Nov. 3, 1988, 102 Stat. 3030.)

Sections that reference this section: None

§930. Dismissal

(a) After notice and a hearing, the court may dismiss a case under this chapter for cause, including—
    (1) want of prosecution;
    (2) unreasonable delay by the debtor that is prejudicial to creditors;
    (3) failure to propose a plan within the time fixed under *section 941* of this title;

(4) if a plan is not accepted within any time fixed by the court;

(5) denial of confirmation of a plan under *section 943(b)* of this title and denial of additional time for filing another plan or a modification of a plan; or

(6) if the court has retained jurisdiction after confirmation of a plan—

(A) material default by the debtor with respect to a term of such plan; or

(B) termination of such plan by reason of the occurrence of a condition specified in such plan.

(b) The court shall dismiss a case under this chapter if confirmation of a plan under this chapter is refused.

(Pub. L. 95–598, Nov. 6, 1978, 92 Stat. 2623, § 927; Pub. L. 98–353, title III, § 496, July 10, 1984, 98 Stat. 384; renumbered § 930, Pub. L. 100–597, § 7(1), Nov. 3, 1988, 102 Stat. 3029.)

Sections that reference this section: None

Subchapter III: The Plan

§941. Filing of plan

The debtor shall file a plan for the adjustment of the debtor's debts. If such a plan is not filed with the petition, the debtor shall file such a plan at such later time as the court fixes.

(Pub. L. 95–598, Nov. 6, 1978, 92 Stat. 2624.)

Sections that reference this section: 930

§942. Modification of plan

The debtor may modify the plan at any time before confirmation, but may not modify the plan so that the plan as modified fails to meet the requirements of this chapter. After the debtor files a modification, the plan as modified becomes the plan.

(Pub. L. 95–598, Nov. 6, 1978, 92 Stat. 2624.)

Sections that reference this section: None

§943. Confirmation

(a) A special tax payer may object to confirmation of a plan.

(b) The court shall confirm the plan if—

(1) the plan complies with the provisions of this title made applicable by *sections 103(e)* and 901 of this title;

(2) the plan complies with the provisions of this chapter;

(3) all amounts to be paid by the debtor or by any person for services or expenses in the case or incident to the plan have been fully disclosed and are reasonable;

(4) the debtor is not prohibited by law from taking any action necessary to carry out the plan;

(5) except to the extent that the holder of a particular claim has agreed to a different treatment of such claim, the plan provides that on the effective date of the plan each holder of a claim of a kind specified in *section 507(a)(2)* of this title will receive on account of such claim cash equal to the allowed amount of such claim;

(6) any regulatory or electoral approval necessary under applicable nonbankruptcy law in order to carry out any provision of the plan has been obtained, or such provision is expressly conditioned on such approval; and

(7) the plan is in the best interests of creditors and is feasible.

(Pub. L. 95–598, Nov. 6, 1978, 92 Stat. 2624; Pub. L. 98–353, title III, § 497, July 10, 1984, 98 Stat. 384; Pub. L. 100–597, § 10, Nov. 3, 1988, 102 Stat. 3030; Pub. L. 109–8, title XV, § 1502(a)(6), Apr. 20, 2005, 119 Stat. 216.)

Sections that reference this section: 347, 930

§944. Effect of confirmation

(a) The provisions of a confirmed plan bind the debtor and any creditor, whether or not—

(1) a proof of such creditor's claim is filed or deemed filed under *section 501* of this title;

(2) such claim is allowed under *section 502* of this title; or

(3) such creditor has accepted the plan.

(b) Except as provided in subsection (c) of this section, the debtor is discharged from all debts as of the time when—

(1) the plan is confirmed;

(2) the debtor deposits any consideration to be distributed under the plan with a disbursing agent appointed by the court; and

(3) the court has determined—

(A) that any security so deposited will constitute, after distribution, a valid legal obligation of the debtor; and

(B) that any provision made to pay or secure payment of such obligation is valid.

(c) The debtor is not discharged under subsection (b) of this section from any debt—

(1) excepted from discharge by the plan or order confirming the plan; or

(2) owed to an entity that, before confirmation of the plan, had neither notice nor actual knowledge of the case.

(Pub. L. 95–598, Nov. 6, 1978, 92 Stat. 2624.)

Sections that reference this section: None

§945. Continuing jurisdiction and closing of the case

(a) The court may retain jurisdiction over the case for such period of time as is necessary for the successful implementation of the plan.

(b) Except as provided in subsection (a) of this section, the court shall close the case when administration of the case has been completed.

(Pub. L. 95–598, Nov. 6, 1978, 92 Stat. 2625; Pub. L. 98–353, title III, § 498, July 10, 1984, 98 Stat. 384.)

Sections that reference this section: None

§946. Effect of exchange of securities before the date of the filing of the petition

The exchange of a new security under the plan for a claim covered by the plan, whether such exchange occurred before or after the date of the filing of the petition, does not limit or impair the effectiveness of the plan or of any provision of this chapter. The amount and number specified in *section 1126(c)* of this title include the amount and number of claims formerly held by a creditor that has participated in any such exchange.

(Pub. L. 95–598, Nov. 6, 1978, 92 Stat. 2625.)

Sections that reference this section: None

CHAPTER 11: REORGANIZATION

Subchapter I: Officers and Administration

§1101. Definitions for this chapter

In this chapter—

(1) "debtor in possession" means debtor except when a person that has qualified under *section 322* of this title is serving as trustee in the case;

(2) "substantial consummation" means—

(A) transfer of all or substantially all of the property proposed by the plan to be transferred;

(B) assumption by the debtor or by the successor to the debtor under the plan of the business or of the management of all or substantially all of the property dealt with by the plan; and

(C) commencement of distribution under the plan.

(Pub. L. 95–598, Nov. 6, 1978, 92 Stat. 2626.)

Sections that reference this section: None

§1102. Creditors' and equity security holders' committees

(a)

(1) Except as provided in paragraph (3), as soon as practicable after the order for relief under chapter 11 of this title, the United States trustee shall appoint a committee of creditors holding unsecured claims and may appoint additional committees of creditors or of equity security holders as the United States trustee deems appropriate.

(2) On request of a party in interest, the court may order the appointment of additional committees of creditors or of equity security holders if necessary to assure adequate representation of creditors or of equity security holders. The United States trustee shall appoint any such committee.

(3) Unless the court for cause orders otherwise, a committee of creditors may not be appointed in a small business case or a case under subchapter V of this chapter.

(4) On request of a party in interest and after notice and a hearing, the court may order the United States trustee to change the membership of a committee appointed under this subsection, if the court determines that the change is necessary to ensure adequate representation of creditors or equity security holders. The court may order the United States trustee to increase the number of members of a committee to include a creditor that is a small business concern (as described in section 3(a)(1) of the Small Business Act), if the court determines that the creditor holds claims (of the kind represented by the committee) the aggregate amount of which, in comparison to the annual gross revenue of that creditor, is disproportionately large.

(b)

(1) A committee of creditors appointed under subsection (a) of this section shall ordinarily consist of the persons, willing to serve, that hold the seven largest claims against the debtor of the kinds represented on such committee, or of the members of a committee organized by creditors before the commencement of the case under this chapter, if such committee was fairly chosen and is representative of the different kinds of claims to be represented.

(2) A committee of equity security holders appointed under subsection (a)(2) of this section shall ordinarily consist of the persons, willing to serve, that hold the seven largest amounts of equity securities of the debtor of the kinds represented on such committee.

(3) A committee appointed under subsection (a) shall—

(A) provide access to information for creditors who—

(i) hold claims of the kind represented by that committee; and

(ii) are not appointed to the committee;

(B) solicit and receive comments from the creditors described in subparagraph (A); and

(C) be subject to a court order that compels any additional report or disclosure to be made to the creditors described in subparagraph (A).

(Pub. L. 95–598, Nov. 6, 1978, 92 Stat. 2626; Pub. L. 98–353, title III, § 499, July 10, 1984, 98 Stat. 384; Pub. L. 99–554, title II, § 221, Oct. 27, 1986, 100 Stat. 3101; Pub. L. 103–394, title II, § 217(b), Oct. 22, 1994, 108 Stat. 4127; Pub. L. 109–8, title IV, §§ 405, 432(b), Apr. 20, 2005, 119 Stat. 105, 110; Pub. L. 116–54, § 4(a)(11), Aug. 23, 2019, 133 Stat. 1086.)

Sections that reference this section: 101, 1103, 1114, 1181, 328, 503

§1103. Powers and duties of committees

(a) At a scheduled meeting of a committee appointed under *section 1102* of this title, at which a majority of the members of such committee are present, and with the court's approval, such committee may select and authorize the employment by such committee of one or more attorneys, accountants, or other agents, to represent or perform services for such committee.

(b) An attorney or accountant employed to represent a committee appointed under *section 1102* of this title may not, while employed by such committee, represent any other entity having an adverse interest in connection with the case. Representation of one or more creditors of the same class as represented by the committee shall not per se constitute the representation of an adverse interest.

(c) A committee appointed under *section 1102* of this title may—

(1) consult with the trustee or debtor in possession concerning the administration of the case;

(2) investigate the acts, conduct, assets, liabilities, and financial condition of the debtor, the operation of the debtor's business and the desirability of the continuance of such business, and any other matter relevant to the case or to the formulation of a plan;

(3) participate in the formulation of a plan, advise those represented by such committee of such committee's determinations as to any plan formulated, and collect and file with the court acceptances or rejections of a plan;

(4) request the appointment of a trustee or examiner under *section 1104* of this title; and

(5) perform such other services as are in the interest of those represented.

(d) As soon as practicable after the appointment of a committee under *section 1102* of this title, the trustee shall meet with such committee to transact such business as may be necessary and proper.

(Pub. L. 95–598, Nov. 6, 1978, 92 Stat. 2627; Pub. L. 98–353, title III, §§ 324, 500, July 10, 1984, 98 Stat. 358, 384.)

Sections that reference this section: None

§1104. Appointment of trustee or examiner

(a) At any time after the commencement of the case but before confirmation of a plan, on request of a party in interest or the United States trustee, and after notice and a hearing, the court shall order the appointment of a trustee—

   (1) for cause, including fraud, dishonesty, incompetence, or gross mismanagement of the affairs of the debtor by current management, either before or after the commencement of the case, or similar cause, but not including the number of holders of securities of the debtor or the amount of assets or liabilities of the debtor; or

   (2) if such appointment is in the interests of creditors, any equity security holders, and other interests of the estate, without regard to the number of holders of securities of the debtor or the amount of assets or liabilities of the debtor.

(b)

   (1) Except as provided in *section 1163* of this title, on the request of a party in interest made not later than 30 days after the court orders the appointment of a trustee under subsection (a), the United States trustee shall convene a meeting of creditors for the purpose of electing one disinterested person to serve as trustee in the case. The election of a trustee shall be conducted in the manner provided in subsections (a), (b), and (c) of *section 702* of this title.

   (2)

      (A) If an eligible, disinterested trustee is elected at a meeting of creditors under paragraph (1), the United States trustee shall file a report certifying that election.

      (B) Upon the filing of a report under subparagraph (A)—

         (i) the trustee elected under paragraph (1) shall be considered to have been selected and appointed for purposes of this section; and

         (ii) the service of any trustee appointed under subsection (a) shall terminate.

      (C) The court shall resolve any dispute arising out of an election described in subparagraph (A).

(c) If the court does not order the appointment of a trustee under this section, then at any time before the confirmation of a plan, on request of a party in interest or the United States trustee, and after notice and a hearing, the court shall order the appointment of an examiner to conduct such an investigation of the debtor as is appropriate, including an investigation of any allegations of fraud, dishonesty, incompetence, misconduct, mismanagement, or irregularity in the management of the affairs of the debtor of or by current or former management of the debtor, if—

   (1) such appointment is in the interests of creditors, any equity security holders, and other interests of the estate; or

   (2) the debtor's fixed, liquidated, unsecured debts, other than debts for goods, services, or taxes, or owing to an insider, exceed $5,000,000.

(d) If the court orders the appointment of a trustee or an examiner, if a trustee or an examiner dies or resigns during the case or is removed under *section 324* of this title, or if a trustee fails to qualify under *section 322* of this title, then the United States trustee, after consultation with parties in interest, shall appoint, subject to the court's approval, one disinterested person other than the United States trustee to serve as trustee or examiner, as the case may be, in the case.

(e) The United States trustee shall move for the appointment of a trustee under subsection (a) if there are reasonable grounds to suspect that current members of the governing body of the debtor, the debtor's chief executive or chief financial officer, or members of the governing body who selected the debtor's chief executive or chief financial officer, participated in actual fraud, dishonesty, or criminal conduct in the management of the debtor or the debtor's public financial reporting.

(Pub. L. 95–598, Nov. 6, 1978, 92 Stat. 2627; Pub. L. 99–554, title II, § 222, Oct. 27, 1986, 100 Stat. 3102; Pub. L. 103–394, title II, § 211(a), title V, § 501(d)(30), Oct. 22, 1994, 108 Stat. 4125, 4146; Pub. L. 109–8, title IV, §§ 416, 442(b), title XIV, § 1405, Apr. 20, 2005, 119 Stat.

107, 116, 215; Pub. L. 111–327, § 2(a)(30), Dec. 22, 2010, 124 Stat. 3560.)

Sections that reference this section: 1103, 1106, 1112, 1115, 1522

§1105. Termination of trustee's appointment

At any time before confirmation of a plan, on request of a party in interest or the United States trustee, and after notice and a hearing, the court may terminate the trustee's appointment and restore the debtor to possession and management of the property of the estate and of the operation of the debtor's business.

(Pub. L. 95–598, Nov. 6, 1978, 92 Stat. 2628; Pub. L. 98–353, title III, § 501, July 10, 1984, 98 Stat. 384; Pub. L. 99–554, title II, § 223, Oct. 27, 1986, 100 Stat. 3102.)

Sections that reference this section: None

§1106. Duties of trustee and examiner

(a) A trustee shall—

(1) perform the duties of the trustee, as specified in paragraphs (2), (5), (7), (8), (9), (10), (11), and (12) of *section 704(a)*;

(2) if the debtor has not done so, file the list, schedule, and statement required under *section 521(a)(1)* of this title;

(3) except to the extent that the court orders otherwise, investigate the acts, conduct, assets, liabilities, and financial condition of the debtor, the operation of the debtor's business and the desirability of the continuance of such business, and any other matter relevant to the case or to the formulation of a plan;

(4) as soon as practicable—

(A) file a statement of any investigation conducted under paragraph (3) of this subsection, including any fact ascertained pertaining to fraud, dishonesty, incompetence, misconduct, mismanagement, or irregularity in the management of the affairs of the debtor, or to a cause of action available to the estate; and

(B) transmit a copy or a summary of any such statement to any creditors' committee or equity security holders' committee, to any indenture trustee, and to such other entity as the court designates;

(5) as soon as practicable, file a plan under *section 1121* of this title, file a report of why the trustee will not file a plan, or recommend conversion of the case to a case under chapter 7, 12, or 13 of this title or dismissal of the case;

(6) for any year for which the debtor has not filed a tax return required by law, furnish, without personal liability, such information as may be required by the governmental unit with which such tax return was to be filed, in light of the condition of the debtor's books and records and the availability of such information;

(7) after confirmation of a plan, file such reports as are necessary or as the court orders; and

(8) if with respect to the debtor there is a claim for a domestic support obligation, provide the applicable notice specified in subsection (c).

(b) An examiner appointed under *section 1104(d)* of this title shall perform the duties specified in paragraphs (3) and (4) of subsection (a) of this section, and, except to the extent that the court orders otherwise, any other duties of the trustee that the court orders the debtor in possession not to perform.

(c)

(1) In a case described in subsection (a)(8) to which subsection (a)(8) applies, the trustee shall—

(A)

(i) provide written notice to the holder of the claim described in subsection (a)(8) of such claim and of the right of such holder to use the services of the State child support enforcement agency established under sections 464 and 466 of the Social Security Act for the State in which such holder resides, for assistance in collecting child support during and after the case under this title; and

(ii) include in the notice required by clause (i) the address and telephone number of such State child support enforcement agency;

(B)

(i) provide written notice to such State child support enforcement agency of such claim; and

(ii) include in the notice required by clause (i) the name, address, and telephone number of such holder; and

(C) at such time as the debtor is granted a discharge under *section 1141*, provide written notice to such holder and to such State child support enforcement agency of—

(i) the granting of the discharge;

(ii) the last recent known address of the debtor;

(iii) the last recent known name and address of the debtor's employer; and

(iv) the name of each creditor that holds a claim that—

(I) is not discharged under paragraph (2), (4), or (14A) of *section 523(a)*; or

(II) was reaffirmed by the debtor under *section 524(c)*.

(2)

(A) The holder of a claim described in subsection (a)(8) or the State child enforcement support agency of the State in which such holder resides may request from a creditor described in paragraph (1)(C)(iv) the last known address of the debtor.

(B) Notwithstanding any other provision of law, a creditor that makes a disclosure of a last known address of a debtor in connection with a request made under subparagraph (A) shall not be liable by reason of making such disclosure.

(Pub. L. 95–598, Nov. 6, 1978, 92 Stat. 2628; Pub. L. 98–353, title III, §§ 311(b)(1), 502, July 10, 1984, 98 Stat. 355, 384; Pub. L. 99–554, title II, § 257(c), Oct. 27, 1986, 100 Stat. 3114; Pub. L. 103–394, title II, § 211(b), Oct. 22, 1994, 108 Stat. 4125; Pub. L. 109–8, title II, § 219(b), title IV, § 446(c), title XI, § 1105(b), Apr. 20, 2005, 119 Stat. 56, 118, 192; Pub. L. 111–327, § 2(a)(31), Dec. 22, 2010, 124 Stat. 3560.)

Sections that reference this section: 1107, 1183, 1184, 1202, 1203, 1302

§1107. Rights, powers, and duties of debtor in possession

(a) Subject to any limitations on a trustee serving in a case under this chapter, and to such limitations or conditions as the court prescribes, a debtor in possession shall have all the rights, other than the right to compensation under *section 330* of this title, and powers, and shall perform all the functions and duties, except the duties specified in *sections 1106(a)(2)*, (3), and (4) of this title, of a trustee serving in a case under this chapter.

(b) Notwithstanding *section 327(a)* of this title, a person is not disqualified for employment under *section 327* of this title by a debtor in possession solely because of such person's employment by or representation of the debtor before the commencement of the case.

(Pub. L. 95–598, Nov. 6, 1978, 92 Stat. 2628; Pub. L. 98–353, title III, § 503, July 10, 1984, 98 Stat. 384.)

Sections that reference this section: None

§1108. Authorization to operate business

Unless the court, on request of a party in interest and after notice and a hearing, orders otherwise, the trustee may operate the debtor's business.

(Pub. L. 95–598, Nov. 6, 1978, 92 Stat. 2629; Pub. L. 98–353, title III, § 504, July 10, 1984, 98 Stat. 384.)

Sections that reference this section: None

§1109. Right to be heard

(a) The Securities and Exchange Commission may raise and may appear and be heard on any issue in a case under this chapter, but the Securities and Exchange Commission may not appeal from any judgment, order, or decree entered in the case.

(b) A party in interest, including the debtor, the trustee, a creditors' committee, an equity security holders' committee, a creditor, an equity security holder, or any indenture trustee, may raise and may appear and be heard on any issue in a case under this chapter.

(Pub. L. 95–598, Nov. 6, 1978, 92 Stat. 2629; Pub. L. 119–27, § 11(f), July 18, 2025, 139 Stat. 458.)

Sections that reference this section: None

§1110. Aircraft equipment and vessels

(a)

(1) Except as provided in paragraph (2) and subject to subsection (b), the right of a secured party with a security interest in equipment described in paragraph (3), or of a lessor or conditional vendor of such equipment, to take possession of such equipment in compliance with a security agreement, lease, or conditional sale contract, and to enforce any of its other rights or remedies, under such security agreement, lease, or conditional sale contract, to sell, lease, or otherwise retain or dispose of such equipment, is not limited or otherwise affected by any other provision of this title or by any power of the court.

(2) The right to take possession and to enforce the other rights and remedies described in paragraph (1) shall be subject to *section 362* if—

(A) before the date that is 60 days after the date of the order for relief under this chapter, the trustee, subject to the approval of the court, agrees to perform all obligations of the debtor under such security agreement, lease, or conditional sale contract; and

(B) any default, other than a default of a kind specified in *section 365(b)(2)*, under such security agreement, lease, or conditional sale contract—

(i) that occurs before the date of the order is cured before the expiration of such 60-day period;

(ii) that occurs after the date of the order and before the expiration of such 60-day period is cured before the later of—

(I) the date that is 30 days after the date of the default; or

(II) the expiration of such 60-day period; and

(iii) that occurs on or after the expiration of such 60-day period is cured in compliance with the terms of such security agreement, lease, or conditional sale contract, if a cure is permitted under that agreement, lease, or contract.

(3) The equipment described in this paragraph —

(A) is—

(i) an aircraft, aircraft engine, propeller, appliance, or spare part (as defined in section 40102 of title 49) that is subject to a security interest granted by, leased to, or conditionally sold to a debtor that, at the time such transaction is entered into, holds an air carrier operating certificate issued pursuant to chapter 447 of title 49 for aircraft capable of carrying 10 or more individuals or 6,000 pounds or more of cargo; or

(ii) a vessel documented under chapter 121 of title 46 that is subject to a security interest granted by, leased to, or conditionally sold to a debtor that is a water carrier that, at the time such transaction is entered into, holds a certificate of public convenience and necessity or permit issued by the Department of Transportation; and

(B) includes all records and documents relating to such equipment that are required, under the terms of the security agreement, lease, or conditional sale contract, to be surrendered or returned by the debtor in connection with the surrender or return of such equipment.

(4) Paragraph (1) applies to a secured party, lessor, or conditional vendor acting in its own behalf or acting as trustee or otherwise in behalf of another party.

(b) The trustee and the secured party, lessor, or conditional vendor whose right to take possession is protected under subsection (a) may agree, subject to the approval of the court, to extend the 60-day period specified in subsection (a)(1).

(c)

(1) In any case under this chapter, the trustee shall immediately surrender and return to a secured party, lessor, or conditional vendor, described in subsection (a)(1), equipment described in subsection (a)(3), if at any time

after the date of the order for relief under this chapter such secured party, lessor, or conditional vendor is entitled pursuant to subsection (a)(1) to take possession of such equipment and makes a written demand for such possession to the trustee.

(2) At such time as the trustee is required under paragraph (1) to surrender and return equipment described in subsection (a)(3), any lease of such equipment, and any security agreement or conditional sale contract relating to such equipment, if such security agreement or conditional sale contract is an executory contract, shall be deemed rejected.

(d) With respect to equipment first placed in service on or before October 22, 1994, for purposes of this section—

(1) the term "lease" includes any written agreement with respect to which the lessor and the debtor, as lessee, have expressed in the agreement or in a substantially contemporaneous writing that the agreement is to be treated as a lease for Federal income tax purposes; and

(2) the term "security interest" means a purchase-money equipment security interest.

(Pub. L. 95–598, Nov. 6, 1978, 92 Stat. 2629; Pub. L. 103–272, § 5(c), July 5, 1994, 108 Stat. 1373; Pub. L. 103–394, title II, § 201(a), Oct. 22, 1994, 108 Stat. 4119; Pub. L. 106–181, title VII, § 744(b), Apr. 5, 2000, 114 Stat. 177; Pub. L. 109–304, § 17(b)(2), Oct. 6, 2006, 120 Stat. 1707.)

Sections that reference this section: None

§1111. Claims and interests

(a) A proof of claim or interest is deemed filed under *section 501* of this title for any claim or interest that appears in the schedules filed under *section 521(a)(1)* or *1106*(a)(2) of this title, except a claim or interest that is scheduled as disputed, contingent, or unliquidated.

(b)

(1)

(A) A claim secured by a lien on property of the estate shall be allowed or disallowed under *section 502* of this title the same as if the holder of such claim had recourse against the debtor on account of such claim, whether or not such holder has such recourse, unless —

(i) the class of which such claim is a part elects, by at least two-thirds in amount and more than half in number of allowed claims of such class, application of paragraph (2) of this subsection; or

(ii) such holder does not have such recourse and such property is sold under *section 363* of this title or is to be sold under the plan.

(B) A class of claims may not elect application of paragraph (2) of this subsection if—

(i) the interest on account of such claims of the holders of such claims in such property is of inconsequential value; or

(ii) the holder of a claim of such class has recourse against the debtor on account of such claim and such property is sold under *section 363* of this title or is to be sold under the plan.

(2) If such an election is made, then notwithstanding *section 506(a)* of this title, such claim is a secured claim to the extent that such claim is allowed.

(Pub. L. 95–598, Nov. 6, 1978, 92 Stat. 2630; Pub. L. 111–327, § 2(a)(32), Dec. 22, 2010, 124 Stat. 3561.)

Sections that reference this section: 1129, 927

§1112. Conversion or dismissal

(a) The debtor may convert a case under this chapter to a case under chapter 7 of this title unless—

(1) the debtor is not a debtor in possession;

(2) the case originally was commenced as an involuntary case under this chapter; or

(3) the case was converted to a case under this chapter other than on the debtor's request.

(b)

(1) Except as provided in paragraph (2) and subsection (c), on request of a party in interest, and after notice and a hearing, the court shall convert a case under this chapter to a case under chapter 7 or dismiss a case under this chapter, whichever is in the best interests of creditors and the estate, for cause unless the court determines that

the appointment under *section 1104(a)* of a trustee or an examiner is in the best interests of creditors and the estate.

(2) The court may not convert a case under this chapter to a case under chapter 7 or dismiss a case under this chapter if the court finds and specifically identifies unusual circumstances establishing that converting or dismissing the case is not in the best interests of creditors and the estate, and the debtor or any other party in interest establishes that—

(A) there is a reasonable likelihood that a plan will be confirmed within the timeframes established in *sections 1121(e)* and *1129*(e) of this title, or if such sections do not apply, within a reasonable period of time; and

(B) the grounds for converting or dismissing the case include an act or omission of the debtor other than under paragraph (4)(A)—

(i) for which there exists a reasonable justification for the act or omission; and

(ii) that will be cured within a reasonable period of time fixed by the court.

(3) The court shall commence the hearing on a motion under this subsection not later than 30 days after filing of the motion, and shall decide the motion not later than 15 days after commencement of such hearing, unless the movant expressly consents to a continuance for a specific period of time or compelling circumstances prevent the court from meeting the time limits established by this paragraph.

(4) For purposes of this subsection, the term "cause" includes—

(A) substantial or continuing loss to or diminution of the estate and the absence of a reasonable likelihood of rehabilitation;

(B) gross mismanagement of the estate;

(C) failure to maintain appropriate insurance that poses a risk to the estate or to the public;

(D) unauthorized use of cash collateral substantially harmful to 1 or more creditors;

(E) failure to comply with an order of the court;

(F) unexcused failure to satisfy timely any filing or reporting requirement established by this title or by any rule applicable to a case under this chapter;

(G) failure to attend the meeting of creditors convened under *section 341(a)* or an examination ordered under rule 2004 of the Federal Rules of Bankruptcy Procedure without good cause shown by the debtor;

(H) failure timely to provide information or attend meetings reasonably requested by the United States trustee (or the bankruptcy administrator, if any);

(I) failure timely to pay taxes owed after the date of the order for relief or to file tax returns due after the date of the order for relief;

(J) failure to file a disclosure statement, or to file or confirm a plan, within the time fixed by this title or by order of the court;

(K) failure to pay any fees or charges required under chapter 123 of title 28;

(L) revocation of an order of confirmation under *section 1144*;

(M) inability to effectuate substantial consummation of a confirmed plan;

(N) material default by the debtor with respect to a confirmed plan;

(O) termination of a confirmed plan by reason of the occurrence of a condition specified in the plan; and

(P) failure of the debtor to pay any domestic support obligation that first becomes payable after the date of the filing of the petition.

(c) The court may not convert a case under this chapter to a case under chapter 7 of this title if the debtor is a farmer or a corporation that is not a moneyed, business, or commercial corporation, unless the debtor requests such conversion.

(d) The court may convert a case under this chapter to a case under chapter 12 or 13 of this title only if—

(1) the debtor requests such conversion;

(2) the debtor has not been discharged under *section 1141(d)* of this title; and

(3) if the debtor requests conversion to chapter 12 of this title, such conversion is equitable.

(e) Except as provided in subsections (c) and (f), the court, on request of the United States trustee, may convert a case under this chapter to a case under chapter 7 of this title or may dismiss a case under this chapter, whichever is in the best interest of creditors and the estate if the debtor in a voluntary case fails to file, within fifteen days after the filing of the petition commencing such case or such additional time as the court may allow, the information required by paragraph (1) of *section 521(a)*, including a list containing the names and addresses of the holders of the twenty largest unsecured claims (or of all unsecured claims if there are fewer than twenty unsecured claims), and the approximate dollar amounts of each of such claims.

(f) Notwithstanding any other provision of this section, a case may not be converted to a case under another chapter of this title unless the debtor may be a debtor under such chapter.

(Pub. L. 95–598, Nov. 6, 1978, 92 Stat. 2630; Pub. L. 98–353, title III, § 505, July 10, 1984, 98 Stat. 384; Pub. L. 99–554, title II, §§ 224, 256, Oct. 27, 1986, 100 Stat. 3102, 3114; Pub. L. 103–394, title II, § 217(c), Oct. 22, 1994, 108 Stat. 4127; Pub. L. 109–8, title IV, § 442(a), Apr. 20, 2005, 119 Stat. 115; Pub. L. 111–327, § 2(a)(33), Dec. 22, 2010, 124 Stat. 3561.)

Sections that reference this section: 348, 365, 706, 726

§1113. Rejection of collective bargaining agreements

(a) The debtor in possession, or the trustee if one has been appointed under the provisions of this chapter, other than a trustee in a case covered by subchapter IV of this chapter and by title I of the Railway Labor Act, may assume or reject a collective bargaining agreement only in accordance with the provisions of this section.

(b)

(1) Subsequent to filing a petition and prior to filing an application seeking rejection of a collective bargaining agreement, the debtor in possession or trustee (hereinafter in this section "trustee" shall include a debtor in possession), shall—

(A) make a proposal to the authorized representative of the employees covered by such agreement, based on the most complete and reliable information available at the time of such proposal, which provides for those necessary modifications in the employees benefits and protections that are necessary to permit the reorganization of the debtor and assures that all creditors, the debtor and all of the affected parties are treated fairly and equitably; and

(B) provide, subject to subsection (d)(3), the representative of the employees with such relevant information as is necessary to evaluate the proposal.

(2) During the period beginning on the date of the making of a proposal provided for in paragraph (1) and ending on the date of the hearing provided for in subsection (d)(1), the trustee shall meet, at reasonable times, with the authorized representative to confer in good faith in attempting to reach mutually satisfactory modifications of such agreement.

(c) The court shall approve an application for rejection of a collective bargaining agreement only if the court finds that—

(1) the trustee has, prior to the hearing, made a proposal that fulfills the requirements of subsection (b)(1);

(2) the authorized representative of the employees has refused to accept such proposal without good cause; and

(3) the balance of the equities clearly favors rejection of such agreement.

(d)

(1) Upon the filing of an application for rejection the court shall schedule a hearing to be held not later than fourteen days after the date of the filing of such application. All interested parties may appear and be heard at such hearing. Adequate notice shall be provided to such parties at least ten days before the date of such hearing. The court may extend the time for the commencement of such hearing for a period not exceeding seven days where the circumstances of the case, and the interests of justice require such extension, or for additional periods of time to which the trustee and representative agree.

(2) The court shall rule on such application for rejection within thirty days after the date of the commencement of the hearing. In the interests of justice, the court may extend such time for ruling for such additional pe-

riod as the trustee and the employees' representative may agree to. If the court does not rule on such application within thirty days after the date of the commencement of the hearing, or within such additional time as the trustee and the employees' representative may agree to, the trustee may terminate or alter any provisions of the collective bargaining agreement pending the ruling of the court on such application.

(3) The court may enter such protective orders, consistent with the need of the authorized representative of the employee to evaluate the trustee's proposal and the application for rejection, as may be necessary to prevent disclosure of information provided to such representative where such disclosure could compromise the position of the debtor with respect to its competitors in the industry in which it is engaged.

(e) If during a period when the collective bargaining agreement continues in effect, and if essential to the continuation of the debtor's business, or in order to avoid irreparable damage to the estate, the court, after notice and a hearing, may authorize the trustee to implement interim changes in the terms, conditions, wages, benefits, or work rules provided by a collective bargaining agreement. Any hearing under this paragraph shall be scheduled in accordance with the needs of the trustee. The implementation of such interim changes shall not render the application for rejection moot.

(f) No provision of this title shall be construed to permit a trustee to unilaterally terminate or alter any provisions of a collective bargaining agreement prior to compliance with the provisions of this section.

(Added Pub. L. 98–353, title III, § 541(a), July 10, 1984, 98 Stat. 390.)

Sections that reference this section: None

§1114. Payment of insurance benefits to retired employees

(a) For purposes of this section, the term "retiree benefits" means payments to any entity or person for the purpose of providing or reimbursing payments for retired employees and their spouses and dependents, for medical, surgical, or hospital care benefits, or benefits in the event of sickness, accident, disability, or death under any plan, fund, or program (through the purchase of insurance or otherwise) maintained or established in whole or in part by the debtor prior to filing a petition commencing a case under this title.

(b)

(1) For purposes of this section, the term "authorized representative" means the authorized representative designated pursuant to subsection (c) for persons receiving any retiree benefits covered by a collective bargaining agreement or subsection (d) in the case of persons receiving retiree benefits not covered by such an agreement.

(2) Committees of retired employees appointed by the court pursuant to this section shall have the same rights, powers, and duties as committees appointed under *sections 1102* and *1103* of this title for the purpose of carrying out the purposes of sections 1114 and 1129(a)(13) and, as permitted by the court, shall have the power to enforce the rights of persons under this title as they relate to retiree benefits.

(c)

(1) A labor organization shall be, for purposes of this section, the authorized representative of those persons receiving any retiree benefits covered by any collective bargaining agreement to which that labor organization is signatory, unless (A) such labor organization elects not to serve as the authorized representative of such persons, or (B) the court, upon a motion by any party in interest, after notice and hearing, determines that different representation of such persons is appropriate.

(2) In cases where the labor organization referred to in paragraph (1) elects not to serve as the authorized representative of those persons receiving any retiree benefits covered by any collective bargaining agreement to which that labor organization is signatory, or in cases where the court, pursuant to paragraph (1) finds different representation of such persons appropriate, the court, upon a motion by any party in interest, and after notice and a hearing, shall appoint a committee of retired employees if the debtor seeks to modify or not pay the retiree benefits or if the court otherwise determines that it is appropriate, from among such persons, to serve as the authorized

representative of such persons under this section.

(d) The court, upon a motion by any party in interest, and after notice and a hearing, shall order the appointment of a committee of retired employees if the debtor seeks to modify or not pay the retiree benefits or if the court otherwise determines that it is appropriate, to serve as the authorized representative, under this section, of those persons receiving any retiree benefits not covered by a collective bargaining agreement. The United States trustee shall appoint any such committee.

(e)

(1) Notwithstanding any other provision of this title, the debtor in possession, or the trustee if one has been appointed under the provisions of this chapter (hereinafter in this section "trustee" shall include a debtor in possession), shall timely pay and shall not modify any retiree benefits, except that—

(A) the court, on motion of the trustee or authorized representative, and after notice and a hearing, may order modification of such payments, pursuant to the provisions of subsections (g) and (h) of this section, or

(B) the trustee and the authorized representative of the recipients of those benefits may agree to modification of such payments,

after which such benefits as modified shall continue to be paid by the trustee.

(2) Any payment for retiree benefits required to be made before a plan confirmed under *section 1129* of this title is effective has the status of an allowed administrative expense as provided in *section 503* of this title.

(f)

(1) Subsequent to filing a petition and prior to filing an application seeking modification of the retiree benefits, the trustee shall—

(A) make a proposal to the authorized representative of the retirees, based on the most complete and reliable information available at the time of such proposal, which provides for those necessary modifications in the retiree benefits that are necessary to permit the reorganization of the debtor and assures that all creditors, the debtor and all of the affected parties are treated fairly and equitably; and

(B) provide, subject to subsection (k)(3), the representative of the retirees with such relevant information as is necessary to evaluate the proposal.

(2) During the period beginning on the date of the making of a proposal provided for in paragraph (1), and ending on the date of the hearing provided for in subsection (k)(1), the trustee shall meet, at reasonable times, with the authorized representative to confer in good faith in attempting to reach mutually satisfactory modifications of such retiree benefits.

(g) The court shall enter an order providing for modification in the payment of retiree benefits if the court finds that—

(1) the trustee has, prior to the hearing, made a proposal that fulfills the requirements of subsection (f);

(2) the authorized representative of the retirees has refused to accept such proposal without good cause; and

(3) such modification is necessary to permit the reorganization of the debtor and assures that all creditors, the debtor, and all of the affected parties are treated fairly and equitably, and is clearly favored by the balance of the equities;

except that in no case shall the court enter an order providing for such modification which provides for a modification to a level lower than that proposed by the trustee in the proposal found by the court to have complied with the requirements of this subsection and subsection (f): *Provided, however*, That at any time after an order is entered providing for modification in the payment of retiree benefits, or at any time after an agreement modifying such benefits is made between the trustee and the authorized representative of the recipients of such benefits, the authorized representative may apply to the court for an order increasing those benefits which order shall be granted if the increase in retiree benefits sought is consistent with the standard set forth in paragraph (3): *Provided further*, That neither the trustee nor the authorized representative is precluded from making more than one motion for a modification order governed by this subsection.

(h)

(1) Prior to a court issuing a final order under subsection (g) of this section, if essential to the continuation of the debtor's business, or in order to avoid irreparable damage to the estate, the court, after notice and a hearing, may authorize the trustee to implement interim modifications in retiree benefits.

(2) Any hearing under this subsection shall be scheduled in accordance with the needs of the trustee.

(3) The implementation of such interim changes does not render the motion for modification moot.

(i) No retiree benefits paid between the filing of the petition and the time a plan confirmed under *section 1129* of this title becomes effective shall be deducted or offset from the amounts allowed as claims for any benefits which remain unpaid, or from the amounts to be paid under the plan with respect to such claims for unpaid benefits, whether such claims for unpaid benefits are based upon or arise from a right to future unpaid benefits or from any benefits not paid as a result of modifications allowed pursuant to this section.

(j) No claim for retiree benefits shall be limited by *section 502(b)(7)* of this title.

(k)

(1) Upon the filing of an application for modifying retiree benefits, the court shall schedule a hearing to be held not later than fourteen days after the date of the filing of such application. All interested parties may appear and be heard at such hearing. Adequate notice shall be provided to such parties at least ten days before the date of such hearing. The court may extend the time for the commencement of such hearing for a period not exceeding seven days where the circumstances of the case, and the interests of justice require such extension, or for additional periods of time to which the trustee and the authorized representative agree.

(2) The court shall rule on such application for modification within ninety days after the date of the commencement of the hearing. In the interests of justice, the court may extend such time for ruling for such additional period as the trustee and the authorized representative may agree to. If the court does not rule on such application within ninety days after the date of the commencement of the hearing, or within such additional time as the trustee and the authorized representative may agree to, the trustee may implement the proposed modifications pending the ruling of the court on such application.

(3) The court may enter such protective orders, consistent with the need of the authorized representative of the retirees to evaluate the trustee's proposal and the application for modification, as may be necessary to prevent disclosure of information provided to such representative where such disclosure could compromise the position of the debtor with respect to its competitors in the industry in which it is engaged.

(l) If the debtor, during the 180-day period ending on the date of the filing of the petition—

(1) modified retiree benefits; and

(2) was insolvent on the date such benefits were modified;

the court, on motion of a party in interest, and after notice and a hearing, shall issue an order reinstating as of the date the modification was made, such benefits as in effect immediately before such date unless the court finds that the balance of the equities clearly favors such modification.

(m) This section shall not apply to any retiree, or the spouse or dependents of such retiree, if such retiree's gross income for the twelve months preceding the filing of the bankruptcy petition equals or exceeds $250,000, unless such retiree can demonstrate to the satisfaction of the court that he is unable to obtain health, medical, life, and disability coverage for himself, his spouse, and his dependents who would otherwise be covered by the employer's insurance plan, comparable to the coverage provided by the employer on the day before the filing of a petition under this title.

(Added Pub. L. 100–334, § 2(a), June 16, 1988, 102 Stat. 610; amended Pub. L. 109–8, title IV, § 447, title XIV, § 1403, Apr. 20, 2005, 119 Stat. 118, 215.)

Sections that reference this section: 1129

§1115. Property of the estate

(a) In a case in which the debtor is an individual, property of the estate includes, in addition to the property specified in *section 541*—

(1) all property of the kind specified in *section 541* that the debtor acquires after the commencement of the case but before the case is closed, dismissed, or converted to a case under chapter 7, 12, or 13, whichever occurs first; and

(2) earnings from services performed by the debtor after the commencement of the case but before the case is closed, dismissed, or converted to a case under chapter 7, 12, or 13, whichever occurs first.

(b) Except as provided in *section 1104* or a confirmed plan or order confirming a plan, the debtor shall remain in possession of all property of the estate.

(Added Pub. L. 109–8, title III, § 321(a)(1), Apr. 20, 2005, 119 Stat. 94.)

Sections that reference this section: 1129

§1116. Duties of trustee or debtor in possession in small business cases

In a small business case, a trustee or the debtor in possession, in addition to the duties provided in this title and as otherwise required by law, shall—

(1) append to the voluntary petition or, in an involuntary case, file not later than 7 days after the date of the order for relief—

(A) its most recent balance sheet, statement of operations, cash-flow statement, and Federal income tax return; or

(B) a statement made under penalty of perjury that no balance sheet, statement of operations, or cash-flow statement has been prepared and no Federal tax return has been filed;

(2) attend, through its senior management personnel and counsel, meetings scheduled by the court or the United States trustee, including initial debtor interviews, scheduling conferences, and meetings of creditors convened under *section 341* unless the court, after notice and a hearing, waives that requirement upon a finding of extraordinary and compelling circumstances;

(3) timely file all schedules and statements of financial affairs, unless the court, after notice and a hearing, grants an extension, which shall not extend such time period to a date later than 30 days after the date of the order for relief, absent extraordinary and compelling circumstances;

(4) file all postpetition financial and other reports required by the Federal Rules of Bankruptcy Procedure or by local rule of the district court;

(5) subject to *section 363(c)(2)*, maintain insurance customary and appropriate to the industry;

(6)

(A) timely file tax returns and other required government filings; and

(B) subject to *section 363(c)(2)*, timely pay all taxes entitled to administrative expense priority except those being contested by appropriate proceedings being diligently prosecuted; and

(7) allow the United States trustee, or a designated representative of the United States trustee, to inspect the debtor's business premises, books, and records at reasonable times, after reasonable prior written notice, unless notice is waived by the debtor.

(Added Pub. L. 109–8, title IV, § 436(a), Apr. 20, 2005, 119 Stat. 112.)

Sections that reference this section: 1187

Subchapter II: The Plan

§1121. Who may file a plan

(a) The debtor may file a plan with a petition commencing a voluntary case, or at any time in a voluntary case or an involuntary case.

(b) Except as otherwise provided in this section, only the debtor may file a plan until after 120 days after the date of the order for relief under this chapter.

(c) Any party in interest, including the debtor, the trustee, a creditors' committee, an equity security holders' committee, a creditor, an equity security holder, or any indenture trustee, may file a plan if and only if—

(1) a trustee has been appointed under this chapter;

(2) the debtor has not filed a plan before 120 days after the date of the order for relief under this chapter; or

(3) the debtor has not filed a plan that has been accepted, before 180 days after the date of the order for relief under this chapter, by each class of claims or interests that is impaired under the plan.

(d)

(1) Subject to paragraph (2), on request of a party in interest made within the respective periods specified in subsections (b) and (c) of this section and after notice and a hearing, the court may for cause reduce or increase the 120-day period or the 180-day period referred to in this section.

(2)

(A) The 120-day period specified in paragraph (1) may not be extended beyond a date that is 18 months after the date of the order for relief under this chapter.

(B) The 180-day period specified in paragraph (1) may not be extended beyond a date that is 20 months after the date of the order for relief under this chapter.

(e) In a small business case—

(1) only the debtor may file a plan until after 180 days after the date of the order for relief, unless that period is—

(A) extended as provided by this subsection, after notice and a hearing; or

(B) the court, for cause, orders otherwise;

(2) the plan and a disclosure statement (if any) shall be filed not later than 300 days after the date of the order for relief; and

(3) the time periods specified in paragraphs (1) and (2), and the time fixed in *section 1129(e)* within which the plan shall be confirmed, may be extended only if—

(A) the debtor, after providing notice to parties in interest (including the United States trustee), demonstrates by a preponderance of the evidence that it is more likely than not that the court will confirm a plan within a reasonable period of time;

(B) a new deadline is imposed at the time the extension is granted; and

(C) the order extending time is signed before the existing deadline has expired.

(Pub. L. 95–598, Nov. 6, 1978, 92 Stat. 2631; Pub. L. 98–353, title III, § 506, July 10, 1984, 98 Stat. 385; Pub. L. 99–554, title II, § 283(u), Oct. 27, 1986, 100 Stat. 3118; Pub. L. 103–394, title II, § 217(d), Oct. 22, 1994, 108 Stat. 4127; Pub. L. 109–8, title IV, §§ 411, 437, Apr. 20, 2005, 119 Stat. 106, 113.)

Sections that reference this section: 1106, 1112, 1127, 1129, 307

§1122. Classification of claims or interests

(a) Except as provided in subsection (b) of this section, a plan may place a claim or an interest in a particular class only if such claim or interest is substantially similar to the other claims or interests of such class.

(b) A plan may designate a separate class of claims consisting only of every unsecured claim that is less than or reduced to an amount that the court approves as reasonable and necessary for administrative convenience.

(Pub. L. 95–598, Nov. 6, 1978, 92 Stat. 2631.)

Sections that reference this section: 1123, 1127, 1129, 1193, 1222, 1322

§1123. Contents of plan

(a) Notwithstanding any otherwise applicable nonbankruptcy law, a plan shall—

(1) designate, subject to *section 1122* of this title, classes of claims, other than claims of a kind specified in *section 507(a)(2), 507*(a)(3), or 507(a)(8) of this title, and classes of interests;

(2) specify any class of claims or interests that is not impaired under the plan;

(3) specify the treatment of any class of claims or interests that is impaired under the plan;

(4) provide the same treatment for each claim or interest of a particular class, unless the holder of a particular claim or interest agrees to a less favorable treatment of such particular claim or interest;

(5) provide adequate means for the plan's implementation, such as—

(A) retention by the debtor of all or any part of the property of the estate;

(B) transfer of all or any part of the property of the estate to one or more entities, whether organized before or after the confirmation of such plan;

(C) merger or consolidation of the debtor with one or more persons;

(D) sale of all or any part of the property of the estate, either subject to or free of any lien, or the distribution of all or any part of the property of the estate among those having an interest in such property of the estate;

(E) satisfaction or modification of any lien;

(F) cancellation or modification of any indenture or similar instrument;

(G) curing or waiving of any default;

(H) extension of a maturity date or a change in an interest rate or other term of outstanding securities;

(I) amendment of the debtor's charter; or

(J) issuance of securities of the debtor, or of any entity referred to in subparagraph (B) or (C) of this paragraph, for cash, for property, for existing securities, or in exchange for claims or interests, or for any other appropriate purpose;

(6) provide for the inclusion in the charter of the debtor, if the debtor is a corporation, or of any corporation referred to in paragraph (5)(B) or (5)(C) of this subsection, of a provision prohibiting the issuance of nonvoting equity securities, and providing, as to the several classes of securities possessing voting power, an appropriate distribution of such power among such classes, including, in the case of any class of equity securities having a preference over another class of equity securities with respect to dividends, adequate provisions for the election of directors representing such preferred class in the event of default in the payment of such dividends;

(7) contain only provisions that are consistent with the interests of creditors and equity security holders and with public policy with respect to the manner of selection of any officer, director, or trustee under the plan and any successor to such officer, director, or trustee; and

(8) in a case in which the debtor is an individual, provide for the payment to creditors under the plan of all or such portion of earnings from personal services performed by the debtor after the commencement of the case or other future income of the debtor as is necessary for the execution of the plan.

(b) Subject to subsection (a) of this section, a plan may—

(1) impair or leave unimpaired any class of claims, secured or unsecured, or of interests;

(2) subject to *section 365* of this title, provide for the assumption, rejection, or assignment of any executory contract or unexpired lease of the debtor not previously rejected under such section;

(3) provide for—

(A) the settlement or adjustment of any claim or interest belonging to the debtor or to the estate; or

(B) the retention and enforcement by the debtor, by the trustee, or by a representative of the estate appointed for such purpose, of any such claim or interest;

(4) provide for the sale of all or substantially all of the property of the estate, and the distribution of the proceeds of such sale among holders of claims or interests;

(5) modify the rights of holders of secured claims, other than a claim secured only by a security interest in real property that is the debtor's principal residence, or of holders of unsecured claims, or leave unaffected the rights of holders of any class of claims; and

(6) include any other appropriate provision not inconsistent with the applicable provisions of this title.

(c) In a case concerning an individual, a plan proposed by an entity other than the debtor may not provide for the use, sale, or lease of property exempted under *section 522* of this title, unless the debtor consents to such use, sale, or lease.

(d) Notwithstanding subsection (a) of this section and *sections 506(b)*, *1129*(a)(7), and 1129(b) of this title, if it is proposed in a plan to cure a default the amount necessary to cure the default shall be determined in accordance with the underlying agreement and applicable nonbankruptcy law.

(Pub. L. 95–598, Nov. 6, 1978, 92 Stat. 2631; Pub. L. 98–353, title III, § 507, July 10, 1984, 98 Stat. 385; Pub. L. 103–394, title II, § 206, title III, §§ 304(h)(6), 305(a), title V, § 501(d)(31), Oct. 22, 1994, 108 Stat. 4123, 4134, 4146; Pub. L. 109–8, title III, § 321(b), title XV, § 1502(a)(7), Apr. 20, 2005, 119 Stat. 95, 216.)

Sections that reference this section: 1124, 1172, 1190, 1193

§1124. Impairment of claims or interests

Except as provided in *section 1123(a)(4)* of this title, a class of claims or interests is impaired under a plan unless, with respect to each claim or interest of such class, the plan—

(1) leaves unaltered the legal, equitable, and contractual rights to which such claim or interest entitles the holder of such claim or interest; or

(2) notwithstanding any contractual provision or applicable law that entitles the holder of such claim or interest to demand or receive accelerated payment of such claim or interest after the occurrence of a default—

(A) cures any such default that occurred before or after the commencement of the case under this title, other than a default of a kind specified in *section 365(b)(2)* of this title or of a kind that *section 365(b)(2)* expressly does not require to be cured;

(B) reinstates the maturity of such claim or interest as such maturity existed before such default;

(C) compensates the holder of such claim or interest for any damages incurred as a result of any reasonable reliance by such holder on such contractual provision or such applicable law;

(D) if such claim or such interest arises from any failure to perform a nonmonetary obligation, other than a default arising from failure to operate a nonresidential real property lease subject to *section 365(b)(1)(A)*, compensates the holder of such claim or such interest (other than the debtor or an insider) for any actual pecuniary loss incurred by such holder as a result of such failure; and

(E) does not otherwise alter the legal, equitable, or contractual rights to which such claim or interest entitles the holder of such claim or interest.

(Pub. L. 95–598, Nov. 6, 1978, 92 Stat. 2633; Pub. L. 98–353, title III, § 508, July 10, 1984, 98 Stat. 385; Pub. L. 103–394, title II, § 213(d), Oct. 22, 1994, 108 Stat. 4126; Pub. L. 109–8, title III, § 328(b), Apr. 20, 2005, 119 Stat. 100.)

Sections that reference this section: None

§1125. Postpetition disclosure and solicitation

(a) In this section—

(1) "adequate information" means information of a kind, and in sufficient detail, as far as is reasonably practicable in light of the nature and history of the debtor and the condition of the debtor's books and records, including a discussion of the potential material Federal tax consequences of the plan to the debtor, any successor to the debtor, and a hypothetical investor typical of the holders of claims or interests in the case, that would enable such a hypothetical investor of the relevant class to make an informed judgment about the plan, but adequate information need not include such information about any other possible or proposed plan and in determining whether a disclosure statement provides adequate information, the court shall consider the complexity of the case, the benefit of additional information to creditors and other parties in interest, and the cost of providing additional information; and

(2) "investor typical of holders of claims or interests of the relevant class" means investor having—

(A) a claim or interest of the relevant class;

(B) such a relationship with the debtor as the holders of other claims or interests of such class generally have; and

(C) such ability to obtain such information from sources other than the disclosure required by this section as holders of claims or interests in such class generally have.

(b) An acceptance or rejection of a plan may not be solicited after the commencement of the case under this title from a holder of a claim or interest with respect to such claim or interest, unless, at the time of or before such solicitation, there is transmitted to such holder the plan or a summary of the plan, and a written disclosure statement approved, after notice and a hearing, by the court as containing adequate information. The court may approve a disclosure statement without a valuation of the debtor or an appraisal of the debtor's assets.

(c) The same disclosure statement shall be transmitted to each holder of a claim or interest of a particular class, but there may be transmitted different disclosure statements, differing in amount, detail, or kind of information, as between classes.

(d) Whether a disclosure statement required under subsection (b) of this section contains adequate information is not governed by any otherwise applicable nonbankruptcy law, rule, or regulation, but an agency or official whose duty is to administer or enforce such a law, rule, or regulation may be heard on the issue of whether a disclosure statement contains adequate information. Such an agency or official may not appeal from, or otherwise seek review of, an order approving a disclosure statement.

(e) A person that solicits acceptance or rejection of a plan, in good faith and in compliance with the applicable provisions of this title, or that participates, in good faith and in compliance with the applicable provisions of this title, in the offer, issuance, sale, or purchase of a security, offered or sold under the plan, of the debtor, of an affiliate participating in a joint plan with the debtor, or of a newly organized successor to the debtor under the plan, is not liable, on account of such solicitation or participation, for violation of any applicable law, rule, or regulation governing solicitation of acceptance or rejection of a plan or the offer, issuance, sale, or purchase of securities.

(f) Notwithstanding subsection (b), in a small business case—

(1) the court may determine that the plan itself provides adequate information and that a separate disclosure statement is not necessary;

(2) the court may approve a disclosure statement submitted on standard forms approved by the court or adopted under section 2075 of title 28; and

(3)

(A) the court may conditionally approve a disclosure statement subject to final approval after notice and a hearing;

(B) acceptances and rejections of a plan may be solicited based on a conditionally approved disclosure statement if the debtor provides adequate information to each holder of a claim or interest that is solicited, but a conditionally approved disclosure statement shall be mailed not later than 25 days before the date of the hearing on confirmation of the plan; and

(C) the hearing on the disclosure statement may be combined with the hearing on confirmation of a plan.

(g) Notwithstanding subsection (b), an acceptance or rejection of the plan may be solicited from a holder of a claim or interest if such solicitation complies with applicable nonbankruptcy law and if such holder was solicited before the commencement of the case in a manner complying with applicable nonbankruptcy law.

(Pub. L. 95–598, Nov. 6, 1978, 92 Stat. 2633; Pub. L. 98–353, title III, § 509, July 10, 1984, 98 Stat. 385; Pub. L. 103–394, title II, § 217(e), Oct. 22, 1994, 108 Stat. 4127; Pub. L. 109–8, title IV, §§ 408, 431, title VII, § 717, Apr. 20, 2005, 119 Stat. 106, 109, 131.)

Sections that reference this section: 1126, 1127, 1145, 1187

§1126. Acceptance of plan

(a) The holder of a claim or interest allowed under *section 502* of this title may accept or reject a plan. If the United States is a creditor or equity security holder, the Secretary of the Treasury may accept or reject the plan on behalf of the United States.

(b) For the purposes of subsections (c) and (d) of this section, a holder of a claim or interest that has accepted or rejected the plan before the commencement of the case under this title is deemed to have accepted or rejected such plan, as the case may be, if—

(1) the solicitation of such acceptance or rejection was in compliance with any applicable nonbankruptcy law, rule, or regulation governing the adequacy of disclosure in connection with such solicitation; or

(2) if there is not any such law, rule, or regulation, such acceptance or rejection was solicited after disclosure to such holder of adequate information, as defined in *section 1125(a)* of this title.

(c) A class of claims has accepted a plan if such plan has been accepted by creditors, other than any entity designated under subsection (e) of this section, that hold at least two-thirds in amount and more than one-half in number of the allowed claims of such class held by creditors, other than any entity designated under subsection (e) of this section, that have accepted or rejected such plan.

(d) A class of interests has accepted a plan if such plan has been accepted by holders of such interests, other than any entity designated under subsection (e) of this section, that hold at least two-thirds in amount of the allowed interests of such class held by holders of such interests, other than any entity designated under subsection (e) of this section, that have accepted or rejected such plan.

(e) On request of a party in interest, and after notice and a hearing, the court may designate any entity whose acceptance or rejection of such plan was not in good faith, or was not solicited or procured in good faith or in accordance with the provisions of this title.

(f) Notwithstanding any other provision of this section, a class that is not impaired under a plan, and each holder of a claim or interest of such class, are conclusively presumed to have accepted the plan, and solicitation of acceptances with respect to such class from the holders of claims or interests of such class is not required.

(g) Notwithstanding any other provision of this section, a class is deemed not to have accepted a plan if such plan provides that the claims or interests of such class do not entitle the holders of such claims or interests to receive or retain any property under the plan on account of such claims or interests.

(Pub. L. 95–598, Nov. 6, 1978, 92 Stat. 2634; Pub. L. 98–353, title III, § 510, July 10, 1984, 98 Stat. 386.)

Sections that reference this section: 946

§1127. Modification of plan

(a) The proponent of a plan may modify such plan at any time before confirmation, but may not modify such plan so that such plan as modified fails to meet the requirements of *sections 1122* and *1123* of this title. After the proponent of a plan files a modification of such plan with the court, the plan as modified becomes the plan.

(b) The proponent of a plan or the reorganized debtor may modify such plan at any time after confirmation of such plan and before substantial consummation of such plan, but may not modify such plan so that such plan as modified fails to meet the requirements of *sections 1122* and *1123* of this title. Such plan as modified under this subsection becomes the plan only if circumstances warrant such modification and the court, after notice and a hearing, confirms such plan as modified, under *section 1129* of this title.

(c) The proponent of a modification shall comply with *section 1125* of this title with respect to the plan as modified.

(d) Any holder of a claim or interest that has accepted or rejected a plan is deemed to have accepted or rejected, as the case may be, such plan as modified, unless, within the time fixed by the court, such holder changes such holder's previous acceptance or rejection.

(e) If the debtor is an individual, the plan may be modified at any time after confirmation of the plan but before the completion of payments under the plan, whether or not the plan has been substantially consummated, upon request of the debtor, the trustee, the United States trustee, or the holder of an allowed unsecured claim, to—

  (1) increase or reduce the amount of payments on claims of a particular class provided for by the plan;

  (2) extend or reduce the time period for such payments; or

  (3) alter the amount of the distribution to a creditor whose claim is provided for by the plan to the extent necessary to take account of any payment of such claim made other than under the plan.

(f)

  (1) *Sections 1121* through 1128 and the requirements of *section 1129* apply to any modification under subsection (e).

  (2) The plan, as modified, shall become the plan only after there has been disclosure under *section 1125* as the court may direct, notice and a hearing, and such modification is approved.

(Pub. L. 95–598, Nov. 6, 1978, 92 Stat. 2635; Pub. L. 98–353, title III, § 511, July 10, 1984, 98 Stat. 386; Pub. L. 109–8, title III, § 321(e), Apr. 20, 2005, 119 Stat. 96; Pub. L. 111–327, § 2(a)(34), Dec. 22, 2010, 124 Stat. 3561.)

Sections that reference this section: 1129, 1141

§1128. Confirmation hearing

(a) After notice, the court shall hold a hearing on confirmation of a plan.

(b) A party in interest may object to confirmation of a plan.

(Pub. L. 95–598, Nov. 6, 1978, 92 Stat. 2635.)

Sections that reference this section: 362

§1129. Confirmation of plan

(a) The court shall confirm a plan only if all of the following requirements are met:

  (1) The plan complies with the applicable provisions of this title.

  (2) The proponent of the plan complies with the applicable provisions of this title.

(3) The plan has been proposed in good faith and not by any means forbidden by law.

(4) Any payment made or to be made by the proponent, by the debtor, or by a person issuing securities or acquiring property under the plan, for services or for costs and expenses in or in connection with the case, or in connection with the plan and incident to the case, has been approved by, or is subject to the approval of, the court as reasonable.

(5)

(A)

(i) The proponent of the plan has disclosed the identity and affiliations of any individual proposed to serve, after confirmation of the plan, as a director, officer, or voting trustee of the debtor, an affiliate of the debtor participating in a joint plan with the debtor, or a successor to the debtor under the plan; and

(ii) the appointment to, or continuance in, such office of such individual, is consistent with the interests of creditors and equity security holders and with public policy; and

(B) the proponent of the plan has disclosed the identity of any insider that will be employed or retained by the reorganized debtor, and the nature of any compensation for such insider.

(6) Any governmental regulatory commission with jurisdiction, after confirmation of the plan, over the rates of the debtor has approved any rate change provided for in the plan, or such rate change is expressly conditioned on such approval.

(7) With respect to each impaired class of claims or interests—

(A) each holder of a claim or interest of such class—

(i) has accepted the plan; or

(ii) will receive or retain under the plan on account of such claim or interest property of a value, as of the effective date of the plan, that is not less than the amount that such holder would so receive or retain if the debtor were liquidated under chapter 7 of this title on such date; or

(B) if *section 1111(b)(2)* of this title applies to the claims of such class, each holder of a claim of such class will receive or retain under the plan on account of such claim property of a value, as of the effective date of the plan, that is not less than the value of such holder's interest in the estate's interest in the property that secures such claims.

(8) With respect to each class of claims or interests—

(A) such class has accepted the plan; or

(B) such class is not impaired under the plan.

(9) Except to the extent that the holder of a particular claim has agreed to a different treatment of such claim, the plan provides that—

(A) with respect to a claim of a kind specified in *section 507(a)(2)* or *507*(a)(3) of this title, on the effective date of the plan, the holder of such claim will receive on account of such claim cash equal to the allowed amount of such claim;

(B) with respect to a class of claims of a kind specified in *section 507(a)(1), 507*(a)(4), 507(a)(5), 507(a)(6), or 507(a)(7) of this title, each holder of a claim of such class will receive—

(i) if such class has accepted the plan, deferred cash payments of a value, as of the effective date of the plan, equal to the allowed amount of such claim; or

(ii) if such class has not accepted the plan, cash on the effective date of the plan equal to the allowed amount of such claim;

(C) with respect to a claim of a kind specified in *section 507(a)(8)* of this title, the holder of such claim will receive on account of such claim regular installment payments in cash—

(i) of a total value, as of the effective date of the plan, equal to the allowed amount of such claim;

(ii) over a period ending not later than 5 years after the date of the order for relief under *section 301, 302*, or *303*; and

(iii) in a manner not less favorable than the most favored nonpriority unsecured claim provided for by the plan (other than cash payments made to a class of creditors under *section 1122(b)*); and

(D) with respect to a secured claim which would otherwise meet the description of an unsecured claim of a governmental unit under *section 507(a)(8)*, but for the secured status of that claim, the holder of that claim will receive on account of that claim, cash payments, in the same manner and over the same period, as prescribed in subparagraph (C).

(10) If a class of claims is impaired under the plan, at least one class of claims that is impaired under the plan has accepted the plan, determined without including any acceptance of the plan by any insider.

(11) Confirmation of the plan is not likely to be followed by the liquidation, or the need for further financial reorganization, of the debtor or any successor to the debtor under the plan, unless such liquidation or reorganization is proposed in the plan.

(12) All fees payable under section 1930 of title 28, as determined by the court at the hearing on confirmation of the plan, have been paid or the plan provides for the payment of all such fees on the effective date of the plan.

(13) The plan provides for the continuation after its effective date of payment of all retiree benefits, as that term is defined in *section 1114* of this title, at the level established pursuant to subsection (e)(1)(B) or (g) of *section 1114* of this title, at any time prior to confirmation of the plan, for the duration of the period the debtor has obligated itself to provide such benefits.

(14) If the debtor is required by a judicial or administrative order, or by statute, to pay a domestic support obligation, the debtor has paid all amounts payable under such order or such statute for such obligation that first become payable after the date of the filing of the petition.

(15) In a case in which the debtor is an individual and in which the holder of an allowed unsecured claim objects to the confirmation of the plan—

(A) the value, as of the effective date of the plan, of the property to be distributed under the plan on account of such claim is not less than the amount of such claim; or

(B) the value of the property to be distributed under the plan is not less than the projected disposable income of the debtor (as defined in *section 1325(b)(2)*) to be received during the 5-year period beginning on the date that the first payment is due under the plan, or during the period for which the plan provides payments, whichever is longer.

(16) All transfers of property under the plan shall be made in accordance with any applicable provisions of nonbankruptcy law that govern the transfer of property by a corporation or trust that is not a moneyed, business, or commercial corporation or trust.

(b)

(1) Notwithstanding *section 510(a)* of this title, if all of the applicable requirements of subsection (a) of this section other than paragraph (8) are met with respect to a plan, the court, on request of the proponent of the plan, shall confirm the plan notwithstanding the requirements of such paragraph if the plan does not discriminate unfairly, and is fair and equitable, with respect to each class of claims or interests that is impaired under, and has not accepted, the plan.

(2) For the purpose of this subsection, the condition that a plan be fair and equitable with respect to a class includes the following requirements:

(A) With respect to a class of secured claims, the plan provides—

(i)

(I) that the holders of such claims retain the liens securing such claims, whether the property subject to such liens is retained by the debtor or transferred to another entity, to the extent of the allowed amount of such claims; and

(II) that each holder of a claim of such class receive on account of such claim deferred cash payments totaling at least the allowed amount of such claim, of a value, as of the effective date of the plan, of at least the value of such holder's interest in the estate's interest in such property;

(ii) for the sale, subject to *section 363(k)* of this title, of any property that is subject to the liens securing such claims, free and clear of such liens, with such liens to attach to the proceeds of such sale, and the treatment of such liens on proceeds under clause (i) or (iii) of this subparagraph; or

(iii) for the realization by such holders of the indubitable equivalent of such claims.

(B) With respect to a class of unsecured claims—

(i) the plan provides that each holder of a claim of such class receive or retain on account of such claim property of a value, as of the effective date of the plan, equal to the allowed amount of such claim; or

(ii) the holder of any claim or interest that is junior to the claims of such class will not receive or retain under the plan on account of such junior claim or interest any property, except that in a case in which the debtor is an individual, the debtor may retain property included in the estate under *section 1115*, subject to the requirements of subsection (a)(14) of this section.

(C) With respect to a class of interests—

(i) the plan provides that each holder of an interest of such class receive or retain on account of such interest property of a value, as of the effective date of the plan, equal to the greatest of the allowed amount of any fixed liquidation preference to which such holder is entitled, any fixed redemption price to which such holder is entitled, or the value of such interest; or

(ii) the holder of any interest that is junior to the interests of such class will not receive or retain under the plan on account of such junior interest any property.

(c) Notwithstanding subsections (a) and (b) of this section and except as provided in *section 1127(b)* of this title, the court may confirm only one plan, unless the order of confirmation in the case has been revoked under *section 1144* of this title. If the requirements of subsections (a) and (b) of this section are met with respect to more than one plan, the court shall consider the preferences of creditors and equity security holders in determining which plan to confirm.

(d) Notwithstanding any other provision of this section, on request of a party in interest that is a governmental unit, the court may not confirm a plan if the principal purpose of the plan is the avoidance of taxes or the avoidance of the application of section 5 of the Securities Act of 1933. In any hearing under this subsection, the governmental unit has the burden of proof on the issue of avoidance.

(e) In a small business case, the court shall confirm a plan that complies with the applicable provisions of this title and that is filed in accordance with *section 1121(e)* not later than 45 days after the plan is filed unless the time for confirmation is extended in accordance with *section 1121(e)(3)*.

(Pub. L. 95–598, Nov. 6, 1978, 92 Stat. 2635; Pub. L. 98–353, title III, § 512, July 10, 1984, 98 Stat. 386; Pub. L. 99–554, title II, §§ 225, 283(v), Oct. 27, 1986, 100 Stat. 3102, 3118; Pub. L. 100–334, § 2(b), June 16, 1988, 102 Stat. 613; Pub. L. 103–394, title III, § 304(h)(7), title V, § 501(d)(32), Oct. 22, 1994, 108 Stat. 4134, 4146; Pub. L. 109–8, title II, § 213(1), title III, § 321(c), title IV, § 438, title VII, § 710, title XII, § 1221(b), title XV, § 1502(a)(8), Apr. 20, 2005, 119 Stat. 52, 95, 113, 127, 196, 216; Pub. L. 111–327, § 2(a)(35), Dec. 22, 2010, 124 Stat. 3561.)

Sections that reference this section: 1114, 1121, 1127, 1146, 1173, 1191, 524

Subchapter III: Postconfirmation Matters

§1141. Effect of confirmation

(a) Except as provided in subsections (d)(2) and (d)(3) of this section, the provisions of a confirmed plan bind the debtor, any entity issuing securities under the plan, any entity acquiring property under the plan, and any creditor, equity security holder, or general partner in the debtor, whether or not the claim or interest of such creditor, equity security holder, or general partner is impaired under the plan and whether or not such creditor, equity security holder, or general partner has accepted the plan.

(b) Except as otherwise provided in the plan or the order confirming the plan, the confirmation of a plan vests all of the property of the estate in the debtor.

(c) Except as provided in subsections (d)(2) and (d)(3) of this section and except as otherwise provided in the plan or in the order confirming the plan, after confirmation of a plan, the property dealt with by the plan is free and clear of all claims and interests of creditors, equity security holders, and of general partners in the debtor.

(d)

(1) Except as otherwise provided in this subsection, in the plan, or in the order confirming the plan, the confirmation of a plan—

(A) discharges the debtor from any debt that arose before the date of such confirmation, and any debt of a kind specified in *section 502(g)*, *502*(h), or 502(i) of this title, whether or not—

(i) a proof of the claim based on such debt is filed or deemed filed under *section 501* of this title;

(ii) such claim is allowed under *section 502* of this title; or

(iii) the holder of such claim has accepted the plan; and

(B) terminates all rights and interests of equity security holders and general partners provided for by the plan.

(2) A discharge under this chapter does not discharge a debtor who is an individual from any debt excepted from discharge under *section 523* of this title.

(3) The confirmation of a plan does not discharge a debtor if—

(A) the plan provides for the liquidation of all or substantially all of the property of the estate;

(B) the debtor does not engage in business after consummation of the plan; and

(C) the debtor would be denied a discharge under *section 727(a)* of this title if the case were a case under chapter 7 of this title.

(4) The court may approve a written waiver of discharge executed by the debtor after the order for relief under this chapter.

(5) In a case in which the debtor is an individual—

(A) unless after notice and a hearing the court orders otherwise for cause, confirmation of the plan does not discharge any debt provided for in the plan until the court grants a discharge on completion of all payments under the plan;

(B) at any time after the confirmation of the plan, and after notice and a hearing, the court may grant a discharge to the debtor who has not completed payments under the plan if—

(i) the value, as of the effective date of the plan, of property actually distributed under the plan on account of each allowed unsecured claim is not less than the amount that would have been paid on such claim if the estate of the debtor had been liquidated under chapter 7 on such date;

(ii) modification of the plan under *section 1127* is not practicable; and

(iii) subparagraph (C) permits the court to grant a discharge; and

(C) the court may grant a discharge if, after notice and a hearing held not more than 10 days before the date of the entry of the order granting the discharge, the court finds that there is no reasonable cause to believe that—

(i) *section 522(q)(1)* may be applicable to the debtor; and

(ii) there is pending any proceeding in which the debtor may be found guilty of a felony of the kind described in *section 522(q)(1)(A)* or liable for a debt of the kind described in *section 522(q)(1)(B)*;

and if the requirements of subparagraph (A) or (B) are met.

(6) Notwithstanding paragraph (1), the confirmation of a plan does not discharge a debtor that is a corporation from any debt—

(A) of a kind specified in paragraph (2)(A) or (2)(B) of *section 523(a)* that is owed to a domestic governmental unit, or owed to a person as the result of an action filed under subchapter III of chapter 37 of title 31 or any similar State statute; or

(B) for a tax or customs duty with respect to which the debtor—

(i) made a fraudulent return; or

(ii) willfully attempted in any manner to evade or to defeat such tax or such customs duty.

(Pub. L. 95–598, Nov. 6, 1978, 92 Stat. 2638; Pub. L. 98–353, title III, § 513, July 10, 1984, 98 Stat. 387; Pub. L. 109–8, title III, §§ 321(d), 330(b), title VII, § 708, Apr. 20, 2005, 119 Stat. 95, 101, 126; Pub. L. 111–327, § 2(a)(36), Dec. 22, 2010, 124 Stat. 3561.)

Sections that reference this section: 1106, 1112, 1181, 1192, 524, 727

§1142. Implementation of plan

(a) Notwithstanding any otherwise applicable nonbankruptcy law, rule, or regulation relating to financial condition, the debtor and any entity organized or to be organized for the purpose of carrying out the plan shall carry out the plan and shall comply with any orders of the court.

(b) The court may direct the debtor and any other necessary party to execute or deliver or to join in the execution or delivery of any instrument required to effect a transfer of property dealt with by a confirmed plan, and to perform any other act, including the satisfaction of any lien, that is necessary for the consummation of the plan.

(Pub. L. 95–598, Nov. 6, 1978, 92 Stat. 2639; Pub. L. 98–353, title III, § 514(a), (c), (d), July 10, 1984, 98 Stat. 387.)

Sections that reference this section: None

§1143. Distribution

If a plan requires presentment or surrender of a security or the performance of any other act as a condition to participation in distribution under the plan, such action shall be taken not later than five years after the date of the entry of the order of confirmation. Any entity that has not within such time presented or surrendered such entity's security or taken any such other action that the plan requires may not participate in distribution under the plan.

(Pub. L. 95–598, Nov. 6, 1978, 92 Stat. 2639.)

Sections that reference this section: None

§1144. Revocation of an order of confirmation

On request of a party in interest at any time before 180 days after the date of the entry of the order of confirmation, and after notice and a hearing, the court may revoke such order if and only if such order was procured by fraud. An order under this section revoking an order of confirmation shall—

(1) contain such provisions as are necessary to protect any entity acquiring rights in good faith reliance on the order of confirmation; and

(2) revoke the discharge of the debtor.

(Pub. L. 95–598, Nov. 6, 1978, 92 Stat. 2639; Pub. L. 98–353, title III, § 515, July 10, 1984, 98 Stat. 387.)

Sections that reference this section: 1112, 1129, 524

§1145. Exemption from securities laws

(a) Except with respect to an entity that is an underwriter as defined in subsection (b) of this section, section 5 of the Securities Act of 1933 and any State or local law requiring registration for offer or sale of a security or registration or licensing of an issuer of, underwriter of, or broker or dealer in, a security do not apply to—

(1) the offer or sale under a plan of a security of the debtor, of an affiliate participating in a joint plan with the debtor, or of a successor to the debtor under the plan—

(A) in exchange for a claim against, an interest in, or a claim for an administrative expense in the case concerning, the debtor or such affiliate; or

(B) principally in such exchange and partly for cash or property;

(2) the offer of a security through any warrant, option, right to subscribe, or conversion privilege that was sold in the manner specified in paragraph (1) of this subsection, or the sale of a security upon the exercise of such a warrant, option, right, or privilege;

(3) the offer or sale, other than under a plan, of a security of an issuer other than the debtor or an affiliate, if—

(A) such security was owned by the debtor on the date of the filing of the petition;

(B) the issuer of such security is—

(i) required to file reports under section 13 or 15(d) of the Securities Exchange Act of 1934; and

(ii) in compliance with the disclosure and reporting provision of such applicable section; and

(C) such offer or sale is of securities that do not exceed—

(i) during the two-year period immediately following the date of the filing of the petition, four percent of the securities of such class outstanding on such date; and

(ii) during any 180-day period following such two-year period, one percent of the securities outstanding at the beginning of such 180-day period; or

(4) a transaction by a stockbroker in a security that is executed after a transaction of a kind specified in paragraph (1) or (2) of this subsection in such security and before the expiration of 40 days after the first date on which such security was bona fide offered to the public by the issuer or by or through an underwriter, if such stockbroker provides, at the time of or before such transaction by such stockbroker, a disclosure statement approved under *section 1125* of this title, and, if the court orders, information supplementing such disclosure statement.

(b)

(1) Except as provided in paragraph (2) of this subsection and except with respect to ordinary trading transactions of an entity that is not an issuer, an entity is an underwriter under section 2(a)(11) of the Securities Act of 1933, if such entity—

(A) purchases a claim against, interest in, or claim for an administrative expense in the case concerning, the debtor, if such purchase is with a view to distribution of any security received or to be received in exchange for such a claim or interest;

(B) offers to sell securities offered or sold under the plan for the holders of such securities;

(C) offers to buy securities offered or sold under the plan from the holders of such securities, if such offer to buy is—

(i) with a view to distribution of such securities; and

(ii) under an agreement made in connection with the plan, with the consummation of the plan, or with the offer or sale of securities under the plan; or

(D) is an issuer, as used in such section 2(a)(11), with respect to such securities.

(2) An entity is not an underwriter under section 2(a)(11) of the Securities Act of 1933 or under paragraph (1) of this subsection with respect to an agreement that provides only for—

(A)

(i) the matching or combining of fractional interests in securities offered or sold under the plan into whole interests; or

(ii) the purchase or sale of such fractional interests from or to entities receiving such fractional interests under the plan; or

(B) the purchase or sale for such entities of such fractional or whole interests as are necessary to adjust for any remaining fractional interests after such matching.

(3) An entity other than an entity of the kind specified in paragraph (1) of this subsection is not an underwriter under section 2(a)(11) of the Securities Act of 1933 with respect to any securities offered or sold to such entity in the manner specified in subsection (a)(1) of this section.

(c) An offer or sale of securities of the kind and in the manner specified under subsection (a)(1) of this section is deemed to be a public offering.

(d) The Trust Indenture Act of 1939 does not apply to a note issued under the plan that matures not later than one year after the effective date of the plan.

(Pub. L. 95–598, Nov. 6, 1978, 92 Stat. 2639; Pub. L. 98–353, title III, § 516, July 10, 1984, 98 Stat. 387; Pub. L. 103–394, title V, § 501(d)(33), Oct. 22, 1994, 108 Stat. 4146; Pub. L. 111–327, § 2(a)(37), Dec. 22, 2010, 124 Stat. 3561.)

Sections that reference this section: 364

§1146. Special tax provisions

(a) The issuance, transfer, or exchange of a security, or the making or delivery of an instrument of transfer under a plan confirmed under *section 1129* or *1191* of this title, may not be taxed under any law imposing a stamp tax or similar tax.

(b) The court may authorize the proponent of a plan to request a determination, limited to questions of law, by a State or local governmental unit charged with responsibility for collection or determination of a tax on or measured by income, of the tax effects, under *section 346* of this title and under the law imposing such tax, of the plan. In the event of an actual controversy, the court may declare such effects after the earlier of—

(1) the date on which such governmental unit responds to the request under this subsection; or

(2) 270 days after such request.

(Pub. L. 95–598, Nov. 6, 1978, 92 Stat. 2641; Pub. L. 98–353, title III, § 517, July 10, 1984, 98 Stat. 388; Pub. L. 109–8, title VII, § 719(b)(3), Apr. 20, 2005, 119 Stat. 133; Pub. L. 116–54, § 4(a)(12), Aug. 23, 2019, 133 Stat. 1086.)

Sections that reference this section: None

Subchapter IV: Railroad Reorganization

§1161. Inapplicability of other sections

Sections 341, 343, 1102(a)(1), 1104, 1105, 1107, 1129(a)(7), and 1129(c) of this title do not apply in a case concerning a railroad.

(Pub. L. 95–598, Nov. 6, 1978, 92 Stat. 2641.)

Sections that reference this section: 103

§1162. Definition

In this subchapter, "Board" means the "Surface Transportation Board".

(Added Pub. L. 104–88, title III, § 302(1), Dec. 29, 1995, 109 Stat. 943.)

Sections that reference this section: None

§1163. Appointment of trustee

As soon as practicable after the order for relief the Secretary of Transportation shall submit a list of five disinterested persons that are qualified and willing to serve as trustees in the case. The United States trustee shall appoint one of such persons to serve as trustee in the case.

(Pub. L. 95–598, Nov. 6, 1978, 92 Stat. 2641; Pub. L. 99–554, title II, § 226, Oct. 27, 1986, 100 Stat. 3102.)

Sections that reference this section: 1104

§1164. Right to be heard

The Board, the Department of Transportation, and any State or local commission having regulatory jurisdiction over the debtor may raise and may appear and be heard on any issue in a case under this chapter, but may not appeal from any judgment, order, or decree entered in the case.

(Pub. L. 95–598, Nov. 6, 1978, 92 Stat. 2641; Pub. L. 104–88, title III, § 302(2), Dec. 29, 1995, 109 Stat. 943.)

Sections that reference this section: None

§1165. Protection of the public interest

In applying *sections 1166, 1167, 1169, 1170, 1171, 1172*, 1173, and 1174 of this title, the court and the trustee shall consider the public interest in addition to the interests of the debtor, creditors, and equity security holders.

(Pub. L. 95–598, Nov. 6, 1978, 92 Stat. 2641.)

Sections that reference this section: None

§1166. Effect of subtitle IV of title 49 and of Federal, State, or local regulations

Except with respect to abandonment under *section 1170* of this title, or merger, modification of the financial structure of the debtor, or issuance or sale of securities under a plan, the trustee and the debtor are subject to the provisions of subtitle IV of title 49 that are applicable to railroads, and the trustee is subject to orders of any Federal, State, or local regulatory body to the same extent as the debtor would be if a petition commencing the case under this chapter had not been filed, but—

(1) any such order that would require the expenditure, or the incurring of an obligation for the expenditure, of money from the estate is not effective unless approved by the court; and

(2) the provisions of this chapter are subject to section 601(b) of the Regional Rail Reorganization Act of 1973.

(Pub. L. 95–598, Nov. 6, 1978, 92 Stat. 2642; Pub. L. 97–449, § 5(a)(2), Jan. 12, 1983, 96 Stat. 2442; Pub. L. 98–353, title III, § 518, July 10, 1984, 98 Stat. 388; Pub. L. 103–394, title V, § 501(d)(34), Oct. 22, 1994, 108 Stat. 4146.)

Sections that reference this section: 1165

§1167. Collective bargaining agreements

Notwithstanding *section 365* of this title, neither the court nor the trustee may change the wages or working conditions of employees of the debtor established by a collective bargaining agreement that is subject to the Railway Labor Act except in accordance with section 6 of such Act.

(Pub. L. 95–598, Nov. 6, 1978, 92 Stat. 2642; Pub. L. 103–394, title V, § 501(d)(35), Oct. 22, 1994, 108 Stat. 4146.)

Sections that reference this section: None

§1168. Rolling stock equipment

(a)

(1) The right of a secured party with a security interest in or of a lessor or conditional vendor of equipment described in paragraph (2) to take possession of such equipment in compliance with an equipment security agreement, lease, or conditional sale contract, and to enforce any of its other rights or remedies under such security agreement, lease, or conditional sale contract, to sell, lease, or otherwise retain or dispose of such equipment, is not limited or otherwise affected by any other provision of this title or by any power of the court, except that right to take possession and enforce those other rights and remedies shall be subject to *section 362*, if—

(A) before the date that is 60 days after the date of commencement of a case under this chapter, the trustee, subject to the court's approval, agrees to perform all obligations of the debtor under such security agreement, lease, or conditional sale contract; and

(B) any default, other than a default of a kind described in *section 365(b)(2)*, under such security agreement, lease, or conditional sale contract—

(i) that occurs before the date of commencement of the case and is an event of default therewith is cured before the expiration of such 60-day period;

(ii) that occurs or becomes an event of default after the date of commencement of the case and before the expiration of such 60-day period is cured before the later of—

(I) the date that is 30 days after the date of the default or event of the default; or

(II) the expiration of such 60-day period; and

(iii) that occurs on or after the expiration of such 60-day period is cured in accordance with the terms of such security agreement, lease, or conditional sale contract, if cure is permitted under that agreement, lease, or conditional sale contract.

(2) The equipment described in this paragraph —

(A) is rolling stock equipment or accessories used on rolling stock equipment, including superstructures or racks, that is subject to a security interest granted by, leased to, or conditionally sold to a debtor; and

(B) includes all records and documents relating to such equipment that are required, under the terms of the security agreement, lease, or conditional sale contract, that is to be surrendered or returned by the debtor in connection with the surrender or return of such equipment.

(3) Paragraph (1) applies to a secured party, lessor, or conditional vendor acting in its own behalf or acting as trustee or otherwise in behalf of another party.

(b) The trustee and the secured party, lessor, or conditional vendor whose right to take possession is protected under subsection (a) may agree, subject to the court's approval, to extend the 60-day period specified in subsection (a)(1).

(c)

(1) In any case under this chapter, the trustee shall immediately surrender and return to a secured party, lessor, or conditional vendor, described in subsection (a)(1), equipment described in subsection (a)(2), if at any time after the date of commencement of the case under this chapter such secured party, lessor, or conditional vendor is entitled pursuant to subsection (a)(1) to take possession of such equipment and makes a written demand for such possession of the trustee.

(2) At such time as the trustee is required under paragraph (1) to surrender and return equipment described in subsection (a)(2), any lease of such equipment, and any security agreement or conditional sale contract relating to such equipment, if such security agreement or conditional sale contract is an executory contract, shall be deemed rejected.

(d) With respect to equipment first placed in service on or prior to October 22, 1994, for purposes of this section—

(1) the term "lease" includes any written agreement with respect to which the lessor and the debtor, as lessee, have expressed in the agreement or in a substantially contemporaneous writing that the agreement is to be treated as a lease for Federal income tax purposes; and

(2) the term "security interest" means a purchase-money equipment security interest.

(e) With respect to equipment first placed in service after October 22, 1994, for purposes of this section, the term "rolling stock equipment" includes rolling stock equipment that is substantially rebuilt and accessories used on such equipment.

(Pub. L. 95–598, Nov. 6, 1978, 92 Stat. 2642; Pub. L. 98–353, title III, § 519, July 10, 1984, 98 Stat. 388; Pub. L. 103–394, title II, § 201(b), Oct. 22, 1994, 108 Stat. 4120; Pub. L. 106–181, title VII, § 744(a), Apr. 5, 2000, 114 Stat. 175.)

Sections that reference this section: None

§1169. Effect of rejection of lease of railroad line

(a) Except as provided in subsection (b) of this section, if a lease of a line of railroad under which the debtor is the lessee is rejected under *section 365* of this title, and if the trustee, within such time as the court fixes, and with the court's approval, elects not to operate the leased line, the lessor under such lease, after such approval, shall operate the line.

(b) If operation of such line by such lessor is impracticable or contrary to the public interest, the court, on request of such lessor, and after notice and a hearing, shall order the trustee to continue operation of such line for the account of such lessor until abandonment is ordered under *section 1170* of this title, or until such operation is otherwise lawfully terminated, whichever occurs first.

(c) During any such operation, such lessor is deemed a carrier subject to the provisions of subtitle IV of title 49 that are applicable to railroads.

(Pub. L. 95–598, Nov. 6, 1978, 92 Stat. 2643; Pub. L. 97–449, § 5(a)(3), Jan. 12, 1983, 96 Stat. 2442; Pub. L. 98–353, title III, § 520, July 10, 1984, 98 Stat. 388.)

Sections that reference this section: None

§1170. Abandonment of railroad line

(a) The court, after notice and a hearing, may authorize the abandonment of all or a portion of a railroad line if such abandonment is—

(1)

(A) in the best interest of the estate; or

(B) essential to the formulation of a plan; and

(2) consistent with the public interest.

(b) If, except for the pendency of the case under this chapter, such abandonment would require approval by the Board under a law of the United States, the trustee shall initiate an appropriate application for such abandonment with the Board. The court may fix a time within which the Board shall report to the court on such application.

(c) After the court receives the report of the Board, or the expiration of the time fixed under subsection (b) of this section, whichever occurs first, the court may authorize such abandonment, after notice to the Board, the Secretary of Transportation, the trustee, any party in interest that has requested notice, any affected shipper or community, and any other entity prescribed by the court, and a hearing.

(d)

(1) Enforcement of an order authorizing such abandonment shall be stayed until the time for taking an appeal has expired, or, if an appeal is timely taken, until such order has become final.

(2) If an order authorizing such abandonment is appealed, the court, on request of a party in interest, may authorize suspension of service on a line or a portion of a line pending the determination of such appeal, after notice to the Board, the Secretary of Transportation, the trustee, any party in interest that has requested notice, any affected shipper or community, and any other entity prescribed by the court, and a hearing. An appellant may not obtain a stay of the enforcement of an order authorizing such suspension by the giving of a supersedeas bond or otherwise, during the pendency of such appeal.

(e)

(1) In authorizing any abandonment of a railroad line under this section, the court shall require the rail carrier to provide a fair arrangement at least as protective of the interests of employees as that established under section 11326(a) of title 49.

(2) Nothing in this subsection shall be deemed to affect the priorities or timing of payment of employee protection which might have existed in the absence of this subsection.

(Pub. L. 95–598, Nov. 6, 1978, 92 Stat. 2643; Pub. L. 96–448, title II, § 227(a), Oct. 14, 1980, 94 Stat. 1931; Pub. L. 98–353, title III, § 521, July 10, 1984, 98 Stat. 388; Pub. L. 104–88, title III, § 302(2), Dec. 29, 1995, 109 Stat. 943; Pub. L. 109–8, title XII, § 1217, Apr. 20, 2005, 119 Stat. 195.)

Sections that reference this section: 1166, 1169, 1172

§1171. Priority claims

(a) There shall be paid as an administrative expense any claim of an individual or of the personal representative of a deceased individual against the debtor or the estate, for personal injury to or death of such individual arising out of the operation of the debtor or the estate, whether such claim arose before or after the commencement of the case.

(b) Any unsecured claim against the debtor that would have been entitled to priority if a receiver in equity of the property of the debtor had been appointed by a Federal court on the date of the order for relief under this title shall be entitled to the same priority in the case under this chapter.

(Pub. L. 95–598, Nov. 6, 1978, 92 Stat. 2643; Pub. L. 98–353, title III, § 522, July 10, 1984, 98 Stat. 388.)

Sections that reference this section: None

§1172. Contents of plan

(a) In addition to the provisions required or permitted under *section 1123* of this title, a plan—

(1) shall specify the extent to and the means by which the debtor's rail service is proposed to be continued, and the extent to which any of the debtor's rail service is proposed to be terminated; and

(2) may include a provision for—

(A) the transfer of any or all of the operating railroad lines of the debtor to another operating railroad; or

(B) abandonment of any railroad line in accordance with *section 1170* of this title.

(b) If, except for the pendency of the case under this chapter, transfer of, or operation of or over, any of the debtor's rail lines by an entity other than the debtor or a successor to the debtor under the plan would require approval by the Board under a law of the United States, then a plan may not propose such a transfer or such operation unless the proponent of the plan initiates an appropriate application for such a transfer or such operation with the Board and, within such time as the court may fix, not exceeding 180 days, the Board, with or without a hearing, as the Board may determine, and with or without modification or condition, approves such application, or does not act on such application. Any action or order of the Board approving, modifying, conditioning, or disapproving such application is subject to review by the court only under *sections 706(2)(A)*, *706*(2)(B), 706(2)(C), and 706(2)(D) of title 5.

(c)

(1) In approving an application under subsection (b) of this section, the Board shall require the rail carrier to provide a fair arrangement at least as protective of the interests of employees as that established under section 11326(a) of title 49.

(2) Nothing in this subsection shall be deemed to affect the priorities or timing of payment of employee protection which might have existed in the absence of this subsection.

(Pub. L. 95–598, Nov. 6, 1978, 92 Stat. 2644; Pub. L. 96–448, title II, § 227(b), Oct. 14, 1980, 94 Stat. 1931; Pub. L. 104–88, title III, § 302(2), Dec. 29, 1995, 109 Stat. 943; Pub. L. 109–8, title XII, § 1218, Apr. 20, 2005, 119 Stat. 195.)

Sections that reference this section: None

§1173. Confirmation of plan

(a) The court shall confirm a plan if—

(1) the applicable requirements of *section 1129* of this title have been met;

(2) each creditor or equity security holder will receive or retain under the plan property of a value, as of the effective date of the plan, that is not less than the value of property that each such creditor or equity security holder would so receive or retain if all of the operating railroad lines of the debtor were sold, and the proceeds of such sale, and the other property of the estate, were distributed under chapter 7 of this title on such date;

(3) in light of the debtor's past earnings and the probable prospective earnings of the reorganized debtor, there will be adequate coverage by such prospective earnings of any fixed charges, such as interest on debt, amortization of funded debt, and rent for leased railroads, provided for by the plan; and

(4) the plan is consistent with the public interest.

(b) If the requirements of subsection (a) of this section are met with respect to more than one plan, the court shall confirm the plan that is most likely to maintain adequate rail service in the public interest.

(Pub. L. 95–598, Nov. 6, 1978, 92 Stat. 2644; Pub. L. 98–353, title III, § 523, July 10, 1984, 98 Stat. 388.)

Sections that reference this section: 1174

§1174. Liquidation

On request of a party in interest and after notice and a hearing, the court may, or, if a plan has not been confirmed under *section 1173* of this title before five years after the date of the order for relief, the court shall, order the trustee to cease the debtor's operation and to collect and reduce to money all of the property of the estate in the same manner as if the case were a case under chapter 7 of this title.

(Pub. L. 95–598, Nov. 6, 1978, 92 Stat. 2644.)

Sections that reference this section: None

Subchapter V: Small Business Debtor Reorganization

§1181. Inapplicability of other sections

(a) In General.—

Sections 105(d), *1101*(1), 1104, 1105, 1106, 1107, 1108, 1115, 1116, 1121, 1123(a)(8), 1123(c), 1127, 1129(a)(15), 1129(b), 1129(c), 1129(e), and 1141(d)(5) of this title do not apply in a case under this subchapter.

(b) Court Authority.—

Unless the court for cause orders otherwise, paragraphs (1), (2), and (4) of *section 1102(a)* and *sections 1102(b)*, *1103*, and *1125* of this title do not apply in a case under this subchapter.

(c) Special Rule for Discharge.—

If a plan is confirmed under *section 1191(b)* of this title, *section 1141(d)* of this title shall not apply, except as provided in *section 1192* of this title.

(Added Pub. L. 116–54, § 2(a), Aug. 23, 2019, 133 Stat. 1079.)

Sections that reference this section: 1187

§1182. Definitions

In this subchapter:

(1) Debtor.—

The term "debtor" means a small business debtor.

(2) Debtor in possession.—

The term "debtor in possession" means the debtor, unless removed as debtor in possession under *section 1185(a)* of this title.

(Added Pub. L. 116–54, § 2(a), Aug. 23, 2019, 133 Stat. 1079; amended Pub. L. 116–136, div. A, title I, § 1113(a)(1), (5), Mar. 27, 2020, 134 Stat. 310, 311; Pub. L. 117–151, § 2(d), (i)(1)(B), June 21, 2022, 136 Stat. 1298, 1300.)

Sections that reference this section: 103

§1183. Trustee

(a) In General.—

If the United States trustee has appointed an individual under section 586(b) of title 28 to serve as standing trustee in cases under this subchapter, and if such individual qualifies as a trustee under *section 322* of this title, then that individual shall serve as trustee in any case under this subchapter. Otherwise, the United States trustee shall appoint one disinterested person to serve as trustee in the case or the United States trustee may serve as trustee in the case, as necessary.

(b) Duties.—

The trustee shall—

(1) perform the duties specified in paragraphs (2), (5), (6), (7), and (9) of *section 704(a)* of this title;

(2) perform the duties specified in paragraphs (3), (4), and (7) of *section 1106(a)* of this title, if the court, for cause and on request of a party in interest, the trustee, or the United States trustee, so orders;

(3) appear and be heard at the status conference under *section 1188* of this title and any hearing that concerns—

(A) the value of property subject to a lien;

(B) confirmation of a plan filed under this subchapter;

(C) modification of the plan after confirmation; or

(D) the sale of property of the estate;

(4) ensure that the debtor commences making timely payments required by a plan confirmed under this subchapter;

(5) if the debtor ceases to be a debtor in possession—

(A) perform the duties specified in *section 704(a)(8)* and paragraphs (1), (2), and (6) of *section 1106(a)* of this title; and

(B) be authorized to operate the business of the debtor;

(6) if there is a claim for a domestic support obligation with respect to the debtor, perform the duties specified in *section 704(c)* of this title; and

(7) facilitate the development of a consensual plan of reorganization.

(c) Termination of Trustee Service.—

(1) In general.—

If the plan of the debtor is confirmed under *section 1191(a)* of this title, the service of the trustee in the case shall terminate when the plan has been substantially consummated, except that the United States trustee may reappoint a trustee as needed for performance of duties under subsection (b)(3)(C) of this section and *section 1185(a)* of this title.

(2) Service of notice of substantial consummation.—

Not later than 14 days after the plan of the debtor is substantially consummated, the debtor shall file with the court and serve on the trustee, the United States trustee, and all parties in interest notice of such substantial consummation.

(Added Pub. L. 116–54, § 2(a), Aug. 23, 2019, 133 Stat. 1079; amended Pub. L. 117–151, § 2(e), June 21, 2022, 136 Stat. 1299.)

Sections that reference this section: None

§1184. Rights and powers of a debtor in possession

Subject to such limitations or conditions as the court may prescribe, a debtor in possession shall have all the rights, other than the right to compensation under *section 330* of this title, and powers, and shall perform all functions and duties, except the duties specified in paragraphs (2), (3), and (4) of *section 1106(a)* of this title, of a trustee serving in a case under this chapter, including operating the business of the debtor.

(Added Pub. L. 116–54, § 2(a), Aug. 23, 2019, 133 Stat. 1080.)

Sections that reference this section: None

§1185. Removal of debtor in possession

(a) In General.—

On request of a party in interest, and after notice and a hearing, the court shall order that the debtor shall not be a debtor in possession for cause, including fraud, dishonesty, incompetence, or gross mismanagement of the affairs of the debtor, either before or after the date of commencement of the case, or for failure to perform the obligations of the debtor under a plan confirmed under this subchapter.

(b) Reinstatement.—

On request of a party in interest, and after notice and a hearing, the court may reinstate the debtor in possession.

(Added Pub. L. 116–54, § 2(a), Aug. 23, 2019, 133 Stat. 1080.)

Sections that reference this section: 1182, 1183, 1186

§1186. Property of the estate

(a) Inclusions.—

If a plan is confirmed under *section 1191(b)* of this title, property of the estate includes, in addition to the property specified in *section 541* of this title—

(1) all property of the kind specified in that section that the debtor acquires after the date of commencement of the case but before the case is closed, dismissed, or converted to a case under chapter 7, 12, or 13 of this title, whichever occurs first; and

(2) earnings from services performed by the debtor after the date of commencement of the case but before the case is closed, dismissed, or converted to a case under chapter 7, 12, or 13 of this title, whichever occurs first.

(b) Debtor Remaining in Possession.—

Except as provided in *section 1185* of this title, a plan confirmed under this subchapter, or an order confirming a plan under this subchapter, the debtor shall remain in possession of all property of the estate.

(Added Pub. L. 116–54, § 2(a), Aug. 23, 2019, 133 Stat. 1081.)

Sections that reference this section: None

§1187. Duties and reporting requirements of debtors

(a) Filing Requirements.—

Upon electing to be a debtor under this subchapter, the debtor shall file the documents required by subparagraphs (A) and (B) of *section 1116(1)* of this title.

(b) Other Applicable Provisions.—

A debtor, in addition to the duties provided in this title and as otherwise required by law, shall comply with the requirements of *section 308* and paragraphs (2), (3), (4), (5), (6), and (7) of *section 1116* of this title.

(c) Separate Disclosure Statement Exemption.—

If the court orders under *section 1181(b)* of this title that *section 1125* of this title applies, *section 1125(f)* of this title shall apply.

(Added Pub. L. 116–54, § 2(a), Aug. 23, 2019, 133 Stat. 1081.)

Sections that reference this section: None

§1188. Status conference

(a) In General.—

Except as provided in subsection (b), not later than 60 days after the entry of the order for relief under this chapter, the court shall hold a status conference to further the expeditious and economical resolution of a case under this subchapter.

(b) Exception.—

The court may extend the period of time for holding a status conference under subsection (a) if the need for an extension is attributable to circumstances for which the debtor should not justly be held accountable.

(c) Report.—

Not later than 14 days before the date of the status conference under subsection (a), the debtor shall file with the court and serve on the trustee and all parties in interest a report that details the efforts the debtor has undertaken and will undertake to attain a consensual plan of reorganization.

(Added Pub. L. 116–54, § 2(a), Aug. 23, 2019, 133 Stat. 1081.)

Sections that reference this section: 1183

§1189. Filing of the plan

(a) Who May File a Plan.—

Only the debtor may file a plan under this subchapter.

(b) Deadline.—

The debtor shall file a plan not later than 90 days after the order for relief under this chapter, except that the court may extend the period if the need for the extension is attributable to circumstances for which the debtor should not justly be held accountable.

(Added Pub. L. 116–54, § 2(a), Aug. 23, 2019, 133 Stat. 1081.)

Sections that reference this section: None

§1190. Contents of plan

A plan filed under this subchapter—

(1) shall include—

(A) a brief history of the business operations of the debtor;

(B) a liquidation analysis; and

(C) projections with respect to the ability of the debtor to make payments under the proposed plan of reorganization;

(2) shall provide for the submission of all or such portion of the future earnings or other future income of the debtor to the supervision and control of the trustee as is necessary for the execution of the plan; and

(3) notwithstanding *section 1123(b)(5)* of this title, may modify the rights of the holder of a claim secured only by a security interest in real property that is the principal residence of the debtor if the new value received in connection with the granting of the security interest was—

(A) not used primarily to acquire the real property; and

(B) used primarily in connection with the small business of the debtor.

(Added Pub. L. 116–54, § 2(a), Aug. 23, 2019, 133 Stat. 1082.)

Sections that reference this section: None

§1191. Confirmation of plan

(a) Terms.—

The court shall confirm a plan under this subchapter only if all of the requirements of *section 1129(a)*, other than paragraph (15) of that section, of this title are met.

(b) Exception.—

Notwithstanding *section 510(a)* of this title, if all of the applicable requirements of *section 1129(a)* of this title, other than paragraphs (8), (10), and (15) of that section, are met with respect to a plan, the court, on request of the debtor, shall confirm the plan notwithstanding the requirements of such paragraphs if the plan does not discriminate unfairly, and is fair and equitable, with respect to each class of claims or interests that is impaired under, and has not accepted, the plan.

(c) Rule of Construction.—

For purposes of this section, the condition that a plan be fair and equitable with respect to each class of claims or interests includes the following requirements:

(1) With respect to a class of secured claims, the plan meets the requirements of *section 1129(b)(2)(A)* of this title.

(2) As of the effective date of the plan—

(A) the plan provides that all of the projected disposable income of the debtor to be received in the 3-year period, or such longer period not to exceed 5 years as the court may fix, beginning on the date that the first payment is due under the plan will be applied to make payments under the plan; or

(B) the value of the property to be distributed under the plan in the 3-year period, or such longer period not to exceed 5 years as the court may fix, beginning on the date on which the first distribution is due under the plan is not less than the projected disposable income of the debtor.

(3)

(A) The debtor will be able to make all payments under the plan; or

(B)

(i) there is a reasonable likelihood that the debtor will be able to make all payments under the plan; and

(ii) the plan provides appropriate remedies, which may include the liquidation of nonexempt assets, to protect the holders of claims or interests in the event that the payments are not made.

(d) Disposable Income.—

For purposes of this section, the term "disposable income" means the income that is received by the debtor and that is not reasonably necessary to be expended—

(1) for—

(A) the maintenance or support of the debtor or a dependent of the debtor; or

(B) a domestic support obligation that first becomes payable after the date of the filing of the petition; or

(2) for the payment of expenditures necessary for the continuation, preservation, or operation of the business of the debtor.

(e) Special Rule.—

Notwithstanding *section 1129(a)(9)(A)* of this title, a plan that provides for the payment through the plan of a claim of a kind specified in paragraph (2) or (3) of *section 507(a)* of this title may be confirmed under subsection (b) of this section.

(Added Pub. L. 116–54, § 2(a), Aug. 23, 2019, 133 Stat. 1082; amended Pub. L. 116–260, div. N, title III, § 320(c), (f)(2)(A)(iii), Dec. 27, 2020, 134 Stat. 2016, 2017; Pub. L. 117–151, § 2(f), June 21, 2022, 136 Stat. 1299.)

Sections that reference this section: 1181, 1183, 1186, 1192, 1193, 1194

§1192. Discharge

If the plan of the debtor is confirmed under *section 1191(b)* of this title, as soon as practicable after completion by the debtor of all payments due within the first 3 years of the plan, or such longer period not to exceed 5 years as the court may fix, unless the court approves a written waiver of discharge executed by the debtor after the order for relief under this chapter, the court shall grant the debtor a discharge of all debts provided in *section 1141(d)(1)(A)* of this title, and all other debts allowed under *section 503* of this title and provided for in the plan, except any debt—

(1) on which the last payment is due after the first 3 years of the plan, or such other time not to exceed 5 years fixed by the court; or

(2) of the kind specified in *section 523(a)* of this title.

(Added Pub. L. 116–54, § 2(a), Aug. 23, 2019, 133 Stat. 1083.)

Sections that reference this section: 1181

§1193. Modification of plan

(a) Modification Before Confirmation.—

The debtor may modify a plan at any time before confirmation, but may not modify the plan so that the plan as modified fails to meet the requirements of *sections 1122* and *1123* of this title, with the exception of subsection (a)(8) of such *section 1123*. After the modification is filed with the court, the plan as modified becomes the plan.

(b) Modification After Confirmation.—

If a plan has been confirmed under *section 1191(a)* of this title, the debtor may modify the plan at any time after confirmation of the plan and before substantial consummation of the plan, but may not modify the plan so that the plan as modified fails to meet the requirements of *sections 1122* and *1123* of this title, with the exception of subsection (a)(8) of such *section 1123*. The plan, as modified under this subsection, becomes the plan only if circumstances warrant the modification and the court, after notice and a hearing, confirms the plan as modified under *section 1191(a)* of this title.

(c) Certain Other Modifications.—

If a plan has been confirmed under *section 1191(b)* of this title, the debtor may modify the plan at any time within 3 years, or such longer time not to exceed 5 years, as fixed by the court, but may not modify the plan so that the plan as modified fails to meet the requirements of *section 1191(b)* of this title. The plan as modified under this subsection becomes the plan only if circumstances warrant such modification and the court, after notice and a hearing, confirms such plan, as modified, under *section 1191(b)* of this title.

(d) Holders of a Claim or Interest.—

If a plan has been confirmed under *section 1191(a)* of this title, any holder of a claim or interest that has accepted or rejected the plan is deemed to have accepted or rejected, as the case may be, the plan as modified, unless, within the time fixed by the court, such holder changes the previous acceptance or rejection of the holder.

(Added Pub. L. 116–54, § 2(a), Aug. 23, 2019, 133 Stat. 1083.)

Sections that reference this section: None

§1194. Payments

(a) Retention and Distribution by Trustee.—

Payments and funds received by the trustee shall be retained by the trustee until confirmation or denial of confirmation of a plan. If a plan is confirmed, the trustee shall distribute any such payment in accordance with the plan. If a plan is not confirmed, the trustee shall return any such payments to the debtor after deducting—

(1) any unpaid claim allowed under *section 503(b)* of this title;

(2) any payment made for the purpose of providing adequate protection of an interest in property due to the holder of a secured claim; and

(3) any fee owing to the trustee.

(b) Other Plans.—

If a plan is confirmed under *section 1191(b)* of this title, except as otherwise provided in the plan or in the order confirming the plan, the trustee shall make payments to creditors under the plan.

(c) Payments Prior to Confirmation.—

Prior to confirmation of a plan, the court, after notice and a hearing, may authorize the trustee to make payments to the holder of a secured claim for the purpose of providing adequate protection of an interest in property.

(Added Pub. L. 116–54, § 2(a), Aug. 23, 2019, 133 Stat. 1084.)

Sections that reference this section: None

§1195. Transactions with professionals

Notwithstanding *section 327(a)* of this title, a person is not disqualified for employment under *section 327* of this title, by a debtor solely because that person holds a claim of less than $10,000 that arose prior to commencement of the case.

(Added Pub. L. 116–54, § 2(a), Aug. 23, 2019, 133 Stat. 1084.)

Sections that reference this section: None

CHAPTER 12: ADJUSTMENT OF DEBTS OF A FAMILY FARMER OR FISHERMAN WITH REGULAR ANNUAL INCOME

Subchapter I: Officers, Administration, and the Estate

§1201. Stay of action against codebtor

(a) Except as provided in subsections (b) and (c) of this section, after the order for relief under this chapter, a creditor may not act, or commence or continue any civil action, to collect all or any part of a consumer debt of the debtor from any individual that is liable on such debt with the debtor, or that secured such debt, unless—

(1) such individual became liable on or secured such debt in the ordinary course of such individual's business; or

(2) the case is closed, dismissed, or converted to a case under chapter 7 of this title.

(b) A creditor may present a negotiable instrument, and may give notice of dishonor of such an instrument.

(c) On request of a party in interest and after notice and a hearing, the court shall grant relief from the stay provided by subsection (a) of this section with respect to a creditor, to the extent that —

(1) as between the debtor and the individual protected under subsection (a) of this section, such individual received the consideration for the claim held by such creditor;

(2) the plan filed by the debtor proposes not to pay such claim; or

(3) such creditor's interest would be irreparably harmed by continuation of such stay.

(d) Twenty days after the filing of a request under subsection (c)(2) of this section for relief from the stay provided by subsection (a) of this section, such stay is terminated with respect to the party in interest making such request, unless the debtor or any individual that is liable on such debt with the debtor files and serves upon such party in interest a written objection to the taking of the proposed action.

(Added and amended Pub. L. 99–554, title II, § 255, title III, § 302(f), Oct. 27, 1986, 100 Stat. 3105, 3124; Pub. L. 103–65, § 1, Aug. 6, 1993,

107 Stat. 311; Pub. L. 105–277, div. C, title I, § 149(a), Oct. 21, 1998, 112 Stat. 2681–610; Pub. L. 106–5, § 1(1), (2), Mar. 30, 1999, 113 Stat. 9; Pub. L. 106–70, § 1, Oct. 9, 1999, 113 Stat. 1031; Pub. L. 107–8, § 1, May 11, 2001, 115 Stat. 10; Pub. L. 107–17, § 1, June 26, 2001, 115 Stat. 151; Pub. L. 107–170, § 1, May 7, 2002, 116 Stat. 133; Pub. L. 107–171, title X, § 10814(a), May 13, 2002, 116 Stat. 532; Pub. L. 107–377, § 2(a), Dec. 19, 2002, 116 Stat. 3115; Pub. L. 108–73, § 2(a), Aug. 15, 2003, 117 Stat. 891; Pub. L. 108–369, § 2(a), Oct. 25, 2004, 118 Stat. 1749; Pub. L. 109–8, title X, § 1001(a)(1), (c), Apr. 20, 2005, 119 Stat. 185, 186.)

Sections that reference this section: 108

§1202. Trustee

(a) If the United States trustee has appointed an individual under section 586(b) of title 28 to serve as standing trustee in cases under this chapter and if such individual qualifies as a trustee under *section 322* of this title, then such individual shall serve as trustee in any case filed under this chapter. Otherwise, the United States trustee shall appoint one disinterested person to serve as trustee in the case or the United States trustee may serve as trustee in the case if necessary.

(b) The trustee shall—

(1) perform the duties specified in *sections 704(a)(2), 704*(a)(3), 704(a)(5), 704(a)(6), 704(a)(7), and 704(a)(9) of this title;

(2) perform the duties specified in *section 1106(a)(3)* and *1106*(a)(4) of this title if the court, for cause and on request of a party in interest, the trustee, or the United States trustee, so orders;

(3) appear and be heard at any hearing that concerns—

(A) the value of property subject to a lien;

(B) confirmation of a plan;

(C) modification of the plan after confirmation; or

(D) the sale of property of the estate;

(4) ensure that the debtor commences making timely payments required by a confirmed plan;

(5) if the debtor ceases to be a debtor in possession, perform the duties specified in *sections 704(a)(8), 1106*(a)(1), 1106(a)(2), 1106(a)(6), 1106(a)(7), and 1203; and

(6) if with respect to the debtor there is a claim for a domestic support obligation, provide the applicable notice specified in subsection (c).

(c)

(1) In a case described in subsection (b)(6) to which subsection (b)(6) applies, the trustee shall—

(A)

(i) provide written notice to the holder of the claim described in subsection (b)(6) of such claim and of the right of such holder to use the services of the State child support enforcement agency established under sections 464 and 466 of the Social Security Act for the State in which such holder resides, for assistance in collecting child support during and after the case under this title; and

(ii) include in the notice provided under clause (i) the address and telephone number of such State child support enforcement agency;

(B)

(i) provide written notice to such State child support enforcement agency of such claim; and

(ii) include in the notice provided under clause (i) the name, address, and telephone number of such holder; and

(C) at such time as the debtor is granted a discharge under *section 1228*, provide written notice to such holder and to such State child support enforcement agency of—

(i) the granting of the discharge;

(ii) the last recent known address of the debtor;

(iii) the last recent known name and address of the debtor's employer; and

(iv) the name of each creditor that holds a claim that—

(I) is not discharged under paragraph (2), (4), or (14A) of *section 523(a)*; or

(II) was reaffirmed by the debtor under *section 524(c)*.

(2)

(A) The holder of a claim described in subsection (b)(6) or the State child support enforcement agency of the State in which such holder resides may request from a creditor described in paragraph (1)(C)(iv) the last known address of the debtor.

(B) Notwithstanding any other provision of law, a creditor that makes a disclosure of a last known address of a debtor in connection with a request made under subparagraph (A) shall not be liable by reason of making that disclosure.

(Added and amended Pub. L. 99–554, title II, §§ 227, 255, title III, § 302(f), Oct. 27, 1986, 100 Stat. 3103, 3106, 3124; Pub. L. 103–65, § 1, Aug. 6, 1993, 107 Stat. 311; Pub. L. 105–277, div. C, title I, § 149(a), Oct. 21, 1998, 112 Stat. 2681–610; Pub. L. 106–5, § 1(1), (2), Mar. 30, 1999, 113 Stat. 9; Pub. L. 106–70, § 1, Oct. 9, 1999, 113 Stat. 1031; Pub. L. 107–8, § 1, May 11, 2001, 115 Stat. 10; Pub. L. 107–17, § 1, June 26, 2001, 115 Stat. 151; Pub. L. 107–170, § 1, May 7, 2002, 116 Stat. 133; Pub. L. 107–171, title X, § 10814(a), May 13, 2002, 116 Stat. 532; Pub. L. 107–377, § 2(a), Dec. 19, 2002, 116 Stat. 3115; Pub. L. 108–73, § 2(a), Aug. 15, 2003, 117 Stat. 891; Pub. L. 108–369, § 2(a), Oct. 25, 2004, 118 Stat. 1749; Pub. L. 109–8, title II, § 219(c), title X, § 1001(a)(1), (c), Apr. 20, 2005, 119 Stat. 57, 185, 186; Pub. L. 111–327, § 2(a)(38), Dec. 22, 2010, 124 Stat. 3561.)

Sections that reference this section: 1226, 326

§1203. Rights and powers of debtor

Subject to such limitations as the court may prescribe, a debtor in possession shall have all the rights, other than the right to compensation under *section 330*, and powers, and shall perform all the functions and duties, except the duties specified in paragraphs (3) and (4) of *section 1106(a)*, of a trustee serving in a case under chapter 11, including operating the debtor's farm or commercial fishing operation.

(Added and amended Pub. L. 99–554, title II, § 255, title III, § 302(f), Oct. 27, 1986, 100 Stat. 3107, 3124; Pub. L. 103–65, § 1, Aug. 6, 1993, 107 Stat. 311; Pub. L. 105–277, div. C, title I, § 149(a), Oct. 21, 1998, 112 Stat. 2681–610; Pub. L. 106–5, § 1(1), (2), Mar. 30, 1999, 113 Stat. 9; Pub. L. 106–70, § 1, Oct. 9, 1999, 113 Stat. 1031; Pub. L. 107–8, § 1, May 11, 2001, 115 Stat. 10; Pub. L. 107–17, § 1, June 26, 2001, 115 Stat. 151; Pub. L. 107–170, § 1, May 7, 2002, 116 Stat. 133; Pub. L. 107–171, title X, § 10814(a), May 13, 2002, 116 Stat. 532; Pub. L. 107–377, § 2(a), Dec. 19, 2002, 116 Stat. 3115; Pub. L. 108–73, § 2(a), Aug. 15, 2003, 117 Stat. 891; Pub. L. 108–369, § 2(a), Oct. 25, 2004, 118 Stat. 1749; Pub. L. 109–8, title X, §§ 1001(a)(1), (c), 1007(c)(2), Apr. 20, 2005, 119 Stat. 185, 186, 188.)

Sections that reference this section: None

§1204. Removal of debtor as debtor in possession

(a) On request of a party in interest, and after notice and a hearing, the court shall order that the debtor shall not be a debtor in possession for cause, including fraud, dishonesty, incompetence, or gross mismanagement of the affairs of the debtor, either before or after the commencement of the case.

(b) On request of a party in interest, and after notice and a hearing, the court may reinstate the debtor in possession.

(Added and amended Pub. L. 99–554, title II, § 255, title III, § 302(f), Oct. 27, 1986, 100 Stat. 3107, 3124; Pub. L. 103–65, § 1, Aug. 6, 1993, 107 Stat. 311; Pub. L. 105–277, div. C, title I, § 149(a), Oct. 21, 1998, 112 Stat. 2681–610; Pub. L. 106–5, § 1(1), (2), Mar. 30, 1999, 113 Stat. 9; Pub. L. 106–70, § 1, Oct. 9, 1999, 113 Stat. 1031; Pub. L. 107–8, § 1, May 11, 2001, 115 Stat. 10; Pub. L. 107–17, § 1, June 26, 2001, 115 Stat. 151; Pub. L. 107–170, § 1, May 7, 2002, 116 Stat. 133; Pub. L. 107–171, title X, § 10814(a), May 13, 2002, 116 Stat. 532; Pub. L. 107–377, § 2(a), Dec. 19, 2002, 116 Stat. 3115; Pub. L. 108–73, § 2(a), Aug. 15, 2003, 117 Stat. 891; Pub. L. 108–369, § 2(a), Oct. 25, 2004, 118 Stat. 1749; Pub. L. 109–8, title X, § 1001(a)(1), (c), Apr. 20, 2005, 119 Stat. 185, 186.)

Sections that reference this section: 1207

§1205. Adequate protection

(a) *Section 361* does not apply in a case under this chapter.

(b) In a case under this chapter, when adequate protection is required under *section 362, 363,* or *364* of this title of an interest of an entity in property, such adequate protection may be provided by—

(1) requiring the trustee to make a cash payment or periodic cash payments to such entity, to the extent that the stay under *section 362* of this title, use, sale, or lease under *section 363* of this title, or any grant of a lien under *section 364* of this title results in a decrease in the value of property securing a claim or of an entity's ownership interest in property;

(2) providing to such entity an additional or replacement lien to the extent that such stay, use, sale, lease, or grant results in a decrease in the value of property securing a claim or of an entity's ownership interest in property;

(3) paying to such entity for the use of farmland the reasonable rent customary in the community where the property is located, based upon the rental value, net income, and earning capacity of the property; or

(4) granting such other relief, other than entitling such entity to compensation allowable under *section 503(b)(1)* of this title as an administrative expense, as will adequately protect the value of property securing a claim or of such entity's ownership interest in property.

(Added and amended Pub. L. 99–554, title II, § 255, title III, § 302(f), Oct. 27, 1986, 100 Stat. 3107, 3124; Pub. L. 103–65, § 1, Aug. 6, 1993, 107 Stat. 311; Pub. L. 105–277, div. C, title I, § 149(a), Oct. 21, 1998, 112 Stat. 2681–610; Pub. L. 106–5, § 1(1), (2), Mar. 30, 1999, 113 Stat. 9; Pub. L. 106–70, § 1, Oct. 9, 1999, 113 Stat. 1031; Pub. L. 107–8, § 1, May 11, 2001, 115 Stat. 10; Pub. L. 107–17, § 1, June 26, 2001, 115 Stat. 151; Pub. L. 107–170, § 1, May 7, 2002, 116 Stat. 133; Pub. L. 107–171, title X, § 10814(a), May 13, 2002, 116 Stat. 532; Pub. L. 107–377, § 2(a), Dec. 19, 2002, 116 Stat. 3115; Pub. L. 108–73, § 2(a), Aug. 15, 2003, 117 Stat. 891; Pub. L. 108–369, § 2(a), Oct. 25, 2004, 118 Stat. 1749; Pub. L. 109–8, title X, § 1001(a)(1), (c), Apr. 20, 2005, 119 Stat. 185, 186.)

Sections that reference this section: None

§1206. Sales free of interests

After notice and a hearing, in addition to the authorization contained in *section 363(f)*, the trustee in a case under this chapter may sell property under *section 363(b)* and (c) free and clear of any interest in such property of an entity other than the estate if the property is farmland, farm equipment, or property used to carry out a commercial fishing operation (including a commercial fishing vessel), except that the proceeds of such sale shall be subject to such interest.

(Added and amended Pub. L. 99–554, title II, § 255, title III, § 302(f), Oct. 27, 1986, 100 Stat. 3108, 3124; Pub. L. 103–65, § 1, Aug. 6, 1993, 107 Stat. 311; Pub. L. 105–277, div. C, title I, § 149(a), Oct. 21, 1998, 112 Stat. 2681–610; Pub. L. 106–5, § 1(1), (2), Mar. 30, 1999, 113 Stat. 9; Pub. L. 106–70, § 1, Oct. 9, 1999, 113 Stat. 1031; Pub. L. 107–8, § 1, May 11, 2001, 115 Stat. 10; Pub. L. 107–17, § 1, June 26, 2001, 115 Stat. 151; Pub. L. 107–170, § 1, May 7, 2002, 116 Stat. 133; Pub. L. 107–171, title X, § 10814(a), May 13, 2002, 116 Stat. 532; Pub. L. 107–377, § 2(a), Dec. 19, 2002, 116 Stat. 3115; Pub. L. 108–73, § 2(a), Aug. 15, 2003, 117 Stat. 891; Pub. L. 108–369, § 2(a), Oct. 25, 2004, 118 Stat. 1749; Pub. L. 109–8, title X, §§ 1001(a)(1), (c), 1007(c)(3), Apr. 20, 2005, 119 Stat. 185, 186, 188.)

Sections that reference this section: None

§1207. Property of the estate

(a) Property of the estate includes, in addition to the property specified in *section 541* of this title—

(1) all property of the kind specified in such section that the debtor acquires after the commencement of the case but before the case is closed, dismissed, or converted to a case under chapter 7 of this title, whichever occurs first; and

(2) earnings from services performed by the debtor after the commencement of the case but before the case is closed, dismissed, or converted to a case under chapter 7 of this title, whichever occurs first.

(b) Except as provided in *section 1204*, a confirmed plan, or an order confirming a plan, the debtor shall remain in possession of all property of the estate.

(Added and amended Pub. L. 99–554, title II, § 255, title III, § 302(f), Oct. 27, 1986, 100 Stat. 3108, 3124; Pub. L. 103–65, § 1, Aug. 6, 1993, 107 Stat. 311; Pub. L. 105–277, div. C, title I, § 149(a), Oct. 21, 1998, 112 Stat. 2681–610; Pub. L. 106–5, § 1(1), (2), Mar. 30, 1999, 113 Stat. 9; Pub. L. 106–70, § 1, Oct. 9, 1999, 113 Stat. 1031; Pub. L. 107–8, § 1, May 11, 2001, 115 Stat. 10; Pub. L. 107–17, § 1, June 26, 2001, 115 Stat. 151; Pub. L. 107–170, § 1, May 7, 2002, 116 Stat. 133; Pub. L. 107–171, title X, § 10814(a), May 13, 2002, 116 Stat. 532; Pub. L. 107–377, § 2(a), Dec. 19, 2002, 116 Stat. 3115; Pub. L. 108–73, § 2(a), Aug. 15, 2003, 117 Stat. 891; Pub. L. 108–369, § 2(a), Oct. 25, 2004, 118 Stat. 1749; Pub. L. 109–8, title X, § 1001(a)(1), (c), Apr. 20, 2005, 119 Stat. 185, 186.)

Sections that reference this section: 1230

§1208. Conversion or dismissal

(a) The debtor may convert a case under this chapter to a case under chapter 7 of this title at any time. Any waiver of the right to convert under this subsection is unenforceable.

(b) On request of the debtor at any time, if the case has not been converted under *section 706* or *1112* of this title, the court shall dismiss a case under this chapter. Any waiver of the right to dismiss under this subsection is unenforceable.

(c) On request of a party in interest, and after notice and a hearing, the court may dismiss a case under this chapter for cause, including—

(1) unreasonable delay, or gross mismanagement, by the debtor that is prejudicial to creditors;

(2) nonpayment of any fees and charges required under chapter 123 of title 28;

(3) failure to file a plan timely under *section 1221* of this title;

(4) failure to commence making timely payments required by a confirmed plan;

(5) denial of confirmation of a plan under *section 1225* of this title and denial of a request made for additional time for filing another plan or a modification of a plan;

(6) material default by the debtor with respect to a term of a confirmed plan;

(7) revocation of the order of confirmation under *section 1230* of this title, and denial of confirmation of a modified plan under *section 1229* of this title;

(8) termination of a confirmed plan by reason of the occurrence of a condition specified in the plan;

(9) continuing loss to or diminution of the estate and absence of a reasonable likelihood of rehabilitation; and

(10) failure of the debtor to pay any domestic support obligation that first becomes payable after the date of the filing of the petition.

(d) On request of a party in interest, and after notice and a hearing, the court may dismiss a case under this chapter or convert a case under this chapter to a case under chapter 7 of this title upon a showing that the debtor has committed fraud in connection with the case.

(e) Notwithstanding any other provision of this section, a case may not be converted to a case under another chapter of this title unless the debtor may be a debtor under such chapter.

(Added and amended Pub. L. 99–554, title II, § 255, title III, § 302(f), Oct. 27, 1986, 100 Stat. 3108, 3124; Pub. L. 103–65, § 1, Aug. 6, 1993, 107 Stat. 311; Pub. L. 105–277, div. C, title I, § 149(a), Oct. 21, 1998, 112 Stat. 2681–610; Pub. L. 106–5, § 1(1), (2), Mar. 30, 1999, 113 Stat. 9; Pub. L. 106–70, § 1, Oct. 9, 1999, 113 Stat. 1031; Pub. L. 107–8, § 1, May 11, 2001, 115 Stat. 10; Pub. L. 107–17, § 1, June 26, 2001, 115 Stat. 151; Pub. L. 107–170, § 1, May 7, 2002, 116 Stat. 133; Pub. L. 107–171, title X, § 10814(a), May 13, 2002, 116 Stat. 532; Pub. L. 107–377, § 2(a), Dec. 19, 2002, 116 Stat. 3115; Pub. L. 108–73, § 2(a), Aug. 15, 2003, 117 Stat. 891; Pub. L. 108–369, § 2(a), Oct. 25, 2004, 118 Stat. 1749; Pub. L. 109–8, title II, § 213(2), title X, § 1001(a)(1), (c), Apr. 20, 2005, 119 Stat. 52, 185, 186.)

Sections that reference this section: None

Subchapter II: The Plan

§1221. Filing of plan

The debtor shall file a plan not later than 90 days after the order for relief under this chapter, except that the court may extend such period if the need for an extension is attributable to circumstances for which the debtor should not justly be held accountable.

(Added and amended Pub. L. 99–554, title II, § 255, title III, § 302(f), Oct. 27, 1986, 100 Stat. 3109, 3124; Pub. L. 103–65, §§ 1, 2, Aug. 6, 1993, 107 Stat. 311; Pub. L. 105–277, div. C, title I, § 149(a), Oct. 21, 1998, 112 Stat. 2681–610; Pub. L. 106–5, § 1(1), (2), Mar. 30, 1999, 113 Stat. 9; Pub. L. 106–70, § 1, Oct. 9, 1999, 113 Stat. 1031; Pub. L. 107–8, § 1, May 11, 2001, 115 Stat. 10; Pub. L. 107–17, § 1, June 26, 2001, 115 Stat. 151; Pub. L. 107–170, § 1, May 7, 2002, 116 Stat. 133; Pub. L. 107–171, title X, § 10814(a), May 13, 2002, 116 Stat. 532; Pub. L. 107–377, § 2(a), Dec. 19, 2002, 116 Stat. 3115; Pub. L. 108–73, § 2(a), Aug. 15, 2003, 117 Stat. 891; Pub. L. 108–369, § 2(a), Oct. 25, 2004, 118 Stat. 1749; Pub. L. 109–8, title X, § 1001(a)(1), (c), Apr. 20, 2005, 119 Stat. 185, 186.)

Sections that reference this section: 1208

§1222. Contents of plan

(a) The plan shall—

(1) provide for the submission of all or such portion of future earnings or other future income of the debtor to the supervision and control of the trustee as is necessary for the execution of the plan;

(2) provide for the full payment, in deferred cash payments, of all claims entitled to priority under *section 507*, unless the holder of a particular claim agrees to a different treatment of that claim;

(3) if the plan classifies claims and interests, provide the same treatment for each claim or interest within a particular class unless the holder of a particular claim or interest agrees to less favorable treatment;

(4) notwithstanding any other provision of this section, a plan may provide for less than full payment of all amounts owed for a claim entitled to priority under *section 507(a)(1)(B)* only if the plan provides that all of the debtor's projected disposable income for a 5-year period beginning on the date that the first payment is due under the plan will be applied to make payments under the plan; and

(5) subject to *section 1232*, provide for the treatment of any claim by a governmental unit of a kind described in *section 1232(a)*.

(b) Subject to subsections (a) and (c) of this section, the plan may—

(1) designate a class or classes of unsecured claims, as provided in *section 1122* of this title, but may not discriminate unfairly against any class so designated; however, such plan may treat claims for a consumer debt of the debtor if an individual is liable on such consumer debt with the debtor differently than other unsecured claims;

(2) modify the rights of holders of secured claims, or of holders of unsecured claims, or leave unaffected the rights of holders of any class of claims;

(3) provide for the curing or waiving of any default;

(4) provide for payments on any unsecured claim to be made concurrently with payments on any secured claim or any other unsecured claim;

(5) provide for the curing of any default within a reasonable time and maintenance of payments while the case is pending on any unsecured claim or secured claim on which the last payment is due after the date on which the final payment under the plan is due;

(6) subject to *section 365* of this title, provide for the assumption, rejection, or assignment of any executory contract or unexpired lease of the debtor not previously rejected under such section;

(7) provide for the payment of all or part of a claim against the debtor from property of the estate or property of the debtor;

(8) provide for the sale of all or any part of the property of the estate or the distribution of all or any part of the property of the estate among those having an interest in such property;

(9) provide for payment of allowed secured claims consistent with *section 1225(a)(5)* of this title, over a period exceeding the period permitted under section 1222(c);

(10) provide for the vesting of property of the estate, on confirmation of the plan or at a later time, in the debtor or in any other entity;

(11) provide for the payment of interest accruing after the date of the filing of the petition on unsecured claims that are nondischargeable under *section 1228(a)*, except that such interest may be paid only to the extent that the debtor has disposable income available to pay such interest after making provision for full payment of all allowed claims; and

(12) include any other appropriate provision not inconsistent with this title.

(c) Except as provided in subsections (b)(5) and (b)(9), the plan may not provide for payments over a period that is longer than three years unless the court for cause approves a longer period, but the court may not approve a period that is longer than five years.

(d) Notwithstanding subsection (b)(2) of this section and *sections 506(b)* and *1225*(a)(5) of this title, if it is proposed in a plan to cure a default, the amount necessary to cure the default, shall be determined in accordance with the underlying agreement and applicable nonbankruptcy law.

(Added and amended Pub. L. 99–554, title II, § 255, title III, § 302(f), Oct. 27, 1986, 100 Stat. 3109, 3124; Pub. L. 103–65, § 1, Aug. 6, 1993, 107 Stat. 311; Pub. L. 103–394, title III, § 305(b), Oct. 22, 1994, 108 Stat. 4134; Pub. L. 105–277, div. C, title I, § 149(a), Oct. 21, 1998, 112 Stat. 2681–610; Pub. L. 106–5, § 1(1), (2), Mar. 30, 1999, 113 Stat. 9; Pub. L. 106–70, § 1, Oct. 9, 1999, 113 Stat. 1031; Pub. L. 107–8, § 1, May 11, 2001, 115 Stat. 10; Pub. L. 107–17, § 1, June 26, 2001, 115 Stat. 151; Pub. L. 107–170, § 1, May 7, 2002, 116 Stat. 133; Pub. L. 107–171, title X, § 10814(a), May 13, 2002, 116 Stat. 532; Pub. L. 107–377, § 2(a), Dec. 19, 2002, 116 Stat. 3115; Pub. L. 108–73, § 2(a), Aug. 15, 2003, 117 Stat. 891; Pub. L. 108–369, § 2(a), Oct. 25, 2004, 118 Stat. 1749; Pub. L. 109–8, title II, § 213(3), (4), title X, §§ 1001(a)(1), (c), 1003(a), Apr. 20, 2005, 119 Stat. 52, 185, 186; Pub. L. 115–72, div. B, § 1005(b)(1)(A), Oct. 26, 2017, 131 Stat. 1233.)

Sections that reference this section: 1223, 1225, 1228, 1229

§1223. Modification of plan before confirmation

(a) The debtor may modify the plan at any time before confirmation, but may not modify the plan so that the plan as modified fails to meet the requirements of *section 1222* of this title.

(b) After the debtor files a modification under this section, the plan as modified becomes the plan.

(c) Any holder of a secured claim that has accepted or rejected the plan is deemed to have accepted or rejected, as the case may be, the plan as modified, unless the modification provides for a change in the rights of such holder from what such rights were under the plan before modification, and such holder changes such holder's previous acceptance or rejection.

(Added and amended Pub. L. 99–554, title II, § 255, title III, § 302(f), Oct. 27, 1986, 100 Stat. 3110, 3124; Pub. L. 103–65, § 1, Aug. 6, 1993, 107 Stat. 311; Pub. L. 105–277, div. C, title I, § 149(a), Oct. 21, 1998, 112 Stat. 2681–610; Pub. L. 106–5, § 1(1), (2), Mar. 30, 1999, 113 Stat. 9; Pub. L. 106–70, § 1, Oct. 9, 1999, 113 Stat. 1031; Pub. L. 107–8, § 1, May 11, 2001, 115 Stat. 10; Pub. L. 107–17, § 1, June 26, 2001, 115 Stat. 151; Pub. L. 107–170, § 1, May 7, 2002, 116 Stat. 133; Pub. L. 107–171, title X, § 10814(a), May 13, 2002, 116 Stat. 532; Pub. L. 107–377, § 2(a), Dec. 19, 2002, 116 Stat. 3115; Pub. L. 108–73, § 2(a), Aug. 15, 2003, 117 Stat. 891; Pub. L. 108–369, § 2(a), Oct. 25, 2004, 118 Stat. 1749; Pub. L. 109–8, title X, § 1001(a)(1), (c), Apr. 20, 2005, 119 Stat. 185, 186.)

Sections that reference this section: None

§1224. Confirmation hearing

After expedited notice, the court shall hold a hearing on confirmation of the plan. A party in interest, the trustee, or the United States trustee may object to the confirmation of the plan. Except for cause, the hearing shall be concluded not later than 45 days after the filing of the plan.

(Added and amended Pub. L. 99–554, title II, § 255, title III, § 302(f), Oct. 27, 1986, 100 Stat. 3110, 3124; Pub. L. 103–65, § 1, Aug. 6, 1993, 107 Stat. 311; Pub. L. 105–277, div. C, title I, § 149(a), Oct. 21, 1998, 112 Stat. 2681–610; Pub. L. 106–5, § 1(1), (2), Mar. 30, 1999, 113 Stat. 9; Pub. L. 106–70, § 1, Oct. 9, 1999, 113 Stat. 1031; Pub. L. 107–8, § 1, May 11, 2001, 115 Stat. 10; Pub. L. 107–17, § 1, June 26, 2001, 115 Stat. 151; Pub. L. 107–170, § 1, May 7, 2002, 116 Stat. 133; Pub. L. 107–171, title X, § 10814(a), May 13, 2002, 116 Stat. 532; Pub. L. 107–377, § 2(a), Dec. 19, 2002, 116 Stat. 3115; Pub. L. 108–73, § 2(a), Aug. 15, 2003, 117 Stat. 891; Pub. L. 108–369, § 2(a), Oct. 25, 2004, 118 Stat. 1749; Pub. L. 109–8, title X, § 1001(a)(1), (c), Apr. 20, 2005, 119 Stat. 185, 186.)

Sections that reference this section: None

§1225. Confirmation of plan

(a) Except as provided in subsection (b), the court shall confirm a plan if—

(1) the plan complies with the provisions of this chapter and with the other applicable provisions of this title;

(2) any fee, charge, or amount required under chapter 123 of title 28, or by the plan, to be paid before confirmation, has been paid;

(3) the plan has been proposed in good faith and not by any means forbidden by law;

(4) the value, as of the effective date of the plan, of property to be distributed under the plan on account of each allowed unsecured claim is not less than the amount that would be paid on such claim if the estate of the debtor were liquidated under chapter 7 of this title on such date;

(5) with respect to each allowed secured claim provided for by the plan—

(A) the holder of such claim has accepted the plan;

(B)

(i) the plan provides that the holder of such claim retain the lien securing such claim; and

(ii) the value, as of the effective date of the plan, of property to be distributed by the trustee or the debtor under the plan on account of such claim is not less than the allowed amount of such claim; or

(C) the debtor surrenders the property securing such claim to such holder;

(6) the debtor will be able to make all payments under the plan and to comply with the plan; and

(7) the debtor has paid all amounts that are required to be paid under a domestic support obligation and that first become payable after the date of the filing of the petition if the debtor is required by a judicial or administrative order, or by statute, to pay such domestic support obligation.

(b)

(1) If the trustee or the holder of an allowed unsecured claim objects to the confirmation of the plan, then the court may not approve the plan unless, as of the effective date of the plan—

(A) the value of the property to be distributed under the plan on account of such claim is not less than the amount of such claim;

(B) the plan provides that all of the debtor's projected disposable income to be received in the three-year period, or such longer period as the court may approve under *section 1222(c)*, beginning on the date that the first payment is due under the plan will be applied to make payments under the plan; or

(C) the value of the property to be distributed under the plan in the 3-year period, or such longer period as the court may approve under *section 1222(c)*, beginning on the date that the first distribution is due under the plan is not less than the debtor's projected disposable income for such period.

(2) For purposes of this subsection, "disposable income" means income which is received by the debtor and which is not reasonably necessary to be expended—

(A) for the maintenance or support of the debtor or a dependent of the debtor or for a domestic support obligation that first becomes payable after the date of the filing of the petition; or

(B) for the payment of expenditures necessary for the continuation, preservation, and operation of the debtor's business.

(c) After confirmation of a plan, the court may order any entity from whom the debtor receives income to pay all or any part of such income to the trustee.

(Added and amended Pub. L. 99–554, title II, § 255, title III, § 302(f), Oct. 27, 1986, 100 Stat. 3110, 3124; Pub. L. 103–65, § 1, Aug. 6, 1993, 107 Stat. 311; Pub. L. 105–277, div. C, title I, § 149(a), Oct. 21, 1998, 112 Stat. 2681–610; Pub. L. 106–5, § 1(1), (2), Mar. 30, 1999, 113 Stat. 9; Pub. L. 106–70, § 1, Oct. 9, 1999, 113 Stat. 1031; Pub. L. 107–8, § 1, May 11, 2001, 115 Stat. 10; Pub. L. 107–17, § 1, June 26, 2001, 115 Stat. 151; Pub. L. 107–170, § 1, May 7, 2002, 116 Stat. 133; Pub. L. 107–171, title X, § 10814(a), May 13, 2002, 116 Stat. 532; Pub. L. 107–377, § 2(a), Dec. 19, 2002, 116 Stat. 3115; Pub. L. 108–73, § 2(a), Aug. 15, 2003, 117 Stat. 891; Pub. L. 108–369, § 2(a), Oct. 25, 2004, 118 Stat. 1749; Pub. L. 109–8, title II, §§ 213(5), 218, title X, §§ 1001(a)(1), (c), 1006(a), Apr. 20, 2005, 119 Stat. 52, 55, 185–187; Pub. L. 116–260, div. N, title III, § 320(d), (f)(2)(A)(iv), Dec. 27, 2020, 134 Stat. 2016, 2017.)

Sections that reference this section: 1208, 1222, 1229, 1230, 1231, 1232

§1226. Payments

(a) Payments and funds received by the trustee shall be retained by the trustee until confirmation or denial of confirmation of a plan. If a plan is confirmed, the trustee shall distribute any such payment in accordance with the plan. If a plan is not confirmed, the trustee shall return any such payments to the debtor, after deducting—

(1) any unpaid claim allowed under *section 503(b)* of this title; and

(2) if a standing trustee is serving in the case, the percentage fee fixed for such standing trustee.

(b) Before or at the time of each payment to creditors under the plan, there shall be paid—

(1) any unpaid claim of the kind specified in *section 507(a)(2)* of this title; and

(2) if a standing trustee appointed under *section 1202(c)* of this title is serving in the case, the percentage fee fixed for such standing trustee under *section 1202(d)* of this title.

(c) Except as otherwise provided in the plan or in the order confirming the plan, the trustee shall make payments to creditors under the plan.

(Added and amended Pub. L. 99–554, title II, § 255, title III, § 302(f), Oct. 27, 1986, 100 Stat. 3111, 3124; Pub. L. 103–65, § 1, Aug. 6, 1993, 107 Stat. 311; Pub. L. 103–394, title V, § 501(d)(36), Oct. 22, 1994, 108 Stat. 4147; Pub. L. 105–277, div. C, title I, § 149(a), Oct. 21, 1998, 112 Stat. 2681–610; Pub. L. 106–5, § 1(1), (2), Mar. 30, 1999, 113 Stat. 9; Pub. L. 106–70, § 1, Oct. 9, 1999, 113 Stat. 1031; Pub. L. 107–8, § 1, May 11, 2001, 115 Stat. 10; Pub. L. 107–17, § 1, June 26, 2001, 115 Stat. 151; Pub. L. 107–170, § 1, May 7, 2002, 116 Stat. 133; Pub. L. 107–171, title X, § 10814(a), May 13, 2002, 116 Stat. 532; Pub. L. 107–377, § 2(a), Dec. 19, 2002, 116 Stat. 3115; Pub. L. 108–73, § 2(a), Aug. 15, 2003, 117 Stat. 891; Pub. L. 108–369, § 2(a), Oct. 25, 2004, 118 Stat. 1749; Pub. L. 109–8, title X, § 1001(a)(1), (c), title XV, § 1502(a)(9), Apr. 20, 2005, 119 Stat. 185, 186, 217.)

Sections that reference this section: None

§1227. Effect of confirmation

(a) Except as provided in *section 1228(a)* of this title, the provisions of a confirmed plan bind the debtor, each creditor, each equity security holder, and each general partner in the debtor, whether or not the claim of such creditor, such equity security holder, or such general partner in the debtor is provided for by the plan, and whether or not such creditor, such equity security holder, or such general partner in the debtor has objected to, has accepted, or has rejected the plan.

(b) Except as otherwise provided in the plan or the order confirming the plan, the confirmation of a plan vests all of the property of the estate in the debtor.

(c) Except as provided in *section 1228(a)* of this title and except as otherwise provided in the plan or in the order confirming the plan, the property vesting in the debtor under subsection (b) of this section is free and clear of any claim or interest of any creditor provided for by the plan.

(Added and amended Pub. L. 99–554, title II, § 255, title III, § 302(f), Oct. 27, 1986, 100 Stat. 3112, 3124; Pub. L. 103–65, § 1, Aug. 6, 1993, 107 Stat. 311; Pub. L. 105–277, div. C, title I, § 149(a), Oct. 21, 1998, 112 Stat. 2681–610; Pub. L. 106–5, § 1(1), (2), Mar. 30, 1999, 113 Stat. 9; Pub. L. 106–70, § 1, Oct. 9, 1999, 113 Stat. 1031; Pub. L. 107–8, § 1, May 11, 2001, 115 Stat. 10; Pub. L. 107–17, § 1, June 26, 2001, 115 Stat. 151; Pub. L. 107–170, § 1, May 7, 2002, 116 Stat. 133; Pub. L. 107–171, title X, § 10814(a), May 13, 2002, 116 Stat. 532; Pub. L. 107–377, § 2(a), Dec. 19, 2002, 116 Stat. 3115; Pub. L. 108–73, § 2(a), Aug. 15, 2003, 117 Stat. 891; Pub. L. 108–369, § 2(a), Oct. 25, 2004, 118 Stat. 1749; Pub. L. 109–8, title X, § 1001(a)(1), (c), Apr. 20, 2005, 119 Stat. 185, 186.)

Sections that reference this section: None

§1228. Discharge

(a) Subject to subsection (d), as soon as practicable after completion by the debtor of all payments under the plan, and in the case of a debtor who is required by a judicial or administrative order, or by statute, to pay a domestic support obligation, after such debtor certifies that all amounts payable under such order or such statute that are due on or before the date of the certification (including amounts due before the petition was filed, but only to the extent provided for by the plan) have been paid, other than payments to holders of allowed claims provided for under *section 1222(b)(5)* or *1222*(b)(9) of this title, unless the court approves a written waiver of discharge executed by the debtor after the order for relief under this chapter, the court shall grant the debtor a discharge of all debts provided for by the plan, allowed under *section 503* of this title, or disallowed under *section 502* of this title, except any debt—

(1) provided for under *section 1222(b)(5)* or *1222*(b)(9) of this title; or

(2) of a kind specified in *section 523(a)* of this title, except as provided in *section 1232(c)*.

(b) Subject to subsection (d), at any time after the confirmation of the plan and after notice and a hearing, the court may grant a discharge to a debtor that has not completed payments under the plan only if—

(1) the debtor's failure to complete such payments is due to circumstances for which the debtor should not justly be held accountable;

(2) the value, as of the effective date of the plan, of property actually distributed under the plan on account of each allowed unsecured claim is not less than the amount that would have been paid on such claim if the estate of the debtor had been liquidated under chapter 7 of this title on such date; and

(3) modification of the plan under *section 1229* of this title is not practicable.

(c) A discharge granted under subsection (b) of this section discharges the debtor from all unsecured debts provided for by the plan or disallowed under *section 502* of this title, except any debt—

(1) provided for under *section 1222(b)(5)* or *1222*(b)(9) of this title; or

(2) of a kind specified in *section 523(a)* of this title, except as provided in *section 1232(c)*.

(d) On request of a party in interest before one year after a discharge under this section is granted, and after notice and a hearing, the court may revoke such discharge only if—

(1) such discharge was obtained by the debtor through fraud; and

(2) the requesting party did not know of such fraud until after such discharge was granted.

(e) After the debtor is granted a discharge, the court shall terminate the services of any trustee serving in the case.

(f) The court may not grant a discharge under this chapter unless the court after notice and a hearing held not more than 10 days before the date of the entry of the order granting the discharge finds that there is no reasonable cause to believe that—

(1) *section 522(q)(1)* may be applicable to the debtor; and

(2) there is pending any proceeding in which the debtor may be found guilty of a felony of the kind described in *section 522(q)(1)(A)* or liable for a debt of the kind described in *section 522(q)(1)(B)*.

(Added and amended Pub. L. 99–554, title II, § 255, title III, § 302(f), Oct. 27, 1986, 100 Stat. 3112, 3124; Pub. L. 103–65, § 1, Aug. 6, 1993, 107 Stat. 311; Pub. L. 105–277, div. C, title I, § 149(a), Oct. 21, 1998, 112 Stat. 2681–610; Pub. L. 106–5, § 1(1), (2), Mar. 30, 1999, 113 Stat. 9; Pub. L. 106–70, § 1, Oct. 9, 1999, 113 Stat. 1031; Pub. L. 106–518, title II, § 208, Nov. 13, 2000, 114 Stat. 2415; Pub. L. 107–8, § 1, May 11, 2001, 115 Stat. 10; Pub. L. 107–17, § 1, June 26, 2001, 115 Stat. 151; Pub. L. 107–170, § 1, May 7, 2002, 116 Stat. 133; Pub. L. 107–171, title X, § 10814(a), May 13, 2002, 116 Stat. 532; Pub. L. 107–377, § 2(a), Dec. 19, 2002, 116 Stat. 3115; Pub. L. 108–73, § 2(a), Aug. 15, 2003, 117 Stat. 891; Pub. L. 108–369, § 2(a), Oct. 25, 2004, 118 Stat. 1749; Pub. L. 109–8, title II, § 213(6), title III, § 330(c), title X, § 1001(a)(1), (c), Apr. 20, 2005, 119 Stat. 53, 101, 185, 186; Pub. L. 115–72, div. B, § 1005(b)(1)(B), Oct. 26, 2017, 131 Stat. 1233.)

Sections that reference this section: 1202, 1222, 1227, 1232, 727

§1229. Modification of plan after confirmation

(a) At any time after confirmation of the plan but before the completion of payments under such plan, the plan may be modified, on request of the debtor, the trustee, or the holder of an allowed unsecured claim, to—

(1) increase or reduce the amount of payments on claims of a particular class provided for by the plan;

(2) extend or reduce the time for such payments;

(3) alter the amount of the distribution to a creditor whose claim is provided for by the plan to the extent necessary to take account of any payment of such claim other than under the plan; or

(4) provide for the payment of a claim described in *section 1232(a)* that arose after the date on which the petition was filed.

(b)

(1) *Sections 1222(a), 1222*(b), and 1223(c) of this title and the requirements of *section 1225(a)* of this title apply to any modification under subsection (a) of this section.

(2) The plan as modified becomes the plan unless, after notice and a hearing, such modification is disapproved.

(c) A plan modified under this section may not provide for payments over a period that expires after three years after the time that the first payment under the original confirmed plan was due, unless the court, for cause, approves a longer period, but the court may not approve a period that expires after five years after such time.

(d) A plan may not be modified under this section—

(1) to increase the amount of any payment due before the plan as modified becomes the plan;

(2) by anyone except the debtor, based on an increase in the debtor's disposable income, to increase the amount of payments to unsecured creditors required for a particular month so that the aggregate of such payments exceeds the debtor's disposable income for such month; or

(3) in the last year of the plan by anyone except the debtor, to require payments that would leave the debtor with insufficient funds to carry on the farming operation after the plan is completed.

(Added and amended Pub. L. 99–554, title II, § 255, title III, § 302(f), Oct. 27, 1986, 100 Stat. 3113, 3124; Pub. L. 103–65, § 1, Aug. 6, 1993, 107 Stat. 311; Pub. L. 105–277, div. C, title I, § 149(a), Oct. 21, 1998, 112 Stat. 2681–610; Pub. L. 106–5, § 1(1), (2), Mar. 30, 1999, 113 Stat. 9; Pub. L. 106–70, § 1, Oct. 9, 1999, 113 Stat. 1031; Pub. L. 107–8, § 1, May 11, 2001, 115 Stat. 10; Pub. L. 107–17, § 1, June 26, 2001, 115 Stat. 151; Pub. L. 107–170, § 1, May 7, 2002, 116 Stat. 133; Pub. L. 107–171, title X, § 10814(a), May 13, 2002, 116 Stat. 532; Pub. L. 107–377, § 2(a), Dec. 19, 2002, 116 Stat. 3115; Pub. L. 108–73, § 2(a), Aug. 15, 2003, 117 Stat. 891; Pub. L. 108–369, § 2(a), Oct. 25, 2004, 118 Stat. 1749; Pub. L. 109–8, title X, §§ 1001(a)(1), (c), 1006(b), Apr. 20, 2005, 119 Stat. 185–187; Pub. L. 115–72, div. B, § 1005(b)(1)(C), Oct. 26, 2017, 131 Stat. 1234.)

Sections that reference this section: 1208, 1228, 1230

§1230. Revocation of an order of confirmation

(a) On request of a party in interest at any time within 180 days after the date of the entry of an order of confirmation under *section 1225* of this title, and after notice and a hearing, the court may revoke such order if such order was procured by fraud.

(b) If the court revokes an order of confirmation under subsection (a) of this section, the court shall dispose of the case under *section 1207* of this title, unless, within the time fixed by the court, the debtor proposes and the court confirms a modification of the plan under *section 1229* of this title.

(Added and amended Pub. L. 99–554, title II, § 255, title III, § 302(f), Oct. 27, 1986, 100 Stat. 3113, 3124; Pub. L. 103–65, § 1, Aug. 6, 1993, 107 Stat. 311; Pub. L. 105–277, div. C, title I, § 149(a), Oct. 21, 1998, 112 Stat. 2681–610; Pub. L. 106–5, § 1(1), (2), Mar. 30, 1999, 113 Stat. 9; Pub. L. 106–70, § 1, Oct. 9, 1999, 113 Stat. 1031; Pub. L. 107–8, § 1, May 11, 2001, 115 Stat. 10; Pub. L. 107–17, § 1, June 26, 2001, 115 Stat. 151; Pub. L. 107–170, § 1, May 7, 2002, 116 Stat. 133; Pub. L. 107–171, title X, § 10814(a), May 13, 2002, 116 Stat. 532; Pub. L. 107–377, § 2(a), Dec. 19, 2002, 116 Stat. 3115; Pub. L. 108–73, § 2(a), Aug. 15, 2003, 117 Stat. 891; Pub. L. 108–369, § 2(a), Oct. 25, 2004, 118 Stat. 1749; Pub. L. 109–8, title X, § 1001(a)(1), (c), Apr. 20, 2005, 119 Stat. 185, 186.)

Sections that reference this section: 1208

§1231. Special tax provisions

(a) The issuance, transfer, or exchange of a security, or the making or delivery of an instrument of transfer under a plan confirmed under *section 1225* of this title, may not be taxed under any law imposing a stamp tax or similar tax.

(b) The court may authorize the proponent of a plan to request a determination, limited to questions of law, by any governmental unit charged with responsibility for collection or determination of a tax on or measured by income, of the tax effects, under *section 346* of this title and under the law imposing such tax, of the plan. In the event of an actual controversy, the court may declare such effects after the earlier of—

(1) the date on which such governmental unit responds to the request under this subsection; or

(2) 270 days after such request.

(Added and amended Pub. L. 99–554, title II, § 255, title III, § 302(f), Oct. 27, 1986, 100 Stat. 3113, 3124; Pub. L. 103–65, § 1, Aug. 6, 1993, 107 Stat. 311; Pub. L. 105–277, div. C, title I, § 149(a), Oct. 21, 1998, 112 Stat. 2681–610; Pub. L. 106–5, § 1(1), (2), Mar. 30, 1999, 113 Stat. 9; Pub. L. 106–70, § 1, Oct. 9, 1999, 113 Stat. 1031; Pub. L. 107–8, § 1, May 11, 2001, 115 Stat. 10; Pub. L. 107–17, § 1, June 26, 2001, 115 Stat. 151; Pub. L. 107–170, § 1, May 7, 2002, 116 Stat. 133; Pub. L. 107–171, title X, § 10814(a), May 13, 2002, 116 Stat. 532; Pub. L. 107–377, § 2(a), Dec. 19, 2002, 116 Stat. 3115; Pub. L. 108–73, § 2(a), Aug. 15, 2003, 117 Stat. 891; Pub. L. 108–369, § 2(a), Oct. 25, 2004, 118 Stat. 1749; Pub. L. 109–8, title VII, § 719(b)(4), title X, §§ 1001(a)(1), (c), 1003(b), Apr. 20, 2005, 119 Stat. 133, 185, 186.)

Sections that reference this section: None

§1232. Claim by a governmental unit based on the disposition of property used in a farming operation

(a) Any unsecured claim of a governmental unit against the debtor or the estate that arises before the filing of the petition, or that arises after the filing of the petition and before the debtor's discharge under *section 1228*, as a result of the sale, transfer, exchange, or other disposition of any property used in the debtor's farming operation —

(1) shall be treated as an unsecured claim arising before the date on which the petition is filed;

(2) shall not be entitled to priority under *section 507*;

(3) shall be provided for under a plan; and

(4) shall be discharged in accordance with *section 1228*.

(b) For purposes of applying *sections 1225(a)(4), 1228*(b)(2), and 1229(b)(1) to a claim described in subsection (a) of this section, the amount that would be paid on such claim if the estate of the debtor were liquidated in a case under chapter 7 of this title shall be the amount that would be paid by the estate in a chapter 7 case if the claim were an unsecured claim arising before the date on which the petition was filed and were not entitled to priority under *section 507*.

(c) For purposes of applying *sections 523(a), 1228*(a)(2), and 1228(c)(2) to a claim described in subsection (a) of this section, the claim shall not be treated as a claim of a kind specified in subparagraph (A) or (B) of *section 523(a)(1)*.

(d)

(1) A governmental unit may file a proof of claim for a claim described in subsection (a) that arises after the date on which the petition is filed.

(2) If a debtor files a tax return after the filing of the petition for a period in which a claim described in subsection (a) arises, and the claim relates to the tax return, the debtor shall serve notice of the claim on the governmental unit charged with the responsibility for the collection of the tax at the address and in the manner designated in *section 505(b)(1)*. Notice under this paragraph shall state that the debtor has filed a petition under this chapter, state the name and location of the court in which the case under this chapter is pending, state the amount of the claim, and include a copy of the filed tax return and documentation supporting the calculation of the claim.

(3) If notice of a claim has been served on the governmental unit in accordance with paragraph (2), the governmental unit may file a proof of claim not later than 180 days after the date on which such notice was served. If the governmental unit has not filed a timely proof of the claim, the debtor or trustee may file proof of the claim that is consistent with the notice served under paragraph (2). If a proof of claim is filed by the debtor or trustee under this paragraph, the governmental unit may not amend the proof of claim.

(4) A claim filed under this subsection shall be determined and shall be allowed under subsection (a), (b), or (c) of *section 502*, or disallowed under subsection (d) or (e) of *section 502*, in the same manner as if the claim had arisen immediately before the date of the filing of the petition.

(Added Pub. L. 115–72, div. B, § 1005(a), Oct. 26, 2017, 131 Stat. 1232.)

Sections that reference this section: 1222, 1228, 1229

CHAPTER 13: ADJUSTMENT OF DEBTS OF AN INDIVIDUAL WITH REGULAR INCOME

Subchapter I: Officers, Administration, and the Estate

§1301. Stay of action against codebtor

(a) Except as provided in subsections (b) and (c) of this section, after the order for relief under this chapter, a creditor may not act, or commence or continue any civil action, to collect all or any part of a consumer debt of the debtor from any individual that is liable on such debt with the debtor, or that secured such debt, unless—

(1) such individual became liable on or secured such debt in the ordinary course of such individual's business; or

(2) the case is closed, dismissed, or converted to a case under chapter 7 or 11 of this title.

(b) A creditor may present a negotiable instrument, and may give notice of dishonor of such an instrument.

(c) On request of a party in interest and after notice and a hearing, the court shall grant relief from the stay provided by subsection (a) of this section with respect to a creditor, to the extent that —

(1) as between the debtor and the individual protected under subsection (a) of this section, such individual received the consideration for the claim held by such creditor;

(2) the plan filed by the debtor proposes not to pay such claim; or

(3) such creditor's interest would be irreparably harmed by continuation of such stay.

(d) Twenty days after the filing of a request under subsection (c)(2) of this section for relief from the stay provided by subsection (a) of this section, such stay is terminated with respect to the party in interest making such request, unless the debtor or any individual that is liable on such debt with the debtor files and serves upon such party in interest a written objection to the taking of the proposed action.

(Pub. L. 95–598, Nov. 6, 1978, 92 Stat. 2645; Pub. L. 98–353, title III, §§ 313, 524, July 10, 1984, 98 Stat. 355, 388.)

Sections that reference this section: 365

§1302. Trustee

(a) If the United States trustee appoints an individual under section 586(b) of title 28 to serve as standing trustee in cases under this chapter and if such individual qualifies under *section 322* of this title, then such individual shall serve as trustee in the case. Otherwise, the United States trustee shall appoint one disinterested person to serve as trustee in the case or the United States trustee may serve as a trustee in the case.

(b) The trustee shall—

(1) perform the duties specified in *sections 704(a)(2), 704*(a)(3), 704(a)(4), 704(a)(5), 704(a)(6), 704(a)(7), and 704(a)(9) of this title;

(2) appear and be heard at any hearing that concerns—

(A) the value of property subject to a lien;

(B) confirmation of a plan; or

(C) modification of the plan after confirmation;

(3) dispose of, under regulations issued by the Director of the Administrative Office of the United States Courts, moneys received or to be received in a case under chapter XIII of the Bankruptcy Act;

(4) advise, other than on legal matters, and assist the debtor in performance under the plan;

(5) ensure that the debtor commences making timely payments under *section 1326* of this title; and

(6) if with respect to the debtor there is a claim for a domestic support obligation, provide the applicable notice specified in subsection (d).

(c) If the debtor is engaged in business, then in addition to the duties specified in subsection (b) of this section, the trustee shall perform the duties specified in *sections 1106(a)(3)* and *1106*(a)(4) of this title.

(d)

(1) In a case described in subsection (b)(6) to which subsection (b)(6) applies, the trustee shall—

(A)

(i) provide written notice to the holder of the claim described in subsection (b)(6) of such claim and of the right of such holder to use the services of the State child support enforcement agency established under sections 464 and 466 of the Social Security Act for the State in which such holder resides, for assistance in collecting child support during and after the case under this title; and

(ii) include in the notice provided under clause (i) the address and telephone number of such State child support enforcement agency;

(B)

(i) provide written notice to such State child support enforcement agency of such claim; and

(ii) include in the notice provided under clause (i) the name, address, and telephone number of such holder; and

(C) at such time as the debtor is granted a discharge under *section 1328*, provide written notice to such holder and to such State child support enforcement agency of—

(i) the granting of the discharge;

(ii) the last recent known address of the debtor;

(iii) the last recent known name and address of the debtor's employer; and

(iv) the name of each creditor that holds a claim that—

(I) is not discharged under paragraph (2) or (4) of *section 523(a)*; or

(II) was reaffirmed by the debtor under *section 524(c)*.

(2)

(A) The holder of a claim described in subsection (b)(6) or the State child support enforcement agency of the State in which such holder resides may request from a creditor described in paragraph (1)(C)(iv) the last known address of the debtor.

(B) Notwithstanding any other provision of law, a creditor that makes a disclosure of a last known address of a debtor in connection with a request made under subparagraph (A) shall not be liable by reason of making that disclosure.

(Pub. L. 95–598, Nov. 6, 1978, 92 Stat. 2645; Pub. L. 98–353, title III, §§ 314, 525, July 10, 1984, 98 Stat. 356, 388; Pub. L. 99–554, title II, §§ 228, 283(w), Oct. 27, 1986, 100 Stat. 3103, 3118; Pub. L. 103–394, title V, § 501(d)(37), Oct. 22, 1994, 108 Stat. 4147; Pub. L. 109–8, title II, § 219(d), Apr. 20, 2005, 119 Stat. 58; Pub. L. 111–327, § 2(a)(39), Dec. 22, 2010, 124 Stat. 3561.)

Sections that reference this section: None

§1303. Rights and powers of debtor

Subject to any limitations on a trustee under this chapter, the debtor shall have, exclusive of the trustee, the rights and powers of a trustee under *sections 363(b), 363*(d), 363(e), 363(f), and 363(*l*), of this title.

(Pub. L. 95–598, Nov. 6, 1978, 92 Stat. 2646.)

Sections that reference this section: None

§1304. Debtor engaged in business

(a) A debtor that is self-employed and incurs trade credit in the production of income from such employment is engaged in business.

(b) Unless the court orders otherwise, a debtor engaged in business may operate the business of the debtor and, subject to any limitations on a trustee under *sections 363(c)* and *364* of this title and to such limitations or conditions as the court prescribes, shall have, exclusive of the trustee, the rights and powers of the trustee under such sections.

(c) A debtor engaged in business shall perform the duties of the trustee specified in *section 704(a)(8)* of this title.

(Pub. L. 95–598, Nov. 6, 1978, 92 Stat. 2646; Pub. L. 98–353, title III, §§ 311(b)(2), 526, July 10, 1984, 98 Stat. 355, 389; Pub. L. 111–327, § 2(a)(40), Dec. 22, 2010, 124 Stat. 3562.)

Sections that reference this section: None

§1305. Filing and allowance of postpetition claims

(a) A proof of claim may be filed by any entity that holds a claim against the debtor—

(1) for taxes that become payable to a governmental unit while the case is pending; or

(2) that is a consumer debt, that arises after the date of the order for relief under this chapter, and that is for property or services necessary for the debtor's performance under the plan.

(b) Except as provided in subsection (c) of this section, a claim filed under subsection (a) of this section shall be allowed or disallowed under *section 502* of this title, but shall be determined as of the date such claim arises, and shall be allowed under *section 502(a)*, *502*(b), or 502(c) of this title, or disallowed under *section 502(d)* or *502*(e) of this title, the same as if such claim had arisen before the date of the filing of the petition.

(c) A claim filed under subsection (a)(2) of this section shall be disallowed if the holder of such claim knew or should have known that prior approval by the trustee of the debtor's incurring the obligation was practicable and was not obtained.

(Pub. L. 95–598, Nov. 6, 1978, 92 Stat. 2647.)

Sections that reference this section: 1322, 1328

§1306. Property of the estate

(a) Property of the estate includes, in addition to the property specified in *section 541* of this title—

(1) all property of the kind specified in such section that the debtor acquires after the commencement of the case but before the case is closed, dismissed, or converted to a case under chapter 7, 11, or 12 of this title, whichever occurs first; and

(2) earnings from services performed by the debtor after the commencement of the case but before the case is closed, dismissed, or converted to a case under chapter 7, 11, or 12 of this title, whichever occurs first.

(b) Except as provided in a confirmed plan or order confirming a plan, the debtor shall remain in possession of all property of the estate.

(Pub. L. 95–598, Nov. 6, 1978, 92 Stat. 2647; Pub. L. 99–554, title II, § 257(u), Oct. 27, 1986, 100 Stat. 3116.)

Sections that reference this section: None

§1307. Conversion or dismissal

(a) The debtor may convert a case under this chapter to a case under chapter 7 of this title at any time. Any waiver of the right to convert under this subsection is unenforceable.

(b) On request of the debtor at any time, if the case has not been converted under *section 706, 1112*, or *1208* of this title, the court shall dismiss a case under this chapter. Any waiver of the right to dismiss under this subsection is unenforceable.

(c) Except as provided in subsection (f) of this section, on request of a party in interest or the United States trustee and after notice and a hearing, the court may convert a case under this chapter to a case under chapter 7 of this title, or may dismiss a case under this chapter, whichever is in the best interests of creditors and the estate, for cause, including—

(1) unreasonable delay by the debtor that is prejudicial to creditors;

(2) nonpayment of any fees and charges required under chapter 123 of title 28;

(3) failure to file a plan timely under *section 1321* of this title;

(4) failure to commence making timely payments under *section 1326* of this title;

(5) denial of confirmation of a plan under *section 1325* of this title and denial of a request made for additional time for filing another plan or a modification of a plan;

(6) material default by the debtor with respect to a term of a confirmed plan;

(7) revocation of the order of confirmation under *section 1330* of this title, and denial of confirmation of a modified plan under *section 1329* of this title;

(8) termination of a confirmed plan by reason of the occurrence of a condition specified in the plan other than completion of payments under the plan;

(9) only on request of the United States trustee, failure of the debtor to file, within fifteen days, or such additional time as the court may allow, after the filing of the petition commencing such case, the information required by paragraph (1) of *section 521(a)*;

(10) only on request of the United States trustee, failure to timely file the informa-

tion required by paragraph (2) of *section 521(a)*; or

(11) failure of the debtor to pay any domestic support obligation that first becomes payable after the date of the filing of the petition.

(d) Except as provided in subsection (f) of this section, at any time before the confirmation of a plan under *section 1325* of this title, on request of a party in interest or the United States trustee and after notice and a hearing, the court may convert a case under this chapter to a case under chapter 11 or 12 of this title.

(e) Upon the failure of the debtor to file a tax return under *section 1308*, on request of a party in interest or the United States trustee and after notice and a hearing, the court shall dismiss a case or convert a case under this chapter to a case under chapter 7 of this title, whichever is in the best interest of the creditors and the estate.

(f) The court may not convert a case under this chapter to a case under chapter 7, 11, or 12 of this title if the debtor is a farmer, unless the debtor requests such conversion.

(g) Notwithstanding any other provision of this section, a case may not be converted to a case under another chapter of this title unless the debtor may be a debtor under such chapter.

(Pub. L. 95–598, Nov. 6, 1978, 92 Stat. 2647; Pub. L. 98–353, title III, §§ 315, 527, July 10, 1984, 98 Stat. 356, 389; Pub. L. 99–554, title II, §§ 229, 257(v), Oct. 27, 1986, 100 Stat. 3103, 3116; Pub. L. 109–8, title II, § 213(7), title VII, § 716(c), Apr. 20, 2005, 119 Stat. 53, 130; Pub. L. 111–327, § 2(a)(41), Dec. 22, 2010, 124 Stat. 3562.)

Sections that reference this section: 1330

§1308. Filing of prepetition tax returns

(a) Not later than the day before the date on which the meeting of the creditors is first scheduled to be held under *section 341(a)*, if the debtor was required to file a tax return under applicable nonbankruptcy law, the debtor shall file with appropriate tax authorities all tax returns for all taxable periods ending during the 4-year period ending on the date of the filing of the petition.

(b)

(1) Subject to paragraph (2), if the tax returns required by subsection (a) have not been filed by the date on which the meeting of creditors is first scheduled to be held under *section 341(a)*, the trustee may hold open that meeting for a reasonable period of time to allow the debtor an additional period of time to file any unfiled returns, but such additional period of time shall not extend beyond—

(A) for any return that is past due as of the date of the filing of the petition, the date that is 120 days after the date of that meeting; or

(B) for any return that is not past due as of the date of the filing of the petition, the later of—

(i) the date that is 120 days after the date of that meeting; or

(ii) the date on which the return is due under the last automatic extension of time for filing that return to which the debtor is entitled, and for which request is timely made, in accordance with applicable nonbankruptcy law.

(2) After notice and a hearing, and order entered before the tolling of any applicable filing period determined under paragraph (1), if the debtor demonstrates by a preponderance of the evidence that the failure to file a return as required under paragraph (1) is attributable to circumstances beyond the control of the debtor, the court may extend the filing period established by the trustee under paragraph (1) for—

(A) a period of not more than 30 days for returns described in paragraph (1)(A); and

(B) a period not to extend after the applicable extended due date for a return described in paragraph (1)(B).

(c) For purposes of this section, the term "return" includes a return prepared pursuant to subsection (a) or (b) of section 6020 of the Internal Revenue Code of 1986, or a similar State or local law, or a written stipulation to a judgment or a final order entered by a nonbankruptcy tribunal.

(Added Pub. L. 109–8, title VII, § 716(b)(1), Apr. 20, 2005, 119 Stat. 129; amended Pub. L. 111–327, § 2(a)(42), Dec. 22, 2010, 124 Stat. 3562.)

Sections that reference this section: 1307, 1325, 502

Subchapter II: The Plan

§1321. Filing of plan

The debtor shall file a plan.

(Pub. L. 95–598, Nov. 6, 1978, 92 Stat. 2648.)

Sections that reference this section: 1307

§1322. Contents of plan

(a) The plan—

(1) shall provide for the submission of all or such portion of future earnings or other future income of the debtor to the supervision and control of the trustee as is necessary for the execution of the plan;

(2) shall provide for the full payment, in deferred cash payments, of all claims entitled to priority under *section 507* of this title, unless the holder of a particular claim agrees to a different treatment of such claim;

(3) if the plan classifies claims, shall provide the same treatment for each claim within a particular class; and

(4) notwithstanding any other provision of this section, may provide for less than full payment of all amounts owed for a claim entitled to priority under *section 507(a)(1)(B)* only if the plan provides that all of the debtor's projected disposable income for a 5-year period beginning on the date that the first payment is due under the plan will be applied to make payments under the plan.

(b) Subject to subsections (a) and (c) of this section, the plan may—

(1) designate a class or classes of unsecured claims, as provided in *section 1122* of this title, but may not discriminate unfairly against any class so designated; however, such plan may treat claims for a consumer debt of the debtor if an individual is liable on such consumer debt with the debtor differently than other unsecured claims;

(2) modify the rights of holders of secured claims, other than a claim secured only by a security interest in real property that is the debtor's principal residence, or of holders of unsecured claims, or leave unaffected the rights of holders of any class of claims;

(3) provide for the curing or waiving of any default;

(4) provide for payments on any unsecured claim to be made concurrently with payments on any secured claim or any other unsecured claim;

(5) notwithstanding paragraph (2) of this subsection, provide for the curing of any default within a reasonable time and maintenance of payments while the case is pending on any unsecured claim or secured claim on which the last payment is due after the date on which the final payment under the plan is due;

(6) provide for the payment of all or any part of any claim allowed under *section 1305* of this title;

(7) subject to *section 365* of this title, provide for the assumption, rejection, or assignment of any executory contract or unexpired lease of the debtor not previously rejected under such section;

(8) provide for the payment of all or part of a claim against the debtor from property of the estate or property of the debtor;

(9) provide for the vesting of property of the estate, on confirmation of the plan or at a later time, in the debtor or in any other entity;

(10) provide for the payment of interest accruing after the date of the filing of the petition on unsecured claims that are nondischargeable under *section 1328(a)*, except that such interest may be paid only to the extent that the debtor has disposable income available to pay such interest after making provision for full payment of all allowed claims; and

(11) include any other appropriate provision not inconsistent with this title.

(c) Notwithstanding subsection (b)(2) and applicable nonbankruptcy law—

(1) a default with respect to, or that gave rise to, a lien on the debtor's principal residence may be cured under paragraph (3) or (5) of subsection (b) until such residence is sold at a foreclosure sale that is conducted in accordance with applicable nonbankruptcy law; and

(2) in a case in which the last payment on the original payment schedule for a claim

secured only by a security interest in real property that is the debtor's principal residence is due before the date on which the final payment under the plan is due, the plan may provide for the payment of the claim as modified pursuant to *section 1325(a)(5)* of this title.

(d)

(1) If the current monthly income of the debtor and the debtor's spouse combined, when multiplied by 12, is not less than—

(A) in the case of a debtor in a household of 1 person, the median family income of the applicable State for 1 earner;

(B) in the case of a debtor in a household of 2, 3, or 4 individuals, the highest median family income of the applicable State for a family of the same number or fewer individuals; or

(C) in the case of a debtor in a household exceeding 4 individuals, the highest median family income of the applicable State for a family of 4 or fewer individuals, plus $925 per month for each individual in excess of 4,

the plan may not provide for payments over a period that is longer than 5 years.

(2) If the current monthly income of the debtor and the debtor's spouse combined, when multiplied by 12, is less than—

(A) in the case of a debtor in a household of 1 person, the median family income of the applicable State for 1 earner;

(B) in the case of a debtor in a household of 2, 3, or 4 individuals, the highest median family income of the applicable State for a family of the same number or fewer individuals; or

(C) in the case of a debtor in a household exceeding 4 individuals, the highest median family income of the applicable State for a family of 4 or fewer individuals, plus $925 per month for each individual in excess of 4,

the plan may not provide for payments over a period that is longer than 3 years, unless the court, for cause, approves a longer period, but the court may not approve a period that is longer than 5 years.

(e) Notwithstanding subsection (b)(2) of this section and *sections 506(b)* and *1325*(a)(5) of this title, if it is proposed in a plan to cure a default, the amount necessary to cure the default, shall be determined in accordance with the underlying agreement and applicable nonbankruptcy law.

(f) A plan may not materially alter the terms of a loan described in *section 362(b)(19)* and any amounts required to repay such loan shall not constitute "disposable income" under *section 1325*.

(Pub. L. 95–598, Nov. 6, 1978, 92 Stat. 2648; Pub. L. 98–353, title III, §§ 316, 528, July 10, 1984, 98 Stat. 356, 389; Pub. L. 103–394, title III, §§ 301, 305(c), Oct. 22, 1994, 108 Stat. 4131, 4134; Pub. L. 109–8, title II, §§ 213(8), (9), 224(d), title III, § 318(1), Apr. 20, 2005, 119 Stat. 53, 65, 93; Pub. L. 111–327, § 2(a)(43), Dec. 22, 2010, 124 Stat. 3562.)

Sections that reference this section: 1323, 1328, 1329

§1323. Modification of plan before confirmation

(a) The debtor may modify the plan at any time before confirmation, but may not modify the plan so that the plan as modified fails to meet the requirements of *section 1322* of this title.

(b) After the debtor files a modification under this section, the plan as modified becomes the plan.

(c) Any holder of a secured claim that has accepted or rejected the plan is deemed to have accepted or rejected, as the case may be, the plan as modified, unless the modification provides for a change in the rights of such holder from what such rights were under the plan before modification, and such holder changes such holder's previous acceptance or rejection.

(Pub. L. 95–598, Nov. 6, 1978, 92 Stat. 2649.)

Sections that reference this section: None

§1324. Confirmation hearing

(a) Except as provided in subsection (b) and after notice, the court shall hold a hearing on confirmation of the plan. A party in interest may object to confirmation of the plan.

(b) The hearing on confirmation of the plan may be held not earlier than 20 days and not later than 45 days after the date of the meeting of creditors under *section 341(a)*, unless the court determines that it would be in the best interests of the creditors and the estate to hold such hearing at an earlier date and there is no objection to such earlier date.

(Pub. L. 95–598, Nov. 6, 1978, 92 Stat. 2649; Pub. L. 98–353, title III, § 529, July 10, 1984, 98 Stat. 389; Pub. L. 99–554, title II, § 283(x), Oct. 27, 1986, 100 Stat. 3118; Pub. L. 109–8, title III, § 317, Apr. 20, 2005, 119 Stat. 92.)

Sections that reference this section: None

§1325. Confirmation of plan

(a) Except as provided in subsection (b), the court shall confirm a plan if—

(1) The plan complies with the provisions of this chapter and with the other applicable provisions of this title;

(2) any fee, charge, or amount required under chapter 123 of title 28, or by the plan, to be paid before confirmation, has been paid;

(3) the plan has been proposed in good faith and not by any means forbidden by law;

(4) the value, as of the effective date of the plan, of property to be distributed under the plan on account of each allowed unsecured claim is not less than the amount that would be paid on such claim if the estate of the debtor were liquidated under chapter 7 of this title on such date;

(5) with respect to each allowed secured claim provided for by the plan—

(A) the holder of such claim has accepted the plan;

(B)

(i) the plan provides that—

(I) the holder of such claim retain the lien securing such claim until the earlier of—

(aa) the payment of the underlying debt determined under nonbankruptcy law; or

(bb) discharge under *section 1328*; and

(II) if the case under this chapter is dismissed or converted without completion of the plan, such lien shall also be retained by such holder to the extent recognized by applicable nonbankruptcy law;

(ii) the value, as of the effective date of the plan, of property to be distributed under the plan on account of such claim is not less than the allowed amount of such claim; and

(iii) if—

(I) property to be distributed pursuant to this subsection is in the form of periodic payments, such payments shall be in equal monthly amounts; and

(II) the holder of the claim is secured by personal property, the amount of such payments shall not be less than an amount sufficient to provide to the holder of such claim adequate protection during the period of the plan; or

(C) the debtor surrenders the property securing such claim to such holder;

(6) the debtor will be able to make all payments under the plan and to comply with the plan;

(7) the action of the debtor in filing the petition was in good faith;

(8) the debtor has paid all amounts that are required to be paid under a domestic support obligation and that first become payable after the date of the filing of the petition if the debtor is required by a judicial or administrative order, or by statute, to pay such domestic support obligation; and

(9) the debtor has filed all applicable Federal, State, and local tax returns as required by *section 1308*.

For purposes of paragraph (5), *section 506* shall not apply to a claim described in that paragraph if the creditor has a purchase money security interest securing the debt that is the subject of the claim, the debt was incurred within the 910-day period preceding the date of the filing of the petition, and the collateral for that debt consists of a motor vehicle (as defined in section 30102 of title 49) acquired for the personal use of the debtor, or if collateral for that debt consists of any other thing of value, if the debt was incurred during the 1-year period preceding that filing.

(b)

(1) If the trustee or the holder of an allowed unsecured claim objects to the confirmation of the plan, then the court may not approve the plan unless, as of the effective date of the plan—

(A) the value of the property to be distributed under the plan on account of such claim is not less than the amount of such claim; or

(B) the plan provides that all of the debtor's projected disposable income to be received in the applicable commitment period beginning on the date that the first payment is due under the plan will be applied to make payments to unsecured creditors under the plan.

(2) For purposes of this subsection, the term "disposable income" means current monthly income received by the debtor (other than child support payments, foster care payments, or disability payments for a dependent child made in accordance with applicable nonbankruptcy law to the extent reasonably necessary to be expended for such child) less amounts reasonably necessary to be expended—

(A)

(i) for the maintenance or support of the debtor or a dependent of the debtor, or for a domestic support obligation, that first becomes payable after the date the petition is filed; and

(ii) for charitable contributions (that meet the definition of "charitable contribution" under *section 548(d)(3)*) to a qualified religious or charitable entity or organization (as defined in *section 548(d)(4)*) in an amount not to exceed 15 percent of gross income of the debtor for the year in which the contributions are made; and

(B) if the debtor is engaged in business, for the payment of expenditures necessary for the continuation, preservation, and operation of such business.

(3) Amounts reasonably necessary to be expended under paragraph (2), other than subparagraph (A)(ii) of paragraph (2), shall be determined in accordance with subparagraphs (A) and (B) of *section 707(b)(2)*, if the debtor has current monthly income, when multiplied by 12, greater than—

(A) in the case of a debtor in a household of 1 person, the median family income of the applicable State for 1 earner;

(B) in the case of a debtor in a household of 2, 3, or 4 individuals, the highest median family income of the applicable State for a family of the same number or fewer individuals; or

(C) in the case of a debtor in a household exceeding 4 individuals, the highest median family income of the applicable State for a family of 4 or fewer individuals, plus $925 per month for each individual in excess of 4.

(4) For purposes of this subsection, the "applicable commitment period"—

(A) subject to subparagraph (B), shall be—

(i) 3 years; or

(ii) not less than 5 years, if the current monthly income of the debtor and the debtor's spouse combined, when multiplied by 12, is not less than—

(I) in the case of a debtor in a household of 1 person, the median family income of the applicable State for 1 earner;

(II) in the case of a debtor in a household of 2, 3, or 4 individuals, the highest median family income of the applicable State for a family of the same number or fewer individuals; or

(III) in the case of a debtor in a household exceeding 4 individuals, the highest median family income of the applicable State for a family of

4 or fewer individuals, plus $925 per month for each individual in excess of 4; and

(B) may be less than 3 or 5 years, whichever is applicable under subparagraph (A), but only if the plan provides for payment in full of all allowed unsecured claims over a shorter period.

(c) After confirmation of a plan, the court may order any entity from whom the debtor receives income to pay all or any part of such income to the trustee.

(Pub. L. 95–598, Nov. 6, 1978, 92 Stat. 2649; Pub. L. 98–353, title III, §§ 317, 530, July 10, 1984, 98 Stat. 356, 389; Pub. L. 99–554, title II, § 283(y), Oct. 27, 1986, 100 Stat. 3118; Pub. L. 105–183, § 4(a), June 19, 1998, 112 Stat. 518; Pub. L. 109–8, title I, § 102(g), (h), title II, § 213(10), title III, §§ 306(a), (b), 309(c)(1), 318(2), (3), title VII, § 716(a), Apr. 20, 2005, 119 Stat. 33, 53, 80, 83, 93, 129; Pub. L. 109–439, § 2, Dec. 20, 2006, 120 Stat. 3285; Pub. L. 111–327, § 2(a)(44), Dec. 22, 2010, 124 Stat. 3562; Pub. L. 116–136, div. A, title I, § 1113(b)(1)(B), (2)(A)(ii), Mar. 27, 2020, 134 Stat. 311, 312; Pub. L. 116–260, div. N, title III, § 320(e), (f)(2)(A)(v), Dec. 27, 2020, 134 Stat. 2016, 2017.)

Sections that reference this section: 1129, 1307, 1322, 1329, 1330, 541

§1326. Payments

(a)

(1) Unless the court orders otherwise, the debtor shall commence making payments not later than 30 days after the date of the filing of the plan or the order for relief, whichever is earlier, in the amount—

(A) proposed by the plan to the trustee;

(B) scheduled in a lease of personal property directly to the lessor for that portion of the obligation that becomes due after the order for relief, reducing the payments under subparagraph (A) by the amount so paid and providing the trustee with evidence of such payment, including the amount and date of payment; and

(C) that provides adequate protection directly to a creditor holding an allowed claim secured by personal property to the extent the claim is attributable to the purchase of such property by the debtor for that portion of the obligation that becomes due after the order for relief, reducing the payments under subparagraph (A) by the amount so paid and providing the trustee with evidence of such payment, including the amount and date of payment.

(2) A payment made under paragraph (1)(A) shall be retained by the trustee until confirmation or denial of confirmation. If a plan is confirmed, the trustee shall distribute any such payment in accordance with the plan as soon as is practicable. If a plan is not confirmed, the trustee shall return any such payments not previously paid and not yet due and owing to creditors pursuant to paragraph (3) to the debtor, after deducting any unpaid claim allowed under *section 503(b)*.

(3) Subject to *section 363*, the court may, upon notice and a hearing, modify, increase, or reduce the payments required under this subsection pending confirmation of a plan.

(4) Not later than 60 days after the date of filing of a case under this chapter, a debtor retaining possession of personal property subject to a lease or securing a claim attributable in whole or in part to the purchase price of such property shall provide the lessor or secured creditor reasonable evidence of the maintenance of any required insurance coverage with respect to the use or ownership of such property and continue to do so for so long as the debtor retains possession of such property.

(b) Before or at the time of each payment to creditors under the plan, there shall be paid—

(1) any unpaid claim of the kind specified in *section 507(a)(2)* of this title;

(2) if a standing trustee appointed under section 586(b) of title 28 is serving in the case, the percentage fee fixed for such standing trustee under section 586(e)(1)(B) of title 28; and

(3) if a chapter 7 trustee has been allowed compensation due to the conversion or dismissal of the debtor's prior case pursuant to *section 707(b)*, and some portion of that compensation remains unpaid in a case converted to this chapter or in the case dismissed under *section 707(b)* and refiled under this chapter, the amount of any such unpaid compensation, which shall be paid monthly—

(A) by prorating such amount over the remaining duration of the plan; and

(B) by monthly payments not to exceed the greater of—

(i) $25; or

(ii) the amount payable to unsecured nonpriority creditors, as provided by the plan, multiplied by 5 percent, and the result divided by the number of months in the plan.

(c) Except as otherwise provided in the plan or in the order confirming the plan, the trustee shall make payments to creditors under the plan.

(d) Notwithstanding any other provision of this title —

(1) compensation referred to in subsection (b)(3) is payable and may be collected by the trustee under that paragraph, even if such amount has been discharged in a prior case under this title; and

(2) such compensation is payable in a case under this chapter only to the extent permitted by subsection (b)(3).

(Pub. L. 95–598, Nov. 6, 1978, 92 Stat. 2650; Pub. L. 98–353, title III, §§ 318(a), 531, July 10, 1984, 98 Stat. 357, 389; Pub. L. 99–554, title II, §§ 230, 283(z), Oct. 27, 1986, 100 Stat. 3103, 3118; Pub. L. 103–394, title III, § 307, Oct. 22, 1994, 108 Stat. 4135; Pub. L. 109–8, title III, § 309(c)(2), title XII, § 1224, title XV, § 1502(a)(10), Apr. 20, 2005, 119 Stat. 83, 199, 217.)

Sections that reference this section: 1302, 1307

§1327. Effect of confirmation

(a) The provisions of a confirmed plan bind the debtor and each creditor, whether or not the claim of such creditor is provided for by the plan, and whether or not such creditor has objected to, has accepted, or has rejected the plan.

(b) Except as otherwise provided in the plan or the order confirming the plan, the confirmation of a plan vests all of the property of the estate in the debtor.

(c) Except as otherwise provided in the plan or in the order confirming the plan, the property vesting in the debtor under subsection (b) of this section is free and clear of any claim or interest of any creditor provided for by the plan.

(Pub. L. 95–598, Nov. 6, 1978, 92 Stat. 2650.)

Sections that reference this section: None

§1328. Discharge

(a) Subject to subsection (d), as soon as practicable after completion by the debtor of all payments under the plan, and in the case of a debtor who is required by a judicial or administrative order, or by statute, to pay a domestic support obligation, after such debtor certifies that all amounts payable under such order or such statute that are due on or before the date of the certification (including amounts due before the petition was filed, but only to the extent provided for by the plan) have been paid, unless the court approves a written waiver of discharge executed by the debtor after the order for relief under this chapter, the court shall grant the debtor a discharge of all debts provided for by the plan or disallowed under *section 502* of this title, except any debt—

(1) provided for under *section 1322(b)(5);*

(2) of the kind specified in *section 507(a)(8)(C)* or in paragraph (1)(B), (1)(C), (2), (3), (4), (5), (8), or (9) of *section 523(a);*

(3) for restitution, or a criminal fine, included in a sentence on the debtor's conviction of a crime; or

(4) for restitution, or damages, awarded in a civil action against the debtor as a result of willful or malicious injury by the debtor that caused personal injury to an individual or the death of an individual.

(b) Subject to subsection (d), at any time after the confirmation of the plan and after notice and a hearing, the court may grant a discharge to a debtor that has not completed payments under the plan only if—

(1) the debtor's failure to complete such payments is due to circumstances for which the debtor should not justly be held accountable;

(2) the value, as of the effective date of the plan, of property actually distributed under the plan on account of each allowed unsecured claim is not less than the amount that would have been paid on such claim if the estate of the debtor had been liquidated under chapter 7 of this title on such date; and

(3) modification of the plan under *section 1329* of this title is not practicable.

(c) A discharge granted under subsection (b) of this section discharges the debtor from all unsecured debts provided for by the plan or disallowed under *section 502* of this title, except any debt—

(1) provided for under *section 1322(b)(5)* of this title; or

(2) of a kind specified in *section 523(a)* of this title.

(d) Notwithstanding any other provision of this section, a discharge granted under this section does not discharge the debtor from any debt based on an allowed claim filed under *section 1305(a)(2)* of this title if prior approval by the trustee of the debtor's incurring such debt was practicable and was not obtained.

(e) On request of a party in interest before one year after a discharge under this section is granted, and after notice and a hearing, the court may revoke such discharge only if—

(1) such discharge was obtained by the debtor through fraud; and

(2) the requesting party did not know of such fraud until after such discharge was granted.

(f) Notwithstanding subsections (a) and (b), the court shall not grant a discharge of all debts provided for in the plan or disallowed under *section 502,* if the debtor has received a discharge—

(1) in a case filed under chapter 7, 11, or 12 of this title during the 4-year period preceding the date of the order for relief under this chapter, or

(2) in a case filed under chapter 13 of this title during the 2-year period preceding the date of such order.

(g)

(1) The court shall not grant a discharge under this section to a debtor unless after filing a petition the debtor has completed an instructional course concerning personal financial management described in *section 111*.

(2) Paragraph (1) shall not apply with respect to a debtor who is a person described in *section 109(h)(4)* or who resides in a district for which the United States trustee (or the bankruptcy administrator, if any) determines that the approved instructional courses are not adequate to service the additional individuals who would otherwise be required to complete such instructional course by reason of the requirements of paragraph (1).

(3) The United States trustee (or the bankruptcy administrator, if any) who makes a determination described in paragraph (2) shall review such determination not later than 1 year after the date of such determination, and not less frequently than annually thereafter.

(h) The court may not grant a discharge under this chapter unless the court after notice and a hearing held not more than 10 days before the date of the entry of the order granting the discharge finds that there is no reasonable cause to believe that—

(1) *section 522(q)(1)* may be applicable to the debtor; and

(2) there is pending any proceeding in which the debtor may be found guilty of a felony of the kind described in *section 522(q)(1)(A)* or liable for a debt of the kind described in *section 522(q)(1)(B).*

(Pub. L. 95–598, Nov. 6, 1978, 92 Stat. 2650; Pub. L. 98–353, title III, § 532, July 10, 1984, 98 Stat. 389; Pub. L. 101–508, title III, § 3007(b)(1), Nov. 5, 1990, 104 Stat. 1388–28; Pub. L. 101–581, §§ 2(b), 3, Nov. 15, 1990, 104 Stat. 2865; Pub. L. 101–647, title XXXI, §§ 3102(b), 3103, Nov. 29, 1990, 104 Stat. 4916; Pub. L. 103–394, title III, § 302, title V, § 501(d)(38), Oct. 22, 1994, 108 Stat. 4132, 4147; Pub. L. 109–8, title I, § 106(c), title II, § 213(11), title III, §§ 312(2), 314(b), 330(d), title VII, § 707, Apr. 20, 2005, 119 Stat. 38, 53, 87, 88, 102, 126; Pub. L. 116–260, div. FF, title X, § 1001(b), Dec. 27, 2020, 134 Stat. 3217.)

Sections that reference this section: 1302, 1322, 1325

§1329. Modification of plan after confirmation

(a) At any time after confirmation of the plan but before the completion of payments under such plan, the plan may be modified, upon request of the debtor, the trustee, or the holder of an allowed unsecured claim, to—

(1) increase or reduce the amount of payments on claims of a particular class provided for by the plan;

(2) extend or reduce the time for such payments;

(3) alter the amount of the distribution to a creditor whose claim is provided for by the plan to the extent necessary to take account of any payment of such claim other than under the plan; or

(4) reduce amounts to be paid under the plan by the actual amount expended by the debtor to purchase health insurance for the debtor (and for any dependent of the debtor if

such dependent does not otherwise have health insurance coverage) if the debtor documents the cost of such insurance and demonstrates that—

(A) such expenses are reasonable and necessary;

(B)

(i) if the debtor previously paid for health insurance, the amount is not materially larger than the cost the debtor previously paid or the cost necessary to maintain the lapsed policy; or

(ii) if the debtor did not have health insurance, the amount is not materially larger than the reasonable cost that would be incurred by a debtor who purchases health insurance, who has similar income, expenses, age, and health status, and who lives in the same geographical location with the same number of dependents who do not otherwise have health insurance coverage; and

(C) the amount is not otherwise allowed for purposes of determining disposable income under *section 1325(b)* of this title;

and upon request of any party in interest, files proof that a health insurance policy was purchased.

(b)

(1) *Sections 1322(a), 1322*(b), and 1323(c) of this title and the requirements of *section 1325(a)* of this title apply to any modification under subsection (a) of this section.

(2) The plan as modified becomes the plan unless, after notice and a hearing, such modification is disapproved.

(c) A plan modified under this section may not provide for payments over a period that expires after the applicable commitment period under *section 1325(b)(1)(B)* after the time that the first payment under the original confirmed plan was due, unless the court, for cause, approves a longer period, but the court may not approve a period that expires after five years after such time.

(Pub. L. 95–598, Nov. 6, 1978, 92 Stat. 2651; Pub. L. 98–353, title III, §§ 319, 533, July 10, 1984, 98 Stat. 357, 389; Pub. L. 109–8, title I, § 102(i), title III, § 318(4), Apr. 20, 2005, 119 Stat. 34, 94; Pub. L. 116–136, div. A, title I, § 1113(b)(1)(C), (2)(A)(iii), Mar. 27, 2020, 134 Stat. 311, 312; Pub. L. 116–260, div. FF, title X, § 1001(e), Dec. 27, 2020, 134 Stat. 3218; Pub. L. 117–5, § 2(b)(1), Mar. 27, 2021, 135 Stat. 249.)

Sections that reference this section: 1307, 1328, 1330

§1330. Revocation of an order of confirmation

(a) On request of a party in interest at any time within 180 days after the date of the entry of an order of confirmation under *section 1325* of this title, and after notice and a hearing, the court may revoke such order if such order was procured by fraud.

(b) If the court revokes an order of confirmation under subsection (a) of this section, the court shall dispose of the case under *section 1307* of this title, unless, within the time fixed by the court, the debtor proposes and the court confirms a modification of the plan under *section 1329* of this title.

(Pub. L. 95–598, Nov. 6, 1978, 92 Stat. 2651.)

Sections that reference this section: 1307

CHAPTER 15: ANCILLARY AND OTHER CROSS-BORDER CASES

§1501. Purpose and scope of application

(a) The purpose of this chapter is to incorporate the Model Law on Cross-Border Insolvency so as to provide effective mechanisms for dealing with cases of cross-border insolvency with the objectives of—

(1) cooperation between—

(A) courts of the United States, United States trustees, trustees, examiners, debtors, and debtors in possession; and

(B) the courts and other competent authorities of foreign countries involved in cross-border insolvency cases;

(2) greater legal certainty for trade and investment;

(3) fair and efficient administration of cross-border insolvencies that protects the interests of all creditors, and other interested entities, including the debtor;

(4) protection and maximization of the value of the debtor's assets; and

(5) facilitation of the rescue of financially troubled businesses, thereby protecting investment and preserving employment.

(b) This chapter applies where—

(1) assistance is sought in the United States by a foreign court or a foreign representative in connection with a foreign proceeding;

(2) assistance is sought in a foreign country in connection with a case under this title;

(3) a foreign proceeding and a case under this title with respect to the same debtor are pending concurrently; or

(4) creditors or other interested persons in a foreign country have an interest in requesting the commencement of, or participating in, a case or proceeding under this title.

(c) This chapter does not apply to—

(1) a proceeding concerning an entity, other than a foreign insurance company, identified by exclusion in *section 109(b)*;

(2) an individual, or to an individual and such individual's spouse, who have debts within the limits specified in *section 109(e)* and who are citizens of the United States or aliens lawfully admitted for permanent residence in the United States; or

(3) an entity subject to a proceeding under the Securities Investor Protection Act of 1970, a stockbroker subject to subchapter III of chapter 7 of this title, or a commodity broker subject to subchapter IV of chapter 7 of this title.

(d) The court may not grant relief under this chapter with respect to any deposit, escrow, trust fund, or other security required or permitted under any applicable State insurance law or regulation for the benefit of claim holders in the United States.

(Added Pub. L. 109–8, title VIII, § 801(a), Apr. 20, 2005, 119 Stat. 135.)

Sections that reference this section: 1525, 1526, 1530

Subchapter I: General Provisions

§1502. Definitions

For the purposes of this chapter, the term—

(1) "debtor" means an entity that is the subject of a foreign proceeding;

(2) "establishment" means any place of operations where the debtor carries out a nontransitory economic activity;

(3) "foreign court" means a judicial or other authority competent to control or supervise a foreign proceeding;

(4) "foreign main proceeding" means a foreign proceeding pending in the country where the debtor has the center of its main interests;

(5) "foreign nonmain proceeding" means a foreign proceeding, other than a foreign main proceeding, pending in a country where the debtor has an establishment;

(6) "trustee" includes a trustee, a debtor in possession in a case under any chapter of this title, or a debtor under chapter 9 of this title;

(7) "recognition" means the entry of an order granting recognition of a foreign main proceeding or foreign nonmain proceeding under this chapter; and

(8) "within the territorial jurisdiction of the United States", when used with reference to property of a debtor, refers to tangible property located within the territory of the United States and intangible property deemed under applicable

nonbankruptcy law to be located within that territory, including any property subject to attachment or garnishment that may properly be seized or garnished by an action in a Federal or State court in the United States.

(Added Pub. L. 109–8, title VIII, § 801(a), Apr. 20, 2005, 119 Stat. 135.)

Sections that reference this section: 1517

§1503. International obligations of the United States

To the extent that this chapter conflicts with an obligation of the United States arising out of any treaty or other form of agreement to which it is a party with one or more other countries, the requirements of the treaty or agreement prevail.

(Added Pub. L. 109–8, title VIII, § 801(a), Apr. 20, 2005, 119 Stat. 136.)

Sections that reference this section: None

§1504. Commencement of ancillary case

A case under this chapter is commenced by the filing of a petition for recognition of a foreign proceeding under *section 1515*.

(Added Pub. L. 109–8, title VIII, § 801(a), Apr. 20, 2005, 119 Stat. 136.)

Sections that reference this section: 1509

§1505. Authorization to act in a foreign country

A trustee or another entity (including an examiner) may be authorized by the court to act in a foreign country on behalf of an estate created under *section 541*. An entity authorized to act under this section may act in any way permitted by the applicable foreign law.

(Added Pub. L. 109–8, title VIII, § 801(a), Apr. 20, 2005, 119 Stat. 136.)

Sections that reference this section: 103

§1506. Public policy exception

Nothing in this chapter prevents the court from refusing to take an action governed by this chapter if the action would be manifestly contrary to the public policy of the United States.

(Added Pub. L. 109–8, title VIII, § 801(a), Apr. 20, 2005, 119 Stat. 136.)

Sections that reference this section: 1517

§1507. Additional assistance

(a) Subject to the specific limitations stated elsewhere in this chapter the court, if recognition is granted, may provide additional assistance to a foreign representative under this title or under other laws of the United States.

(b) In determining whether to provide additional assistance under this title or under other laws of the United States, the court shall consider whether such additional assistance, consistent with the principles of comity, will reasonably assure—

 (1) just treatment of all holders of claims against or interests in the debtor's property;

 (2) protection of claim holders in the United States against prejudice and inconvenience in the processing of claims in such foreign proceeding;

 (3) prevention of preferential or fraudulent dispositions of property of the debtor;

 (4) distribution of proceeds of the debtor's property substantially in accordance with the order prescribed by this title; and

 (5) if appropriate, the provision of an opportunity for a fresh start for the individual that such foreign proceeding concerns.

(Added Pub. L. 109–8, title VIII, § 801(a), Apr. 20, 2005, 119 Stat. 136.)

Sections that reference this section: None

§1508. Interpretation

In interpreting this chapter, the court shall consider its international origin, and the need to promote an application of this chapter that is consistent with the application of similar statutes adopted by foreign jurisdictions.

(Added Pub. L. 109–8, title VIII, § 801(a), Apr. 20, 2005, 119 Stat. 137.)

Sections that reference this section: None

Subchapter II: Access of Foreign Representatives and Creditors to the Court

§1509. Right of direct access

(a) A foreign representative may commence a case under *section 1504* by filing directly with the court a petition for recognition of a foreign proceeding under *section 1515*.

(b) If the court grants recognition under *section 1517*, and subject to any limitations that the court may impose consistent with the policy of this chapter—
  (1) the foreign representative has the capacity to sue and be sued in a court in the United States;
  (2) the foreign representative may apply directly to a court in the United States for appropriate relief in that court; and
  (3) a court in the United States shall grant comity or cooperation to the foreign representative.

(c) A request for comity or cooperation by a foreign representative in a court in the United States other than the court which granted recognition shall be accompanied by a certified copy of an order granting recognition under *section 1517*.

(d) If the court denies recognition under this chapter, the court may issue any appropriate order necessary to prevent the foreign representative from obtaining comity or cooperation from courts in the United States.

(e) Whether or not the court grants recognition, and subject to *sections 306* and *1510*, a foreign representative is subject to applicable nonbankruptcy law.

(f) Notwithstanding any other provision of this section, the failure of a foreign representative to commence a case or to obtain recognition under this chapter does not affect any right the foreign representative may have to sue in a court in the United States to collect or recover a claim which is the property of the debtor.

(Added Pub. L. 109–8, title VIII, § 801(a), Apr. 20, 2005, 119 Stat. 137.)

Sections that reference this section: 103

§1510. Limited jurisdiction

The sole fact that a foreign representative files a petition under *section 1515* does not subject the foreign representative to the jurisdiction of any court in the United States for any other purpose.

(Added Pub. L. 109–8, title VIII, § 801(a), Apr. 20, 2005, 119 Stat. 138.)

Sections that reference this section: None

§1511. Commencement of case under section 301, 302, or 303

(a) Upon recognition, a foreign representative may commence—
  (1) an involuntary case under *section 303*; or
  (2) a voluntary case under *section 301* or *302*, if the foreign proceeding is a foreign main proceeding.

(b) The petition commencing a case under subsection (a) must be accompanied by a certified copy of an order granting recognition. The court where the petition for recognition has been filed must be advised of the foreign representative's intent to commence a case under subsection (a) prior to such commencement.

(Added Pub. L. 109–8, title VIII, § 801(a), Apr. 20, 2005, 119 Stat. 138; amended Pub. L. 111–327, § 2(a)(45), Dec. 22, 2010, 124 Stat. 3562.)

Sections that reference this section: None

§1512. Participation of a foreign representative in a case under this title

Upon recognition of a foreign proceeding, the foreign representative in the recognized proceeding is entitled to participate as a party in interest in a case regarding the debtor under this title.

(Added Pub. L. 109–8, title VIII, § 801(a), Apr. 20, 2005, 119 Stat. 138.)

Sections that reference this section: None

§1513. Access of foreign creditors to a case under this title

(a) Foreign creditors have the same rights regarding the commencement of, and participation in, a case under this title as domestic creditors.

(b)
  (1) Subsection (a) does not change or codify present law as to the priority of claims under *section 507* or *726*, except that the claim of a foreign creditor under those sections shall not be given a lower priority than that of general unsecured claims without priority solely because the holder of such claim is a foreign creditor.
  (2)
    (A) Subsection (a) and paragraph (1) do not change or codify present law as to the allowability of foreign revenue

claims or other foreign public law claims in a proceeding under this title.

(B) Allowance and priority as to a foreign tax claim or other foreign public law claim shall be governed by any applicable tax treaty of the United States, under the conditions and circumstances specified therein.

(Added Pub. L. 109–8, title VIII, § 801(a), Apr. 20, 2005, 119 Stat. 138.)

Sections that reference this section: None

§1514. Notification to foreign creditors concerning a case under this title

(a) Whenever in a case under this title notice is to be given to creditors generally or to any class or category of creditors, such notice shall also be given to the known creditors generally, or to creditors in the notified class or category, that do not have addresses in the United States. The court may order that appropriate steps be taken with a view to notifying any creditor whose address is not yet known.

(b) Such notification to creditors with foreign addresses described in subsection (a) shall be given individually, unless the court considers that, under the circumstances, some other form of notification would be more appropriate. No letter or other formality is required.

(c) When a notification of commencement of a case is to be given to foreign creditors, such notification shall—

(1) indicate the time period for filing proofs of claim and specify the place for filing such proofs of claim;

(2) indicate whether secured creditors need to file proofs of claim; and

(3) contain any other information required to be included in such notification to creditors under this title and the orders of the court.

(d) Any rule of procedure or order of the court as to notice or the filing of a proof of claim shall provide such additional time to creditors with foreign addresses as is reasonable under the circumstances.

(Added Pub. L. 109–8, title VIII, § 801(a), Apr. 20, 2005, 119 Stat. 138.)

Sections that reference this section: None

Subchapter III: Recognition of a Foreign Proceeding and Relief

§1515. Application for recognition

(a) A foreign representative applies to the court for recognition of a foreign proceeding in which the foreign representative has been appointed by filing a petition for recognition.

(b) A petition for recognition shall be accompanied by—

(1) a certified copy of the decision commencing such foreign proceeding and appointing the foreign representative;

(2) a certificate from the foreign court affirming the existence of such foreign proceeding and of the appointment of the foreign representative; or

(3) in the absence of evidence referred to in paragraphs (1) and (2), any other evidence acceptable to the court of the existence of such foreign proceeding and of the appointment of the foreign representative.

(c) A petition for recognition shall also be accompanied by a statement identifying all foreign proceedings with respect to the debtor that are known to the foreign representative.

(d) The documents referred to in paragraphs (1) and (2) of subsection (b) shall be translated into English. The court may require a translation into English of additional documents.

(Added Pub. L. 109–8, title VIII, § 801(a), Apr. 20, 2005, 119 Stat. 139.)

Sections that reference this section: 1504, 1509, 1510, 1516, 1517, 305

§1516. Presumptions concerning recognition

(a) If the decision or certificate referred to in *section 1515(b)* indicates that the foreign proceeding is a foreign proceeding and that the person or body is a foreign representative, the court is entitled to so presume.

(b) The court is entitled to presume that documents submitted in support of the petition for recognition are authentic, whether or not they have been legalized.

(c) In the absence of evidence to the contrary, the debtor's registered office, or habitual residence in the case of an individual, is presumed to be the center of the debtor's main interests.

(Added Pub. L. 109–8, title VIII, § 801(a), Apr. 20, 2005, 119 Stat. 139.)

Sections that reference this section: None

§1517. Order granting recognition

(a) Subject to *section 1506*, after notice and a hearing, an order recognizing a foreign proceeding shall be entered if—

(1) such foreign proceeding for which recognition is sought is a foreign main proceeding or foreign nonmain proceeding within the meaning of *section 1502*;

(2) the foreign representative applying for recognition is a person or body; and

(3) the petition meets the requirements of *section 1515*.

(b) Such foreign proceeding shall be recognized—

(1) as a foreign main proceeding if it is pending in the country where the debtor has the center of its main interests; or

(2) as a foreign nonmain proceeding if the debtor has an establishment within the meaning of *section 1502* in the foreign country where the proceeding is pending.

(c) A petition for recognition of a foreign proceeding shall be decided upon at the earliest possible time. Entry of an order recognizing a foreign proceeding constitutes recognition under this chapter.

(d) The provisions of this subchapter do not prevent modification or termination of recognition if it is shown that the grounds for granting it were fully or partially lacking or have ceased to exist, but in considering such action the court shall give due weight to possible prejudice to parties that have relied upon the order granting recognition. A case under this chapter may be closed in the manner prescribed under *section 350*.

(Added Pub. L. 109–8, title VIII, § 801(a), Apr. 20, 2005, 119 Stat. 139.)

Sections that reference this section: 1509

§1518. Subsequent information

From the time of filing the petition for recognition of a foreign proceeding, the foreign representative shall file with the court promptly a notice of change of status concerning—

(1) any substantial change in the status of such foreign proceeding or the status of the foreign representative's appointment; and

(2) any other foreign proceeding regarding the debtor that becomes known to the foreign representative.

(Added Pub. L. 109–8, title VIII, § 801(a), Apr. 20, 2005, 119 Stat. 140.)

Sections that reference this section: None

§1519. Relief that may be granted upon filing petition for recognition

(a) From the time of filing a petition for recognition until the court rules on the petition, the court may, at the request of the foreign representative, where relief is urgently needed to protect the assets of the debtor or the interests of the creditors, grant relief of a provisional nature, including—

(1) staying execution against the debtor's assets;

(2) entrusting the administration or realization of all or part of the debtor's assets located in the United States to the foreign representative or another person authorized by the court, including an examiner, in order to protect and preserve the value of assets that, by their nature or because of other circumstances, are perishable, susceptible to devaluation or otherwise in jeopardy; and

(3) any relief referred to in paragraph (3), (4), or (7) of *section 1521(a)*.

(b) Unless extended under *section 1521(a)(6)*, the relief granted under this section terminates when the petition for recognition is granted.

(c) It is a ground for denial of relief under this section that such relief would interfere with the administration of a foreign main proceeding.

(d) The court may not enjoin a police or regulatory act of a governmental unit, including a criminal action or proceeding, under this section.

(e) The standards, procedures, and limitations applicable to an injunction shall apply to relief under this section.

(f) The exercise of rights not subject to the stay arising under *section 362(a)* pursuant to paragraph (6), (7), (17), or (27) of *section 362(b)* or pursuant to *section 362(o)* shall not be stayed by any order of a court or administrative agency in any proceeding under this chapter.

(Added Pub. L. 109–8, title VIII, § 801(a), Apr. 20, 2005, 119 Stat. 140; amended Pub. L. 111–327, § 2(a)(46), Dec. 22, 2010, 124 Stat. 3562.)

Sections that reference this section: 1521, 1522, 1529, 1530

§1520. Effects of recognition of a foreign main proceeding

(a) Upon recognition of a foreign proceeding that is a foreign main proceeding—

(1) *sections 361* and *362* apply with respect to the debtor and the property of the debtor that is within the territorial jurisdiction of the United States;

(2) *sections 363, 549,* and *552* apply to a transfer of an interest of the debtor in property that is within the territorial jurisdiction of the United States to the same extent that the sections would apply to property of an estate;

(3) unless the court orders otherwise, the foreign representative may operate the debtor's business and may exercise the rights and powers of a trustee under and to the extent provided by *sections 363* and *552*; and

(4) *section 552* applies to property of the debtor that is within the territorial jurisdiction of the United States.

(b) Subsection (a) does not affect the right to commence an individual action or proceeding in a foreign country to the extent necessary to preserve a claim against the debtor.

(c) Subsection (a) does not affect the right of a foreign representative or an entity to file a petition commencing a case under this title or the right of any party to file claims or take other proper actions in such a case.

(Added Pub. L. 109–8, title VIII, § 801(a), Apr. 20, 2005, 119 Stat. 141.)

Sections that reference this section: 1521, 1522, 1529

§1521. Relief that may be granted upon recognition

(a) Upon recognition of a foreign proceeding, whether main or nonmain, where necessary to effectuate the purpose of this chapter and to protect the assets of the debtor or the interests of the creditors, the court may, at the request of the foreign representative, grant any appropriate relief, including—

(1) staying the commencement or continuation of an individual action or proceeding concerning the debtor's assets, rights, obligations or liabilities to the extent they have not been stayed under *section 1520(a);*

(2) staying execution against the debtor's assets to the extent it has not been stayed under *section 1520(a);*

(3) suspending the right to transfer, encumber or otherwise dispose of any assets of the debtor to the extent this right has not been suspended under *section 1520(a);*

(4) providing for the examination of witnesses, the taking of evidence or the delivery of information concerning the debtor's assets, affairs, rights, obligations or liabilities;

(5) entrusting the administration or realization of all or part of the debtor's assets within the territorial jurisdiction of the United States to the foreign representative or another person, including an examiner, authorized by the court;

(6) extending relief granted under *section 1519(a);* and

(7) granting any additional relief that may be available to a trustee, except for relief available under *sections 522, 544, 545, 547, 548, 550,* and 724(a).

(b) Upon recognition of a foreign proceeding, whether main or nonmain, the court may, at the request of the foreign representative, entrust the distribution of all or part of the debtor's assets located in the United States to the foreign representative or another person, including an examiner, authorized by the court, provided that the court is satisfied that the interests of creditors in the United States are sufficiently protected.

(c) In granting relief under this section to a representative of a foreign nonmain proceeding, the court must be satisfied that the relief relates to assets that, under the law of the United States, should be administered in the foreign nonmain proceeding or concerns information required in that proceeding.

(d) The court may not enjoin a police or regulatory act of a governmental unit, including a criminal action or proceeding, under this section.

(e) The standards, procedures, and limitations applicable to an injunction shall apply to relief under paragraphs (1), (2), (3), and (6) of subsection (a).

(f) The exercise of rights not subject to the stay arising under *section 362(a)* pursuant to paragraph (6), (7), (17), or (27) of *section 362(b)* or pursuant to *section 362(o)* shall not be stayed by any order of a court or administrative agency in any proceeding under this chapter.

(Added Pub. L. 109–8, title VIII, § 801(a), Apr. 20, 2005, 119 Stat. 141; amended Pub. L. 111–327, § 2(a)(47), Dec. 22, 2010, 124 Stat. 3562.)

Sections that reference this section: 1519

§1522. Protection of creditors and other interested persons

(a) The court may grant relief under *section 1519* or *1521*, or may modify or terminate relief under subsection (c), only if the interests of the creditors and other interested entities, including the debtor, are sufficiently protected.

(b) The court may subject relief granted under *section 1519* or *1521*, or the operation of the debtor's business under *section 1520(a)(3)*, to conditions it considers appropriate, including the giving of security or the filing of a bond.

(c) The court may, at the request of the foreign representative or an entity affected by relief granted under *section 1519* or *1521*, or at its own motion, modify or terminate such relief.

(d) *Section 1104(d)* shall apply to the appointment of an examiner under this chapter. Any examiner shall comply with the qualification requirements imposed on a trustee by *section 322*.

(Added Pub. L. 109–8, title VIII, § 801(a), Apr. 20, 2005, 119 Stat. 142.)

Sections that reference this section: None

§1523. Actions to avoid acts detrimental to creditors

(a) Upon recognition of a foreign proceeding, the foreign representative has standing in a case concerning the debtor pending under another chapter of this title to initiate actions under *sections 522, 544, 545, 547, 548, 550*, 553, and 724(a).

(b) When a foreign proceeding is a foreign nonmain proceeding, the court must be satisfied that an action under subsection (a) relates to assets that, under United States law, should be administered in the foreign nonmain proceeding.

(Added Pub. L. 109–8, title VIII, § 801(a), Apr. 20, 2005, 119 Stat. 142.)

Sections that reference this section: None

§1524. Intervention by a foreign representative

Upon recognition of a foreign proceeding, the foreign representative may intervene in any proceedings in a State or Federal court in the United States in which the debtor is a party.

(Added Pub. L. 109–8, title VIII, § 801(a), Apr. 20, 2005, 119 Stat. 142.)

Sections that reference this section: None

Subchapter IV: Cooperation with Foreign Courts and Foreign Representatives

§1525. Cooperation and direct communication between the court and foreign courts or foreign representatives

(a) Consistent with *section 1501*, the court shall cooperate to the maximum extent possible with a foreign court or a foreign representative, either directly or through the trustee.

(b) The court is entitled to communicate directly with, or to request information or assistance directly from, a foreign court or a foreign representative, subject to the rights of a party in interest to notice and participation.

(Added Pub. L. 109–8, title VIII, § 801(a), Apr. 20, 2005, 119 Stat. 143.)

Sections that reference this section: 1527, 1528, 1529, 1530

§1526. Cooperation and direct communication between the trustee and foreign courts or foreign representatives

(a) Consistent with *section 1501*, the trustee or other person, including an examiner, authorized by the court, shall, subject to the supervision of the court, cooperate to the maximum extent possible with a foreign court or a foreign representative.

(b) The trustee or other person, including an examiner, authorized by the court is entitled, subject to the supervision of the court, to communicate directly with a foreign court or a foreign representative.

(Added Pub. L. 109–8, title VIII, § 801(a), Apr. 20, 2005, 119 Stat. 143.)

Sections that reference this section: None

§1527. Forms of cooperation

Cooperation referred to in *sections 1525* and *1526* may be implemented by any appropriate means, including—

(1) appointment of a person or body, including an examiner, to act at the direction of the court;

(2) communication of information by any means considered appropriate by the court;

(3) coordination of the administration and supervision of the debtor's assets and affairs;

(4) approval or implementation of agreements concerning the coordination of proceedings; and

(5) coordination of concurrent proceedings regarding the same debtor.

(Added Pub. L. 109–8, title VIII, § 801(a), Apr. 20, 2005, 119 Stat. 143.)

Sections that reference this section: None

Subchapter V: Concurrent Proceedings

§1528. Commencement of a case under this title after recognition of a foreign main proceeding

After recognition of a foreign main proceeding, a case under another chapter of this title may be commenced only if the debtor has assets in the United States. The effects of such case shall be restricted to the assets of the debtor that are within the territorial jurisdiction of the United States and, to the extent necessary to implement cooperation and coordination under *sections 1525, 1526,* and *1527,* to other assets of the debtor that are within the jurisdiction of the court under *sections 541(a)* of this title, and 1334(e) of title 28, to the extent that such other assets are not subject to the jurisdiction and control of a foreign proceeding that has been recognized under this chapter.

(Added Pub. L. 109–8, title VIII, § 801(a), Apr. 20, 2005, 119 Stat. 143.)

Sections that reference this section: 1529

§1529. Coordination of a case under this title and a foreign proceeding

If a foreign proceeding and a case under another chapter of this title are pending concurrently regarding the same debtor, the court shall seek cooperation and coordination under *sections 1525, 1526,* and *1527,* and the following shall apply:

(1) If the case in the United States is pending at the time the petition for recognition of such foreign proceeding is filed—

(A) any relief granted under *section 1519* or *1521* must be consistent with the relief granted in the case in the United States; and

(B) *section 1520* does not apply even if such foreign proceeding is recognized as a foreign main proceeding.

(2) If a case in the United States under this title commences after recognition, or after the date of the filing of the petition for recognition, of such foreign proceeding—

(A) any relief in effect under *section 1519* or *1521* shall be reviewed by the court and shall be modified or terminated if inconsistent with the case in the United States; and

(B) if such foreign proceeding is a foreign main proceeding, the stay and suspension referred to in *section 1520(a)* shall be modified or terminated if inconsistent with the relief granted in the case in the United States.

(3) In granting, extending, or modifying relief granted to a representative of a foreign nonmain proceeding, the court must be satisfied that the relief relates to assets that, under the laws of the United States, should be administered in the foreign nonmain proceeding or concerns information required in that proceeding.

(4) In achieving cooperation and coordination under *sections 1528* and 1529, the court may grant any of the relief authorized under *section 305*.

(Added Pub. L. 109–8, title VIII, § 801(a), Apr. 20, 2005, 119 Stat. 144; amended Pub. L. 111–327, § 2(a)(48), Dec. 22, 2010, 124 Stat. 3562.)

Sections that reference this section: None

§1530. Coordination of more than 1 foreign proceeding

In matters referred to in *section 1501,* with respect to more than 1 foreign proceeding regarding the debtor, the court shall seek cooperation and coordination under *sections 1525, 1526,* and *1527,* and the following shall apply:

(1) Any relief granted under *section 1519* or *1521* to a representative of a foreign nonmain proceeding after recognition of a foreign main proceed-

ing must be consistent with the foreign main proceeding.

(2) If a foreign main proceeding is recognized after recognition, or after the filing of a petition for recognition, of a foreign nonmain proceeding, any relief in effect under *section 1519* or *1521* shall be reviewed by the court and shall be modified or terminated if inconsistent with the foreign main proceeding.

(3) If, after recognition of a foreign nonmain proceeding, another foreign nonmain proceeding is recognized, the court shall grant, modify, or terminate relief for the purpose of facilitating coordination of the proceedings.

(Added Pub. L. 109–8, title VIII, § 801(a), Apr. 20, 2005, 119 Stat. 144.)

Sections that reference this section: None

§1531. Presumption of insolvency based on recognition of a foreign main proceeding

In the absence of evidence to the contrary, recognition of a foreign main proceeding is, for the purpose of commencing a proceeding under *section 303*, proof that the debtor is generally not paying its debts as such debts become due.

(Added Pub. L. 109–8, title VIII, § 801(a), Apr. 20, 2005, 119 Stat. 144.)

Sections that reference this section: None

§1532. Rule of payment in concurrent proceedings

Without prejudice to secured claims or rights in rem, a creditor who has received payment with respect to its claim in a foreign proceeding pursuant to a law relating to insolvency may not receive a payment for the same claim in a case under any other chapter of this title regarding the debtor, so long as the payment to other creditors of the same class is proportionately less than the payment the creditor has already received.

(Added Pub. L. 109–8, title VIII, § 801(a), Apr. 20, 2005, 119 Stat. 145.)

Sections that reference this section: None

Appendix: Adjustment of Dollar Amounts (90 Fed. Reg. 8941, 10643)

Federal Register / Vol. 90, No. 22 / Tuesday, February 4, 2025 / Notices 8941

results is three business days after the issuance of Commerce's results. If comments contain business proprietary information (BPI), they must conform with the requirements of §§ 201.6, 207.3, and 207.7 of the Commission's rules. The Commission's *Handbook on Filing Procedures*, available on the Commission's website at *https://www.usitc.gov/documents/handbook_on_filing_procedures.pdf*, elaborates upon the Commission's procedures with respect to filings.

In accordance with §§ 201.16(c) and 207.3 of the rules, each document filed by a party to the reviews must be served on all other parties to the reviews (as identified by either the public or BPI service list), and a certificate of service must be timely filed. The Secretary will not accept a document for filing without a certificate of service.

Determination.—The Commission has determined these reviews are extraordinarily complicated and therefore has determined to exercise its authority to extend the review period by up to 90 days pursuant to 19 U.S.C. 1675(c)(5)(B).

Authority: These reviews are being conducted under authority of title VII of the Act; this notice is published pursuant to § 207.62 of the Commission's rules.

By order of the Commission.

Issued: January 29, 2025.

Lisa Barton,

Secretary to the Commission.

[FR Doc. 2025–02170 Filed 2–3–25; 8:45 am]

BILLING CODE 7020–02–P

JUDICIAL CONFERENCE OF THE UNITED STATES

Adjustment of Certain Dollar Amounts Applicable to Bankruptcy Cases

AGENCY: Judicial Conference of the United States.

ACTION: Notice of adjusted dollar amounts.

SUMMARY: Certain dollar amounts in the United States Code applicable to bankruptcy cases are adjusted to reflect the change in the Consumer Price Index for All Urban Consumers for the most recent 3-year period ending immediately before January 1, 2025.

DATES: The dollar amounts are adjusted on April 1, 2025.

FOR FURTHER INFORMATION CONTACT: Gary D. Streeting, Senior Attorney, Judicial Services Office, Administrative Office of the United States Courts, Thurgood Marshall Federal Judiciary Building, One Columbus Circle NE, Room 4–270, Washington, DC 20544, Telephone (202) 502–1800, or by email at *Judicial_Services_Office@ao.uscourts.gov.*

SUPPLEMENTARY INFORMATION: Section 104 of title 11, United States Code, provides for an automatic three-year adjustment of dollar amounts in certain sections of titles 11 and 28. Notice is hereby given, pursuant to 11 U.S.C. 104(b), that the next such adjustment will occur on April 1, 2025. Effective on that date, the dollar amounts in effect under sections 101(3), 101(18), 101(19A), 101(51D), 109(e), 303(b), 507(a), 522(d), 522(f)(3), 522(f)(4), 522(n), 522(p), 522(q), 523(a)(2)(C), 541(b), 547(c)(9), 707(b), 1182(1), 1322(d), 1325(b), and 1326(b)(3) of title 11, and section 1409(b) of title 28, United States Code, are adjusted as set forth in the chart below to reflect the change in the Consumer Price Index for All Urban Consumers, published by the Department of Labor, for the 3-year period ending immediately before January 1, 2025, rounded to the nearest $25. This adjustment does not apply with respect to cases commenced before April 1, 2025. Seven Official Bankruptcy Forms (106C, 107, 122A–2, 122C–2, 201, 207, and 410) and two Director's Forms (2000 and 2830) will also be amended to reflect these adjusted dollar amounts.

(Authority: 11 U.S.C. 104.)

Dated: January 30, 2025.

Joseph T. Phillips,

Chief, Judicial Services Office.

Affected sections of Titles 11 and 28 U.S.C.	Dollar amount to be adjusted	New (adjusted) dollar amount [1]
11 U.S.C.:		
Section 101(3)	$226,850	$256,800.
Section 101(18)	$11,097,350 (each time it appears)	$12,562,250 (each time it appears).
Section 101(19A)	$2,268,550 (each time it appears)	$2,568,000 (each time it appears).
Section 101(51D)	$3,024,725 (each time it appears)	$3,424,000 (each time it appears).
Section 109(e)	$465,275 (each time it appears)	$526,700 (each time it appears).
	$1,395,875 (each time it appears)	$1,580,125 (each time it appears).
Section 303(b)	$18,600 (each time it appears)	$21,050 (each time it appears).
Section 507(a)		
paragraph (4)	$15,150	$17,150.
paragraph (5)(B)(i)	$15,150	$17,150.
paragraph (6)	$7,475	$8,450.
paragraph (7)	$3,350	$3,800.
Section 522(d)		
paragraph (1)	$27,900	$31,575.
paragraph (2)	$4,450	$5,025.
paragraph (3)	$700	$800.
	$14,875	$16,850.
paragraph (4)	$1,875	$2,125.
paragraph (5)	$1,475	$1,675.
	$13,950	$15,800.
paragraph (6)	$2,800	$3,175.
paragraph (8)	$14,875	$16,850.
paragraph (11)(D)	$27,900	$31,575.
Section 522(f)(3)	$7,575	$8,575.
Section 522(f)(4)	$800 (each time it appears)	$900 (each time it appears).
Section 522(n)	$1,512,350	$1,711,975.
Section 522(p)	$189,050	$214,000.
Section 522(q)	$189,050	$214,000.
Section 523(a)(2)(C)		
paragraph (i)(I)	$800	$900.
paragraph (i)(II)	$1,100	$1,250.
Section 541(b)	$7,575 (each time it appears)	$8,575 (each time it appears).

Affected sections of Titles 11 and 28 U.S.C.	Dollar amount to be adjusted	New (adjusted) dollar amount [1]
Section 547(c)(9)	$7,575	$8,575.
Section 707(b)		
paragraph (2)(A)(i)(I)	$9,075	$10,275.
paragraph (2)(A)(i)(II)	$15,150	$17,150.
paragraph (2)(A)(ii)(IV)	$2,275	$2,575.
paragraph (2)(B)(iv)(I)	$9,075	$10,275.
paragraph (2)(B)(iv)(II)	$15,150	$17,150.
paragraph (5)(B)	$1,525	$1,725.
paragraph (6)(C)	$825	$925.
paragraph (7)(A)(iii)	$825	$925.
Section 1182(1)	(2)	
Section 1322(d)	$825 (each time it appears)	$925 (each time it appears).
Section 1325(b)	$825 (each time it appears)	$925 (each time it appears).
Section 1326(b)(3)	$25	$25.
28 U.S.C.:		
Section 1409(b)	$1,525	$1,725.
	$22,700	$27,750.
	$25,700	$31,425

[1] The New (Adjusted) Dollar Amounts reflect a 13.2004 percent increase, rounded to the nearest $25.

[2] There is no dollar amount currently set forth in 11 U.S.C. 1182(1). Most recently, the Bankruptcy Threshold Adjustment and Technical Corrections Act (BTATCA) (Pub. L. 117–151, 136 Stat. 1298) added a dollar amount to that section, but the BTATCA provision that included the dollar amount sunset on June 21, 2024.

[FR Doc. 2025–02207 Filed 2–3–25; 8:45 am]

BILLING CODE 2210–55–P

DEPARTMENT OF JUSTICE

Antitrust Division

Notice Pursuant to the National Cooperative Research and Production Act of 1993—ODVA, Inc.

Notice is hereby given that, on January 8, 2025, pursuant to Section 6(a) of the National Cooperative Research and Production Act of 1993, 15 U.S.C. 4301 *et seq.* ("the Act"), ODVA, Inc. ("ODVA") has filed written notifications simultaneously with the Attorney General and the Federal Trade Commission disclosing changes in its membership. The notifications were filed for the purpose of extending the Act's provisions limiting the recovery of antitrust plaintiffs to actual damages under specified circumstances. Specifically, Aerotech, Inc., Pittsburgh, PA; JVL A/S, Birkerød, KINGDOM OF DENMARK; Simco (Nederland) B.V., Lochem, Gelderland, NETHERLANDS; Fortinet, Inc., Sunnyvale, CA; Shenzhen Blue Dynamics Precision Co., Ltd., Shenzhen, PEOPLE'S REPUBLIC OF CHINA; NITTOKU CO., LTD., Saitama, JAPAN; and MicroVision, Inc., Redmond, WA, have been added as parties to this venture.

Also, Nanjing Decowell Automation Co., Ltd., Nanjing, PEOPLE'S REPUBLIC OF CHINA; Beijing Tianma Intelligent Control Technology Co., Ltd., Beijing, PEOPLE'S REPUBLIC OF CHINA; Hanwha Corporation, Seoul, REPUBLIC OF KOREA; and Perinet GmbH, Berlin, GERMANY, have withdrawn as parties to this venture.

No other changes have been made in either the membership or planned activity of the group research project. Membership in this group research project remains open, and ODVA intends to file additional written notifications disclosing all changes in membership.

On June 21, 1995, ODVA filed its original notification pursuant to Section 6(a) of the Act. The Department of Justice published a notice in the **Federal Register** pursuant to Section 6(b) of the Act on February 15, 1996 (61 FR 6039).

The last notification was filed with the Department on October 18, 2024. A notice was published in the **Federal Register** pursuant to Section 6(b) of the Act on January 24, 2025 (90 FR 8143).

Suzanne Morris,

Deputy Director Civil Enforcement Operations, Antitrust Division.

[FR Doc. 2025–02190 Filed 2–3–25; 8:45 am]

BILLING CODE 4410–11–P

DEPARTMENT OF JUSTICE

Antitrust Division

Notice Pursuant to the National Cooperative Research and Production Act of 1993—Customer Experience Hub

Notice is hereby given that, on January 3, 2025, pursuant to section 6(a) of the National Cooperative Research and Production Act of 1993, 15 U.S.C. 4301 *et seq.* ("the Act"), The Customer Experience Hub ("CX Hub") has filed written notifications simultaneously with the Attorney General and the Federal Trade Commission disclosing changes in its membership. The notifications were filed for the purpose of extending the Act's provisions limiting the recovery of antitrust plaintiffs to actual damages under specified circumstances.

Specifically, Access Pediatric LLC, Gainesville, FL; Advanced Telesensors, Inc., Austin, TX; The Susan G. Komen Breast Cancer Foundation, Inc., Dallas, TX; The Wistar Institute of Anatomy and Biology, Philadelphia, PA; ViVBioTech LLC, Sacramento, CA; Biogenesis, Palo Alto, CA; CARIN Alliance, Washington, DC; CellChorus, Inc., Houston, TX; ELHS Institute, Inc., Palo Alto, CA; Global Coalition on Aging, New York, NY; Handzin, Inc., San Fransisco, CA; Health in her HUE, New York, NY; Landmark Bio PBLLC, Watertown, MA; LastMinute, Inc., Brookline, MA; Netrias LLC, Annapolis, MD; Patientory, Inc., Atlanta, GA; Performance Hypothesis LLC, Atlanta, GA; and SmarTechNexus Foundation, Baltimore, MD have been added as parties to this venture.

No other changes have been made in either the membership or planned activity of the group research project. Membership in this group research project remains open, and the CX Hub intends to file additional written notifications disclosing all changes in membership.

On January 11, 2024, the CX Hub filed its original notification pursuant to section 6(a) of the Act. The Department of Justice published a notice in the **Federal Register** pursuant to section 6(b) of the Act on April 16, 2024 (89 FR 26929).

The last notification was filed with the Department on October 1, 2024. A

Federal Register / Vol. 90, No. 36 / Tuesday, February 25, 2025 / Notices 10643

Comments should address whether issuance of the relief specifically requested by the complainant in this investigation would affect the public health and welfare in the United States, competitive conditions in the United States economy, the production of like or directly competitive articles in the United States, or United States consumers.

In particular, the Commission is interested in comments that:

(i) explain how the articles potentially subject to the requested remedial orders are used in the United States;

(ii) identify any public health, safety, or welfare concerns in the United States relating to the requested remedial orders;

(iii) identify like or directly competitive articles that complainant, its licensees, or third parties make in the United States which could replace the subject articles if they were to be excluded;

(iv) indicate whether complainant, complainant's licensees, and/or third party suppliers have the capacity to replace the volume of articles potentially subject to the requested exclusion order and/or a cease and desist order within a commercially reasonable time; and

(v) explain how the requested remedial orders would impact United States consumers.

Written submissions on the public interest must be filed no later than by close of business, eight calendar days after the date of publication of this notice in the **Federal Register**. There will be further opportunities for comment on the public interest after the issuance of any final initial determination in this investigation. Any written submissions on other issues must also be filed by no later than the close of business, eight calendar days after publication of this notice in the **Federal Register**. Complainant may file replies to any written submissions no later than three calendar days after the date on which any initial submissions were due, notwithstanding § 201.14(a) of the Commission's Rules of Practice and Procedure. No other submissions will be accepted, unless requested by the Commission. Any submissions and replies filed in response to this Notice are limited to five (5) pages in length, inclusive of attachments.

Persons filing written submissions must file the original document electronically on or before the deadlines stated above. Submissions should refer to the docket number ("Docket No. 3811") in a prominent place on the cover page and/or the first page. (*See* Handbook for Electronic Filing Procedures, Electronic Filing Procedures [1]). Please note the Secretary's Office will accept only electronic filings during this time. Filings must be made through the Commission's Electronic Document Information System (EDIS, *https://edis.usitc.gov*). No in-person paper-based filings or paper copies of any electronic filings will be accepted until further notice. Persons with questions regarding filing should contact the Secretary at *EDIS3Help@usitc.gov*.

Any person desiring to submit a document to the Commission in confidence must request confidential treatment. All such requests should be directed to the Secretary to the Commission and must include a full statement of the reasons why the Commission should grant such treatment. *See* 19 CFR 201.6. Documents for which confidential treatment by the Commission is properly sought will be treated accordingly. All information, including confidential business information and documents for which confidential treatment is properly sought, submitted to the Commission for purposes of this Investigation may be disclosed to and used: (i) by the Commission, its employees and Offices, and contract personnel (a) for developing or maintaining the records of this or a related proceeding, or (b) in internal investigations, audits, reviews, and evaluations relating to the programs, personnel, and operations of the Commission including under 5 U.S.C. appendix 3; or (ii) by U.S. Government employees and contract personnel,[2] solely for cybersecurity purposes. All nonconfidential written submissions will be available for public inspection at the Office of the Secretary and on EDIS.[3]

This action is taken under the authority of section 337 of the Tariff Act of 1930, as amended (19 U.S.C. 1337), and of §§ 201.10 and 210.8(c) of the Commission's Rules of Practice and Procedure (19 CFR 201.10, 210.8(c)).

By order of the Commission.

Issued: February 20, 2025.

Lisa Barton,

Secretary to the Commission.

[FR Doc. 2025–03046 Filed 2–24–25; 8:45 am]

BILLING CODE 7020–02–P

[1] Handbook for Electronic Filing Procedures: *https://www.usitc.gov/documents/handbook_on_filing_procedures.pdf*.

[2] All contract personnel will sign appropriate nondisclosure agreements.

[3] Electronic Document Information System (EDIS): *https://edis.usitc.gov*.

JUDICIAL CONFERENCE OF THE UNITED STATES

Adjustment of Certain Dollar Amounts Applicable to Bankruptcy Cases

Correction

In notice document, 2025–02207, appearing on pages 8941–8942 in the issue of Tuesday, February 4, 2025, make the following corrections:

1. On page 8942, in the second column, in the last line of the table, "$25,700" should read "$27,750".

2. On the same page, in the third column, in the second line from the bottom of the table, "$27,750" should read "$25,700".

[FR Doc. C1–2025–02207 Filed 2–24–25; 8:45 am]

BILLING CODE 1505–01–D

NATIONAL CREDIT UNION ADMINISTRATION

Sunshine Act Meetings

TIME AND DATE: 10:00 a.m., Thursday, February 27, 2025.

PLACE: Board Room, 7th Floor, Room 7B, 1775 Duke Street (All visitors must use Diagonal Road Entrance), Alexandria, VA 22314–3428.

STATUS: Open.

MATTERS TO BE CONSIDERED:

1. Board Briefing, Share Insurance Fund Quarterly Report.

2. NCUA Board Vice Chairman Designation.

CONTACT PERSON FOR MORE INFORMATION: Melane Conyers-Ausbrooks, Secretary of the Board, Telephone: 703–518–6304.

Melane Conyers-Ausbrooks,

Secretary of the Board.

[FR Doc. 2025–03087 Filed 2–21–25; 11:15 am]

BILLING CODE 7535–01–P

NUCLEAR REGULATORY COMMISSION

[NRC–2025–0027]

Monthly Notice; Applications and Amendments to Facility Operating Licenses and Combined Licenses Involving No Significant Hazards Considerations; Correction

AGENCY: Nuclear Regulatory Commission.

ACTION: Monthly notice; correction.

SUMMARY: The U.S. Nuclear Regulatory Commission (NRC) is correcting a notice that was published in the **Federal Register** on February 18, 2025, regarding the publication of the regular monthly

Index to United States Bankruptcy Code

www.ingramcontent.com/pod-product-compliance
Ingram Content Group UK Ltd.
Pitfield, Milton Keynes, MK11 3LW, UK
UKHW051452290926
15471UKWH00008B/1157

9 781640 021716